NO[N] [LEAGUE]
FOOTBALL TABLES
OF SOUTH EAST
ENGLAND
1894-2017

EDITOR
Michael Robinson

FOREWORD

Following the success of our 'Non-League Football Tables' series of books, the first of which was published in 2002, we have long considered introducing a number of regionalised titles about various football leagues both past and present. The first book in such a series, 'Non-League Football Tables of South West England 1892-2015' was published in 2015 and the second book, 'Non-League Football Tables of North-West England 1889-2016' was published in 2016. Both of these books are available for purchase at our address shown below, each priced £11.99.

This third book, of a planned series of six, covers eight football leagues from the South East of England. The earliest of these commenced in 1894 and a number of the other leagues included continue to operate to this day.

The Leagues which currently form the apex of the 'Non-League Pyramid', namely the National League (formerly called the Football Conference) and its three feeder leagues (Northern Premier, Southern Premier & Isthmian) will continue to be covered by our yearly 'Non-League Football Tables' books.

We are indebted to Mick Blakeman for providing tables for the various Leagues included in this book.

British Library Cataloguing in Publication Data
A catalogue record for this book is available from the British Library

ISBN: 978-1-86223-367-6

Printed in the UK by 4edge Ltd.

CONTENTS

KENT LEAGUE 1894-1959

The Kent League was formed in March 1894 following a meeting held at Anderton's Hotel, London, to gauge support.

Notes on the tables below:

1.   Until 1939, some clubs fielded their first team in both the Kent League and another league (usually the Southern or South-Eastern League), whilst other clubs with first teams in those leagues fielded their reserves in the Kent League. In the tables below, reserve sides are noted but it is possible that during that period, some clubs' first teams may have fulfilled their reserve sides' fixtures.

2.   Before the First World War and just afterwards, Kent League clubs' reserve sides were sometimes referred to as "A" sides. Below, they are always referred to as "Reserves" while only third teams are referred to as "A" sides.

3.   Some Kent League tables published at the time, or subsequently, contained errors. Recent research has enabled many to be corrected but where it has not been possible to correct the errors, totals are shown in italics below the relevant columns.

4.   Promoted clubs are shown in **bold type**, relegated clubs are shown in ***bold italics***.

1894-95

Division One

Chatham	16	11	3	2	55	23	25
Royal Engineers Training Battalion	16	8	5	3	50	23	21
Folkestone	16	8	3	5	30	29	19
Gravesend United	16	6	5	5	54	33	17
Sheppey United	16	8	1	7	37	28	17
Sittingbourne	16	7	2	7	30	37	16
Ashford United	16	6	2	8	35	41	14
Dartford	16	5	2	9	30	39	12
Maidstone	16	1	1	14	14	84	3
					335	*337*	

Test matches   (27th April 1895)

Dartford v Sheppey United Reserves	4-0
(Played at Swanscombe)	
Swanscombe v Maidstone	2-0
(Played at the Sheppey United ground, Sheerness)	

Swanscombe were promoted to Division One. New Brompton, Northfleet United and Woolwich Arsenal Reserves also joined Division One while Maidstone left.

Division Two

Swanscombe	16	12	3	1	60	13	27
Sheppey United Reserves	16	11	2	3	50	16	24
Cray Wanderers	16	10	2	4	48	25	22
Chatham Reserves	16	8	2	6	51	28	18
Sittingbourne Reserves	16	6	2	8	24	36	14
Faversham	16	4	5	7	31	30	13
Dover	16	4	5	7	35	42	13
Sevenoaks	16	3	2	11	18	91	8
Folkestone Harveians	16	2	1	13	19	55	5

Maidstone Church Institute, Maidstone Invicta and Folkestone Reserves joined while Chatham Reserves and Sevenoaks left.

1895-96

Division One

Northfleet United	22	16	2	4	85	31	34
Woolwich Arsenal Reserves	22	16	1	5	76	39	31
Folkestone	22	12	4	6	46	34	28
Chatham	22	12	3	7	49	30	27
Royal Engineers Training Battalion	22	9	5	8	47	39	23
Sheppey United	22	9	5	8	48	42	23
New Brompton	22	9	3	10	36	42	21
Gravesend United	22	10	4	8	36	41	20
Dartford	22	8	3	11	52	69	19
Sittingbourne	22	4	5	13	40	72	13
Swanscombe	22	3	4	15	19	62	10
Ashford United	22	3	3	16	34	69	9
					568	*570*	

Woolwich Arsenal Reserves had 2 points deducted for fielding ineligible players.
Gravesend United had 4 points deducted for fielding ineligible players.

Test matches

Ashford United v Faversham	5-0
Swanscombe v Cray Wanderers	6-0

Division Two

Sheppey United Reserves	16	12	3	1	42	11	27
Faversham	16	13	1	2	54	24	27
Cray Wanderers	16	12	0	4	56	21	24
Dover	16	6	5	5	38	31	17
Sittingbourne Reserves	16	6	2	8	32	39	14
Maidstone Invicta	16	4	3	9	31	39	11
Folkestone Harveians	16	4	2	10	26	50	10
Maidstone Church Institute	16	4	2	10	18	42	10
Folkestone Reserves	16	2	0	14	14	53	4
					311	*310*	

1896: THE FORMATION OF THE THAMES & MEDWAY COMBINATION

Chatham, New Brompton and Sheppey United were playing in both the Southern League and the Kent League and Gravesend United and Northfleet United were elected to the Southern League for 1896-97. These 5 clubs wished to field their reserves in the Kent League but had a lesser status than Woolwich Arsenal (of the Football League) and were refused permission. They then resigned from the Kent League and formed a rival competition, the Thames and Medway Combination.

Dartford and Royal Engineers Training Battalion also moved to the Southern League and Swanscombe resigned, leaving only 4 clubs in Division One.

Five clubs – Cray Wanderers, Dover, Faversham, Maidstone Church Institute and Maidstone Invicta, were therefore promoted from Division Two to form a 9-club First Division for the 1896-97 season.

Sheppey United Reserves and Folkestone Harveians also left Division Two but Cray Wanderers Reserves, Faversham Reserves, Herne Bay and New Brompton Reserves joined to form a 6-club Second Division.

1896-97

Division One

Woolwich Arsenal Reserves	16	13	3	0	81	11	29
Folkestone	16	10	4	2	46	21	24
Sittingbourne	16	8	2	6	30	33	18
Dover	16	7	3	6	39	32	15
Ashford United	16	5	5	6	33	34	15
Faversham	16	5	4	7	38	45	14
Cray Wanderers	16	6	1	9	44	37	13
Maidstone Invicta	16	4	5	7	29	41	13
Maidstone Church Institute	16	0	1	15	9	95	1

Dover had 2 points deducted for fielding an ineligible player.
Maidstone Invicta and Maidstone Church Institute merged to form Maidstone United.
Woolwich Arsenal Reserves left the league and Swanscombe joined.

Division Two

New Brompton Reserves	10	8	1	1	49	8	17
Sittingbourne Reserves	10	8	1	1	47	11	17
Faversham Reserves	10	4	3	3	23	24	11
Cray Wanderers Reserves	10	2	2	6	19	31	6
Folkestone Reserves	10	1	3	6	10	54	5
Herne Bay	10	1	2	7	6	26	4

New Brompton Reserves and Cray Wanderers Reserves left the league.
Brompton United, Dover Reserves, New Brompton Excelsior and Sheppey United Reserves all joined.

1897-98

Division One

Swanscombe	14	10	2	2	31	12	22
Maidstone United	14	8	1	5	34	22	17
Sittingbourne	14	6	4	4	30	23	16
Ashford United	14	6	3	5	27	28	15
Dover	14	3	6	5	22	23	12
Faversham	14	3	6	5	25	31	12
Cray Wanderers	14	3	3	8	26	36	9
Folkestone	14	3	3	8	15	29	9
					210	204	

Dartford, Northfleet United and Royal Engineers Training Department returned from the Southern League and Woolwich Arsenal Reserves also returned. Bromley joined from the London League and Royal West Kent Regiment also joined.

Division Two

Sittingbourne Reserves	12	9	1	2	38	9	19
Faversham Reserves	12	6	3	3	33	26	15
Sheppey United Reserves	11	7	0	4	52	17	14
Folkestone Reserves	12	4	2	6	32	21	10
New Brompton Excelsior	9	2	4	3	13	23	8
Dover Reserves	8	2	0	6	12	38	4
Herne Bay	10	2	0	8	6	45	4
					186	179	

Brompton United resigned in January 1898 and their record was deleted when it stood as follows: 3 1 0 2 2 7 2
Results of missing games have not been traced but it is known that Sheppey United Reserves finished as runners-up at the end of the season.

Division Two disbanded at the end of the season.

Herne Bay moved to the East Kent League.

1898-99

Maidstone United	24	15	4	5	77	28	34
Dover	24	15	4	5	78	30	34
Woolwich Arsenal Reserves	24	12	10	2	55	25	34
Dartford	24	14	4	6	61	46	32
Sittingbourne	24	11	4	9	50	38	26
Royal West Kent Regiment	24	10	6	8	40	31	26
Folkestone	24	10	4	10	53	47	24
Ashford United	24	9	6	9	54	56	24
Cray Wanderers	24	8	8	8	47	58	24
Swanscombe	24	8	7	9	38	42	23
Royal Engineers United	24	5	3	16	33	72	13
Faversham	24	4	4	16	31	88	12
Bromley	24	2	2	20	33	89	6

During the season, Northfleet United resigned and their record was deleted when it stood as: 7 3 2 2 26 19 8
Royal Engineers Training Battalion changed their name to Royal Engineers United.
Bromley returned to the London League, swapping places with Deptford Town. Royal Engineers United and Royal West Kent Regiment both left the league and Royal North Lancashire Fusiliers joined.

1899-1900

Maidstone United	20	14	2	4	43	20	30
Woolwich Arsenal Reserves	20	13	2	5	46	23	26
Dover	20	11	3	6	48	29	25
Deptford Town	20	10	2	8	37	42	22
Sittingbourne	20	8	4	8	42	30	20
Folkestone	20	7	5	8	37	33	19
Dartford	20	7	5	8	44	40	19
Faversham	20	8	2	10	31	41	18
Ashford United	19	6	2	11	32	51	14
Cray Wanderers	19	5	2	12	22	50	12
Swanscombe	20	5	1	14	21	44	11

Woolwich Arsenal Reserves had 2 points deducted for fielding an ineligible player.

Royal North Lancashire Fusiliers resigned after playing 3 games as the regiment was posted to the Transvaal to fight in the Boer War.

Ashford United vs Cray Wanderers was not played.

Dartford changed their name to Dartford United. Woolwich Arsenal Reserves and Deptford Town moved to the London League and Faversham also left. Erith joined the league and Sheppey United rejoined.

1900-01

Maidstone United	16	14	0	2	54	6	28
Sittingbourne	16	9	4	3	29	21	22
Sheppey United	16	10	1	5	45	20	21
Ashford United	16	8	3	5	35	21	19
Folkestone	16	7	4	5	28	29	18
Cray Wanderers	16	7	0	9	27	33	14
Dartford United	16	3	4	9	23	37	10
Swanscombe	16	2	3	11	12	58	7
Erith	16	2	1	13	17	45	5

Dover were declared bankrupt and resigned 27th October 1900. Their record was deleted:

	3	1	0	2	-	-	2

Gravesend United joined from the Southern League. Chatham resigned from that League in December and disbanded but reformed as Chatham Amateurs in 1901 and joined the Kent League.

1901-02

Cray Wanderers	20	15	2	3	69	22	32
Sittingbourne	20	15	2	3	44	13	32
Maidstone United	20	13	2	5	56	27	28
Sheppey United	20	12	1	7	45	36	25
Ashford United	19	9	2	8	47	31	20
Erith	18	7	3	8	38	29	17
Folkestone	20	6	5	9	38	37	17
Chatham Amateurs	20	7	2	11	35	44	16
Swanscombe	19	7	1	11	22	46	13
Dartford	19	3	2	14	14	58	8
Gravesend United	19	1	2	16	23	81	4
					431	424	

Swanscombe had 2 points deducted for fielding an ineligible player.
Three games were not played.

Championship decider　(Chatham, 25th April 1902)

Cray Wanderers vs Sittingbourne　　　　　　　　　　1-0

Chatham Amateurs changed their name to Chatham.
Dartford moved to the West Kent League while Gravesend United and Erith also left the league. Dover joined from the East Kent League.

1902-03

Sittingbourne	16	12	3	1	45	11	27
Chatham	16	12	1	3	47	11	25
Sheppey United	16	11	2	3	32	19	24
Maidstone United	16	7	2	7	32	26	16
Ashford United	16	6	2	8	32	45	14
Cray Wanderers	16	5	1	10	24	43	11
Swanscombe	16	4	2	10	16	39	10
Folkestone	16	3	3	10	23	36	9
Dover	16	2	4	10	19	40	8

Cray Wanderers and Swanscombe both left the league.
New Brompton Amateurs and Tunbridge Wells Rangers joined.

1903-04

Chatham	16	14	2	0	52	12	30
Sheppey United	16	9	3	4	45	19	21
Sittingbourne	16	8	5	3	38	21	21
Maidstone United	16	10	0	6	51	33	20
New Brompton Amateurs	16	7	2	7	33	35	16
Dover	16	7	1	8	28	31	15
Ashford United	16	6	1	9	26	29	13
Tunbridge Wells Rangers	16	2	0	14	18	60	4
Folkestone	16	2	0	14	16	67	4

Folkestone left the league.
Faversham and 8th South Lancashire Regiment both joined the league.

1904-05

Chatham	18	13	4	1	63	14	30
Sheppey United	18	13	2	3	55	18	28
Sittingbourne	18	12	2	4	53	22	26
Maidstone United	18	11	1	6	43	18	23
Ashford United	18	8	4	6	39	37	20
Dover	18	7	3	8	37	43	17
Tunbridge Wells Rangers	18	5	3	10	31	51	13
New Brompton Amateurs	18	4	1	13	23	48	9
8th South Lancashire Regiment	18	3	1	14	18	56	7
Faversham	18	2	3	13	15	70	7

Chatham and Sittingbourne moved to the South-Eastern League and Maidstone United left to play solely in the South-Eastern League.
8th South Lancashire Regiment left the league, being posted overseas.
Gravesend United and Maidstone Church Institute Wanderers joined.

1905-06

Sheppey United	14	11	1	2	52	18	23
Gravesend United	14	10	1	3	44	21	21
Faversham	14	7	5	2	41	26	19
Tunbridge Wells Rangers	14	9	1	4	38	15	17
Ashford United	14	4	3	7	28	29	11
Maidstone Church Institute Wands	14	4	2	8	25	28	10
Dover	14	2	2	10	18	52	6
New Brompton Amateurs	14	1	1	12	12	69	3

Tunbridge Wells Rangers had 2 points deducted for fielding an ineligible player.
Tunbridge Wells Rangers left to play solely in the South-Eastern League.
New Brompton Amateurs also left the league.
Cray Wanderers returned while continuing to play in the West Kent League.
Northfleet United and Royal Naval Depot also joined.

1906-07

Sheppey United	14	11	1	2	35	12	23
Northfleet United	14	9	0	5	37	19	18
Gravesend United	14	7	1	6	42	24	15
Faversham	14	7	1	6	24	22	15
Royal Naval Depot (Chatham)	14	5	3	6	24	25	13
Dover	14	5	1	8	22	31	11
Cray Wanderers	14	4	1	9	20	51	9
Maidstone Church Institute Wands.	14	3	2	9	21	35	8
					225	219	

Ashford United resigned and disbanded after playing 10 games (2 of which were won). Their record was deleted.
Cray Wanderers left the league. Royal Scots joined from the East Kent League and Royal West Kent Regiment also joined.

1907-08

Northfleet United	16	14	1	1	54	13	29
Royal Scots	16	9	6	1	24	11	24
Sheppey United	16	7	3	6	34	26	17
Faversham	16	8	1	7	26	26	17
Maidstone Church Institute Wands.	16	6	2	8	23	34	14
Dover	16	4	6	6	24	40	14
Gravesend United	14	5	1	8	21	26	11
Royal Naval Depot (Chatham)	16	3	3	10	26	33	9
Royal West Kent Regiment	14	2	1	11	12	35	5

Two games not played.
Royal Scots left the league and Tunbridge Wells Rangers returned while continuing in the South-Eastern League.
Maidstone Church Institute Wanderers changed their name to Maidstone Athletic.

1908-09

Northfleet United	16	13	1	2	52	23	27
Gravesend United	16	11	3	2	40	16	25
Tunbridge Wells Rangers	16	10	2	4	58	19	22
Royal West Kent Regiment	16	8	2	6	38	27	18
Royal Naval Depot (Chatham)	16	6	3	7	28	34	15
Sheppey United	16	5	3	8	33	32	13
Faversham	16	4	3	9	24	51	11
Maidstone Athletic	16	3	1	12	18	49	7
Dover	16	2	2	12	14	54	6

Royal West Kent Regiment and Maidstone Athletic both left the league. Maidstone United, Metrogas Athletic and Sittingbourne joined from the South-Eastern League, Depot Battalion Royal Engineers joined from the Southern League and Chatham, Dartford, New Brompton Reserves and Rochester also joined.

A new Second Division formed in two sections, West and East. Tunbridge Wells Rangers moved to Division Two (West) along with 8 new members while Dover and Faversham both moved to Division Two (East) along with 9 new members.

1909-10

Division One

Northfleet United	22	17	2	3	74	31	36
Sittingbourne	22	15	3	4	56	23	33
Dartford	22	12	4	6	41	27	28
New Brompton Reserves	22	11	5	6	55	34	27
Chatham	22	10	7	5	38	28	27
Gravesend United	22	9	5	8	34	35	23
Royal Naval Depot (Chatham)	22	10	2	10	36	52	22
Sheppey United	22	9	2	11	37	34	20
Metrogas Athletic	22	5	6	11	33	46	16
Maidstone United	22	5	3	14	26	53	13
Rochester	22	4	2	16	22	56	10
Depot Battalion Royal Engineers	22	3	3	16	21	54	9

Depot Battalion Royal Engineers and Royal Naval Depot (Chatham) both left the league.

Crystal Palace Reserves joined from the South-Eastern League and Millwall Reserves also joined, while continuing to play in the London League.
Orpington were promoted from Division Two (West) and 1st Royal Irish Rifles were promoted from Division Two (East) taking their place as 2nd Royal Irish Rifles.

Division Two (West)

Orpington	16	13	1	2	64	20	27
Cray Wanderers	16	9	2	5	36	20	20
Plumstead St. John's	16	8	3	5	39	34	19
Tunbridge Wells Rangers	16	8	2	6	39	25	18
Army Service Corps	16	7	2	7	24	31	16
Army Ordnance Corps	16	6	2	8	31	31	14
Northumberland Oddfellows	16	4	5	7	28	39	13
1st Duke of Cornwall's Light Infantry	16	4	3	9	17	37	11
Tonbridge	16	1	4	11	17	58	6

Tunbridge Wells Rangers left to play in the South-Eastern League.
Plumstead St. John's and Northumberland Oddfellows also left the league and Tonbridge Onward joined.

Division Two (East)

1st Royal Irish Rifles	20	14	3	3	75	24	31
Ashford Railway Works	20	14	1	5	75	38	29
Folkestone	19	11	2	6	57	33	24
Whitstable	20	10	2	8	59	50	22
Folkestone Gas	19	10	1	8	32	38	21
3rd Worcestershire Regiment	17	9	1	7	52	46	19
Deal Cinque Ports	20	7	2	11	34	60	16
Ramsgate Town	20	4	6	10	35	56	14
Faversham	20	6	2	12	33	63	14
Herne Bay	19	6	1	12	32	58	13
Dover	20	5	1	14	34	52	11

3rd Worcestershire Regiment were posted overseas and were unable to fulfil their last 3 fixtures.
Dover and Herne Bay left the league. 1st North Staffordshire Regiment and 2nd Kings Royal Rifles both joined.

1910-11

Division One

Millwall Reserves	26	20	2	4	72	24	42
Crystal Palace Reserves	26	20	2	4	86	36	42
New Brompton Reserves	26	17	4	5	58	28	38
Sittingbourne	26	12	7	7	58	46	31
Metrogas Athletic	26	12	6	8	69	53	30
Chatham	26	12	5	9	42	37	29
Gravesend United	26	8	6	12	37	53	22
Rochester	26	9	4	13	41	66	22
Maidstone United	26	9	3	14	44	55	21
Sheppey United	26	7	6	13	49	55	20
2nd Royal Irish Rifles	26	8	3	15	45	65	19
Dartford	26	7	5	14	35	51	19
Northfleet United	26	7	4	15	38	64	18
Orpington	*26*	*3*	*5*	*18*	*42*	*83*	*11*

Championship decider (Played at Woolwich Arsenal)

Millwall Reserves vs Crystal Palace Reserves   1-0

Orpington were relegated to Division Two (West) from where Cray Wanderers were promoted. Bromley joined from the Isthmian League.

Division Two (West)

Army Service Corps	10	8	0	2	34	10	16
Cray Wanderers	**10**	**7**	**0**	**3**	**29**	**19**	**14**
1st Duke of Cornwall's Light Infantry	10	6	1	3	21	9	13
Army Ordnance Corps	10	4	1	5	31	21	9
Tonbridge	10	2	0	8	25	53	4
Tonbridge Onward	10	2	0	8	25	53	4

1st Duke of Cornwall''s Light Infantry and Tonbridge Onward left the league. 2nd Royal Dublin Fusiliers and South Wales Borderers both joined.

Division Two (East)

1st North Staffordshire Regiment	16	12	1	3	56	13	25
2nd Kings Royal Rifles	16	9	3	4	33	28	21
Ashford Railway Works	16	10	0	6	37	16	20
Folkestone	16	7	4	5	26	20	18
Ramsgate Town	16	6	3	7	33	27	15
Folkestone Gas	16	7	1	8	23	35	15
Whitstable	16	6	2	8	27	35	14
Deal Cinque Ports	16	3	6	7	25	32	12
Faversham	16	1	2	13	21	75	4

Canterbury City resigned in December 1910 after playing 7 games. Their record was deleted.

1st North Staffordshire Regiment and Deal Cinque Ports both left the league. Margate joined from the Thanet & District League.

1911-12

Division One

Millwall Reserves	28	24	2	2	98	24	50
New Brompton Reserves	28	17	6	5	64	38	40
Crystal Palace Reserves	28	15	6	7	75	48	36
Chatham	28	14	6	8	56	41	34
Gravesend United	28	12	5	11	54	50	29
Bromley	28	12	5	11	70	68	29
Maidstone United	28	11	7	10	63	64	29
Northfleet United	28	10	5	13	47	48	25
Sittingbourne	28	10	4	14	59	59	24
Metrogas Athletic	28	9	5	14	60	69	23
Rochester	28	9	5	14	33	62	23
Sheppey United	28	9	4	15	60	62	22
Dartford	28	7	7	14	37	61	21
Cray Wanderers	28	8	4	16	44	69	20
2nd Royal Irish Rifles	28	5	5	18	36	93	15

New Brompton Reserves changed their name to Gillingham Reserves.

2nd Royal Irish Rifles left the league and Royal Naval Depot (Chatham) joined.

Division Two (West)

Army Service Corps	10	9	0	1	32	9	18
1st South Wales Borderers	10	5	3	2	26	12	13
2nd Royal Dublin Fusiliers	10	5	2	3	34	13	12
Army Ordnance Corps	10	4	2	4	27	17	10
Orpington	10	2	2	6	17	33	6
Tonbridge	10	0	1	9	8	60	1

Army Service Corps, Orpington and Tonbridge left the league. Deptford Invicta, Snodland Town and Training Battalion Royal Engineers joined.

Division Two (East)

Ashford Railway Works	14	10	1	3	45	19	21
Whitstable	14	8	2	4	34	24	18
Ramsgate Town	14	7	3	4	29	24	17
Folkestone	14	5	4	5	27	18	14
Folkestone Gas	14	6	2	6	22	24	14
2nd Kings Royal Rifles	14	6	2	6	21	24	14
Margate	14	3	2	9	18	41	8
Faversham	14	2	2	10	9	39	6
					205	213	

2nd Kings Royal Rifles and Faversham left the league.
Depot Royal Marines (Deal) joined.

1912-13

Division One

Millwall Reserves	28	20	5	3	79	21	45
Crystal Palace Reserves	28	19	4	5	91	35	42
Royal Naval Depot (Chatham)	28	13	7	8	52	34	33
Northfleet United	28	14	5	9	58	55	33
Dartford	28	14	3	11	66	35	31
Metrogas Athletic	28	10	8	10	45	38	28
Chatham	28	12	4	12	62	54	28
Sittingbourne	28	10	7	11	54	59	27
Gillingham Reserves	28	10	7	11	46	65	27
Maidstone United	28	9	8	11	48	55	26
Sheppey United	28	10	4	14	37	48	24
Gravesend United	28	7	7	14	34	52	21
Bromley	28	9	2	17	45	69	20
Rochester	28	8	2	18	42	81	18
Cray Wanderers	*28*	*6*	*5*	*17*	*41*	*75*	*17*
					800	776	

Cray Wanderers were relegated to Division Two (West) from where 2nd Royal Dublin Fusiliers were promoted. Metrogas Athletic moved to the Athenian League and Gillingham Reserves moved to the South-Eastern League. Tunbridge Wells Rangers joined from the South-Eastern League and Woolwich and Southend United Reserves also joined. Woolwich were a new club formed to use Arsenal's former ground in Plumstead after Arsenal had moved to Highbury. They also joined the London League.

Division Two (West)

2nd Royal Dublin Fusiliers	**10**	**9**	**1**	**0**	**40**	**8**	**19**
Snodland Town	9	7	1	1	28	14	15
Training Battalion Royal Engineers	10	4	0	6	22	34	8
Army Ordnance Corps	10	3	1	6	21	27	7
1st South Wales Borderers	7	1	1	5	10	20	3
Deptford Invicta	8	1	0	7	10	28	2

1st South Wales Borderers were posted abroad and were to resign from the league, leaving 3 games unplayed.
Army Ordnance Corps and Deptford Invicta also left the league.
2nd Essex Regiment, 2nd Royal Dublin Fusiliers Reserves, Dartford Reserves, Depot Battalion Royal Engineers, Royal West Kent Depot, Strood and Woolwich Reserves all joined.

Division Two (East)

Ashford Railway Works	12	7	3	2	26	13	17
Folkestone Gas	12	7	3	2	27	21	17
Folkestone	12	5	4	3	25	14	14
Depot Royal Marines (Deal)	12	5	2	5	26	27	12
Whitstable	12	5	1	6	24	20	11
Margate	12	2	2	8	14	26	6
Ramsgate Town	12	3	1	8	11	31	5
					153	152	

Ramsgate Town had 2 points deducted for fielding an ineligible player.

Championship decider (Played at Folkestone Town)

Ashford Railway Works vs Folkestone Gas   2-0

2nd Lancashire Fusiliers, The Carabiniers and Kings Own Regiment all joined the league.

1913-14

Division One

Crystal Palace Reserves	30	25	1	4	110	25	51
Millwall Reserves	30	18	5	7	79	35	41
Woolwich	30	18	3	9	76	42	39
Northfleet United	30	17	5	8	63	49	37
Chatham	30	15	6	9	75	47	36
Maidstone United	30	17	2	11	64	58	36
Tunbridge Wells Rangers	30	14	5	11	65	66	33
Southend United Reserves	30	12	7	11	45	51	31
Dartford	30	13	3	14	57	57	29
Sittingbourne	30	12	3	15	41	64	27
Gravesend United	30	10	6	14	51	52	26
Sheppey United	30	11	3	16	55	62	25
Bromley	30	9	4	17	36	57	22
Royal Naval Depot (Chatham)	30	8	5	17	40	53	21
2nd Royal Dublin Fusiliers	30	8	4	18	36	57	20
Rochester	30	1	2	27	26	134	4
					919	909	

Northfleet United had 2 points deducted for fielding an ineligible player.

Division Two (West)

Strood	18	13	2	3	46	19	28
Woolwich Reserves	18	9	4	5	40	30	22
2nd Essex Regiment	18	9	2	7	39	25	20
Training Battalion Royal Engineers	18	7	6	5	37	32	20
Snodland Town	18	7	5	6	43	42	19
Cray Wanderers	18	9	1	8	42	47	19
Royal West Kent Depot	18	6	5	7	37	31	17
Depot Battalion Royal Engineers	18	4	5	9	30	46	13
2nd Royal Dublin Fusiliers Reserves	18	3	5	10	35	47	11
Dartford Reserves	18	4	3	11	33	51	11
					390	370	

Division Two (East)

Ashford Railway Works	18	13	3	2	47	16	29
Folkestone	18	13	3	2	49	17	29
2nd Lancashire Fusiliers	18	10	4	4	45	27	24
Margate	**18**	**7**	**5**	**6**	**36**	**34**	**19**
1st Kings Own Regiment	17	6	5	6	32	34	17
Whitstable	17	6	5	6	26	29	17
The Carabiniers	18	4	7	7	36	36	15
Ramsgate Town	18	4	4	10	27	51	12
Depot Royal Marines (Deal)	18	3	4	11	15	45	10
Folkestone Gas	18	3	0	15	23	48	6
					336	337	

1st Kings Own Regiment vs Whitstable was not played.

Championship decider (Played at Folkestone Town)

Ashford Railway Works vs Folkestone   1-0

1914-19

The Kent League was suspended when war was declared and play did not resume until 1919.

1919: CHANGES AFTER THE WAR

Division One

Charlton Athletic joined from the London League and Gillingham Reserves joined from the South-Eastern League. New Brompton, Royal Army Service Corps (Grove Park), Ordnance and Vickers (Crayford) also joined. Margate were promoted from Division Two (East).

Note: Ordnance was the playing name of the Royal Ordnance Factory. Bromley moved to the Athenian League and Crystal Palace Reserves and Millwall Reserves moved to the London Combination. 2nd Royal Dublin Fusiliers, Dartford, Gravesend United, Rochester, Southend United Reserves and Woolwich did not rejoin.

Division Two (West)

Only Depot Battalion Royal Engineers rejoined after the war, along with 5 new members amongst whom were Belvedere & District, a newly formed club.

Of the pre-war clubs who left, Cray Wanderers had joined the South Suburban League.

Division Two (East)

Ashford Railway Works, Depot Royal Marines (Deal), Folkestone and Whitstable rejoined after the war and were joined by 4 new members: Deal Cinque Ports, Depot Machine Gun Corps, Eythorne and S.E.R.M.I. Note: S.E.R.M.I. = South-Eastern and Chatham Railway Mechanics Institute.

1919-20

Division One

Northfleet United	24	19	3	2	70	22	41
Maidstone United	24	16	1	7	50	31	33
Sheppey United	24	14	2	8	63	30	30
Charlton Athletic	24	12	5	7	45	28	29
Gillingham Reserves	24	11	6	7	54	36	28
Chatham	24	13	2	9	46	32	28
Margate	24	8	6	10	48	51	22
Ordnance	24	10	2	12	41	45	22
Royal Naval Depot (Chatham)	24	7	5	12	28	42	19
Tunbridge Wells Rangers	24	8	2	14	41	52	18
Sittingbourne	24	7	4	13	34	52	18
Vickers (Crayford)	24	8	2	14	38	59	18
New Brompton	24	2	2	20	18	87	6
					576	567	

Royal Army Service Corps (Grove Park) resigned after playing 18 games because they were posted elsewhere. Their record was deleted.

Charlton Athletic and Chatham both moved to the Southern League and were replaced by their Reserves. Gillingham Reserves also moved to the Southern League and New Brompton left. Middlesex Regiment, Ramsgate and Royal Marine Light Infantry joined. Folkestone and Ashford Railway Works were promoted from Division Two (East).
Depot Battalion Royal Engineers and Bexleyheath Labour were promoted from Division Two (West), the latter changing their name to Bexleyheath Town.

Division Two (West)

Depot Battalion Royal Engineers	10	9	0	1	44	12	18
Bexleyheath Labour	10	8	1	1	28	6	17
Gravesend Hotspur	10	3	2	5	22	21	8
Belvedere & District	10	2	3	5	18	26	7
Imperial Paper Mills	10	2	2	6	18	24	6
N.F.D.S. & S. Sittingbourne	10	2	0	8	9	50	4

Note: N.F.D.S. & S. = National Federation of Disabled Soldiers & Sailors. They left the league at the end of the season, as did Imperial Paper Mills. 1st Royal Warwickshire Regiment, Erith Oil Works, Maidstone United Reserves, Minster United, Royal Artillery, Sheppey United Reserves and Sittingbourne Paper Mills all joined the league.

Division Two (East)

Ashford Railway Works	14	10	2	2	60	18	22
Folkestone	14	9	3	2	58	19	21
Whitstable	14	8	3	3	29	23	19
Depot Machine Gun Corps	14	8	1	5	50	24	17
Depot Royal Marines (Deal)	14	3	3	8	31	30	9
S.E.R.M.I.	13	4	1	8	23	49	9
Deal Cinque Ports	14	4	0	10	16	75	8
Eythorne	13	2	1	10	13	35	5
					280	273	

S.E.R.M.I. vs Eythorne was not played. Ashford Railway Works Reserves, Dover Sports, Folkestone Reserves, Margate Reserves and Ramsgate Reserves all joined the league. Deal Cinque Ports left.

1920-21

Division One

Charlton Athletic Reserves	32	21	7	4	75	29	49
Maidstone United	32	20	7	5	82	27	47
Northfleet United	32	21	3	8	76	40	45
Ramsgate	31	17	9	5	71	35	43
Folkestone	31	16	7	8	73	38	39
Sittingbourne	32	15	7	10	69	49	37
Sheppey United	32	14	8	10	53	50	36
Margate	32	14	7	11	41	41	35
Tunbridge Wells Rangers	32	12	9	11	60	47	33
Ashford Railway Works	31	13	6	12	50	42	32
Chatham Reserves	32	13	5	14	54	47	31
Ordnance	32	9	7	16	35	68	25
Royal Naval Depot (Chatham)	32	9	6	17	37	57	24
Royal Marine Light Infantry	32	7	9	16	44	62	23
Bexleyheath Town	32	6	8	18	36	82	20
Vickers (Crayford)	32	3	8	21	22	71	14
Depot Battalion Royal Engineers	29	1	3	25	23	108	5
					901	893	

Depot Battalion Royal Engineers left 3 games unplayed. Middlesex Regiment resigned when they were posted to Cologne and their record was deleted. They had previously lost all 17 of their games! Depot Battalion Royal Engineers were relegated to Division Two (West). Charlton Athletic Reserves moved to the London Combination and Ordnance and Vickers (Crayford) also left the league. Chatham returned from the Southern League, replacing their reserves. Dartford and Woolwich also returned.

Division Two (West)

Maidstone United Reserves	14	9	2	3	67	15	20
Royal Artillery	14	9	1	4	44	20	19
Sittingbourne Paper Mills	14	9	0	5	38	24	18
Sheppey United Reserves	14	8	2	4	40	26	18
Belvedere & District	14	7	4	3	27	19	18
Minster United	14	2	4	8	21	50	8
Gravesend Hotspur	14	2	3	9	14	39	7
Erith Oil Works	14	0	4	10	7	60	4
					258	253	

1st Royal Warwickshire Regiment resigned when posted overseas after playing 8 games. Their record was deleted.

Belvedere & District left the league and Erith Oil Works, Gravesend Hotspur and Royal Artillery also left. Sittingbourne Reserves and Training Battalion Royal Engineers both joined.

Division Two (East)

Depot Machine Gun Corps	18	12	2	4	55	19	26
Ramsgate Reserves	18	11	4	3	46	23	26
Dover Sports	18	11	3	4	48	29	25
Eythorne	18	10	1	7	37	43	21
Whitstable	18	8	4	6	45	37	20
Folkestone Reserves	18	8	3	7	42	32	19
Depot Royal Marines (Deal)	18	7	3	8	35	46	17
Ashford Railway Works Reserves	18	4	5	9	38	41	13
S.E.R.M.I.	18	5	2	11	30	67	12
Margate Reserves	18	0	1	17	13	52	1

Dover Sports changed their name to Dover United. Depot Machine Gun Corps and S.E.R.M.I. both left the league. Connaught Rangers joined.

1921-22

Division One

Maidstone United	28	24	3	1	92	12	51
Northfleet United	28	18	6	4	72	36	42
Folkestone	28	17	6	5	59	30	40
Ramsgate	28	13	7	8	52	36	33
Dartford	28	13	7	8	50	40	33
Sheppey United	28	14	3	11	50	27	31
Margate	28	11	8	9	43	36	30
Ashford Railway Works	28	9	11	8	42	40	29
Royal Naval Depot (Chatham)	28	11	5	12	44	48	27
Chatham	28	9	8	11	36	34	26
Sittingbourne	28	7	6	15	40	54	20
Royal Marine Light Infantry	28	5	7	16	31	61	17
Bexleyheath Town	28	7	3	18	26	86	17
Tunbridge Wells Rangers	28	5	6	17	33	58	16
Woolwich	28	2	4	22	16	88	8

Belvedere & District of the London League returned and changed their name to Erith & Belvedere. Gillingham Reserves also returned, from the Southern League.

Division Two (West)

Maidstone United Reserves	12	10	1	1	58	10	21
Sheppey United Reserves	12	7	2	3	25	18	16
Depot Battalion Royal Engineers	12	5	2	5	22	36	12
Sittingbourne Paper Mills	12	4	3	5	23	33	11
Minster United	12	5	0	7	15	27	10
Sittingbourne Reserves	12	4	1	7	20	29	9
Training Battalion Royal Engineers	12	2	1	9	20	30	5

Whitstable transferred from Division Two (East). Dartford Reserves and Tunbridge Wells Rangers Reserves both joined.

Division Two (East)

Dover United	14	10	2	2	44	17	22
Margate Reserves	14	8	3	3	33	19	19
Whitstable	14	7	3	4	29	15	17
Folkestone Reserves	14	6	5	3	38	32	17
Ashford Railway Works Reserves	14	8	0	6	41	27	16
Ramsgate Reserves	14	4	2	8	24	37	10
Depot Royal Marines (Deal)	14	3	2	9	17	40	8
Connaught Rangers	14	1	1	12	11	50	3

Eythorne resigned after losing all 3 of their games played and their record was deleted. Connaught Rangers left the league.

1922-23

Division One

Maidstone United	32	26	4	2	96	10	56
Sittingbourne	32	24	4	4	102	20	52
Dartford	32	17	9	6	41	22	43
Northfleet United	32	17	5	10	88	41	39
Folkestone	32	16	7	9	65	42	39
Ashford Railway Works	32	13	8	11	63	50	34
Royal Naval Depot (Chatham)	32	13	8	11	54	60	34
Sheppey United	32	13	7	12	53	43	33
Gillingham Reserves	32	11	9	12	58	56	31
Chatham	32	12	6	14	60	55	30
Royal Marine Light Infantry	32	12	3	17	43	71	27
Erith & Belvedere	32	10	6	16	39	63	26
Ramsgate	32	9	8	15	40	69	26
Tunbridge Wells Rangers	32	10	3	19	51	79	23
Bexleyheath Town	32	7	7	18	43	77	21
Margate	32	7	6	19	36	72	20
Woolwich	32	3	4	25	25	127	10

Royal Marine Light Infantry changed their name to Royal Marine Depot (Chatham).
Margate were suspended due to financial irregularities. Folkestone moved to the Southern League. Charlton Athletic "A" joined the league.

Division Two (West)

Maidstone United Reserves	18	17	0	1	81	10	34
Dartford Reserves	18	14	1	3	48	20	29
Whitstable	18	11	3	4	57	28	25
Depot Battalion Royal Engineers	18	9	2	7	38	31	20
Minster United	18	7	2	9	36	43	16
Sittingbourne Paper Mills	18	6	4	8	27	35	16
Tunbridge Wells Rangers Reserves	18	5	3	10	23	65	13
Sheppey United Reserves	18	5	2	11	26	44	12
Sittingbourne Reserves	18	4	1	13	23	50	9
Training Battalion Royal Engineers	18	2	2	14	22	55	6

The reserve sides of Dartford, Maidstone United, Sittingbourne and Tunbridge Wells all left the league. Aveling & Porter's, Chatham Reserves, Dartford Amateurs, Faversham Rangers, Faversham Services and Southern Railway Mechanics Institute joined.

Division Two (East)

Folkestone Reserves	10	7	3	0	42	8	17
Dover United	10	7	2	1	40	14	16
Ashford Railway Works Reserves	10	5	0	5	20	24	10
Margate Reserves	10	4	1	5	22	24	9
Ramsgate Reserves	10	2	0	8	10	37	4
Depot Royal Marines (Deal)	10	2	0	8	13	40	4

Ashford Railway Works Reserves, Depot Royal Marines (Deal), Folkestone Reserves and Margate Reserves all left the league. Southern Railway Mechanics Institute joined.

1923-24

Division One

Charlton Athletic "A"	30	25	3	2	79	15	53
Chatham	30	20	4	6	76	35	44
Sittingbourne	30	17	5	8	65	30	39
Northfleet United	30	15	5	10	61	35	35
Maidstone United	30	15	5	10	52	48	35
Sheppey United	30	15	4	11	70	50	34
Ashford Railway Works	30	13	7	10	61	48	33
Dartford	30	14	5	11	60	57	33
Gillingham Reserves	30	13	4	13	56	49	30
Tunbridge Wells Rangers	30	15	0	15	72	72	30
Erith & Belvedere	30	11	4	15	51	69	26
Royal Marine Depot (Chatham)	30	9	6	15	39	55	24
Royal Naval Depot (Chatham)	30	9	5	16	48	63	23
Woolwich	30	7	4	19	31	77	18
Bexleyheath Town	30	5	3	22	32	88	13
Ramsgate	30	3	4	23	34	96	10

Charlton Athletic "A" and Ramsgate both left the league. Margate rejoined

after reforming as Margate Town and Grays Thurrock United joined as a new club. Catford Southend and Grays Athletic also joined.

Division Two (West)

Chatham Reserves	22	16	4	2	66	17	36
Faversham Services	22	12	8	2	53	20	32
Minster United	22	12	5	5	59	29	29
Whitstable	22	10	6	6	52	34	26
Training Battalion Royal Engineers	22	10	5	7	42	31	25
Sittingbourne Paper Mills	22	9	6	7	51	43	24
Depot Battalion Royal Engineers	22	9	5	8	45	45	23
Sheppey United Reserves	22	10	2	10	41	54	22
Aveling & Porter's	22	8	5	9	45	49	21
Dartford Amateurs	22	4	3	15	28	65	11
Faversham Rangers	22	2	5	15	31	65	9
Southern Railway Mechanics Institute	22	2	2	18	32	93	6

Dartford Amateurs, Sheppey United Reserves and Southern Railway Mechanics Institute all left the league.
1st Royal Warwickshire Regiment, Canterbury Waverley, R.A.F. Eastchurch, Royal Naval Depot (Chatham) Reserves and Sittingbourne Reserves joined.

Division Two (East)

Dover United	4	4	0	0	26	3	8
Southern Railway Mechanics Institute	4	1	0	3	11	14	2
Ramsgate Reserves	4	1	0	3	5	25	2

The two sections of the Second Divisions merged to become Division Two (Mid-Kent).
Dover United and Ramsgate Reserves both left the league.

1924-25

Division One

Chatham	34	31	1	2	111	24	63
Northfleet United	34	29	1	4	114	25	59
Dartford	34	21	6	7	77	42	48
Sittingbourne	34	18	7	9	69	40	43
Gillingham Reserves	34	17	6	11	77	52	40
Grays Thurrock United	34	16	8	10	65	46	40
Sheppey United	34	15	9	10	83	62	39
Tunbridge Wells Rangers	34	15	8	11	51	53	38
Catford Southend	34	17	2	15	72	54	36
Grays Athletic	34	11	8	15	55	57	30
Ashford Railway Works	34	12	6	16	56	67	30
Royal Marine Depot (Chatham)	34	9	7	18	48	80	25
Erith & Belvedere	34	8	8	18	64	78	24
Margate Town	34	9	5	20	50	92	23
Bexleyheath Town	34	10	2	22	40	68	22
Royal Naval Depot (Chatham)	34	9	3	22	46	93	21
Maidstone United	34	7	4	23	39	92	18
Woolwich	34	5	3	26	33	125	13

Grays Thurrock United moved to the Southern League and were replaced by their reserves.
1st Royal Warwickshire Regiment were promoted from Division Two (Mid-Kent).

Division Two (Mid-Kent)

1st Royal Warwickshire Regt.	**24**	**18**	**3**	**3**	**88**	**29**	**39**
Whitstable	26	16	6	4	60	35	38
Minster United	25	14	4	7	72	47	32
Depot Battalion Royal Engineers	26	11	7	8	68	58	29
Sittingbourne Paper Mills	26	11	6	9	59	62	28
Training Battalion Royal Engineers	25	9	7	9	64	60	25
Chatham Reserves	26	10	5	11	53	60	25
Faversham Services	26	9	5	12	70	62	23
Aveling & Porter's	26	9	5	12	49	60	23
Faversham Rangers	26	9	5	12	42	64	23
R.A.F. Eastchurch	25	9	4	12	66	66	22
Royal Naval Depot (Chatham) Res.	25	9	3	13	44	69	21
Sittingbourne Reserves	21	4	4	13	30	57	12
Canterbury Waverley	23	4	2	17	53	91	10
					818	**820**	

7 games were not played.
Faversham Services, Royal Naval Depot (Chatham) Reserves and Sittingbourne Reserves all left the league. Rainham joined.

1925-26

Division One

Northfleet United	36	29	3	4	172	48	61
Chatham	36	27	5	4	125	31	59
Sittingbourne	36	23	7	6	122	46	53
Dartford	36	20	5	11	89	55	45
Gillingham Reserves	36	20	3	13	88	60	43
Ashford Railway Works	36	17	7	12	81	76	41
Margate Town	36	15	8	13	81	60	38
Grays Thurrock United Reserves	36	17	3	16	85	72	37
1st Royal Warwickshire Regiment	35	14	8	13	84	76	36
Catford Southend	35	12	9	14	83	67	33
Royal Naval Depot (Chatham)	36	13	6	17	71	96	32
Maidstone United	36	13	4	19	59	116	30
Sheppey United	36	12	4	20	53	104	28
Bexleyheath Town	36	10	7	19	63	92	27
Grays Athletic	36	9	8	19	64	93	26
Erith & Belvedere	36	9	8	19	52	81	26
Tunbridge Wells Rangers	36	10	5	21	68	121	25
Woolwich	36	9	6	21	55	135	24
Royal Marine Depot (Chatham)	36	8	2	26	60	126	18

One game was not played.
Dartford moved to the Southern League, Grays Athletic moved to the London League and 1st Royal Warwickshire Regiment, Catford Southend, Grays Thurrock United Reserves and Woolwich also left the league. The Loyal Regiment joined.

Division Two (Mid-Kent)

Minster United	20	16	1	3	60	28	33
Whitstable	20	14	3	3	74	28	31
Training Battalion Royal Engineers	20	14	0	6	52	41	28
Chatham Reserves	20	10	4	6	51	40	24
R.A.F. Eastchurch	20	9	4	7	64	51	22
Faversham Rangers	20	9	2	9	45	45	20
Canterbury Waverley	20	8	1	11	71	72	17
Depot Battalion Royal Engineers	20	7	3	10	46	57	17
Sittingbourne Paper Mills	20	4	5	11	38	59	13
Rainham	20	3	2	15	35	76	8
Aveling & Porter's	20	2	3	15	31	70	7

Aveling & Porter's and Rainham left the league.
Murston Rangers and Royal Marine Depot (Chatham) Reserves joined.

1926-27

Division One

Chatham	26	20	2	4	70	25	42
Sittingbourne	26	20	0	6	84	35	40
Margate Town	26	18	4	4	70	33	40
Sheppey United	26	15	4	7	64	34	34
Northfleet United	26	15	3	8	79	51	33
Gillingham Reserves	26	13	5	8	57	44	31
Tunbridge Wells Rangers	26	8	6	12	58	66	22
Maidstone United	26	7	8	11	66	82	22
Erith & Belvedere	26	7	6	13	47	62	20
Royal Naval Depot (Chatham)	26	8	4	14	47	63	20
Loyal Regiment	26	8	4	14	44	68	20
Ashford Railway Works	*26*	*8*	*3*	*15*	*36*	*58*	*19*
Bexleyheath Town	26	4	7	15	50	80	15
Royal Marine Depot (Chatham)	26	2	2	22	34	105	6

Catford Southend resigned after playing 10 games. Their record was deleted.
Chatham Reserves and Sittingbourne Paper Mills were promoted from Division Two (Mid-Kent).
Sheppey United moved to the Southern League and were replaced by their Reserves. Chatham, Gillingham Reserves, Northfleet United and Sittingbourne also moved to the Southern League.
Dartford Reserves, Grays Thurrock United Reserves and Tilbury all joined.

Division Two (Mid-Kent)

Chatham Reserves	**20**	**15**	**1**	**4**	**77**	**23**	**31**
R.A.F. Eastchurch	20	14	3	3	75	31	31
Minster United	20	13	2	5	67	35	28
Canterbury Waverley	20	12	1	7	70	52	25
Sittingbourne Paper Mills	**20**	**8**	**2**	**10**	**45**	**41**	**18**
Whitstable	20	9	0	11	46	51	18
Depot Battalion Royal Engineers	20	7	3	10	36	43	17
Training Battalion Royal Engineers	20	6	2	12	48	69	14
Royal Marine Depot (Chatham) Res.	20	7	0	13	46	104	14
Faversham Rangers	20	6	1	13	46	73	13
Murston Rangers	20	5	1	14	49	83	11

Faversham Rangers and Minster United both left the league.
Borstal Athletic and Troy Town Invicta joined.

Division Two (East) was revived with 3 members – Ashford Railway Works (who were relegated from Division One), Chislet Colliery Welfare and Dover United.

1927-28

Division One

Sheppey United Reserves	26	18	2	6	83	47	38
Margate Town	26	14	6	6	68	43	34
Loyal Regiment	26	12	5	9	81	63	29
Bexleyheath Town	26	14	1	11	76	77	29
Dartford Reserves	26	13	2	11	65	53	28
Grays Thurrock United Reserves	26	11	5	10	78	65	27
Tunbridge Wells Rangers	26	12	1	13	72	66	25
Royal Naval Depot (Chatham)	26	10	5	11	68	65	25
Chatham Reserves	26	13	1	12	55	54	25
Erith & Belvedere	26	10	5	11	53	68	25
Tilbury	26	11	2	13	69	76	24
Maidstone United	26	8	4	14	56	81	20
Royal Marine Depot (Chatham)	26	8	2	16	45	77	18
Sittingbourne Paper Mills	26	4	7	15	44	78	15

Chatham Reserves had 2 points deducted for fielding an ineligible player.

Canterbury Waverley were promoted from Division Two (Mid-Kent).
Margate Town closed down with large debts and the Loyal Regiment also left the league. Folkestone Reserves joined.

Division Two (Mid-Kent)

Whitstable	16	11	0	5	44	41	22
Canterbury Waverley	**16**	**10**	**1**	**5**	**57**	**36**	**21**
Training Battalion Royal Engineers	16	9	1	6	50	39	19
Depot Battalion Royal Engineers	16	7	3	6	39	35	17
Borstal Athletic	16	5	4	7	36	40	14
Murston Rangers	16	6	2	8	30	35	14
R.A.F. Eastchurch	16	6	1	9	46	56	13
Troy Town Invicta	16	5	2	9	33	42	12
Royal Marine Depot (Chatham) Res.	16	4	4	8	33	44	12

Division Two (East)

Ashford Railway Works	4	2	1	1	9	9	5
Chislet Colliery Welfare	4	2	0	2	7	8	4
Dover United	4	1	1	2	8	7	3

Division Two (East) closed down and Division Two (Mid-Kent) was renamed Division Two.
Canterbury Waverley Reserves and Aylesford Paper Mills both joined.

1928-29

Division One

Bexleyheath Town	26	16	5	5	61	43	37
Tunbridge Wells Rangers	26	16	4	6	102	48	36
Erith & Belvedere	26	14	4	8	63	51	32
Royal Marine Depot (Chatham)	26	14	3	9	71	54	31
Chatham Reserves	26	12	5	9	58	53	29
Royal Naval Depot (Chatham)	26	11	6	9	73	51	28
Sheppey United Reserves	26	12	0	14	62	71	24
Tilbury	26	9	5	12	58	61	23
Sittingbourne Paper Mills	26	9	5	12	59	73	23
Folkestone Reserves	26	8	6	12	60	72	22
Maidstone United	26	9	4	13	54	70	22
Canterbury Waverley	26	7	5	14	48	79	19
Grays Thurrock United Reserves	26	8	2	16	52	71	18
Dartford Reserves	26	8	4	14	43	67	18

Dartford Reserves had 2 points deducted for fielding an ineligible player. Erith & Belvedere moved to the London League. Chatham returned from the Southern League, replacing their reserves and Gillingham Reserves also returned from the Southern League. Margate joined after reforming and Dover United and Sittingbourne Reserves also joined.

Division Two

R.A.F. Eastchurch	18	14	2	2	73	25	30
Whitstable	18	13	1	4	53	28	27
Borstal Athletic	18	8	4	6	45	33	20
Troy Town Invicta	18	9	2	7	45	40	20
Royal Marine Depot (Chatham) Res.	18	7	5	6	39	38	19
Aylesford Paper Mills	18	8	3	7	40	46	19
Murston Rangers	18	6	3	9	28	44	15
Depot Battalion Royal Engineers	18	5	2	11	42	59	12
Training Battalion Royal Engineers	18	4	4	10	26	40	12
Canterbury Waverley Reserves	18	2	2	14	27	65	6

Tunbridge Wells Rangers Reserves joined the league.

1929-30

Division One

Gillingham Reserves	32	24	4	4	102	43	52
Margate	32	23	3	6	103	33	49
Tunbridge Wells Rangers	32	22	2	8	115	65	46
Dartford Reserves	32	19	4	9	90	45	42
Maidstone United	32	15	7	10	80	67	37
Royal Naval Depot (Chatham)	32	14	5	13	82	73	33
Sittingbourne Reserves	32	13	5	14	66	52	31
Chatham	32	12	7	13	63	63	31
Sheppey United Reserves	32	14	3	15	77	96	31
Bexleyheath Town	32	13	4	15	74	84	30
Sittingbourne Paper Mills	32	11	8	13	70	84	30
Tilbury	32	13	3	16	67	61	29
Royal Marine Depot (Chatham)	32	12	3	17	70	73	27
Dover United	32	11	0	21	67	99	22
Canterbury Waverley	32	8	3	21	65	143	19
Grays Thurrock United Reserves	32	8	2	22	60	129	18
Folkestone Reserves	32	8	1	23	65	106	17

Sittingbourne and Grays Thurrock United joined from the Southern League, replacing their reserves. Northfleet United also joined from the Southern League and Ashford joined as a newly formed club.

Division Two

Aylesford Paper Mills	20	15	2	3	81	24	32
Borstal Athletic	20	12	2	6	48	32	26
Training Battalion Royal Engineers	20	11	4	5	47	33	26
Canterbury Waverley Reserves	20	11	2	7	51	42	24
Tunbridge Wells Rangers Reserves	20	9	2	9	42	33	20
Royal Marine Depot (Chatham) Res.	20	7	4	9	48	44	18
R.A.F. Eastchurch	20	7	3	10	41	60	17
Whitstable	20	7	2	11	43	48	16
Depot Battalion Royal Engineers	20	6	3	11	41	66	15
Troy Town Invicta	20	7	1	12	35	64	15
Murston Rangers	20	4	3	13	26	57	11

Luton joined the league.

1930-31

Division One

Tunbridge Wells Rangers	36	29	4	3	159	23	62
Gillingham Reserves	36	27	5	4	103	44	59
Margate	36	24	10	2	99	27	58
Northfleet United	36	22	3	11	125	58	47
Chatham	36	20	6	10	134	65	46
Ashford	36	16	10	10	93	70	42
Dartford Reserves	36	18	5	13	85	79	41
Sheppey United Reserves	*36*	*17*	*6*	*13*	*85*	*92*	*40*
Sittingbourne	36	15	5	16	93	79	35
Canterbury Waverley	36	14	7	15	79	92	35
Grays Thurrock United	36	12	8	16	87	108	32
Maidstone United	36	14	4	18	72	90	32
Bexleyheath Town	36	13	4	19	72	99	30
Sittingbourne Paper Mills	36	9	6	21	60	110	24
Folkestone Reserves	36	11	1	24	80	123	23
Tilbury	36	10	2	24	57	112	22
Royal Marine Depot (Chatham)	36	8	5	23	69	112	21
Dover United	36	8	4	24	73	142	20
Royal Naval Depot (Chatham)	36	6	3	27	52	152	15

Sittingbourne Paper Mills changed their name to Lloyds (Sittingbourne) and Bexleyheath Town changed their name to Bexleyheath & Welling. Tunbridge Wells Rangers moved to the Southern League and were replaced by their reserves who were promoted from Division Two. Sheppey United rejoined and their reserves moved down to Division Two. Tilbury moved to the London League from where Erith & Belvedere returned.

Division Two

Aylesford Paper Mills	22	18	2	2	64	25	38
Tunbridge Wells Rangers Res.	**22**	**12**	**3**	**7**	**76**	**43**	**27**
Royal Marine Depot (Chatham) Res.	22	11	5	6	67	39	27
Canterbury Waverley Reserves	22	11	5	6	66	43	27
Borstal Athletic	22	11	5	6	62	43	27
Whitstable	22	9	6	7	51	51	24
Luton	21	8	5	8	46	42	21
Training Battalion Royal Engineers	21	8	3	10	41	43	19
Murston Rangers	22	5	5	12	44	65	15
Depot Battalion Royal Engineers	22	7	1	14	36	67	15
Troy Town Invicta	22	3	5	14	35	78	11
R.A.F. Eastchurch	20	3	3	14	31	80	9

R.A.F. Eastchurch could not fulfil their last 2 fixtures as the base was placed in military isolation.

1931-32

Division One

Northfleet United	36	32	2	2	138	22	66
Ashford	36	26	5	5	115	54	57
Tunbridge Wells Rangers Reserves	36	24	7	5	119	37	55
Margate	36	25	4	7	129	38	54
Chatham	36	22	8	6	100	43	52
Folkestone Reserves	36	23	4	9	103	52	50
Dartford Reserves	36	21	6	9	86	50	48
Canterbury Waverley	36	18	3	15	96	79	39
Gillingham Reserves	36	15	7	14	69	62	37
Bexleyheath & Welling	36	12	6	18	59	76	30
Grays Thurrock United	36	13	3	20	56	107	29
Lloyds (Sittingbourne)	36	12	4	20	67	97	28
Maidstone United	36	12	3	21	72	96	27
Royal Marine Depot (Chatham)	36	10	4	22	59	96	24
Sheppey United	36	9	6	21	57	95	24
Erith & Belvedere	36	8	4	24	51	129	20
Royal Naval Depot (Chatham)	36	7	4	25	53	134	18
Sittingbourne	36	6	5	25	43	111	17
Dover United	36	3	3	30	49	143	9

Dover United and Grays Thurrock United left the league. Aylesford Paper Mills were promoted from Division Two.

Division Two

Aylesford Paper Mills	22	17	3	2	89	28	37
Margate Reserves	22	16	4	2	66	27	36
Lloyds (Sittingbourne) Reserves	22	11	7	4	55	33	29
Borstal Athletic	22	12	5	5	61	43	29
Sheppey United Reserves	22	11	4	7	56	51	26
Canterbury Waverley Reserves	22	10	5	7	61	48	25
Chatham Reserves	22	8	6	8	45	35	22
Depot Battalion Royal Engineers	22	10	2	10	54	67	22
Whitstable	22	7	2	13	45	68	16
R.A.F. Eastchurch	22	5	1	16	48	78	11
Sittingbourne Reserves	22	2	2	18	36	85	6
Royal Marine Depot (Chatham) Res.	22	2	1	19	31	84	5

Depot Battalion Royal Engineers and Sittingbourne Reserves both left the league. Maidstone United Reserves, Ramsgate Press Wanderers and Training Battalion Royal Engineers all joined.

1932-33

Division One

Margate	34	28	1	5	112	34	57
Northfleet United	34	28	1	5	126	50	57
Gillingham Reserves	34	22	4	8	130	44	48
Folkestone Reserves	34	20	4	10	114	56	44
Tunbridge Wells Rangers Reserves	34	21	3	10	127	63	43
Chatham	**34**	**17**	**5**	**12**	**95**	**66**	**39**
Dartford Reserves	34	13	7	14	82	64	33
Ashford	34	16	1	17	79	76	33
Bexleyheath & Welling	34	14	5	15	65	77	33
Canterbury Waverley	34	14	4	16	82	89	32
Sittingbourne	34	13	5	16	70	109	31
Erith & Belvedere	34	13	3	18	70	97	29
Sheppey United	34	12	4	18	73	90	28
Maidstone United	34	11	5	18	78	105	27
Aylesford Paper Mills	34	11	5	18	79	112	27
Lloyds (Sittingbourne)	34	10	4	20	62	97	24
Royal Naval Depot (Chatham)	34	9	4	21	64	113	22
Royal Marine Depot (Chatham)	34	1	1	32	32	198	3

Tunbridge Wells Rangers Reserves had 2 points deducted.

Financial troubles caused Chatham to become amateur and the first team voluntarily replaced the Reserves in Division Two, from where Ramsgate Press Wanderers were promoted. London Paper Mills joined the league. Margate joined the Southern League while continuing to play in the Kent League.

Division Two

Sheppey United Reserves	22	14	3	5	94	42	31
Ramsgate Press Wanderers	**22**	**14**	**3**	**5**	**78**	**50**	**31**
Borstal Athletic	22	14	2	6	57	35	30
Canterbury Waverley Reserves	22	13	1	8	65	61	27
Chatham Reserves	22	11	3	8	66	41	25
Lloyds (Sittingbourne) Reserves	22	11	2	9	64	46	24
Training Battalion Royal Engineers	22	11	1	10	56	59	23
Margate Reserves	22	9	2	11	45	40	20
Maidstone United Reserves	22	7	6	9	71	74	20
Whitstable	22	7	4	11	53	72	18
Royal Marine Depot (Chatham) Res.	22	4	3	15	37	105	11
R.A.F. Eastchurch	22	1	2	19	31	92	4

Canterbury Waverley Reserves changed their name to Canterbury Amateurs. Deal Town joined from the Kent Amateur League and Aylesford Paper Mills Reserves and Gravesend United also joined. Margate Reserves left.

1933-34

Division One

London Paper Mills	36	30	2	4	111	42	62
Gillingham Reserves	36	26	4	6	118	50	56
Margate	36	23	3	10	94	58	49
Northfleet United	36	23	2	11	122	47	48
Ramsgate Press Wanderers	36	19	6	11	84	58	44
Royal Naval Depot (Chatham)	36	20	2	14	113	74	42
Dartford Reserves	36	18	5	13	75	63	41
Tunbridge Wells Rangers Reserves	36	16	8	12	76	66	40
Folkestone Reserves	36	15	5	16	102	71	35
Sheppey United	36	16	3	17	74	85	35
Canterbury Waverley	36	14	6	16	79	79	34
Lloyds (Sittingbourne)	36	13	8	15	64	75	34
Sittingbourne	36	11	10	15	57	90	32
Ashford	36	14	3	19	72	92	31
Aylesford Paper Mills	36	12	5	19	57	72	29
Erith & Belvedere	36	10	5	21	82	108	25
Bexleyheath & Welling	36	7	7	22	55	93	21
Maidstone United	36	8	3	25	59	126	19
Royal Marine Depot (Chatham)	*36*	*2*	*3*	*31*	*39*	*184*	*7*

Royal Marine Depot (Chatham) were relegated to Division Two, replacing their reserves. Ramsgate Press Wanderers changed their name to Ramsgate. Cray Wanderers returned from the London League.

Division Two

Whitstable	24	16	5	3	85	41	37
Training Battalion Royal Engineers	24	17	2	5	72	35	36
Aylesford Paper Mills Reserves	24	16	4	4	86	47	36
Gravesend United	24	13	4	7	75	46	30
Canterbury Amateurs	24	11	3	10	73	60	25
Lloyds (Sittingbourne) Reserves	24	9	6	9	57	50	24
Maidstone United Reserves	24	10	3	11	58	68	23
Borstal Athletic	24	8	5	11	51	58	21
Deal Town	24	8	4	12	56	83	20
Sheppey United Reserves	24	8	3	13	59	63	19
Chatham	24	6	4	14	49	75	16
R.A.F. Eastchurch	24	6	3	15	49	85	15
Royal Marine Depot (Chatham) Reserves	24	2	6	16	31	90	10

Maidstone United Reserves left the league and Depot Battalion Royal Engineers joined.

1934-35

Division One

Northfleet United	36	26	7	3	110	30	59
London Paper Mills	36	24	5	7	95	40	53
Margate	36	23	4	9	110	51	50
Gillingham Reserves	36	19	6	11	97	61	44
Ashford	36	16	9	11	72	51	41
Canterbury Waverley	36	16	7	13	86	64	39
Ramsgate	36	16	6	14	69	65	38
Sittingbourne	36	16	4	16	67	76	36
Folkestone Reserves	36	17	1	18	81	77	35
Lloyds (Sittingbourne)	36	13	9	14	65	65	35
Dartford Reserves	36	13	6	17	64	76	32
Erith & Belvedere	36	13	4	19	62	90	30
Bexleyheath & Welling	36	11	7	18	74	93	29
Sheppey United	36	12	5	19	50	90	29
Maidstone United	36	12	4	20	68	90	28
Royal Naval Depot (Chatham)	36	11	6	19	81	109	28
Cray Wanderers	36	13	1	22	63	106	27
Tunbridge Wells Rangers Reserves	36	9	8	19	49	82	26
Aylesford Paper Mills	36	9	7	20	49	96	25

Margate's first team concentrated on the Southern League and their Kent League fixtures were fulfilled by their reserves.

Division Two

Chatham	24	17	3	4	82	34	37
Aylesford Paper Mills Reserves	24	16	5	3	91	46	37
Deal Town	24	15	3	6	102	47	33
Lloyds (Sittingbourne) Reserves	24	14	2	8	74	41	30
Whitstable	24	12	5	7	79	41	29
Canterbury Amateurs	24	12	4	8	81	63	28
Borstal Athletic	24	13	2	9	53	55	28
Sheppey United Reserves	24	11	4	9	64	50	26
Training Battalion Royal Engineers	22	7	3	12	49	66	17
Gravesend United	24	8	1	15	46	100	17
Depot Battalion Royal Engineers	24	5	3	16	48	64	13
R.A.F. Eastchurch	22	3	4	15	32	64	10
Royal Marine Depot (Chatham)	24	1	1	22	18	148	3

Two games were left unplayed.

Division Two closed down as the Kent County F.A. wished to introduce a new Kent Amateur League. Most of the Second Division clubs moved to this new league.

1935-36

Northfleet United	36	26	5	5	158	41	57
Folkestone Reserves	36	27	3	6	129	44	57
Margate Reserves	36	20	8	8	86	48	48
Canterbury Waverley	36	22	3	11	116	59	47
Gillingham Reserves	36	20	5	11	99	58	45
London Paper Mills	36	21	2	13	110	64	44
Cray Wanderers	36	16	7	13	62	83	39
Dartford Reserves	36	16	6	14	80	69	38
Bexleyheath & Welling	36	15	8	13	79	75	38
Lloyds (Sittingbourne)	36	15	8	13	66	71	38
Sittingbourne	36	13	9	14	77	84	35
Ashford	36	12	6	18	84	97	30
Ramsgate	36	12	6	18	61	84	30
Aylesford Paper Mills	36	12	6	18	61	98	30
Tunbridge Wells Rangers Reserves	36	12	5	19	82	120	29
Sheppey United	36	10	5	21	63	87	25
Maidstone United	36	9	6	21	63	122	24
Erith & Belvedere	36	9	3	24	57	97	21
Royal Naval Depot (Chatham)	36	3	3	30	42	174	9

Ramsgate and Royal Naval Depot (Chatham) both left the league.

1936-37

Northfleet United	32	25	2	5	128	29	52
Margate Reserves	32	24	4	4	107	41	52
Lloyds (Sittingbourne)	32	18	6	8	82	61	42
Gillingham Reserves	32	19	2	11	81	50	40
London Paper Mills	32	17	4	11	77	52	38
Ashford	32	16	5	11	76	53	37
Tunbridge Wells Rangers Reserves	32	18	1	13	80	69	37
Bexleyheath & Welling	32	14	5	13	72	54	33
Canterbury Waverley	32	11	8	13	74	63	30
Folkestone Reserves	32	12	4	16	79	99	28
Aylesford Paper Mills	32	12	3	17	68	89	27
Sittingbourne	32	9	8	15	64	86	26
Dartford Reserves	32	10	5	17	64	77	25
Erith & Belvedere	32	9	6	17	46	85	24
Sheppey United	32	8	6	18	44	80	22
Maidstone United	32	7	7	18	55	100	21
Cray Wanderers	32	3	4	25	55	164	10

Margate resigned from the Southern League and replaced their reserves in the Kent League.

The Second Division was revived as the attempt to introduce a new Kent Amateur League had not been successful.

1937-38　Division One

Margate	32	24	4	4	103	31	52
Aylesford Paper Mills	32	24	4	4	102	42	52
Northfleet United	32	23	5	4	116	29	51
London Paper Mills	32	20	9	3	88	35	49
Canterbury Waverley	32	16	8	8	74	53	40
Gillingham Reserves	32	16	3	13	84	63	35
Bexleyheath & Welling	32	14	5	13	68	60	33
Sittingbourne	32	14	4	14	74	64	32
Folkestone Reserves	32	12	6	14	78	85	30
Lloyds (Sittingbourne)	32	11	8	13	69	78	30
Ashford	32	11	6	15	67	75	28
Dartford Reserves	32	8	7	17	51	89	23
Erith & Belvedere	32	9	4	19	47	79	22
Sheppey United	32	9	4	19	46	108	22
Tunbridge Wells Rangers Reserves	32	10	1	21	60	88	21
Maidstone United	32	5	3	24	47	94	13
Cray Wanderers	32	5	1	26	39	130	11
					1213	*1203*	

Margate disbanded and Cray Wanderers moved to the Kent Amateur League.

Division Two

Margate Reserves	20	16	1	3	78	17	33
Lloyds (Sittingbourne) Reserves	20	16	1	3	61	23	33
Chatham	20	12	4	4	48	29	28
Whitstable	20	11	2	7	66	41	24
Aylesford Paper Mills Reserves	20	11	2	7	63	47	24
R.A.F. Eastchurch	20	8	3	9	41	46	19
Medway Corrugated Paper Co.	20	8	1	11	48	43	17
Faversham Invicta	20	6	1	13	50	75	13
Canterbury Waverley Reserves	20	5	3	12	38	60	13
Sheppey United Reserves	20	4	3	13	29	70	11
Southern Railway Athletic (Ashford)	20	2	1	17	22	93	5

Canterbury Waverley Reserves, Sheppey United Reserves and Southern Railway Athletic (Ashford) all left the league. Luton joined from the New Brompton League and Ashford Reserves, Deal Town, Dover, Ramsgate Grenville and Royal Marines Depot (Deal) also joined.

1938-39　Division One

Northfleet United	28	20	4	4	125	38	44
Gillingham Reserves	28	20	2	6	77	29	42
London Paper Mills	28	18	4	6	88	45	40
Ashford	28	16	3	9	89	59	35
Bexleyheath & Welling	28	15	4	9	67	52	34
Erith & Belvedere	28	14	3	11	77	65	31
Aylesford Paper Mills	28	12	5	11	69	67	29
Lloyds (Sittingbourne)	28	12	4	12	78	71	28
Canterbury Waverley	28	11	5	12	71	88	27
Sittingbourne	28	8	7	13	60	74	23
Dartford Reserves	28	8	5	15	56	90	21
Tunbridge Wells Rangers Reserves	28	7	4	17	60	114	18
Maidstone United	28	6	5	17	43	81	17
Folkestone Reserves	*28*	*5*	*6*	*17*	*57*	*85*	*16*
Sheppey United	28	5	5	18	42	101	15

Division Two

Dover	24	20	3	1	80	25	43
Ramsgate Grenville	24	15	4	5	73	43	34
Whitstable	24	10	7	7	56	50	27
Medway Corrugated Paper Co.	24	10	6	8	53	47	26
Deal Town	24	12	1	11	74	57	25
Royal Marines Depot (Deal)	24	10	5	9	59	66	25
Aylesford Paper Mills Reserves	24	11	1	12	65	60	23
Lloyds (Sittingbourne) Reserves	24	10	3	11	65	65	23
Ashford Reserves	24	9	5	10	72	74	23
R.A.F. Eastchurch	24	9	4	11	48	53	22
Chatham	24	7	4	13	36	47	18
Luton	24	9	0	15	46	62	18
Faversham Invicta	24	2	1	21	31	109	5

1939-44

At the end of the 1938-39 season, Folkestone returned to Division One from the Southern League, replacing their reserves who were relegated to Division Two. After re-forming, Margate also returned to Division One and Callenders Athletic and Shorts Sports also joined.
Aylesford Paper Mills Reserves, Chatham, Lloyds (Sittingbourne) Reserves and Royal Marines Depot (Deal) left Division Two and R.A.F. Manston joined.

However, after just 7 days of the 1939-40 season, in which 13 games had been played in Division One and 2 games in Division Two, war was declared and the league suspended all action.

An emergency league was started that operated in most seasons during the war but the majority of sides were military teams who could be moved at short notice. These seasons are not included in the official Kent League records.

The first season when the league was able to include more than a handful of civilian clubs or complete its fixtures was 1944-45.

1944-45

Gillingham	18	14	1	3	77	38	29
Shorts Sports	18	13	2	3	60	25	28
Ford Sports	18	9	3	6	40	36	21
Royal Navy Depot (Chatham)	18	8	2	8	62	49	18
Snowdown Colliery Welfare	18	7	3	8	59	53	17
Royal Marines (Chatham)	18	7	3	8	55	56	17
Gravesend United	18	7	3	8	39	50	17
Training Battalion Royal Engineers	18	8	0	10	45	51	16
Lloyds (Sittingbourne)	18	5	2	11	43	60	12
Dartford Amateurs	18	2	1	15	20	72	5
					500	490	

Coast Regiment resigned after playing 12 games and R.A.F. (D) resigned after playing 8 games.
Their records were deleted.
Ford Sports returned to the London League and Royal Navy Depot (Chatham) also left.
Folkestone Town and Sheppey United returned to the league, 12th I.T.C. Canterbury also joined and Ramsgate Athletic joined as a newly formed club.

1945-46

Gillingham	20	18	1	1	111	33	37
Folkestone Town	20	12	2	6	56	40	26
Gravesend United	20	9	3	8	62	52	21
Royal Marines (Chatham)	20	9	3	8	69	80	21
Sheppey United	20	10	1	9	55	70	21
Shorts Sports	20	9	1	10	47	51	19
12th I.T.C. (Canterbury)	20	8	3	9	53	59	19
Lloyds (Sittingbourne)	20	9	0	11	60	60	18
Ramsgate Athletic	20	7	3	10	51	51	17
Snowdown Colliery Welfare	20	5	1	14	45	80	11
Dartford Amateurs	20	4	2	14	34	79	10
					643	655	

Training Battalion Royal Engineers resigned and their record was deleted.
Gravesend United merged with Northfleet United to form Gravesend & Northfleet who joined the Southern League, while their reserves joined the Kent League. Gillingham returned to the Southern League and were replaced by their reserves. 12th I.T.C. (Canterbury) and Dartford Amateurs both left the league.

Pre-war members Ashford, Deal Town, Dover, Maidstone United, Margate and Sittingbourne returned to the league and Betteshanger Colliery Welfare also joined.

The Second Division was re-formed.

1946-47

Division One

Margate	30	16	9	5	89	46	41
Folkestone Town	30	17	5	8	100	70	39
Sheppey United	30	17	4	9	84	55	38
Maidstone United	30	17	3	10	80	56	37
Ramsgate Athletic	30	16	5	9	69	59	37
Lloyds (Sittingbourne)	30	16	3	11	104	76	35
Gravesend & Northfleet Reserves	30	14	6	10	85	73	34
Shorts Sports	30	12	9	9	81	66	33
Ashford	30	13	6	11	81	72	32
Sittingbourne	30	13	5	12	97	79	31
Gillingham Reserves	30	12	6	12	90	73	30
Snowdown Colliery Welfare	30	9	7	14	56	99	25
Royal Marines (Chatham)	30	11	2	17	75	93	24
Dover	30	7	3	20	46	118	17
Betteshanger Colliery Welfare	30	4	7	19	63	111	15
Deal Town	30	3	6	21	43	97	12

Shorts Sports merged with Chatham United and joined the league as Chatham Town. Canterbury City joined as a newly formed club.

Division Two

Aylesford Paper Mills	**12**	**8**	**2**	**2**	**40**	**18**	**18**
Faversham Town	12	7	2	3	44	23	16
Medway Corrugated Paper Co.	12	7	2	3	32	29	16
Lloyds (Sittingbourne) Reserves	12	7	1	4	40	31	15
Sheppey United Reserves	12	4	1	7	32	38	9
Sittingbourne Reserves	12	2	1	9	32	56	5
Depot Battalion Royal Engineers	12	2	1	9	16	41	5

Depot Battalion Royal Engineers were unable to fulfil their away fixtures with Aylesford Paper Mills and Medway Corrugated Paper Company and their opponents were each awarded 2 points.
Depot Battalion Royal Engineers left the league and Whitstable joined.

Eight First Division sides placed their reserves in Division Two. They were Ashford, Aylesford Paper Mills, Chatham Town, Dover, Folkestone Town, Maidstone United, Margate and Ramsgate Athletic.

1947-48

Division One

Margate	34	24	1	9	103	44	49
Folkestone Town	34	21	5	8	103	43	47
Gillingham Reserves	34	19	5	10	71	45	43
Ramsgate Athletic	34	20	2	12	72	53	42
Maidstone United	34	18	5	11	72	61	41
Lloyds (Sittingbourne)	34	18	3	13	86	74	39
Dover	34	15	8	11	70	60	38
Gravesend & Northfleet Reserves	33	14	10	9	62	54	38
Sittingbourne	34	15	7	12	86	79	37
Chatham Town	34	15	6	13	82	67	36
Canterbury City	34	15	4	15	77	71	34
Ashford	34	12	5	17	59	68	29
Betteshanger Colliery Welfare	33	11	6	16	68	81	28
Deal Town	34	9	8	17	55	79	26
Snowdown Colliery Welfare	34	8	8	18	61	89	24
Sheppey United	34	10	2	22	64	98	22
Aylesford Paper Mills	34	6	8	20	46	99	20
Royal Marines (Chatham)	34	7	3	24	49	121	17

Division Two

Folkestone Town Reserves	26	20	2	4	121	32	42
Margate Reserves	26	19	2	5	105	51	40
Ramsgate Athletic Reserves	26	19	1	6	104	40	39
Maidstone United Reserves	26	17	3	6	66	32	37
Faversham Town	26	15	4	7	66	45	34
Chatham Town Reserves	26	12	5	9	60	51	29
Ashford Reserves	26	12	3	11	62	59	27
Whitstable	26	11	5	10	64	64	27
Aylesford Paper Mills Reserves	26	8	3	15	43	72	19
Sittingbourne Reserves	26	8	3	15	37	76	19
Lloyds (Sittingbourne) Reserves	26	7	4	15	44	72	18
Dover Reserves	26	5	3	18	46	114	13
Medway Corrugated Paper Co.	26	3	5	18	33	91	11
Sheppey United Reserves	26	3	3	20	45	97	9

Medway Corrugated Paper Company and Sheppey United Reserves left the league. The reserves of Betteshanger Colliery Welfare, Canterbury City and Tonbridge all joined as did Kent Agricultural College Sports.

1948-49

Division One

Ashford	34	24	4	6	109	41	52
Dover	34	24	4	6	86	41	52
Ramsgate Athletic	34	25	2	7	104	57	52
Folkestone Town	34	20	8	6	115	55	48
Betteshanger Colliery Welfare	34	21	3	10	77	64	45
Gillingham Reserves	34	17	8	9	85	46	42
Canterbury City	34	16	5	13	90	64	37
Chatham Town	34	15	6	13	78	70	36
Sheppey United	34	14	6	14	75	73	34
Margate	34	14	5	15	84	64	33
Gravesend & Northfleet Reserves	34	14	3	17	61	58	31
Snowdown Colliery Welfare	34	13	5	16	92	96	31
Maidstone United	34	12	6	16	67	85	30
Sittingbourne	34	12	4	18	57	71	28
Lloyds (Sittingbourne)	34	9	5	20	75	95	23
Deal Town	34	7	4	23	41	100	18
Aylesford Paper Mills	34	4	4	26	39	110	12
Royal Marines (Chatham)	34	2	4	28	35	185	8

Lloyds (Sittingbourne) changed their name to Bowater Lloyds. Faversham Town were promoted from Division Two. Gillingham Reserves moved to the Eastern Counties League and Gravesend & Northfleet Reserves moved to the London League.

Division Two

Folkestone Town Reserves	30	21	6	3	104	31	48
Ashford Reserves	30	20	3	7	84	38	43
Canterbury City Reserves	30	19	4	7	94	47	42
Margate Reserves	30	20	1	9	91	54	41
Ramsgate Athletic Reserves	30	18	4	8	114	45	40
Whitstable	30	16	4	10	64	49	36
Dover Reserves	30	14	5	11	77	70	33
Faversham Town	**30**	**13**	**5**	**12**	**67**	**57**	**31**
Tonbridge Reserves	30	13	5	12	64	60	31
Chatham Town Reserves	30	13	3	14	73	71	29
Maidstone United Reserves	30	10	8	12	53	60	28
Aylesford Paper Mills Reserves	30	10	5	15	55	83	25
Lloyds (Sittingbourne) Reserves	30	4	7	19	52	101	15
Betteshanger Colliery Welfare Res.	30	6	3	21	46	103	15
Sittingbourne Reserves	30	3	7	20	37	97	13
Kent Agricultural E.C. Sports	30	4	2	24	40	149	10

Kent Agricultural Education College Sports and Sittingbourne Reserves both left the league. 36th Army Royal Engineers, Luton, Snowdown Colliery Welfare Reserves and Wingets joined.

1949-50

Division One

Ramsgate Athletic	32	26	3	3	118	33	55
Folkestone Town	32	23	5	4	115	33	51
Canterbury City	32	19	6	7	100	53	44
Dover	32	16	10	6	97	46	42
Snowdown Colliery Welfare	32	18	4	10	79	50	40
Margate	32	17	5	10	67	39	39
Ashford	32	15	8	9	83	62	38
Bowater Lloyds	32	13	10	9	80	75	36
Maidstone United	32	13	3	16	78	88	29
Faversham Town	32	12	5	15	54	65	29
Sheppey United	32	8	11	13	56	78	27
Deal Town	32	10	6	16	51	87	26
Sittingbourne	32	10	5	17	46	70	25
Betteshanger Colliery Welfare	32	8	6	18	68	82	22
Chatham Town	32	8	4	20	56	97	20
Aylesford Paper Mills	32	6	5	21	46	105	17
Royal Marines (Chatham)	32	1	2	29	24	155	4

Maidstone United moved to the Corinthian League and Royal Marines (Chatham) also left. Tunbridge Wells United joined from the Kent Amateur League.

Division Two

Whitstable	32	24	3	5	79	34	51
Dover Reserves	32	22	6	4	85	36	50
Ashford Reserves	32	20	4	8	99	48	44
Snowdown Colliery Welfare Res.	31	20	2	9	80	62	42
Canterbury City Reserves	32	19	3	10	100	39	41
Folkestone Town Reserves	32	16	9	7	113	67	41
Margate Reserves	32	15	4	13	81	60	34
Ramsgate Athletic Reserves	32	15	3	14	76	66	33
Luton	32	12	8	12	78	77	32
Wingets	31	12	3	16	56	63	27
Tonbridge Reserves	32	11	5	16	51	62	27
Aylesford Paper Mills Reserves	32	12	2	18	60	85	26
Maidstone United Reserves	32	10	3	19	65	93	23
Bowater Lloyds Reserves	31	10	2	19	72	128	22
Chatham Town Reserves	32	7	7	18	42	93	21
Betteshanger Colliery Welfare Res.	32	6	5	21	65	113	17
36th Army Royal Engineers	29	2	3	24	42	121	7
						1244	1247

36th Army Royal Engineers did not complete their last 3 fixtures and left the league. Three reserve sides: Chatham Town, Maidstone United and Tonbridge, also left and four reserve sides joined: Deal Town, Faversham Town, Tunbridge Wells United and Whitstable.

1950-51

Division One

Folkestone Town	32	26	4	2	114	29	56
Snowdown Colliery Welfare	32	21	7	4	88	33	49
Canterbury City	32	18	7	7	92	48	43
Ashford	32	18	7	7	87	53	43
Dover	32	19	4	9	105	53	42
Margate	32	16	9	7	93	57	41
Sittingbourne	32	17	5	10	75	52	39
Betteshanger Colliery Welfare	32	13	10	9	62	50	36
Ramsgate Athletic	32	13	8	11	69	62	34
Sheppey United	32	9	9	14	46	69	27
Bowater Lloyds	32	11	4	17	56	75	26
Whitstable	32	10	6	16	38	58	26
Deal Town	32	9	7	16	51	70	25
Tunbridge Wells United	32	9	4	19	51	83	22
Chatham Town	32	7	4	21	33	65	18
Faversham Town	32	4	3	25	37	128	11
Aylesford Paper Mills	32	2	2	28	38	159	6
						1135	1144

Ashford changed their name to Ashford Town. Bexleyheath & Welling joined after re-forming and Aylesford Paper Mills left the league.

Division Two

	P	W	D	L	F	A	Pts
Folkestone Town Reserves	30	24	2	4	130	37	50
Canterbury City Reserves	30	23	3	4	119	39	49
Ashford Reserves	30	20	5	5	103	51	45
Margate Reserves	30	16	11	3	94	40	43
Snowdown Colliery Welfare Res.	30	17	7	6	79	46	41
Dover Reserves	30	16	5	9	87	46	37
Betteshanger Colliery Welfare Res.	30	14	4	12	71	69	32
Luton	30	13	3	14	93	72	29
Wingets	30	12	2	16	49	69	26
Whitstable Reserves	30	10	6	14	67	97	26
Tunbridge Wells United Reserves	30	9	7	14	50	66	25
Deal Town Reserves	30	9	5	16	41	72	23
Ramsgate Athletic Reserves	30	10	2	18	62	90	22
Bowater Lloyds Reserves	30	6	3	21	57	115	15
Aylesford Paper Mills Reserves	30	6	1	23	30	103	13
Faversham Town Reserves	30	1	2	27	34	154	4

Aylesford Paper Mills Reserves, Tunbridge Wells United Reserves and Wingets left.
Rochester & Borstal and Sheppey United Reserves joined.

1951-52

Division One

	P	W	D	L	F	A	Pts
Dover	32	23	6	3	109	36	52
Snowdown Colliery Welfare	32	16	9	7	68	35	41
Sheppey United	32	19	3	10	82	57	41
Margate	32	16	7	9	77	49	39
Folkestone Town	32	17	5	10	80	51	39
Sittingbourne	32	17	4	11	74	66	38
Ashford Town	32	17	3	12	63	38	37
Ramsgate Athletic	32	14	9	9	72	47	37
Deal Town	32	15	5	12	70	51	35
Whitstable	32	15	4	13	59	71	34
Betteshanger Colliery Welfare	32	14	4	14	81	73	32
Faversham Town	32	11	6	15	52	77	28
Canterbury City	32	10	7	15	71	70	27
Bowater Lloyds	32	11	5	16	58	79	27
Chatham Town	32	6	3	23	45	99	15
Bexleyheath & Welling	32	4	4	24	28	118	12
Tunbridge Wells United	32	5	0	27	31	109	10
					1120	1126	

Division Two

	P	W	D	L	F	A	Pts
Dover Reserves	28	22	4	2	144	39	48
Margate Reserves	28	23	1	4	103	29	47
Snowdown Colliery Welfare Res.	28	15	6	7	85	48	36
Ramsgate Athletic Reserves	28	16	4	8	96	67	36
Folkestone Town Reserves	28	14	6	8	64	34	34
Canterbury City Reserves	28	14	5	9	77	57	33
Ashford Town Reserves	28	13	6	9	79	64	32
Deal Town Reserves	28	11	7	10	62	55	29
Sheppey United Reserves	28	12	4	12	70	83	28
Faversham Town Reserves	28	8	3	17	54	87	19
Luton	28	8	2	18	54	94	18
Whitstable Reserves	28	7	3	18	35	97	17
Betteshanger Colliery Welfare Res.	28	5	6	17	46	76	16
Rochester & Borstal	28	8	0	20	47	90	16
Bowater Lloyds Reserves	28	3	5	20	39	135	11

Bowater Lloyds Reserves left and Bexleyheath & Welling Reserves, Sittingbourne Reserves and Tunbridge Wells United Reserves joined.

1952-53

Division One

	P	W	D	L	F	A	Pts
Folkestone Town	32	23	5	4	93	28	51
Dover	32	20	8	4	70	41	48
Sittingbourne	32	18	8	6	81	60	44
Betteshanger Colliery Welfare	32	19	5	8	81	46	43
Tunbridge Wells United	32	19	2	11	64	53	40
Deal Town	32	16	6	10	80	42	38
Ashford Town	32	13	9	10	65	48	35
Canterbury City	32	13	9	10	62	57	35
Sheppey United	32	14	7	11	62	64	35
Snowdown Colliery Welfare	32	14	6	12	74	58	34
Margate	32	13	7	12	66	52	33
Ramsgate Athletic	32	7	13	12	51	48	27
Whitstable	32	7	8	17	51	70	22
Faversham Town	32	5	9	18	51	77	19
Bowater Lloyds	32	8	3	21	50	99	19
Bexleyheath & Welling	32	4	4	24	44	102	12
Chatham Town	32	3	3	26	30	130	9

Bowater Lloyds left the league.

Division Two

	P	W	D	L	F	A	Pts
Ashford Town Reserves	30	21	6	3	83	33	48
Margate Reserves	30	18	6	6	84	43	42
Whitstable Reserves	30	19	4	7	80	50	42
Dover Reserves	30	19	4	7	73	50	42
Sittingbourne Reserves	30	17	3	10	86	48	37
Folkestone Town Reserves	30	15	6	9	71	60	36
Snowdown Colliery Welfare Res.	30	14	6	10	67	65	34
Canterbury City Reserves	30	13	7	10	67	52	33
Ramsgate Athletic Reserves	30	10	8	12	63	48	28
Sheppey United Reserves	30	10	5	15	66	82	25
Tunbridge Wells United Reserves	30	11	3	16	54	71	25
Deal Town Reserves	30	9	4	17	41	64	22
Luton	30	8	3	19	55	86	19
Bexleyheath & Welling Reserves	30	6	6	18	52	96	18
Betteshanger Colliery Welfare Res.	30	7	4	19	43	88	18
Faversham Town Reserves	30	2	7	21	40	89	11

Rochester & Borstal resigned after playing 9 games and their record was deleted.
Luton left and Chatham Town Reserves, Herne Bay and Royal Marines Depot (Deal) joined.

1953-54

Division One

	P	W	D	L	F	A	Pts
Deal Town	30	18	8	4	78	33	44
Margate	30	19	6	5	74	36	44
Folkestone Town	30	17	9	4	71	29	43
Snowdown Colliery Welfare	30	15	8	7	54	39	38
Sittingbourne	30	13	10	7	61	40	36
Whitstable	30	14	7	9	56	48	35
Betteshanger Colliery Welfare	30	14	6	10	48	48	34
Ramsgate Athletic	30	13	7	10	62	51	33
Canterbury City	30	14	5	11	52	46	33
Dover	30	13	6	11	57	42	32
Tunbridge Wells United	30	11	3	16	42	64	25
Sheppey United	30	10	3	17	54	72	23
Faversham Town	30	7	5	18	38	72	19
Ashford Town	30	5	7	18	36	50	17
Bexleyheath & Welling	30	5	5	20	38	81	15
Chatham Town	30	3	3	24	32	102	9

Gillingham Reserves returned from the Eastern Counties League.

Division Two

Margate Reserves	34	26	4	4	126	37	56
Dover Reserves	34	19	9	6	89	45	47
Ashford Town Reserves	34	19	8	7	66	43	46
Tunbridge Wells United Reserves	34	17	8	9	100	56	42
Folkestone Town Reserves	34	15	10	9	83	58	40
Sittingbourne Reserves	34	15	10	9	62	48	40
Ramsgate Athletic Reserves	34	17	4	13	71	65	38
Faversham Town Reserves	34	15	7	12	80	79	37
Snowdown Colliery Welfare Res.	34	15	5	14	66	59	35
Whitstable Reserves	34	11	9	14	82	90	31
Canterbury City Reserves	34	12	7	15	60	77	31
Sheppey United Reserves	34	11	8	15	58	77	30
Herne Bay	34	11	8	15	70	79	30
Chatham Town Reserves	34	11	7	16	78	106	29
Bexleyheath & Welling Reserves	34	10	6	18	57	84	26
Betteshanger Colliery Welfare Res.	34	10	3	21	42	88	23
Royal Marines Depot (Deal)	34	5	6	23	58	110	16
Deal Town Reserves	34	4	7	23	33	80	15

1954-55

Division One

Snowdown Colliery Welfare	32	18	9	5	60	36	45
Dover	32	16	11	5	64	38	43
Folkestone Town	32	16	11	5	73	55	43
Sittingbourne	32	18	5	9	77	50	41
Margate	32	17	6	9	82	48	40
Ramsgate Athletic	32	15	8	9	65	49	38
Tunbridge Wells United	32	15	8	9	60	52	38
Gillingham Reserves	32	12	9	11	53	51	33
Canterbury City	32	12	8	12	57	53	32
Bexleyheath & Welling	32	13	6	13	76	71	32
Deal Town	32	10	12	10	66	62	32
Ashford Town	32	11	7	14	49	52	29
Whitstable	32	9	8	15	51	64	26
Faversham Town	32	9	5	18	47	72	23
Betteshanger Colliery Welfare	32	6	8	18	46	68	20
Chatham Town	32	6	4	22	63	121	16
Sheppey United	32	3	7	22	42	89	13

Division Two

Herne Bay	34	28	4	2	121	45	60
Margate Reserves	34	24	6	4	111	39	54
Tunbridge Wells United Reserves	34	20	8	6	105	64	48
Folkestone Town Reserves	34	21	4	9	97	50	46
Ramsgate Athletic Reserves	34	18	9	7	106	65	45
Sittingbourne Reserves	34	21	2	11	114	57	44
Snowdown Colliery Welfare Res.	34	20	2	12	114	57	42
Ashford Town Reserves	34	18	4	12	90	68	40
Dover Reserves	34	15	8	11	88	51	38
Faversham Town Reserves	34	16	4	14	81	82	36
Sheppey United Reserves	34	11	5	18	70	79	27
Canterbury City Reserves	34	12	3	19	66	79	27
Bexleyheath & Welling Reserves	34	10	5	19	79	81	25
Whitstable Reserves	34	9	5	20	67	121	23
Chatham Town Reserves	34	8	2	24	50	146	18
Deal Town Reserves	34	7	1	26	67	110	15
Betteshanger Colliery Welfare Res.	34	6	2	26	38	143	14
Royal Marines Depot (Deal)	34	5	0	29	45	172	10

Bexleyheath & Welling Reserves and Royal Marines Depot (Deal) both left the league. Gillingham "A" joined.

1955-56

Division One

Ramsgate Athletic	32	24	4	4	108	39	52
Margate	32	19	6	7	93	45	44
Snowdown Colliery Welfare	32	20	4	8	91	50	44
Tunbridge Wells United	32	18	7	7	74	49	43
Sittingbourne	32	16	8	8	73	47	40
Deal Town	32	16	6	10	72	61	38
Canterbury City	32	14	8	10	65	56	36
Dover	32	16	3	13	60	56	35
Folkestone Town	32	14	2	14	64	55	34
Bexleyheath & Welling	32	10	11	11	55	58	31
Ashford Town	32	11	7	14	46	58	29
Gillingham Reserves	32	11	6	15	62	57	28
Betteshanger Colliery Welfare	32	9	6	17	44	68	24
Sheppey United	32	8	4	20	43	80	20
Chatham Town	32	7	5	20	48	90	19
Faversham Town	32	5	5	22	37	97	15
Whitstable	32	2	8	22	29	98	12

Division Two

Ashford Town Reserves	32	22	7	3	111	34	51
Herne Bay	32	24	1	7	124	46	49
Dover Reserves	32	23	2	7	102	41	48
Margate Reserves	32	22	2	8	89	45	46
Canterbury City Reserves	32	20	5	7	108	40	45
Folkestone Town Reserves	32	17	8	7	102	58	42
Sittingbourne Reserves	32	17	6	9	92	58	40
Ramsgate Athletic Reserves	32	17	3	12	87	72	37
Tunbridge Wells United Reserves	32	15	4	13	106	72	34
Faversham Town Reserves	32	15	4	13	68	65	34
Sheppey United Reserves	32	11	5	16	65	85	27
Gillingham "A"	32	11	4	17	75	88	26
Snowdown Colliery Welfare Res.	32	11	2	19	54	69	24
Chatham Town Reserves	32	5	4	23	42	109	14
Deal Town Reserves	32	6	2	24	51	129	14
Betteshanger Colliery Welfare Res.	32	3	1	28	34	167	7
Whitstable Reserves	32	2	2	28	37	169	6

Gravesend & Northfleet Reserves joined from the Metropolitan League.

1956-57

Division One

Ramsgate Athletic	32	23	6	3	84	38	52
Tunbridge Wells United	32	21	6	5	80	36	48
Snowdown Colliery Welfare	32	21	4	7	84	42	46
Canterbury City	32	19	3	10	85	58	41
Dover	32	18	4	10	76	50	40
Gillingham Reserves	32	16	5	11	67	56	37
Sittingbourne	32	14	7	11	65	49	35
Margate	32	16	2	14	64	65	34
Folkestone Town	32	10	9	13	58	56	29
Ashford Town	32	13	3	16	59	59	29
Bexleyheath & Welling	32	12	4	16	69	76	28
Faversham Town	32	8	6	18	64	87	22
Deal Town	32	8	6	18	46	79	22
Betteshanger Colliery Welfare	32	8	6	18	41	76	22
Sheppey United	32	6	8	18	44	79	20
Whitstable	32	8	4	20	39	82	20
Chatham Town	32	8	3	21	68	105	19

Herne Bay were promoted from Division Two from where they were replaced by their reserves.

Division Two

Margate Reserves	34	26	4	4	107	43	56
Ramsgate Athletic Reserves	34	21	7	6	95	45	49
Canterbury City Reserves	34	19	9	6	90	50	47
Dover Reserves	34	20	3	11	108	53	43
Ashford Town Reserves	34	19	5	10	84	55	43
Herne Bay	**34**	**16**	**10**	**8**	**89**	**52**	**42**
Gillingham "A"	34	17	7	10	89	60	41
Tunbridge Wells United Reserves	34	17	5	12	88	63	39
Folkestone Town Reserves	34	17	4	13	78	57	38
Sittingbourne Reserves	34	16	5	13	95	61	37
Snowdown Colliery Welfare Res.	34	17	3	14	87	83	37
Faversham Town Reserves	34	17	2	15	75	78	36
Sheppey United Reserves	34	14	3	17	70	83	31
Gravesend & Northfleet Reserves	34	12	4	18	69	48	28
Chatham Town Reserves	34	9	2	23	59	100	20
Whitstable Reserves	34	5	2	27	43	133	12
Deal Town Reserves	34	1	5	28	35	148	7
Betteshanger Colliery Welfare Res.	34	3	0	31	37	186	6

1957-58

Division One

Sittingbourne	34	26	6	2	90	25	58
Folkestone Town	34	22	5	7	103	49	49
Tunbridge Wells United	34	17	9	8	96	63	43
Bexleyheath & Welling	34	20	2	12	115	76	42
Margate	34	18	5	11	101	72	41
Canterbury City	34	16	8	10	69	74	40
Dover	34	14	10	10	61	47	38
Gillingham Reserves	34	15	7	12	64	47	37
Ashford Town	34	16	4	14	75	53	36
Snowdown Colliery Welfare	34	13	8	13	81	76	34
Ramsgate Athletic	34	10	8	16	65	81	28
Herne Bay	34	13	1	20	58	85	27
Betteshanger Colliery Welfare	34	9	8	17	70	97	26
Chatham Town	34	9	8	17	71	105	26
Faversham Town	34	10	6	18	67	102	26
Sheppey United	34	10	5	19	57	88	25
Whitstable	34	4	12	18	48	98	20
Deal Town	34	6	4	24	50	103	16

Division Two

Folkestone Town Reserves	34	27	3	4	104	30	57
Margate Reserves	34	26	5	3	101	44	57
Sittingbourne Reserves	34	19	4	11	81	62	42
Ashford Town Reserves	34	16	9	9	79	53	41
Gillingham "A"	34	17	5	12	79	64	39
Dover Reserves	34	18	1	15	61	62	37
Canterbury City Reserves	34	17	3	14	75	77	37
Tunbridge Wells United Reserves	34	16	4	14	79	77	36
Gravesend & Northfleet Reserves	34	16	3	15	90	67	35
Ramsgate Athletic Reserves	34	17	1	16	94	84	35
Sheppey United Reserves	34	12	8	14	64	72	32
Herne Bay Reserves	34	14	2	18	93	87	30
Whitstable Reserves	34	10	5	19	56	82	25
Faversham Town Reserves	34	10	4	20	63	86	24
Snowdown Colliery Welfare Res.	34	9	5	20	65	110	23
Chatham Town Reserves	34	10	3	21	63	102	23
Deal Town Reserves	34	8	4	22	66	113	20
Betteshanger Colliery Welfare Res.	34	7	5	22	50	91	19

1958-59

Division One

Sittingbourne	34	25	6	3	77	28	56
Margate	34	20	9	5	80	34	49
Ramsgate Athletic	34	22	4	8	84	49	48
Dover	34	20	5	9	74	43	45
Bexleyheath & Welling	34	18	5	11	84	57	41
Folkestone Town	34	17	6	11	78	62	40
Tunbridge Wells United	34	16	8	10	70	65	40
Snowdown Colliery Welfare	34	17	4	13	78	69	38
Canterbury City	34	14	9	11	78	62	37
Gillingham Reserves	34	12	6	16	52	60	30
Faversham Town	34	12	5	17	76	87	29
Chatham Town	34	13	2	19	60	93	28
Betteshanger Colliery Welfare	34	10	7	17	51	63	27
Sheppey United	34	9	7	18	54	84	25
Deal Town	34	7	7	20	53	87	21
Ashford Town	34	7	6	21	53	85	20
Whitstable	34	8	4	22	49	87	20
Herne Bay	34	6	6	22	51	87	18

Division Two

Gravesend & Northfleet Reserves	34	30	1	3	152	31	61
Folkestone Town Reserves	34	22	7	5	111	58	51
Margate Reserves	34	23	4	7	118	60	50
Ashford Town Reserves	34	23	3	8	84	44	49
Dover Reserves	34	20	6	8	70	41	46
Sittingbourne Reserves	34	19	3	12	98	60	41
Faversham Town Reserves	34	18	5	11	89	60	41
Tunbridge Wells United Reserves	34	16	7	11	91	60	39
Sheppey United Reserves	34	13	5	16	89	87	31
Ramsgate Athletic Reserves	34	15	1	18	81	90	31
Herne Bay Reserves	34	11	5	18	61	76	27
Deal Town Reserves	34	11	5	18	60	108	27
Gillingham "A"	34	11	1	22	62	101	23
Snowdown Colliery Welfare Res.	34	8	6	20	50	90	22
Chatham Town Reserves	33	9	3	21	61	109	21
Whitstable Reserves	34	7	5	22	54	122	19
Canterbury City Reserves	33	7	2	24	48	126	16
Betteshanger Colliery Welfare Res.	34	5	5	24	39	95	15

Chatham Town Reserves vs Canterbury City Reserves was not played.

1959: Closure of the Kent League

Folkestone Town, Dover, Margate, Bexleyheath & Welling and Tunbridge Wells United had tried to join the Southern League in 1958 but gave insufficient notice to the Kent League and so their departure was delayed until 1959 when Ashford Town, Ramsgate Athletic and Sittingbourne joined them in the move.

This made it impossible for the Kent League to continue in the same form so Canterbury City joined the Metropolitan League and Gillingham Reserves joined the Football Combination. The remaining 8 clubs helped to form two new leagues to cover the home counties, the Aetolian League and the Seanglian League.

Chatham Town, Deal Town, Faversham Town, Herne Bay, Sheppey United, Snowdown Colliery Welfare and Whitstable joined the Aetolian League and Betteshanger Colliery Welfare joined the Seanglian League.

Of the Second Division clubs, the reserves of Canterbury City, Deal Town, Faversham Town, Herne Bay, Sheppey United and Snowdown Colliery Welfare joined the Aetolian League while the reserves of Ashford Town, Dover, Folkestone, Gravesend & Northfleet, Margate, Ramsgate Athletic, Sittingbourne, Tunbridge Wells United and Gillingham "A" joined the Seanglian League.

The Kent League then closed down.

1966: Revival of the Kent League (as the Kent Premier League)

Following the closure of the Kent League in 1959, those former clubs who had not gained entry to the Southern League found that there was no other league that was suitable both geographically and in playing standard. By the middle of the 1960s, this had led to support for re-forming the Kent League but there were some difficulties in establishing a new league with that title.

Meanwhile, the Thames & Medway Combination (originally established in 1896 – see above), had closed down in 1930 but was revived in 1954 and had continued since then, albeit with a only small membership. In at least one season there were as few as 3 members.

It was therefore decided to change the purpose of the Combination so that it could serve as a new county league for Kent and its title was changed to the Kent Premier League.

There were 3 clubs who fielded their first teams in the Kent Premier League and 11 reserve sides. The 3 first teams were Orpington Athletic and Snowdown Colliery Welfare who played in the Thames & Medway Combination in 1965-66 and Faversham Town who moved from the Greater London League.

The 11 clubs who fielded their reserve sides in the first season of the Kent Premier League were:
Ashford Town, Bexley United (known as Bexleyheath & Welling until 1963), Canterbury City, Deal Town, Folkestone Town, Margate, Ramsgate Athletic, Sheppey United, Sittingbourne, Tonbridge and Tunbridge Wells Rangers (known as Tunbridge Wells United until 1963).

1967-68

Margate Reserves	34	23	4	7	101	34	50
Sittingbourne	34	24	2	8	93	50	50
Brett Sports	34	21	4	9	86	41	46
Tunnel Sports	34	20	5	9	87	42	45
Tunbridge Wells	34	19	7	8	64	45	45
Bexley United Reserves	34	19	3	12	96	62	41
Ramsgate Athletic Reserves	34	16	9	9	82	62	41
Sheppey United Reserves	34	19	2	13	77	61	40
Folkestone Town Reserves	34	16	4	14	54	59	36
Dover Reserves	34	16	3	15	72	64	35
Whitstable Town	34	13	7	14	51	64	33
Faversham Town	34	14	4	16	52	59	32
Tonbridge Reserves	34	10	4	20	41	87	24
Orpington Athletic	34	8	6	20	54	88	22
Ashford Town Reserves	34	7	6	21	44	99	20
Snowdown Colliery Welfare	34	8	3	23	44	90	19
Deal Town Reserves	34	6	7	21	40	88	19
Canterbury City Reserves	34	6	2	26	35	86	14
					1173	1181	

Folkestone Town changed their name to Folkestone.
Ashford Town Reserves, Bexley United Reserves and Dover Reserves left the league. Deal Town replaced their reserves, Chatham Town joined from the Metropolitan League, Crockenhill joined from the Greater London League and Gravesend & Northfleet Reserves also joined.

The league changed its name to the Kent League.

KENT PREMIER LEAGUE 1966-68

1966-67

Margate Reserves	26	21	1	4	90	18	43
Bexley United Reserves	26	18	3	5	79	37	39
Ramsgate Athletic Reserves	26	15	4	7	76	38	34
Snowdown Colliery Welfare	26	15	3	8	60	36	33
Sheppey United Reserves	26	13	6	7	79	50	32
Orpington Athletic	26	12	8	6	68	49	32
Folkestone Town Reserves	26	11	5	10	68	66	27
Faversham Town	26	9	6	11	53	46	24
Sittingbourne Reserves	26	10	3	13	46	72	23
Deal Town Reserves	26	8	4	14	41	74	20
Ashford Town Reserves	26	7	3	16	42	65	17
Tunbridge Wells Rangers Reserves	26	7	3	16	33	70	17
Tonbridge Reserves	26	6	4	16	48	100	16
Canterbury City Reserves	26	2	3	21	32	79	7
					815	800	

Tunbridge Wells Rangers disbanded. A new club just called Tunbridge Wells was formed and replaced Rangers' Reserves. Sittingbourne moved from the Southern League, taking their reserves' place. Brett Sports and Tunnel Sports joined from the Kent Amateur League, Whitstable joined from the Greater London League (changing their name to Whitstable Town) and Dover Reserves also joined.

KENT LEAGUE 1968-2014

1968-69

Brett Sports	34	23	5	6	98	27	51
Tunbridge Wells	34	21	8	5	92	41	50
Margate Reserves	34	20	8	6	89	43	48
Sittingbourne	34	21	6	7	77	40	48
Chatham Town	34	20	6	8	80	52	46
Ramsgate Athletic Reserves	34	18	6	10	90	59	42
Tunnel Sports	34	15	10	9	70	47	40
Sheppey United Reserves	34	17	6	11	75	52	40
Orpington Athletic	34	11	11	12	52	64	33
Faversham Town	34	13	5	16	60	63	31
Whitstable Town	34	14	3	17	61	66	31
Deal Town	34	12	5	17	59	69	29
Canterbury City Reserves	34	11	6	17	51	79	28
Crockenhill	34	11	5	18	57	82	27
Snowdown Colliery Welfare	34	9	8	17	54	60	26
Folkestone Reserves	34	10	4	20	50	88	24
Gravesend & Northfleet Reserves	34	5	3	26	36	125	13
Tonbridge Reserves	34	1	3	30	35	129	5

Canterbury City Reserves, Gravesend & Northfleet Reserves and Tonbridge Reserves all left.
Kent Police joined from the Kent Amateur League.

1969-70

Faversham Town	28	21	5	2	67	21	47
Kent Police	28	18	3	7	80	55	39
Tunnel Sports	28	15	7	6	58	25	37
Sittingbourne	28	15	7	6	60	36	37
Tunbridge Wells	28	10	11	7	56	50	31
Margate Reserves	28	11	8	9	47	49	30
Chatham Town	28	13	2	13	62	53	28
Snowdown Colliery Welfare	28	11	5	12	54	52	27
Whitstable Town	28	10	7	11	44	50	27
Deal Town	28	9	7	12	41	47	25
Ramsgate Athletic Reserves	28	8	7	13	53	62	23
Brett Sports	28	6	9	13	32	55	21
Sheppey United Reserves	28	5	7	16	44	71	17
Crockenhill	28	6	4	18	40	77	16
Folkestone Reserves	28	5	5	18	35	70	15

Orpington Athletic resigned and disbanded during the season and their record was deleted.
Tunnel Sports changed their name to Dartford Amateurs. Slade Green Athletic joined from the Greater London League and Ashford Town Reserves, Bexley United Reserves, Hastings United Reserves and Tonbridge Reserves also joined.

1970-71

Faversham Town	38	28	5	5	116	37	61
Chatham Town	38	23	8	7	102	52	54
Tonbridge Reserves	38	22	9	7	101	51	53
Sittingbourne	38	21	8	9	95	57	50
Margate Reserves	38	18	5	15	66	71	41
Bexley United Reserves	38	15	11	12	64	72	41
Snowdown Colliery Welfare	38	18	4	16	77	63	40
Brett Sports	38	16	7	15	68	67	39
Slade Green Athletic	38	16	6	16	50	68	38
Ashford Town Reserves	38	15	7	16	98	73	37
Kent Police	38	12	13	13	73	78	37
Hastings United Reserves	38	14	9	15	61	67	37
Tunbridge Wells	38	14	8	16	63	64	36
Whitstable Town	38	14	8	16	67	72	36
Dartford Amateurs	38	13	7	18	68	66	33
Ramsgate Athletic Reserves	38	13	5	20	59	80	31
Sheppey United Reserves	38	11	9	18	57	79	31
Folkestone Reserves	38	10	6	22	53	101	26
Crockenhill	38	6	8	24	49	111	20
Deal Town	38	5	9	24	34	90	19
					1421	1419	

Faversham Town moved to the Metropolitan-London League and Snowdown Colliery Welfare also left the league. Dartford Reserves and Dover Reserves joined.

1971-72

Chatham Town	36	24	10	2	107	33	58
Brett Sports	38	26	6	6	90	37	58
Tonbridge Reserves	38	23	9	6	93	59	55
Sittingbourne	38	18	11	9	72	51	47
Kent Police	38	18	10	10	90	56	46
Dartford Amateurs	36	16	13	7	60	41	45
Deal Town	36	15	11	10	90	55	41
Slade Green Athletic	37	15	9	13	49	37	39
Ashford Town Reserves	38	14	11	13	70	79	39
Dover Reserves	37	13	12	12	51	41	38
Dartford Reserves	38	12	13	13	62	67	37
Crockenhill	37	13	6	18	56	70	32
Bexley United Reserves	38	11	9	18	58	77	31
Hastings United Reserves	38	10	10	18	51	86	30
Folkestone Reserves	36	9	11	16	52	77	29
Margate Reserves	38	11	7	20	60	95	29
Tunbridge Wells	38	6	15	17	51	73	27
Whitstable Town	35	9	5	21	45	80	23
Sheppey United Reserves	38	8	7	23	45	87	23
Ramsgate Athletic Reserves	38	6	7	25	49	100	19

Note: The latest table found was after games played on 19th May 1972 when there were still 14 games left to play. The results of 7 of these have been traced and added into the table above. The 7 remaining games are thought not to have been played.
Ramsgate Athletic changed their name to Ramsgate. Sheppey United joined from the Metropolitan-London League, replacing their reserves. Dartford Reserves left and Snowdown Colliery Welfare returned after a season's absence.

1972-73

Sheppey United	38	31	5	2	127	33	67
Sittingbourne	38	26	6	6	108	37	58
Chatham Town	38	24	5	9	92	47	53
Kent Police	36	22	6	8	76	41	50
Brett Sports	38	22	6	10	98	61	50
Dover Reserves	38	19	9	10	64	35	40
Tonbridge Reserves	38	16	8	14	71	67	40
Tunbridge Wells	38	17	5	16	88	68	39
Bexley United Reserves	38	15	7	16	59	57	37
Dartford Amateurs	38	16	5	17	65	71	37
Deal Town	38	16	5	17	65	69	35
Folkestone Reserves	38	15	4	19	65	92	34
Crockenhill	38	14	4	20	67	94	32
Whitstable Town	37	11	9	17	50	83	31
Ramsgate Reserves	37	10	9	18	49	69	29
Snowdown Colliery Welfare	38	11	7	20	44	71	29
Slade Green Athletic	38	9	10	19	55	77	28
Hastings United Reserves	38	9	5	24	53	97	23
Ashford Town Reserves	38	6	10	22	42	113	22
Margate Reserves	38	4	5	29	41	97	13

Deal Town had 2 points deducted and Dover Reserves had 7 points deducted for fielding ineligible players.
Kent Police were unable to play their last 2 games.
Brett Sports moved to the Kent Amateur League and Hastings United Reserves also left. Canterbury City Reserves joined the league.

1973-74

Chatham Town	36	29	4	3	113	31	62
Sittingbourne	36	27	5	4	97	29	59
Sheppey United	36	19	9	8	80	41	47
Bexley United Reserves	36	16	8	12	57	51	40
Dartford Amateurs	36	15	9	12	76	66	39
Crockenhill	36	14	9	13	55	55	37
Margate Reserves	36	14	9	13	64	64	37
Tunbridge Wells	36	15	6	15	71	54	36
Deal Town	36	14	8	14	59	56	36
Kent Police	36	13	9	14	57	60	35
Whitstable Town	36	13	9	14	52	57	35
Slade Green Athletic	36	11	11	14	55	73	33
Tonbridge Reserves	36	14	5	17	38	54	33
Canterbury City Reserves	36	12	7	17	50	62	31
Ashford Town Reserves	36	10	11	15	64	80	31
Dover Reserves	36	9	9	18	45	70	25
Ramsgate Reserves	36	11	2	23	42	78	24
Snowdown Colliery Welfare	36	8	8	20	45	88	24
Folkestone Reserves	36	7	4	25	39	90	18

Dover Reserves had 2 points deducted for fielding ineligible players.
Chatham Town changed their name to Medway. Folkestone changed their name to Folkestone & Shepway. Herne Bay joined from the Athenian League and Bexley United Reserves left the league.

1974-75

Sheppey United	36	27	8	1	99	37	62
Medway	36	27	3	6	93	32	57
Sittingbourne	36	26	2	8	90	37	54
Crockenhill	36	24	5	7	88	40	53
Dartford Amateurs	36	19	8	9	71	46	46
Tunbridge Wells	36	20	5	11	67	48	45
Tonbridge Reserves	36	19	6	11	63	48	44
Whitstable Town	36	15	12	9	60	58	42
Deal Town	36	14	8	14	72	63	36
Herne Bay	36	12	7	17	56	65	31
Ramsgate Reserves	36	12	6	18	59	70	30
Margate Reserves	36	11	7	18	47	73	29
Ashford Town Reserves	36	11	6	19	54	73	28
Kent Police	36	11	5	20	49	61	27
Snowdown Colliery Welfare	36	7	12	17	46	83	26
Canterbury City Reserves	36	9	6	21	61	88	24
Slade Green Athletic	36	7	8	21	37	73	22
Dover Reserves	36	7	7	22	34	75	21
Folkestone & Shepway Reserves	36	2	3	31	23	99	7

Canterbury City Reserves left the league and Maidstone United Reserves joined.

1975-76

Sittingbourne	36	26	5	5	87	38	57
Dartford Amateurs	36	23	10	3	93	42	56
Tunbridge Wells	36	23	9	4	100	37	55
Sheppey United	36	23	9	4	91	44	55
Deal Town	36	23	4	9	75	30	50
Medway	36	22	5	9	91	44	49
Crockenhill	36	20	4	12	84	52	44
Kent Police	36	15	10	11	80	45	40
Snowdown Colliery Welfare	36	17	5	14	64	53	39
Slade Green Athletic	36	15	5	16	51	63	35
Maidstone United Reserves	36	10	14	12	59	62	34
Margate Reserves	36	12	6	18	53	79	30
Herne Bay	36	11	7	18	59	72	29
Whitstable Town	36	10	5	21	61	100	25
Folkestone & Shepway Reserves	36	10	4	22	49	78	24
Ashford Town Reserves	36	8	5	23	57	117	21
Dover Reserves	36	4	9	23	36	92	17
Tonbridge Reserves	36	4	7	25	38	87	15
Ramsgate Reserves	36	2	5	29	38	131	9

Dartford Amateurs changed their name to Dartford Glentworth. Ramsgate joined from the Southern League, replacing their reserves. Margate Reserves, Ashford Town Reserves and Tonbridge Reserves all left. Faversham Town joined from the Athenian League.

1976-77

Medway	32	25	5	2	93	24	55
Sittingbourne	32	21	5	6	68	48	47
Dartford Glentworth	31	19	7	5	73	35	45
Sheppey United	32	17	8	7	70	37	42
Faversham Town	32	16	7	9	53	28	39
Kent Police	32	14	11	7	53	39	39
Maidstone United Reserves	31	15	7	9	56	43	37
Deal Town	32	13	9	10	50	44	35
Crockenhill	32	14	5	13	54	51	33
Ramsgate	32	14	3	15	47	53	31
Tunbridge Wells	32	9	6	17	60	69	24
Whitstable Town	32	10	4	18	37	54	24
Snowdown Colliery Welfare	32	5	13	14	29	52	23
Herne Bay	32	8	5	19	37	69	21
Dover Reserves	32	5	10	17	24	52	20
Slade Green Athletic	32	7	4	21	36	71	18
Folkestone & Shepway Reserves	32	2	5	25	32	87	9

Hythe Town joined from the Kent Amateur League.

1977-78

Faversham Town	34	23	8	3	83	24	54
Sheppey United	34	24	5	5	87	32	53
Tunbridge Wells	34	21	10	3	84	38	52
Hythe Town	34	19	6	9	73	57	44
Maidstone United Reserves	34	18	6	10	58	39	42
Crockenhill	34	16	8	10	62	46	40
Dartford Glentworth	34	15	8	11	59	45	38
Medway	34	15	8	11	53	49	38
Ramsgate	34	12	13	9	54	51	37
Deal Town	34	13	7	14	47	53	33
Whitstable Town	34	13	6	15	52	43	32
Herne Bay	34	9	9	16	39	76	27
Sittingbourne	34	8	9	17	37	60	25
Snowdown Colliery Welfare	34	8	6	20	44	76	22
Slade Green Athletic	34	4	12	18	40	60	20
Folkestone & Shepway Reserves	34	6	7	21	37	61	19
Kent Police	34	6	6	22	34	81	18
Dover Reserves	34	9	0	25	35	87	18

Erith & Belvedere joined from the Athenian League and Cray Wanderers joined from the London-Spartan League. Darenth Heathside also joined from the London-Spartan League where they had been called Heathside Sports.

A new Second Division was formed for reserve sides. Dover Reserves accepted relegation to the new division but Maidstone United Reserves and Folkestone & Shepway Reserves both left.

Goal difference replaced goal average to decide positions when teams finished on the same points from the next season.

1978-79

Division One

Sheppey United	34	22	11	1	73	28	55
Hythe Town	34	21	7	6	71	34	49
Faversham Town	34	22	5	7	71	37	49
Medway	34	18	10	6	64	27	46
Whitstable Town	34	18	7	9	52	35	43
Sittingbourne	34	16	7	11	57	42	39
Tunbridge Wells	34	15	6	13	51	52	36
Darenth Heathside	34	10	12	12	42	38	32
Deal Town	34	13	6	15	40	50	32
Ramsgate	34	14	4	16	42	59	32
Slade Green Athletic	34	8	13	13	46	47	29
Herne Bay	34	10	10	14	47	59	28
Dartford Glentworth	34	9	10	15	40	52	28
Cray Wanderers	34	9	9	16	50	65	27
Erith & Belvedere	34	8	9	17	49	48	25
Kent Police	34	10	4	20	46	67	24
Crockenhill	34	7	7	20	43	73	21
Snowdown Colliery Welfare	*34*	*4*	*7*	*23*	*29*	*102*	*15*

Herne Bay had 2 points and 2 goals deducted for fielding an ineligible player. Medway changed their name to Chatham Town.

Division Two

Medway Reserves	20	16	4	0	59	16	36
Herne Bay Reserves	18	13	2	3	41	24	28
Dover Reserves	20	9	5	6	40	27	23
Faversham Town Reserves	18	8	5	5	28	23	20
Darenth Heathside Reserves	16	8	3	5	34	17	19
Deal Town Reserves	18	5	7	6	19	25	15
Margate Reserves	15	5	4	6	23	22	14
Hythe Town Reserves	18	3	7	8	25	32	13
Cray Wanderers Reserves	13	4	1	8	18	36	9
Sittingbourne Reserves	19	3	3	13	26	50	9
Ramsgate Reserves	16	2	1	13	13	51	5

Not all games were played. The records above are final for the top 3 clubs and for Cray Wanderers Reserves but the remaining clubs' records are shown as at 5th May 1979, which is the latest table found.

Faversham Town Reserves had 1 point and 1 goal deducted for fielding ineligible players. Deal Town Reserves had 2 points and 1 goal deducted for fielding ineligible players.

Margate Reserves left the league. Ashford Town Reserves, Erith & Belvedere Reserves, Hastings United Reserves, Sheppey United Reserves and Whitstable Town Reserves all joined.

1979-80

Division One

Chatham Town	32	23	7	2	69	22	53
Cray Wanderers	32	20	9	3	80	25	49
Hythe Town	32	19	4	9	57	48	42
Darenth Heathside	32	17	7	8	52	34	41
Sittingbourne	32	15	9	8	49	43	39
Sheppey United	32	14	7	11	51	42	35
Whitstable Town	32	14	7	11	43	37	35
Tunbridge Wells	32	15	5	12	50	53	35
Erith & Belvedere	32	11	12	9	34	29	34
Slade Green Athletic	32	11	5	16	48	57	27
Dartford Glentworth	32	8	10	14	33	48	26
Deal Town	32	7	10	15	33	45	24
Herne Bay	32	8	8	16	34	51	24
Faversham Town	32	7	8	17	40	51	22
Crockenhill	32	7	7	18	51	69	21
Ramsgate	32	6	8	18	30	57	20
Kent Police	32	5	7	20	38	81	17

Division Two

Chatham Town Reserves	30	26	3	1	90	9	55
Sheppey United Reserves	30	20	5	5	73	34	45
Sittingbourne Reserves	30	18	4	8	63	34	40
Hastings United Reserves	29	17	6	6	63	35	40
Herne Bay Reserves	30	15	8	7	62	38	38
Darenth Heathside Reserves	29	13	7	9	55	39	33
Erith & Belvedere Reserves	29	13	7	9	48	36	33
Cray Wanderers Reserves	27	13	4	10	48	43	30
Dover Reserves	30	11	5	14	48	57	27
Hythe Town Reserves	29	10	6	13	69	64	26
Deal Town Reserves	30	9	7	14	47	60	25
Ashford Town Reserves	30	7	8	15	40	58	22
Whitstable Town Reserves	30	6	5	19	32	72	17
Ramsgate Reserves	28	4	8	16	29	58	16
Faversham Town Reserves	29	6	2	21	38	74	14
Snowdown Colliery Welfare	30	3	3	24	28	122	9

The 5 outstanding games may not have been played.
Cray Wanderers Reserves and Ramsgate Reserves left the league.
Five new reserve sides joined: Dartford, Dartford Glentworth, Folkestone, Maidstone United and Welling United.

1980-81

Division One

Cray Wanderers	32	24	5	3	92	27	53
Chatham Town	32	22	6	4	61	23	50
Crockenhill	32	20	5	7	63	37	45
Erith & Belvedere	32	19	5	8	57	30	43
Sittingbourne	32	18	5	9	74	29	41
Hythe Town	32	18	5	9	70	45	41
Sheppey United	32	16	9	7	45	33	41
Faversham Town	32	12	11	9	36	28	35
Tunbridge Wells	32	10	9	13	33	49	29
Darenth Heathside	32	9	10	13	45	52	28
Deal Town	32	10	7	15	46	49	27
Slade Green Athletic	32	10	5	17	39	51	25
Dartford Glentworth	32	11	3	18	40	60	25
Whitstable Town	32	7	7	18	33	58	21
Kent Police	32	5	9	18	43	67	19
Herne Bay	32	4	6	22	23	67	14
Ramsgate	32	2	3	27	26	121	7

Dartford Glentworth left the league.

Division Two

Welling United Reserves	36	30	2	4	116	27	62
Maidstone United Reserves	36	28	3	5	120	30	59
Chatham Town Reserves	36	24	5	7	92	34	53
Erith & Belvedere Reserves	36	20	7	9	65	28	47
Dartford Reserves	36	22	3	11	71	44	47
Faversham Town Reserves	36	19	1	16	70	66	39
Darenth Heathside Reserves	36	16	7	13	51	52	39
Folkestone Reserves	36	14	9	13	63	62	37
Deal Town Reserves	36	13	10	13	61	70	36
Sittingbourne Reserves	36	11	13	12	45	42	35
Dover Reserves	36	10	11	15	52	62	31
Sheppey United Reserves	36	12	7	17	55	68	31
Ashford Town Reserves	36	13	5	18	50	76	31
Hythe Town Reserves	36	12	6	18	55	75	30
Whitstable Town Reserves	36	11	4	21	42	78	26
Dartford Glentworth Reserves	36	8	9	19	53	68	25
Hastings United Reserves	36	9	5	22	36	74	23
Herne Bay Reserves	36	7	4	25	43	110	18
Snowdown Colliery Welfare	36	6	3	27	38	112	15

Faversham Town Reserves and Dartford Glentworth Reserves both left the league.

1981-82

Division One

Erith & Belvedere	30	17	10	3	45	22	44
Sittingbourne	30	16	11	3	65	33	43
Chatham Town	30	18	5	7	61	34	41
Sheppey United	30	16	5	9	60	40	37
Crockenhill	30	11	13	6	54	41	35
Slade Green Athletic	30	11	13	6	45	32	35
Whitstable Town	30	11	12	7	48	37	34
Cray Wanderers	30	13	6	11	51	40	32
Deal Town	30	11	10	9	44	36	32
Ramsgate	30	9	9	12	44	47	27
Hythe Town	30	10	7	13	48	52	27
Darenth Heathside	30	10	4	16	37	50	24
Tunbridge Wells	30	8	6	16	36	58	22
Herne Bay	30	7	6	17	36	65	20
Faversham Town	30	4	8	18	26	50	16
Kent Police	30	2	7	21	35	98	11

Erith & Belvedere moved to the Southern League. Alma Swanley and Beckenham Town joined from the London-Spartan League.

Division Two

Maidstone United Reserves	32	27	3	2	123	32	57
Dover Reserves	32	18	6	8	55	38	42
Welling United Reserves	32	18	5	9	88	42	41
Chatham Town Reserves	32	17	6	9	69	42	40
Dartford Reserves	32	16	7	9	68	50	39
Sittingbourne Reserves	32	16	6	10	64	45	38
Erith & Belvedere Reserves	32	16	5	11	58	41	37
Hastings United Reserves	32	15	4	13	55	55	34
Herne Bay Reserves	32	14	5	13	48	51	33
Sheppey United Reserves	32	14	3	15	60	67	31
Folkestone Reserves	32	11	7	14	66	66	29
Darenth Heathside Reserves	32	10	4	18	44	62	24
Hythe Town Reserves	32	10	3	19	42	71	23
Ashford Town Reserves	32	9	4	19	38	55	22
Snowdown Colliery Welfare	32	8	5	19	41	92	21
Whitstable Town Reserves	32	8	4	20	35	76	20
Deal Town Reserves	32	5	3	24	37	106	13

Deal Town Reserves left the league.
Beckenham Town Reserves and Faversham Town Reserves both joined.

1982-83

Division One

Crockenhill	32	19	6	7	55	26	44
Hythe Town	32	18	7	7	66	37	43
Deal Town	32	15	11	6	51	34	41
Sittingbourne	32	15	10	7	70	33	40
Tunbridge Wells	32	14	9	9	52	46	37
Herne Bay	32	13	10	9	33	32	36
Chatham Town	32	12	11	9	42	36	35
Cray Wanderers	32	12	10	10	65	54	34
Beckenham Town	32	12	9	11	47	46	33
Sheppey United	32	13	6	13	51	49	32
Alma Swanley	32	12	8	12	50	49	32
Slade Green Athletic	32	12	7	13	41	35	31
Faversham Town	32	11	5	16	40	53	27
Darenth Heathside	32	5	12	15	27	51	22
Whitstable Town	32	6	9	17	36	59	21
Kent Police	32	6	7	19	34	80	19
Ramsgate	32	4	9	19	22	62	17

Chatham Town moved to the Southern League.

Division Two

Maidstone United Reserves	34	25	5	4	106	42	55
Welling United Reserves	34	23	7	4	85	32	53
Erith & Belvedere Reserves	34	20	8	6	87	39	48
Sheppey United Reserves	34	16	6	12	69	62	38
Darenth Heathside Reserves	34	14	9	11	51	43	37
Beckenham Town Reserves	33	13	9	11	56	51	35
Sittingbourne Reserves	34	15	5	14	67	71	35
Faversham Town Reserves	34	14	7	13	49	54	35
Herne Bay Reserves	34	13	9	12	62	73	35
Chatham Town Reserves	34	12	9	13	48	43	33
Dover Reserves	33	12	9	12	53	53	33
Ashford Town Reserves	34	10	12	12	56	57	32
Hastings United Reserves	34	11	9	14	68	81	31
Dartford Reserves	34	10	9	15	75	80	29
Hythe Town Reserves	34	9	7	18	51	62	25
Folkestone Reserves	34	9	5	20	61	94	23
Snowdown Colliery Welfare	34	4	10	20	42	89	18
Whitstable Town Reserves	34	4	7	23	39	99	15

One game was not played.
Dover disbanded but were replaced by a new club called Dover Athletic. The reserves of Dartford, Maidstone United, Sheppey United and Welling United all left the league and Fisher Athletic Reserves joined.

From the next season, 3 points were awarded for a win instead of 2.

1983-84

Division One

Sittingbourne	30	24	3	3	87	26	75
Sheppey United	30	21	3	6	61	28	66
Hythe Town	30	17	5	8	63	39	56
Cray Wanderers	30	14	7	9	66	40	49
Tunbridge Wells	30	12	7	11	61	44	43
Crockenhill	30	11	10	9	37	34	43
Herne Bay	30	13	4	13	42	43	43
Beckenham Town	30	12	6	12	56	54	42
Deal Town	30	13	3	14	54	54	42
Faversham Town	30	12	6	12	40	41	42
Slade Green Athletic	30	11	4	15	38	52	37
Darenth Heathside	30	9	8	13	44	50	35
Alma Swanley	30	8	10	12	39	50	34
Kent Police	30	8	6	16	27	63	30
Whitstable Town	30	4	9	17	37	62	21
Ramsgate	30	4	3	23	22	94	15

Sheppey United moved to the Southern League. Greenwich Borough joined from the London-Spartan League and Area 4 Metropolitan Police joined from the Kent Amateur League.

Division Two

Fisher Athletic Reserves	28	19	5	4	82	23	59
Sittingbourne Reserves	28	19	2	7	66	38	59
Chatham Town Reserves	28	13	8	7	43	31	47
Hythe Town Reserves	28	14	4	10	67	44	46
Beckenham Town Reserves	28	13	5	10	43	30	44
Hastings United Reserves	28	13	5	10	48	46	44
Erith & Belvedere Reserves	28	13	4	11	48	34	43
Ashford Town Reserves	28	13	4	11	40	35	43
Darenth Heathside Reserves	28	10	8	10	36	39	38
Faversham Town Reserves	28	10	6	12	52	57	36
Snowdown Colliery Welfare	28	9	7	12	35	44	34
Dover Athletic Reserves	28	9	5	14	37	46	32
Folkestone Reserves	28	9	3	16	41	56	30
Herne Bay Reserves	28	6	4	18	29	77	22
Whitstable Town Reserves	28	3	4	21	27	100	13
					694	700	

Fisher Athletic Reserves had 3 points and 6 goals deducted for fielding an ineligible player.
Beckenham Town Reserves and Dover Athletic Reserves both left the league. Canterbury City Reserves, Deal Town Reserves, Sheppey United Reserves and Thanet United (ex-Margate) Reserves all joined.

1984-85

Division One

Tunbridge Wells	32	22	6	4	83	39	72
Hythe Town	32	22	6	4	70	33	72
Sittingbourne	32	21	4	7	77	43	67
Beckenham Town	32	17	8	7	67	46	59
Cray Wanderers	32	17	2	13	59	51	53
Greenwich Borough	32	15	6	11	62	49	51
Faversham Town	32	13	8	11	44	42	47
Darenth Heathside	32	13	7	12	45	43	46
Area 4 Metropolitan Police	32	10	13	9	66	66	43
Whitstable Town	32	12	4	16	43	44	40
Alma Swanley	32	11	7	14	46	49	39
Deal Town	32	9	10	13	50	57	37
Herne Bay	32	7	8	17	43	57	29
Slade Green Athletic	32	7	7	18	35	66	28
Kent Police	32	8	3	21	46	88	27
Crockenhill	32	6	7	19	34	63	25
Ramsgate	32	6	6	20	36	73	24

Alma Swanley had 1 point and 1 goal deducted for fielding an ineligible player, Kent Police had 2 goals deducted for fielding an ineligible player.
Thames Polytechnic joined from the London-Spartan League.

Division Two

Sheppey United Reserves	32	23	6	3	77	25	75
Ashford Town Reserves	32	19	6	7	61	37	63
Erith & Belvedere Reserves	32	19	4	9	61	33	61
Fisher Athletic Reserves	31	19	8	4	68	28	56
Faversham Town Reserves	32	15	6	11	70	56	51
Herne Bay Reserves	31	14	8	9	68	55	50
Hythe Town Reserves	32	14	6	12	53	46	48
Snowdown Colliery Welfare	32	12	7	13	44	47	43
Hastings United Reserves	32	12	6	14	43	53	42
Sittingbourne Reserves	32	12	7	13	68	61	40
Darenth Heathside Reserves	32	10	9	13	53	47	39
Folkestone Reserves	32	10	7	15	51	76	37
Chatham Town Reserves	32	8	12	12	41	49	36
Thanet United Reserves	32	8	7	17	36	56	31
Canterbury City Reserves	32	7	6	19	46	71	27
Deal Town Reserves	32	7	5	20	34	87	26
Whitstable Town Reserves	32	5	4	23	30	97	19

One game was not played.
Fisher Athletic had 9 points and 11 goals deducted for fielding ineligible players. Faversham Town and Herne Bay each had 1 goal deducted for fielding an ineligible player. Sittingbourne had 3 points and 4 goals deducted for fielding ineligible players and Thanet United had 3 goals deducted for the same reason.
Hastings United disbanded. Dover Athletic Reserves and Thames Polytechnic Reserves both joined the league.

1985-86

Division One

Alma Swanley	34	22	9	3	78	39	75
Sittingbourne	34	21	7	6	76	37	70
Crockenhill	34	21	5	8	68	33	68
Darenth Heathside	34	17	11	6	57	32	62
Tunbridge Wells	34	15	13	6	99	58	58
Faversham Town	34	16	6	12	53	50	54
Greenwich Borough	34	13	10	11	51	54	49
Ramsgate	34	12	8	14	50	53	44
Kent Police	34	12	7	15	53	61	43
Thames Polytechnic	34	11	9	14	36	49	42
Herne Bay	34	12	6	16	34	52	42
Hythe Town	34	11	7	16	50	59	40
Area 4 Metropolitan Police	34	12	4	18	54	63	40
Cray Wanderers	34	9	12	13	34	51	39
Beckenham Town	34	10	7	17	43	64	37
Whitstable Town	34	9	9	16	37	52	36
Slade Green Athletic	34	5	10	19	14	42	25
Deal Town	34	6	4	24	36	74	22

Slade Green Athletic changed their name to Slade Green and Area 4 Metropolitan Police changed their name to Metropolitan Police (Hayes)

Division Two

Fisher Athletic Reserves	34	25	5	4	95	34	80
Sheppey United Reserves	34	25	5	4	76	30	80
Sittingbourne Reserves	34	20	7	7	75	38	67
Ashford Town Reserves	34	19	5	10	53	44	62
Faversham Town Reserves	34	16	7	11	67	52	55
Thames Polytechnic Reserves	34	15	7	12	58	55	52
Snowdown Colliery Welfare	34	15	5	14	51	45	50
Folkestone Reserves	34	13	9	12	49	48	48
Darenth Heathside Reserves	34	12	11	11	63	54	47
Thanet United Reserves	34	13	8	13	54	54	47
Erith & Belvedere Reserves	34	13	7	14	58	52	46
Dover Athletic Reserves	34	14	4	16	58	56	46
Hythe Town Reserves	34	14	4	16	63	61	46
Deal Town Reserves	34	8	11	15	42	61	35
Canterbury City Reserves	34	9	7	18	49	71	34
Herne Bay Reserves	34	6	8	20	33	67	26
Whitstable Town Reserves	34	5	8	21	32	86	23
Chatham Town Reserves	34	4	2	28	39	107	14

Canterbury City Reserves and Chatham Town Reserves left the league. Ramsgate Reserves and Hastings Town Reserves both joined.

1986-87

Division One

Greenwich Borough	34	24	6	4	113	36	78
Crockenhill	34	22	9	3	63	31	75
Alma Swanley	34	20	7	7	69	34	67
Ramsgate	34	18	8	8	59	42	62
Herne Bay	34	17	9	8	76	58	60
Sittingbourne	34	17	8	9	60	43	59
Tunbridge Wells	34	14	8	12	56	45	50
Whitstable Town	34	14	8	12	45	47	50
Darenth Heathside	34	13	7	14	53	50	46
Cray Wanderers	34	12	8	14	56	48	44
Hythe Town	34	11	11	12	51	48	44
Slade Green	34	12	6	16	50	51	42
Thames Polytechnic	34	9	6	19	48	72	33
Metropolitan Police (Hayes)	34	9	6	19	37	73	33
Beckenham Town	34	7	10	17	37	61	31
Deal Town	34	8	7	19	45	73	31
Faversham Town	34	7	11	16	31	67	31
Kent Police	34	4	1	29	37	108	13

Faversham Town had 1 goal and 1 point deducted.
Danson (Bexley Borough) joined from the Spartan League.

Division Two

Fisher Athletic Reserves	34	26	4	4	102	29	79
Sittingbourne Reserves	34	22	7	5	75	33	73
Erith & Belvedere Reserves	34	16	13	5	72	49	61
Ashford Town Reserves	34	18	7	9	64	43	61
Snowdown Colliery Welfare	34	17	5	12	55	51	56
Hastings Town Reserves	34	15	7	12	79	62	52
Folkestone Reserves	34	16	3	15	56	60	51
Dover Athletic Reserves	34	14	9	11	72	56	50
Thanet United Reserves	34	12	10	12	72	69	46
Herne Bay Reserves	34	13	7	14	51	57	46
Ramsgate Reserves	34	13	5	16	56	62	44
Darenth Heathside Reserves	34	11	11	12	52	64	44
Thames Polytechnic Reserves	34	12	7	15	62	76	43
Sheppey United Reserves	34	11	8	15	62	62	38
Hythe Town Reserves	34	9	4	21	48	71	31
Deal Town Reserves	34	8	5	21	53	98	29
Faversham Town Reserves	34	6	7	21	49	97	25
Whitstable Town Reserves	34	5	5	24	32	85	20

Fisher Athletic Reserves had 3 points deducted.
Dover Athletic Reservers had 1 point deducted.
Sheppey United Reserves had 3 points deducted.
These 3 clubs also had goals deducted.
Erith & Belvedere Reserves left the league and Beckenham Town Reserves joined.

1987-88

Division One

Greenwich Borough	36	26	5	5	111	50	83
Faversham Town	36	23	7	6	92	36	76
Whitstable Town	36	20	8	8	57	37	68
Sittingbourne	36	17	11	8	68	53	62
Hythe Town	36	19	4	13	70	58	61
Kent Police	36	16	8	12	69	66	56
Cray Wanderers	36	16	7	13	72	51	55
Beckenham Town	36	16	5	15	61	55	53
Tunbridge Wells	36	14	10	12	57	50	52
Ramsgate	36	14	8	14	55	53	50
Darenth Heathside	36	11	11	14	57	58	44
Alma Swanley	36	11	11	14	41	47	44
Metropolitan Police (Hayes)	36	11	8	17	45	61	41
Slade Green	36	10	9	17	54	60	39
Danson (Bexley Borough)	36	10	9	17	44	68	39
Deal Town	36	11	5	20	40	67	38
Thames Polytechnic	36	10	8	18	37	65	38
Herne Bay	36	9	8	19	35	69	35
Crockenhill	36	4	6	26	21	82	18

Chatham Town joined from the Southern League.

Division Two

Fisher Athletic Reserves	34	27	4	3	111	21	85
Ashford Town Reserves	34	23	5	6	77	25	74
Faversham Town Reserves	34	21	4	9	71	38	67
Dover Athletic Reserves	34	19	6	9	64	47	63
Sittingbourne Reserves	34	19	5	10	72	52	62
Darenth Heathside Reserves	34	16	11	7	63	43	59
Snowdown Colliery Welfare	34	16	9	9	59	47	57
Whitstable Town Reserves	34	13	7	14	31	44	46
Sheppey United Reserves	34	14	3	17	57	53	45
Hastings Town Reserves	34	13	6	15	60	69	45
Ramsgate Reserves	34	13	2	19	54	56	41
Deal Town Reserves	34	11	6	17	59	75	39
Folkestone Reserves	34	12	3	19	47	80	39
Beckenham Town Reserves	34	10	3	21	54	74	33
Thames Polytechnic Reserves	34	10	3	21	39	73	33
Thanet United Reserves	34	7	9	18	36	68	30
Hythe Town Reserves	34	8	4	22	41	85	28
Herne Bay Reserves	34	8	2	24	41	86	26

Darenth Heathside Reserves and Fisher Athletic Reserves both left the league. Chatham Town Reserves, Cray Wanderers Reserves and Greenwich Borough Reserves all joined.

1988-89

Division One

Hythe Town	38	29	3	6	133	41	90
Deal Town	38	24	4	10	80	35	76
Faversham Town	38	22	7	9	68	36	73
Darenth Heathside	38	20	8	10	69	44	68
Sittingbourne	38	18	12	8	59	43	66
Alma Swanley	38	18	10	10	66	46	64
Cray Wanderers	38	19	7	12	67	53	64
Whitstable Town	38	18	9	11	75	42	63
Ramsgate	38	19	6	13	66	61	63
Slade Green	38	17	10	11	60	59	61
Tunbridge Wells	38	16	8	14	58	57	56
Kent Police	38	16	5	17	61	74	53
Crockenhill	38	11	12	15	52	51	45
Danson (Bexley Borough)	38	12	5	21	55	67	41
Metropolitan Police (Hayes)	38	11	7	20	50	83	40
Greenwich Borough	38	8	15	15	53	56	36
Beckenham Town	38	8	10	20	41	68	34
Thames Polytechnic	38	8	10	20	44	83	34
Chatham Town	38	3	8	27	41	105	17
Herne Bay	38	3	4	31	27	121	13

Greenwich Borough had 3 points deducted.
Hythe Town moved to the Southern League from where Tonbridge joined.

Division Two

Hythe Town Reserves	36	27	4	5	112	31	79
Ashford Town Reserves	36	24	4	8	67	32	76
Dover Athletic Reserves	36	22	7	7	102	45	73
Hastings Town Reserves	36	21	6	9	83	49	69
Sittingbourne Reserves	36	18	11	7	84	52	65
Sheppey United Reserves	36	19	6	11	89	45	63
Cray Wanderers Reserves	36	19	3	14	75	61	60
Ramsgate Reserves	36	16	7	13	65	60	55
Faversham Town Reserves	36	14	10	12	62	57	52
Thames Polytechnic Reserves	36	12	11	13	50	54	47
Greenwich Borough Reserves	36	15	5	16	62	72	47
Snowdown Colliery Welfare	36	14	9	13	54	60	44
Folkestone Reserves	36	9	10	17	56	77	37
Beckenham Town Reserves	36	10	8	18	39	67	35
Deal Town Reserves	36	9	7	20	37	99	34
Thanet United Reserves	36	7	9	20	47	79	30
Whitstable Town Reserves	36	8	6	22	38	74	30
Chatham Town Reserves	36	6	7	23	42	91	24
Herne Bay Reserves	36	4	6	26	29	104	18

Hythe Town Reserves had 6 points deducted.
Greenwich Borough Reserves had 3 points and 3 goals deducted.
Snowdown Colliery Welfare had 7 points and 7 goals deducted.
Beckenham Town Reserves had 3 points and 4 goals deducted.
Thanet United had 1 goal deducted.
Chatham Town Reserves had 1 point and 1 goal deducted.

Thanet United changed their name back to Margate. Snowdown Colliery Welfare, Hythe Town Reserves, Deal Town Reserves and Chatham Town Reserves left the league. Canterbury City Reserves and Fisher Athletic Reserves both joined.

1989-90

Division One

Faversham Town	38	28	4	6	101	30	88
Sittingbourne	38	27	5	6	85	39	86
Tonbridge	38	26	6	6	87	42	84
Deal Town	38	21	11	6	88	48	74
Alma Swanley	38	22	8	8	80	41	74
Greenwich Borough	38	20	6	12	66	55	65
Tunbridge Wells	38	17	9	12	85	66	60
Whitstable Town	38	17	5	16	51	57	56
Slade Green	38	14	8	16	54	61	50
Darenth Heathside	38	12	12	14	61	64	48
Kent Police	38	13	9	16	60	84	48
Beckenham Town	38	12	10	16	54	60	46
Thames Polytechnic	38	11	11	16	49	61	44
Herne Bay	38	12	7	19	64	62	43
Crockenhill	38	12	6	20	52	75	39
Chatham Town	38	9	8	21	38	84	35
Danson (Bexley Borough)	38	8	9	21	42	58	33
Cray Wanderers	38	7	11	20	48	74	32
Metropolitan Police (Hayes)	38	8	4	26	36	87	28
Ramsgate	38	6	7	25	39	100	25

Greenwich Borough had 1 point and 1 goal deducted.
Crockenhill had 3 points and 4 goals deducted.
Chatham Town had 1 goal deducted.
Metropolitan Police (Hayes) had 2 goals deducted.
Sheppey United joined from the Southern League.

Division Two

Margate Reserves	32	23	3	6	72	34	72
Hastings Town Reserves	32	21	3	8	73	43	66
Canterbury City Reserves	32	20	5	7	73	46	62
Dover Athletic Reserves	32	18	7	7	84	40	61
Sittingbourne Reserves	32	18	3	11	65	35	57
Fisher Athletic Reserves	32	18	6	8	74	39	56
Folkestone Reserves	32	16	7	9	55	47	55
Ashford Town Reserves	32	13	7	12	40	43	46
Greenwich Borough Reserves	32	14	4	14	60	64	46
Beckenham Town Reserves	32	12	5	15	49	47	41
Thames Polytechnic Reserves	32	10	8	14	41	50	38
Whitstable Town Reserves	32	9	6	17	39	61	30
Cray Wanderers Reserves	32	8	6	18	34	66	30
Faversham Town Reserves	32	8	4	20	39	90	28
Sheppey United Reserves	32	8	5	19	35	63	26
Ramsgate Reserves	32	7	3	22	43	79	24
Herne Bay Reserves	32	5	6	21	30	70	21

Canterbury City had 3 points and 1 goal deducted.
Fisher Athletic had 4 points and 5 goals deducted.
Sheppey United had 3 points and 2 goals deducted.
Beckenham Town had 2 goals deducted.
Whitstable Town had 3 points and 1 goal deducted.
Folkestone Reserves and Greenwich Borough Reserves both left the league and Deal Town Reserves joined.

1990-91

Division One

Sittingbourne	40	32	8	0	87	19	104
Cray Wanderers	40	27	11	2	91	33	92
Herne Bay	40	24	11	5	83	28	83
Tonbridge	40	24	8	8	72	33	79
Deal Town	40	23	8	9	88	43	77
Faversham Town	40	20	10	10	62	33	70
Whitstable Town	40	20	8	12	67	44	68
Alma Swanley	40	18	9	13	60	53	63
Slade Green	40	16	10	14	65	49	58
Ramsgate	40	16	9	15	60	63	57
Tunbridge Wells	40	16	6	18	71	79	54
Chatham Town	40	13	9	18	61	71	48
Darenth Heathside	40	12	9	19	44	68	45
Beckenham Town	40	12	7	21	37	54	43
Crockenhill	40	10	11	19	47	89	40
Thames Polytechnic	40	10	7	23	49	76	37
Greenwich Borough	40	10	5	25	49	76	35
Danson (Bexley Borough)	40	7	13	20	41	80	34
Kent Police	40	8	9	23	51	77	33
Metropolitan Police (Hayes)	40	5	10	25	37	89	25
Sheppey United	40	6	4	30	39	105	22

Tonbridge and Crockenhill each had 1 point deducted.
Darenth Heathside had 1 goal deducted.

Sittingbourne moved to the Southern League and Corinthian joined from the Southern League. Danson (Bexley Borough) merged with Furness United of the South London Alliance to form Danson Furness United who continued to play in the Kent League. Thamesmead Town joined from the London-Spartan League.

Division Two

Canterbury City Reserves	30	20	5	5	82	41	62
Ashford Town Reserves	30	17	7	6	65	29	58
Hastings Town Reserves	30	16	8	6	63	37	56
Dover Athletic Reserves	30	18	5	7	61	33	56
Cray Wanderers Reserves	30	16	4	10	58	41	52
Fisher Athletic Reserves	30	16	6	8	70	42	54
Sittingbourne Reserves	30	12	10	8	70	48	43
Thames Polytechnic Reserves	30	12	7	11	48	38	43
Herne Bay Reserves	30	11	8	11	58	58	41
Whitstable Town Reserves	30	9	9	12	46	48	36
Beckenham Town Reserves	30	8	10	12	50	49	34
Margate Reserves	30	9	4	17	50	72	31
Deal Town Reserves	30	9	2	19	54	74	29
Faversham Town Reserves	30	8	5	17	44	94	27
Ramsgate Reserves	30	6	7	17	37	67	25
Sheppey United Reserves	30	3	3	24	25	121	12

Canterbury City had 3 points deducted.
Dover Athletic had 3 points and 3 goals deducted.
Sittingbourne had 3 points and 4 goals deducted.
Faversham Town had 1 point and 2 goals deducted.
Sheppey United had 2 goals deducted.

Margate Reserves and Fisher Athletic Reserves both left the league.
Folkestone Invicta joined from the Kent County League. The reserves of Hythe Town, Thamesmead Town, Chatham Town and Darenth Heathside also joined.

1991-92

Division One

Herne Bay	40	29	6	5	91	34	93
Faversham Town	40	25	11	4	78	33	86
Deal Town	40	26	6	8	119	43	84
Tonbridge	40	26	6	8	93	44	84
Alma Swanley	40	24	11	5	92	49	83
Sheppey United	40	21	11	8	69	44	74
Whitstable Town	40	21	8	11	70	38	71
Slade Green	40	15	12	13	68	56	57
Greenwich Borough	40	15	10	15	77	62	55
Ramsgate	40	16	7	17	62	58	55
Kent Police	40	14	11	15	60	63	53
Tunbridge Wells	40	15	8	17	61	68	53
Corinthian	40	14	8	18	58	63	50
Beckenham Town	40	13	10	17	53	67	49
Thames Polytechnic	40	8	11	21	43	78	35
Crockenhill	40	7	13	20	48	83	34
Thamesmead Town	40	9	7	24	44	100	34
Cray Wanderers	40	8	7	25	38	84	31
Chatham Town	40	7	10	23	41	89	31
Danson Furness United	40	8	6	26	39	94	30
Darenth Heathside	40	6	7	27	42	96	25

Metropolitan Police (Hayes) resigned and their record was deleted when it stood as follows:

	16	2	2	12	12	43	8

Thames Polytechnic moved to the Kent County League because of inadequate ground facilities.

Division Two

Folkestone Invicta	36	29	5	2	122	33	92
Dover Athletic Reserves	36	27	4	5	114	30	85
Hastings Town Reserves	36	24	4	8	117	46	76
Ashford Town Reserves	36	19	6	11	59	45	63
Sittingbourne Reserves	36	20	7	9	98	51	61
Deal Town Reserves	36	16	5	15	84	87	53
Herne Bay Reserves	36	16	4	16	70	86	52
Whitstable Town Reserves	36	15	6	15	61	62	51
Ramsgate Reserves	36	15	5	16	62	66	47
Thames Polytechnic Reserves	36	14	5	17	62	70	47
Cray Wanderers Reserves	36	13	8	15	58	66	47
Darenth Heathside Reserves	36	13	6	17	63	79	45
Canterbury City Reserves	36	12	6	18	62	84	42
Chatham Town Reserves	36	10	11	15	49	65	41
Thamesmead Town Reserves	36	11	7	18	53	74	40
Sheppey United Reserves	36	11	6	19	60	89	39
Beckenham Town Reserves	36	8	5	23	51	83	29
Faversham Town Reserves	36	6	7	23	41	95	25
Hythe Town Reserves	36	8	3	25	44	138	24

Sittingbourne Reserves had 6 points deducted.
Ramsgate Reserves and Hythe Town Reserves each had 3 points deducted.
There were also goal deductions but details of these are not available.

Hythe Town disbanded and 5 more reserve sides left – Ashford Town, Faversham Town, Sheppey United, Sittingbourne and Thames Polytechnic while Folkestone Invicta Reserves and Tonbridge Reserves joined.

1992-93

Division One

	P	W	D	L	F	A	Pts
Tonbridge	40	27	9	4	107	39	90
Herne Bay	40	26	6	8	96	44	84
Sheppey United	40	24	9	7	65	29	81
Deal Town	40	24	7	9	128	60	79
Alma Swanley	40	24	4	12	93	65	76
Chatham Town	40	19	11	10	79	52	68
Danson Furness United	40	18	13	9	58	40	67
Thamesmead Town	40	17	9	14	62	56	60
Beckenham Town	40	17	8	15	64	60	59
Whitstable Town	40	18	4	18	77	64	58
Slade Green	40	15	13	12	71	60	58
Ramsgate	40	17	5	18	78	76	56
Folkestone Invicta	40	16	5	19	78	95	53
Tunbridge Wells	40	13	6	21	66	102	45
Faversham Town	40	11	10	19	44	71	43
Greenwich Borough	40	12	5	23	49	75	41
Cray Wanderers	40	10	8	22	64	79	38
Kent Police	40	10	7	23	56	121	37
Darenth Heathside	40	9	7	24	54	104	34
Corinthian	40	6	8	26	50	95	26
Crockenhill	40	6	8	26	56	108	26

Danson Furness United changed their name to Furness and Tonbridge moved to the Southern League.
Dartford joined the league. They had resigned from the Southern League after 4 games of the 1992-93 season because of financial problems.

Division Two

	P	W	D	L	F	A	Pts
Dover Athletic Reserves	26	21	3	2	81	23	66
Herne Bay Reserves	26	20	2	4	78	27	62
Hastings Town Reserves	26	16	1	9	73	39	49
Beckenham Town Reserves	26	14	5	7	54	41	47
Canterbury City Reserves	26	12	5	9	62	57	41
Thamesmead Town Reserves	26	10	7	9	47	39	37
Whitstable Town Reserves	26	10	4	12	39	57	34
Tonbridge Reserves	26	9	6	11	44	49	33
Darenth Heathside Reserves	26	10	3	13	34	44	33
Folkestone Invicta Reserves	26	7	4	15	36	58	25
Chatham Town Reserves	26	7	3	16	48	59	24
Deal Town Reserves	26	6	5	15	43	66	23
Cray Wanderers Reserves	26	6	4	16	32	70	22
Ramsgate Reserves	26	4	8	14	27	69	20

Cray Wanderers Reserves left the league.

1993-94

Division One

	P	W	D	L	F	A	Pts
Herne Bay	40	33	4	3	102	26	103
Furness	40	23	9	8	94	37	78
Chatham Town	40	23	9	8	86	50	78
Thamesmead Town	40	21	11	8	93	47	74
Alma Swanley	40	22	8	10	90	50	74
Dartford	40	21	11	8	70	44	74
Beckenham Town	40	22	4	14	85	59	70
Corinthian	40	21	6	13	91	51	69
Ramsgate	40	20	6	14	90	67	66
Deal Town	40	18	8	14	102	73	62
Sheppey United	40	17	10	13	69	67	61
Folkestone Invicta	40	17	6	17	83	73	57
Faversham Town	40	14	6	20	68	80	48
Greenwich Borough	40	14	5	21	72	85	47
Whitstable Town	40	12	9	19	68	72	45
Tunbridge Wells	40	11	10	19	54	71	43
Cray Wanderers	40	11	9	20	37	65	42
Crockenhill	40	8	10	22	55	99	33
Slade Green	40	8	7	25	42	87	31
Darenth Heathside	40	5	4	31	38	128	19
Kent Police	40	1	4	35	30	188	7

Crockenhill had 1 point deducted.

Alma Swanley disbanded.
Canterbury City joined from the Southern League.

Division Two

	P	W	D	L	F	A	Pts
Dover Athletic Reserves	24	17	4	3	56	15	55
Herne Bay Reserves	24	17	3	4	51	25	54
Thamesmead Town Reserves	24	13	6	5	53	27	45
Whitstable Town Reserves	24	11	9	4	43	26	41
Tonbridge Reserves	24	11	3	10	47	30	36
Hastings Town Reserves	24	9	8	7	52	50	35
Folkestone Invicta Reserves	24	8	5	11	44	51	29
Beckenham Town Reserves	24	7	6	11	42	50	27
Chatham Town Reserves	24	7	5	12	30	44	26
Deal Town Reserves	24	7	1	16	26	62	22
Darenth Heathside Reserves	24	5	6	13	31	43	21
Canterbury City Reserves	24	5	6	13	30	55	21
Ramsgate Reserves	24	5	6	13	22	49	21

Whitstable Town had 1 point deducted.
Tonbridge changed their name to Tonbridge Angels. Darenth Heathside Reserves left and 3 other reserve sides joined: Corinthian, Faversham Town and Furness.

1994-95

Division One

	P	W	D	L	F	A	Pts
Sheppey United	40	29	9	2	118	32	96
Chatham Town	40	26	10	4	117	41	88
Furness	40	24	9	7	81	33	81
Folkestone Invicta	40	21	11	8	107	51	74
Ramsgate	40	21	11	8	91	45	74
Thamesmead Town	40	21	10	9	87	52	73
Herne Bay	40	19	13	8	68	35	70
Deal Town	40	18	10	12	87	62	64
Whitstable Town	40	17	11	12	83	61	62
Beckenham Town	40	15	11	14	61	61	56
Dartford	40	14	11	15	61	51	53
Corinthian	40	15	8	17	50	63	53
Canterbury City	40	14	6	20	66	80	48
Tunbridge Wells	40	12	11	17	48	66	47
Greenwich Borough	40	13	6	21	71	94	45
Crockenhill	40	10	12	18	45	62	42
Slade Green	40	10	12	18	49	73	42
Faversham Town	40	9	8	23	49	118	35
Cray Wanderers	40	6	14	20	45	76	32
Darenth Heathside	40	3	4	33	30	137	13
Kent Police	*40*	*4*	*1*	*35*	*30*	*153*	*13*

Darenth Heathside disbanded.
Hythe United joined from the Kent County League.

Division Two

	P	W	D	L	F	A	Pts
Thamesmead Town Reserves	28	19	5	4	74	31	62
Dover Athletic Reserves	28	18	5	5	73	44	59
Tonbridge Angels Reserves	28	16	4	8	67	40	49
Herne Bay Reserves	28	15	2	11	69	47	47
Ramsgate Reserves	28	13	8	7	46	39	47
Hastings Town Reserves	28	11	9	8	59	42	42
Chatham Town Reserves	28	12	5	11	57	54	40
Furness Reserves	28	11	7	10	40	37	40
Folkestone Invicta Reserves	28	11	6	11	60	54	39
Beckenham Town Reserves	28	8	8	12	48	56	32
Corinthian Reserves	28	8	6	14	37	56	30
Whitstable Town Reserves	28	6	9	13	49	56	27
Faversham Town Reserves	28	7	5	16	31	61	23
Deal Town Reserves	28	6	4	18	40	78	22
Canterbury City Reserves	28	5	5	18	26	81	20

Tonbridge Angels Reserves and Faversham Town Reserves each had 3 points deducted.
Chatham Town Reserves had 1 point deducted.
Crockenhill Reserves, Margate Reserves and Sittingbourne Reserves joined.

1995-96

1996-97

Division One

Furness	38	27	8	3	87	19	89
Dartford	38	26	11	1	71	21	89
Chatham Town	38	24	5	9	79	48	77
Herne Bay	38	18	10	10	74	44	64
Deal Town	38	17	13	8	72	52	64
Slade Green	38	17	12	9	66	46	63
Sheppey United	38	19	5	14	66	49	62
Whitstable Town	38	17	7	14	85	61	58
Thamesmead Town	38	17	7	14	59	51	58
Folkestone Invicta	38	15	11	12	82	56	56
Greenwich Borough	38	15	7	16	60	66	52
Cray Wanderers	38	16	5	17	70	70	50
Canterbury City	38	14	6	18	48	59	48
Ramsgate	38	13	6	19	62	81	45
Tunbridge Wells	38	10	10	18	45	64	40
Beckenham Town	38	9	9	20	45	60	36
Corinthian	38	9	7	22	53	84	34
Crockenhill	38	8	8	22	51	92	32
Hythe United	38	8	6	24	58	101	30
Faversham Town	38	3	3	32	33	142	12

Cray Wanderers had 3 points deducted.

Dartford moved to the Southern League. Lordswood joined from the Kent County League and Woolwich Town joined from the London-Spartan League.

Division One

Herne Bay	40	23	11	6	73	35	80
Ramsgate	40	24	5	11	82	47	77
Furness	40	23	8	9	66	38	77
Sheppey United	40	22	7	11	74	47	73
Deal Town	40	20	5	15	80	56	65
Folkestone Invicta	40	19	7	14	66	57	64
Whitstable Town	40	17	12	11	61	44	63
Chatham Town	40	16	11	13	60	52	59
Greenwich Borough	40	16	10	14	71	62	58
Faversham Town	40	16	9	15	58	73	57
Beckenham Town	40	15	10	15	49	47	55
Canterbury City	40	15	10	15	47	55	55
Hythe United	40	15	8	17	70	76	53
Thamesmead Town	40	15	8	17	53	61	53
Lordswood	40	14	8	18	57	72	50
Slade Green	40	12	9	19	45	50	45
Woolwich Town	40	10	13	17	40	62	43
Cray Wanderers	40	11	6	23	43	66	39
Crockenhill	40	9	11	20	51	80	38
Tunbridge Wells	40	8	10	22	44	76	34
Corinthian	40	8	6	26	37	71	30

Furness changed their name to Swanley Furness and Woolwich Town changed their name to Erith Town. Vickers Crayford, Dartford Athletic (a.k.a. VCD Athletic) joined from the Kent County League.

Division Two

Hastings Town Reserves	36	26	6	4	127	49	84
Furness Reserves	36	24	5	7	121	36	77
Dover Athletic Reserves	36	23	5	8	104	52	74
Tonbridge Angels Reserves	36	22	7	7	108	48	73
Whitstable Town Reserves	36	22	5	9	107	46	71
Sittingbourne Reserves	36	22	4	10	127	57	70
Thamesmead Town Reserves	36	18	6	12	63	48	60
Folkestone Invicta Reserves	36	18	6	12	84	73	60
Chatham Town Reserves	36	15	10	11	56	59	55
Corinthian Reserves	36	16	4	16	63	58	52
Beckenham Town Reserves	36	15	7	14	62	67	52
Ramsgate Reserves	36	14	4	18	79	84	46
Margate Reserves	36	10	9	17	57	76	39
Herne Bay Reserves	36	12	3	21	49	86	39
Deal Town Reserves	36	12	3	21	73	114	39
Canterbury City Reserves	36	11	5	20	58	86	38
Crockenhill Reserves	36	6	4	26	49	104	22
Faversham Town Reserves	36	5	3	28	41	138	18
Kent Police	36	2	2	32	28	175	8

Kent Police and Canterbury City Reserves both left the league.
Three reserve sides joined: Dartford, Lordswood and Hythe United.

Division Two

Tonbridge Angels Reserves	38	28	6	4	103	41	90
Dartford Reserves	38	26	6	6	100	46	81
Sittingbourne Reserves	38	24	7	7	108	57	79
Furness Reserves	38	22	7	9	73	38	73
Hythe United Reserves	38	18	9	11	76	60	63
Deal Town Reserves	38	18	6	14	80	53	60
Herne Bay Reserves	38	18	6	14	63	54	60
Dover Athletic Reserves	38	18	6	14	62	66	60
Lordswood Reserves	38	18	4	16	77	69	58
Margate Reserves	38	16	8	14	64	66	53
Hastings Town Reserves	38	13	10	15	80	80	49
Crockenhill Reserves	38	15	4	19	67	82	49
Thamesmead Town Reserves	38	13	9	16	59	65	45
Ramsgate Reserves	38	11	11	16	72	90	44
Whitstable Town Reserves	38	10	9	19	56	68	39
Chatham Town Reserves	38	11	8	19	39	72	38
Beckenham Town Reserves	38	11	5	22	61	97	38
Folkestone Invicta Reserves	38	9	6	23	48	100	33
Corinthian Reserves	38	6	6	26	49	87	24
Faversham Town Reserves	38	6	5	27	75	121	23

Dartford Reserves, Margate Reserves, Thamesmead Town Reserves and Chatham Town Reserves all had 3 points deducted.

1997-98

Division One

Herne Bay	42	34	5	3	105	29	107
Folkestone Invicta	42	31	4	7	127	42	97
Sheppey United	42	27	10	5	110	63	91
Swanley Furness	*42*	*22*	*9*	*11*	*86*	*50*	*75*
Greenwich Borough	42	21	11	10	83	42	74
Cray Wanderers	42	20	11	11	70	50	71
Beckenham Town	42	21	7	14	67	54	70
Whitstable Town	42	19	11	12	72	54	68
VCD Athletic	42	17	14	11	88	62	65
Lordswood	42	18	9	15	70	64	63
Tunbridge Wells	42	17	6	19	73	76	57
Thamesmead Town	42	15	9	18	69	70	54
Ramsgate	42	14	9	19	80	85	51
Hythe United	42	15	5	22	75	103	50
Slade Green	42	12	13	17	58	67	49
Deal Town	42	15	4	23	76	97	49
Chatham Town	42	12	12	18	56	66	48
Faversham Town	42	14	12	16	62	68	54
Erith Town	42	12	6	24	48	86	42
Canterbury City	42	8	6	28	45	96	30
Corinthian	42	6	2	34	31	133	20
Crockenhill	42	2	5	35	36	130	11

Faversham Town had 8 points deducted.

Folkestone Invicta moved to the Southern League and Swanley Furness were relegated to Division Two, which was renamed Division One. Corinthian also left the league.

Division Two

Sittingbourne Reserves	36	25	7	4	105	35	82
Tonbridge Angels Reserves	36	24	9	3	93	34	81
Thamesmead Town Reserves	36	22	6	8	67	40	72
Swanley Furness Reserves	36	20	5	11	79	45	65
Folkestone Invicta Reserves	36	20	5	11	69	57	65
Dartford Reserves	36	21	7	8	75	49	64
Dover Athletic Reserves	36	19	6	11	85	49	63
Lordswood Reserves	36	17	8	11	71	51	59
Herne Bay Reserves	36	17	7	12	75	57	58
Margate Reserves	36	16	7	13	60	59	52
Hastings Town Reserves	36	14	7	15	85	69	49
Chatham Town Reserves	36	10	10	16	47	61	40
Ramsgate Reserves	36	11	4	21	60	94	37
Whitstable Town Reserves	36	10	5	21	59	89	35
Hythe United Reserves	36	11	2	23	62	103	35
Corinthian Reserves	36	9	5	22	47	74	32
Beckenham Town Reserves	36	7	6	23	40	86	27
Crockenhill Reserves	36	7	5	24	38	95	26
Deal Town Reserves	36	5	3	28	43	110	18
					1260	*1257*	

Dartford Reserves had 6 points deducted.
Margate Reserves had 3 points deducted.

Faversham Town Reserves resigned during the season and their record was deleted.
Swanley Furness Reserves left the league, being replaced by their relegated first team. Corinthian Reserves and Tonbridge Angels Reserves also left. Canterbury City Reserves and Cray Wanderers Reserves joined.

All Division One grounds had to be floodlit from the next season.

Division One was renamed the Premier Division.
Division Two was renamed Division One.

1998-99

Premier Division

Ramsgate	36	26	5	5	93	24	83
Deal Town	36	24	9	3	78	24	81
Greenwich Borough	36	24	4	8	64	28	76
Thamesmead Town	36	20	14	2	57	19	74
Crockenhill	36	19	10	7	62	38	66
Chatham Town	36	18	11	7	61	40	65
VCD Athletic	36	16	9	11	61	51	57
Whitstable Town	36	15	9	12	60	52	54
Beckenham Town	36	13	11	12	51	47	50
Slade Green	36	11	11	14	58	49	44
Sheppey United	36	11	8	17	50	59	44
Herne Bay	36	9	9	18	34	51	36
Lordswood	36	8	12	16	47	71	36
Cray Wanderers	36	8	9	19	53	66	35
Canterbury City	36	9	8	19	34	73	35
Faversham Town	36	9	5	22	41	80	29
Erith Town	36	8	5	23	33	79	29
Hythe United	36	7	7	22	38	65	28
Tunbridge Wells	36	5	8	23	46	105	23

Crockenhill had 1 point deducted and Cray Wanderers had 2 points awarded.
Faversham Town had 3 points deducted and Sheppey United had 3 points awarded.

Crockenhill moved to the Kent County League.

Division One

Deal Town Reserves	36	28	6	2	114	25	90
Dover Athletic Reserves	36	28	2	6	109	33	86
Margate Reserves	36	23	11	2	85	25	82
Swanley Furness	36	20	4	12	69	46	67
Thamesmead Town Reserves	36	18	9	9	91	65	63
Folkestone Invicta Reserves	36	19	7	10	98	70	64
Ramsgate Reserves	36	17	10	9	74	62	61
Hastings Town Reserves	36	15	9	12	54	67	54
Lordswood Reserves	36	15	6	15	67	69	51
Dartford Reserves	36	14	7	15	60	64	49
Sittingbourne Reserves	36	13	13	10	57	57	46
Chatham Town Reserves	36	13	4	19	57	79	43
Beckenham Town Reserves	36	11	8	17	47	49	39
Herne Bay Reserves	36	10	7	19	53	75	37
Canterbury City Reserves	36	11	4	21	42	91	37
Cray Wanderers Reserves	36	8	6	22	46	83	30
Hythe United Reserves	36	7	3	26	39	99	24
Crockenhill Reserves	36	4	10	22	45	94	22
Whitstable Town Reserves	36	5	3	28	32	86	18

Sittingbourne had 3 points deducted, Beckenham Town had 2 points deducted, Margate had 2 points awarded, Swanley Furness had 3 points awarded and Thamesmead Town had 2 points awarded.

Canterbury City Reserves and Crockenhill Reserves both left the league. Ashford Town Reserves, Erith Town Reserves, Greenwich Borough Reserves and VCD Athletic Reserves all joined.

Division One was divided into two sections, North and South.

1999-2000

Premier Division

Deal Town	34	26	5	3	87	28	83
Thamesmead Town	34	23	6	5	75	29	72
Chatham Town	34	23	3	8	76	40	72
VCD Athletic	34	18	10	6	53	32	64
Ramsgate	34	18	9	7	75	41	63
Greenwich Borough	34	17	5	12	70	44	56
Erith Town	34	16	8	10	56	54	56
Hythe United	34	14	6	14	38	50	48
Sheppey United	34	12	6	16	45	60	45
Beckenham Town	34	12	8	14	45	51	44
Lordswood	34	12	6	16	55	63	42
Herne Bay	34	12	8	14	56	48	41
Cray Wanderers	34	10	3	21	42	80	36
Tunbridge Wells	34	9	6	19	49	72	33
Slade Green	34	8	6	20	41	65	30
Whitstable Town	34	6	9	19	38	56	27
Faversham Town	34	6	6	22	39	70	24
Canterbury City	34	6	6	22	35	92	24

Thamesmead Town and Herne Bay each had 3 points deducted.
Sheppey United and Cray Wanderers each had 3 points awarded.

Division One North

Thamesmead Town Reserves	20	13	3	4	44	16	44
Swanley Furness	20	11	6	3	42	27	38
Ashford Town Reserves	20	10	4	6	36	23	31
Hastings Town Reserves	20	9	4	7	39	36	31
VCD Athletic Reserves	20	8	4	8	36	38	31
Greenwich Borough Reserves	20	7	7	6	37	33	28
Chatham Town Reserves	20	8	4	8	34	44	28
Dartford Reserves	20	7	6	7	33	36	27
Erith Town Reserves	20	5	6	9	24	32	21
Cray Wanderers Reserves	20	4	5	11	30	42	17
Beckenham Town Reserves	20	1	5	14	15	42	8
					370	369	

Swanley Furness had 1 point deducted and Ashford Town Reserves had 3
points deducted.
Thamesmead Town Reserves had 2 points awarded and VCD Athletic
Reserves had 3 points awarded.

Division One South

Deal Town Reserves	18	14	3	1	54	20	45
Dover Athletic Reserves	18	12	3	3	37	16	39
Margate Reserves	18	10	4	4	35	20	34
Ramsgate Reserves	18	9	5	4	27	15	32
Sittingbourne Reserves	18	7	3	8	27	34	24
Whitstable Town Reserves	18	6	4	8	44	36	22
Lordswood Reserves	18	6	4	8	21	25	22
Folkestone Invicta Reserves	18	5	4	9	36	34	19
Herne Bay Reserves	18	2	3	13	21	47	9
Hythe United Reserves	18	2	1	15	17	68	7
					319	315	

Deal Town Reserves left the league.

The two sections merged to form a single Division One once again.

2000-01

Premier Division

Chatham Town	**32**	**23**	**7**	**2**	**76**	**28**	**76**
Herne Bay	32	23	5	4	93	43	74
VCD Athletic	32	21	4	7	74	32	67
Thamesmead Town	32	18	8	6	63	29	62
Ramsgate	32	15	10	7	83	36	55
Tunbridge Wells	32	13	11	8	52	41	50
Beckenham Town	32	13	9	10	48	58	48
Whitstable Town	32	12	9	11	43	44	45
Greenwich Borough	32	12	8	12	46	40	44
Lordswood	32	12	7	13	57	55	43
Erith Town	32	13	4	15	42	49	43
Cray Wanderers	32	10	5	17	39	46	35
Slade Green	32	9	3	20	33	75	30
Hythe United	32	6	11	15	41	46	29
Deal Town	32	7	8	17	41	60	29
Faversham Town	32	6	5	21	33	68	23
Canterbury City	32	0	4	28	15	129	4

Sheppey United resigned from the league and their record was deleted
when it stood as follows: 21   6   3   12   27   38   21
Hythe United changed their name to Hythe Town.
Chatham Town were promoted to the Southern League.
Maidstone United joined from the Kent County League.

Division One

Thamesmead Town Reserves	38	24	10	4	76	31	82
Margate Reserves	38	22	7	9	96	51	73
Folkestone Invicta Reserves	38	20	8	10	95	61	68
VCD Athletic Reserves	38	20	8	10	87	59	68
Herne Bay Reserves	38	20	7	11	89	54	67
Sittingbourne Reserves	38	17	11	10	88	55	65
Dover Athletic Reserves	38	18	10	10	62	45	64
Ramsgate Reserves	38	17	9	12	91	63	60
Ashford Town Reserves	38	16	11	11	67	67	59
Chatham Town Reserves	38	16	8	14	87	78	58
Cray Wanderers Reserves	38	17	4	17	63	71	55
Hastings Town Reserves	38	14	7	17	59	78	52
Lordswood Reserves	38	15	5	18	67	84	50
Dartford Reserves	38	11	13	14	64	66	48
Erith Town Reserves	38	13	7	18	65	82	46
Hythe United Reserves	38	11	5	22	52	95	38
Beckenham Town Reserves	38	9	9	20	52	66	36
Whitstable Town Reserves	38	8	6	24	52	91	30
Greenwich Borough Reserves	38	10	6	22	71	112	28
Swanley Furness	38	3	7	28	49	123	16

Greenwich Borough had 8 points deducted. Sittingbourne and Hastings
Town each had 3 points awarded and Chatham Town and Dartford each
had 2 points deducted.
Swanley Furness changed their name to Furness. Deal Town Reserves and
Tunbridge Wells Reserves both joined the league.

Division One was split into two sections, North and South.

2001-02

Premier Division

Maidstone United	30	20	6	4	72	32	66
VCD Athletic	30	20	6	4	67	31	66
Deal Town	30	19	5	6	79	38	62
Thamesmead Town	30	17	6	7	59	39	57
Cray Wanderers	30	15	6	9	56	44	51
Ramsgate	30	13	5	12	57	50	44
Herne Bay	30	13	5	12	53	49	41
Tunbridge Wells	30	10	10	10	45	46	40
Beckenham Town	30	11	7	12	43	45	40
Whitstable Town	30	9	9	12	43	51	36
Lordswood	30	8	9	13	44	55	36
Slade Green	30	11	2	17	35	47	35
Erith Town	30	10	3	17	42	60	33
Hythe Town	30	8	7	15	31	49	31
Greenwich Borough	30	5	4	21	31	70	19
Faversham Town	30	3	6	21	30	81	15

Herne Bay had 3 points deducted and Lordswood were awarded 3 points.
Canterbury City resigned just before the season started and disbanded.

Division One North

Dartford Reserves	20	13	4	3	51	26	43
Cray Wanderers Reserves	20	14	3	3	46	22	42
VCD Athletic Reserves	20	12	5	3	50	29	41
Chatham Town Reserves	20	10	3	7	33	28	33
Thamesmead Town Reserves	20	10	3	7	40	36	33
Furness	20	8	3	9	45	40	27
Erith Town Reserves	20	7	4	9	38	45	25
Beckenham Town Reserves	20	6	3	11	26	35	24
Tunbridge Wells Reserves	20	6	2	12	35	45	20
Lordswood Reserves	20	3	5	12	32	46	14
Greenwich Borough Reserves	20	3	1	16	23	67	10

Cray Wanderers had 3 points deducted and Beckenham Town had 3 points awarded.
Furness changed their name to Danson Furness.
Greenwich Borough Reserves left the league.
Erith & Belvedere Reserves and Corinthian both joined.

Division One South

Dover Athletic Reserves	20	16	3	1	76	18	53
Ramsgate Reserves	20	11	2	7	52	25	35
Sittingbourne Reserves	20	10	4	6	43	33	34
Deal Town Reserves	20	10	3	7	59	42	33
Ashford Town Reserves	20	8	6	6	43	29	30
Folkestone Invicta Reserves	20	8	4	8	40	37	28
Herne Bay Reserves	20	7	6	7	42	39	27
Hastings Town Reserves	20	7	2	11	45	59	23
Margate Reserves	20	6	4	10	36	54	22
Whitstable Town Reserves	20	5	5	10	32	59	20
Hythe Town Reserves	20	1	3	16	12	85	5

Hythe Town Reserves had 1 point deducted and Dover Athletic Reserves had 2 points awarded.
Hastings Town changed their name to Hastings United.
Maidstone United Reserves joined the league.

2002-03

Premier Division

Faversham Town were suspended by Kent County F.A. for non-payment of fines and left the league after playing 22 matches, but their record stood and final Premier Division positions were decided by average points per game.

	P	W	D	L	F	A	Pts	Ave.
Cray Wanderers	29	19	5	5	68	23	62	2.138
Maidstone United	30	18	9	3	76	31	63	2.100
Thamesmead Town	30	19	6	5	76	39	63	2.100
Deal Town	28	15	9	4	62	40	54	1.929
Ramsgate	30	16	7	7	59	35	55	1.833
Whitstable Town	29	15	8	6	56	45	53	1.828
VCD Athletic	30	13	9	8	51	36	48	1.600
Hythe Town	30	13	6	11	46	54	45	1.500
Slade Green	29	10	5	14	57	54	35	1.207
Beckenham Town	29	9	6	14	41	53	33	1.138
Herne Bay	30	9	7	14	53	54	34	1.133
Tunbridge Wells	29	7	8	14	53	66	29	1.000
Lordswood	30	5	9	16	37	66	24	0.800
Greenwich Borough	30	5	5	20	36	70	20	0.667
Erith Town	29	4	6	19	36	71	18	0.621
Faversham Town	22	2	1	19	18	88	7	0.318

Sevenoaks Town joined from the Kent County League and Sporting Bengal United joined from the London Intermediate League.

Division One North

Cray Wanderers Reserves	22	18	2	2	68	18	56
Thamesmead Town Reserves	21	16	0	5	65	34	48
Danson Furness	22	12	4	6	52	39	40
Corinthian	22	11	3	8	44	40	36
Erith Town Reserves	21	10	3	8	33	39	33
Dartford Reserves	22	10	4	8	30	26	34
Chatham Town Reserves	22	8	6	8	47	38	30
Beckenham Town Reserves	22	7	3	12	40	59	24
Tunbridge Wells Reserves	22	7	3	12	34	56	24
Lordswood Reserves	22	4	6	12	27	44	18
VCD Athletic Reserves	22	5	2	15	44	58	17
Erith & Belvedere Reserves	22	3	4	15	29	62	16

Erith & Belvedere Reserves had 3 points awarded.
One game was not played.

Division One South

Deal Town Reserves	22	13	7	2	55	25	46
Dover Athletic Reserves	22	12	6	4	69	35	42
Herne Bay Reserves	22	11	8	3	47	26	41
Ashford Town Reserves	22	12	3	7	43	26	39
Ramsgate Reserves	22	11	2	9	41	42	35
Hastings United Reserves	22	9	5	8	40	27	32
Sittingbourne Reserves	22	9	2	11	45	69	26
Folkestone Invicta Reserves	22	7	4	11	49	52	25
Maidstone United Reserves	22	6	7	9	38	43	25
Whitstable Town Reserves	22	5	5	12	35	46	23
Margate Reserves	22	5	7	10	29	46	22
Hythe Town Reserves	22	3	2	17	25	79	11

Whitstable Town had 3 points awarded and Sittingbourne had 3 points deducted.
Margate Reserves left the league.
Ground Hoppers and Sevenoaks Town Reserves both joined.

The two sections of the First Division were reorganised into Divisions One and Two. The top 6 of each section moved into Division One and the remaining clubs moved into Division Two.

2003-04

Premier Division

	P	W	D	L	F	A	Pts
Cray Wanderers	32	22	4	6	88	35	70
Thamesmead Town	32	22	3	7	72	38	69
VCD Athletic	32	21	5	6	65	29	68
Maidstone United	32	19	10	3	71	30	67
Whitstable Town	32	19	5	8	77	52	62
Hythe Town	32	17	7	8	51	41	58
Erith Town	32	17	2	13	53	45	53
Greenwich Borough	32	14	8	10	57	53	50
Ramsgate	32	11	11	10	49	46	44
Herne Bay	32	11	7	14	50	49	40
Sevenoaks Town	32	12	1	19	40	57	37
Beckenham Town	32	9	8	15	39	53	35
Lordswood	32	9	5	18	34	68	32
Tunbridge Wells	32	8	6	18	30	57	30
Slade Green	32	7	8	17	42	47	29
Deal Town	32	5	4	23	37	71	19
Sporting Bengal United	32	1	2	29	26	110	5

Cray Wanderers were promoted to the Isthmian League.

Division One

	P	W	D	L	F	A	Pts
Corinthian	22	15	4	3	79	32	49
Dover Athletic Reserves	22	14	4	4	61	30	46
Thamesmead Town Reserves	22	11	4	7	42	25	37
Hastings United Reserves	22	11	1	10	47	53	34
Herne Bay Reserves	21	9	5	7	37	34	32
Cray Wanderers Reserves	22	8	6	8	33	34	30
Ashford Town Reserves	22	8	3	11	29	37	27
Erith Town Reserves	22	7	6	9	32	42	27
Deal Town Reserves	22	7	2	13	29	43	23
Danson Furness	21	6	4	11	30	49	22
Ramsgate Reserves	22	5	7	10	26	52	22
Dartford Reserves	22	5	4	13	30	44	19

Dover Athletic Reserves left the league. Corinthian ceased operating as a separate club, becoming Welling United's reserve side which then joined Division Two.

Division Two

	P	W	D	L	F	A	Pts
Erith & Belvedere Reserves	24	15	6	3	56	21	51
Maidstone United Reserves	24	14	4	6	57	33	46
Beckenham Town Reserves	24	14	4	6	51	30	46
Whitstable Town Reserves	24	13	6	5	50	36	45
Sevenoaks Town Reserves	24	13	5	6	45	39	44
Ground Hoppers	24	13	2	9	59	47	41
Chatham Town Reserves	24	10	8	6	54	37	38
Hythe Town Reserves	24	10	3	11	30	39	33
Folkestone Invicta Reserves	24	7	3	14	43	47	24
Tunbridge Wells Reserves	24	6	4	14	36	67	22
Lordswood Reserves	24	5	3	16	26	54	18
Sittingbourne Reserves	24	4	5	15	27	63	17
VCD Athletic Reserves	24	4	3	17	36	57	15

Ground Hoppers left the league and 3 reserve sides joined – Bromley, Slade Green and Welling United.

2004-05

Premier Division

	P	W	D	L	F	A	Pts
Ramsgate	30	22	4	4	65	27	70
Herne Bay	30	19	5	6	68	41	62
Whitstable Town	30	16	6	8	71	44	54
Maidstone United	30	16	6	8	60	37	54
VCD Athletic	30	16	6	8	67	51	54
Hythe Town	30	14	5	11	46	42	47
Tunbridge Wells	30	12	9	9	45	49	47
Thamesmead Town	30	13	5	12	63	54	44
Greenwich Borough	30	13	4	13	52	54	43
Beckenham Town	30	11	7	12	57	54	39
Sevenoaks Town	30	9	6	15	47	66	33
Slade Green	30	8	6	16	40	56	30
Deal Town	30	8	5	17	40	62	29
Sporting Bengal United	30	8	5	17	42	71	29
Erith Town	30	6	5	19	33	60	23
Lordswood	30	5	4	21	37	65	19

Beckenham Town had 1 point deducted and Tunbridge Wells had 2 points awarded.
Ramsgate were promoted to the Isthmian League.
Erith & Belvedere joined from the Southern League.

Division One

	P	W	D	L	F	A	Pts
Erith & Belvedere Reserves	22	17	0	5	50	16	51
Maidstone United Reserves	22	16	3	3	52	29	51
Cray Wanderers Reserves	22	14	3	5	49	24	45
Thamesmead Town Reserves	22	11	5	6	50	36	38
Ramsgate Reserves	22	10	2	10	32	28	32
Ashford Town Reserves	22	9	2	11	40	45	29
Danson Furness	22	8	5	9	33	39	29
Dartford Reserves	22	8	3	11	32	34	27
Erith Town Reserves	22	5	10	7	33	34	25
Herne Bay Reserves	22	5	4	13	24	47	19
Hastings United Reserves	22	4	3	15	28	67	15
Deal Town Reserves	22	3	4	15	28	52	13

Whitstable Town Reserves and Bromley Reserves were promoted from Division Two.
Danson Furness and Hastings United Reserves both left the league.

Division Two

	P	W	D	L	F	A	Pts
Whitstable Town Reserves	24	16	7	1	47	11	55
Bromley Reserves	24	14	5	5	44	22	44
Beckenham Town Reserves	24	11	6	7	49	32	39
Sevenoaks Town Reserves	24	12	2	10	38	37	38
Slade Green Reserves	24	10	7	7	39	34	37
Chatham Town Reserves	24	10	6	8	50	36	36
VCD Athletic Reserves	24	10	5	9	43	37	35
Folkestone Invicta Reserves	24	9	6	9	49	40	33
Hythe Town Reserves	24	8	8	8	35	39	32
Welling United Reserves	24	7	8	9	25	31	29
Sittingbourne Reserves	24	6	1	17	38	65	22
Tunbridge Wells Reserves	24	6	2	16	29	59	20
Lordswood Reserves	24	4	3	17	26	69	15

Bromley Reserves had 3 points deducted and Sittingbourne Reserves had 3 points awarded.
Beckenham Town Reserves and Welling United Reserves left the league.
Greenwich Borough Reserves and Tilbury Reserves both joined.

2005-06

2006-07

Premier Division

Maidstone United	30	22	6	2	85	23	72
Beckenham Town	30	22	4	4	96	24	70
Thamesmead Town	30	18	6	6	73	41	60
Erith & Belvedere	30	17	7	6	50	31	58
Whitstable Town	30	16	7	7	64	38	55
VCD Athletic	30	15	5	10	51	30	50
Herne Bay	30	14	7	9	52	33	49
Lordswood	30	12	9	9	49	45	45
Deal Town	30	13	4	13	53	62	43
Tunbridge Wells	30	10	7	13	39	41	37
Slade Green	30	9	7	14	31	56	34
Hythe Town	30	7	6	17	41	51	27
Greenwich Borough	30	7	3	20	36	69	24
Erith Town	30	5	5	20	21	65	20
Sporting Bengal United	30	3	6	21	27	107	15
Sevenoaks Town	30	3	5	22	18	70	14

Maidstone United were promoted to the Isthmian League from where Croydon were relegated.
Faversham Town joined from the Kent County League.

Premier Division

Whitstable Town	32	21	7	4	76	40	70
VCD Athletic	32	20	7	5	79	38	67
Croydon	32	20	7	5	58	34	67
Thamesmead Town	32	19	6	7	75	44	63
Greenwich Borough	32	19	6	7	63	38	63
Hythe Town	32	16	8	8	59	35	56
Erith & Belvedere	32	16	8	8	68	50	56
Deal Town	32	14	6	12	68	55	48
Herne Bay	32	12	8	12	51	41	44
Sevenoaks Town	32	12	6	14	50	57	42
Beckenham Town	32	12	4	16	64	52	40
Faversham Town	32	10	6	16	36	55	36
Lordswood	32	8	5	19	40	68	29
Erith Town	32	7	3	22	35	60	24
Tunbridge Wells	32	5	8	19	39	66	23
Slade Green	32	5	8	19	36	68	23
Sporting Bengal United	32	2	5	25	28	124	11

Whitstable Town were promoted to the Isthmian League.
Holmesdale joined from the Kent County League.

Division One

Thamesmead Town Reserves	22	15	5	2	50	23	50
Whitstable Town Reserves	22	13	3	6	46	32	42
Cray Wanderers Reserves	22	11	5	6	51	34	38
Bromley Reserves	22	12	2	8	42	34	38
Dartford Reserves	22	10	5	7	39	27	35
Erith Town Reserves	22	10	4	8	50	42	34
Ramsgate Reserves	22	8	6	8	38	45	30
Ashford Town Reserves	22	8	4	10	38	47	28
Erith & Belvedere Reserves	22	7	6	9	43	47	27
Maidstone United Reserves	22	6	4	12	31	53	22
Herne Bay Reserves	*22*	*3*	*5*	*14*	*25*	*46*	*14*
Deal Town Reserves	*22*	*3*	*3*	*16*	*20*	*43*	*12*

Herne Bay Reserves and Deal Town Reserves relegated to Division Two from where Folkestone Invicta Reserves and Sevenoaks Town Reserves were promoted.

Division One

Thamesmead Town Reserves	22	16	3	3	55	21	51
Bromley Reserves	22	15	3	4	58	27	48
Whitstable Town Reserves	22	14	4	4	49	24	46
Maidstone United Reserves	22	11	4	7	45	25	37
Dartford Reserves	22	10	3	9	31	34	33
Erith & Belvedere Reserves	22	10	2	10	37	34	32
Folkestone Invicta Reserves	22	8	5	9	31	28	29
Erith Town Reserves	22	8	1	13	32	42	25
Ramsgate Reserves	22	7	4	11	31	45	25
Cray Wanderers Reserves	22	6	5	11	38	57	22
Sevenoaks Town Reserves	22	4	7	11	27	33	19
Ashford Town Reserves	*22*	*1*	*3*	*18*	*14*	*78*	*6*

Cray Wanderers Reserves had 1 point deducted.
Bromley Reserves left the league.

Division Two

Folkestone Invicta Reserves	**20**	**14**	**4**	**2**	**53**	**16**	**46**
Sevenoaks Town Reserves	**20**	**11**	**4**	**5**	**32**	**22**	**37**
Chatham Town Reserves	20	11	1	8	47	42	34
Slade Green Reserves	20	9	6	5	36	22	33
Tunbridge Wells Reserves	20	8	7	5	42	34	31
Lordswood Reserves	20	8	4	8	42	39	28
Greenwich Borough Reserves	20	6	5	9	26	37	23
VCD Athletic Reserves	20	6	4	10	27	46	22
Tilbury Reserves	20	5	5	10	26	33	20
Sittingbourne Reserves	20	4	5	11	24	42	17
Hythe Town Reserves	20	3	5	12	24	46	14

Slade Green Reserves left the league.
Three reserve sides joined: Dover Athletic, Faversham Town and Margate.

Division Two

Chatham Town Reserves	**24**	**17**	**6**	**1**	**61**	**24**	**57**
Margate Reserves	**24**	**15**	**4**	**5**	**54**	**29**	**49**
VCD Athletic Reserves	24	12	5	7	46	36	41
Dover Athletic Reserves	24	11	6	7	55	36	39
Hythe Town Reserves	24	11	2	11	55	48	35
Greenwich Borough Reserves	24	10	5	9	48	42	35
Herne Bay Reserves	24	9	6	9	33	47	33
Faversham Town Reserves	24	8	8	8	50	44	32
Deal Town Reserves	24	9	5	10	36	46	32
Sittingbourne Reserves	24	8	6	10	48	49	30
Lordswood Reserves	24	6	5	13	46	65	23
Tilbury Reserves	24	4	4	16	45	70	16
Tunbridge Wells Reserves	24	3	4	17	32	73	13

Tilbury Reserves left the league. Croydon Reserves and Holmesdale Reserves both joined.

2007-08

Premier Division

Thamesmead Town	32	24	6	2	87	36	78
VCD Athletic	32	22	5	5	73	33	71
Beckenham Town	32	21	7	4	80	41	70
Hythe Town	32	20	5	7	85	35	65
Erith Town	32	13	12	7	61	35	51
Herne Bay	32	14	8	10	60	46	50
Erith & Belvedere	32	13	10	9	68	49	49
Greenwich Borough	32	12	10	10	44	36	46
Deal Town	32	12	5	15	62	66	41
Tunbridge Wells	32	12	5	15	53	60	41
Sevenoaks Town	32	9	6	17	57	64	33
Croydon	32	9	5	18	38	61	32
Faversham Town	32	9	4	19	43	79	31
Slade Green	32	8	6	18	38	75	30
Holmesdale	32	6	10	16	40	59	28
Lordswood	32	7	6	19	39	69	27
Sporting Bengal United	32	4	4	24	31	115	16

Thamesmead Town were promoted to Isthmian League.
Norton Sports joined from the Kent County League.

Division One

Thamesmead Town Reserves	22	14	5	3	44	23	47
Dartford Reserves	22	12	4	6	42	28	40
Chatham Town Reserves	22	13	1	8	48	38	40
Maidstone United Reserves	22	11	5	6	50	26	38
Sevenoaks Town Reserves	22	10	6	6	40	33	36
Cray Wanderers Reserves	22	10	5	7	33	36	35
Erith & Belvedere Reserves	22	10	3	9	46	48	33
Whitstable Town Reserves	22	8	4	10	44	42	28
Margate Reserves	22	6	6	10	49	56	24
Folkestone Invicta Reserves	22	7	2	13	31	44	23
Ramsgate Reserves	*22*	*4*	*4*	*14*	*29*	*49*	*16*
Erith Town Reserves	22	2	5	15	22	55	11

Erith Town Reserves left the league.

Division Two

Dover Athletic Reserves	**24**	**18**	**3**	**3**	**67**	**28**	**57**
Ashford Town Reserves	**24**	**14**	**5**	**5**	**68**	**36**	**47**
Greenwich Borough Reserves	24	14	5	5	56	30	47
VCD Athletic Reserves	24	13	6	5	59	30	45
Deal Town Reserves	24	13	4	7	43	29	43
Tunbridge Wells Reserves	24	14	0	10	58	39	42
Holmesdale Reserves	24	13	3	8	37	30	42
Faversham Town Reserves	24	10	2	12	31	49	32
Hythe Town Reserves	24	9	4	11	33	46	31
Sittingbourne Reserves	24	5	4	15	31	55	19
Lordswood Reserves	24	5	4	15	25	61	19
Herne Bay Reserves	24	4	4	16	21	49	16
Croydon Reserves	24	1	2	21	19	66	4

Croydon Reserves had 1 point deducted.
Croydon Reserves and Sittingbourne Reserves both left the league.
Welling United Reserves joined.

2008-09

Premier Division

VCD Athletic	**32**	**22**	**4**	**6**	**68**	**24**	**70**
Hythe Town	32	21	4	7	71	39	67
Greenwich Borough	32	20	4	8	60	45	63
Faversham Town	32	20	2	10	83	40	62
Holmesdale	32	18	7	7	57	30	61
Herne Bay	32	19	3	10	68	50	60
Erith Town	32	14	10	8	59	39	54
Erith & Belvedere	32	16	5	11	67	50	53
Croydon	32	15	4	13	58	40	49
Tunbridge Wells	32	13	6	13	53	50	45
Norton Sports	32	12	4	16	44	57	40
Deal Town	32	10	8	14	57	53	38
Slade Green	32	11	4	17	53	66	37
Sevenoaks Town	32	9	4	19	44	67	31
Beckenham Town	32	8	4	20	54	76	28
Lordswood	32	6	3	23	43	79	21
Sporting Bengal United	32	0	0	32	26	160	0

Greenwich Borough had 1 point deducted and Erith Town were awarded 2 points.
VCD Athletic were promoted to the Isthmian League, Croydon moved to the Combined Counties League and Slade Green disbanded.
Fisher (a new club formed following the demise of Fisher Athletic) joined.

Division One

Thamesmead Town Reserves	22	15	0	7	45	24	45
Cray Wanderers Reserves	22	13	1	8	46	27	40
Dartford Reserves	22	11	4	7	39	26	37
Maidstone United Reserves	22	11	3	8	32	22	36
Ashford Town Reserves	22	11	3	8	36	27	36
Margate Reserves	22	10	4	8	34	35	34
Erith & Belvedere Reserves	22	10	3	9	30	24	33
Dover Athletic Reserves	22	10	2	10	45	45	32
Whitstable Town Reserves	22	8	3	11	25	33	27
Chatham Town Reserves	22	7	5	10	36	43	26
Folkestone Invicta Reserves	*22*	*5*	*2*	*15*	*16*	*47*	*17*
Sevenoaks Town Reserves	*22*	*3*	*6*	*13*	*20*	*51*	*15*

Folkestone Invicta Reserves and Sevenoaks Town Reserves were relegated to Division Two from where Herne Bay Reserves and Holmesdale Reserves were promoted.
Dover Athletic Reserves left the league.

Division Two

Holmesdale Reserves	**20**	**15**	**4**	**1**	**63**	**24**	**49**
Herne Bay Reserves	**20**	**12**	**4**	**4**	**44**	**31**	**40**
Hythe Town Reserves	20	10	5	5	39	30	35
Faversham Town Reserves	20	10	5	5	41	33	35
Tunbridge Wells Reserves	20	10	3	7	45	44	33
Welling United Reserves	**20**	**10**	**2**	**8**	**46**	**32**	**32**
Ramsgate Reserves	20	8	3	9	48	40	27
VCD Athletic Reserves	20	5	2	13	22	43	17
Deal Town Reserves	20	4	6	10	28	42	15
Greenwich Borough Reserves	20	5	1	14	21	41	13
Lordswood Reserves	20	2	3	15	28	65	9

Greenwich Borough Reserves and Deal Town Reserves each had 3 points deducted.
Tunbridge Wells Reserves and Greenwich Borough Reserves both left the league. Beckenham Town Reserves and Erith Town Reserves joined.
Corinthian F.C. had been co-operating with Welling United to help to provide Welling's reserve team but it was now decided that the team would play as Corinthian and as such, they were promoted to the Premier Division.

2009-10

Premier Division

Faversham Town	30	24	2	4	79	23	74
Herne Bay	30	22	2	6	75	36	68
Hythe Town	30	15	8	7	67	36	53
Beckenham Town	30	16	5	9	56	39	53
Greenwich Borough	30	14	8	8	52	39	50
Sevenoaks Town	30	14	4	12	56	50	46
Tunbridge Wells	30	11	8	11	51	50	41
Erith Town	30	11	7	12	52	49	40
Deal Town	30	11	6	13	49	60	39
Holmesdale	30	11	3	16	47	47	36
Norton Sports	30	10	6	14	41	48	36
Erith & Belvedere	30	10	6	14	46	62	36
Fisher	30	9	5	16	41	58	32
Corinthian	30	9	3	18	32	67	30
Sporting Bengal United	30	7	4	19	44	95	25
Lordswood	30	3	9	18	35	64	18

Faversham Town moved to the Isthmian League from where VCD Athletic were relegated.

Division One

Herne Bay Reserves	20	13	5	2	47	26	44
Erith & Belvedere Reserves	20	11	4	5	40	30	37
Maidstone United Reserves	20	10	6	4	35	23	36
Dartford Reserves	20	10	2	8	46	30	32
Cray Wanderers Reserves	20	7	7	6	45	40	28
Thamesmead Town Reserves	20	6	8	6	31	37	26
Ashford Town Reserves	20	6	6	8	27	30	24
Chatham Town Reserves	20	7	3	10	33	37	24
Whitstable Town Reserves	20	5	7	8	45	52	22
Margate Reserves	20	6	3	11	24	46	21
Holmesdale Reserves	*20*	*3*	*1*	*16*	*30*	*52*	*7*

Dartford Reserves and Ashford Town Reserves both left the league.

Division Two

Erith Town Reserves	**18**	**10**	**3**	**5**	**38**	**20**	**33**
Beckenham Town Reserves	**18**	**9**	**5**	**4**	**41**	**25**	**32**
Sevenoaks Town Reserves	18	9	4	5	39	33	31
VCD Athletic Reserves	18	8	4	6	30	25	28
Deal Town Reserves	18	8	4	6	32	32	28
Faversham Town Reserves	18	6	6	6	28	25	24
Lordswood Reserves	18	7	2	9	24	33	23
Folkestone Invicta Reserves	18	5	4	9	28	42	19
Hythe Town Reserves	18	4	4	10	23	36	16
Ramsgate Reserves	18	3	6	9	31	43	15

Greenwich Borough Reserves joined the league.

2010-11

Premier Division

Hythe Town	30	21	5	4	82	33	68
Herne Bay	30	20	8	2	64	30	68
VCD Athletic	30	13	13	4	51	33	52
Greenwich Borough	30	16	2	12	65	42	50
Erith & Belvedere	30	14	7	9	60	40	49
Tunbridge Wells	30	13	6	11	64	48	45
Sevenoaks Town	30	14	3	13	45	50	45
Erith Town	30	11	9	10	54	44	42
Norton Sports	30	10	10	10	52	64	40
Beckenham Town	30	12	3	15	56	55	39
Deal Town	30	10	5	15	39	52	35
Corinthian	30	10	5	15	38	59	35
Lordswood	30	9	7	14	41	50	34
Holmesdale	30	5	8	17	33	54	23
Sporting Bengal United	30	6	5	19	39	92	23
Fisher	30	6	4	20	30	67	22

Norton Sports changed their name to Woodstock Sports.
Hythe Town were promoted to the Isthmian League and Sporting Bengal United moved to the Essex Senior League. Canterbury City and Cray Valley Paper Mills joined from the Kent County League.

Division One

Cray Wanderers Reserves	16	10	3	3	59	19	33
Whitstable Town Reserves	16	7	3	6	36	37	24
Maidstone United Reserves	16	6	5	5	34	40	23
Erith Town Reserves	16	6	4	6	29	25	22
Herne Bay Reserves	16	6	4	6	34	34	22
Thamesmead Town Reserves	16	6	4	6	25	31	22
Chatham Town Reserves	16	5	4	7	26	29	19
Margate Reserves	16	4	6	6	30	41	18
Erith & Belvedere Reserves	16	4	3	9	19	36	15

Beckenham Town Reserves resigned and their record was deleted.
Cray Wanderers Reserves and Thamesmead Town Reserves both left.

Division Two

Faversham Town Reserves	**18**	**15**	**3**	**0**	**58**	**16**	**48**
Deal Town Reserves	**18**	**15**	**2**	**1**	**50**	**11**	**47**
Holmesdale Reserves	18	6	6	6	24	38	24
Lordswood Reserves	18	6	4	8	31	40	22
Sevenoaks Town Reserves	18	6	3	9	33	36	21
Ramsgate Reserves	18	6	3	9	39	45	21
Greenwich Borough Reserves	18	6	2	10	25	40	20
VCD Athletic Reserves	18	5	4	9	31	35	19
Hythe Town Reserves	18	4	4	10	28	39	16
Folkestone Invicta Reserves	18	4	3	11	30	49	15

Hythe Town Reserves, Greenwich Borough Reserves and Sevenoaks Town Reserves all left the league.
Phoenix Sports Reserves, Welling United Reserves and Woodstock Sports Reserves joined.

FORMATION OF THE KENT INVICTA LEAGUE

The feeder competition to the Kent League was the Kent County League but there was a significant gap between the two leagues in terms of both ground facilities and playing standards. Few clubs had been able to make the step up and even fewer had dropped down. It was therefore decided to form a new league to bridge that gap. The new league was called the Kent Invicta League and had 16 founder members who were adjudged to have the best ground facilities and playing standards.

9 of the 16 clubs came from the Kent County League – Premier Division: Bearsted, Bly Spartans, Bridon Ropes, Hollands & Blair, Lewisham Borough, Phoenix Sports, Rusthall, Sutton Athletic and Woodstock Park. Crockenhill and Orpington came from the Kent County League – Division One (West) and Meridian and Seven Acre Sports came from the Kent County League – Division Two (West), Seven Acre Sports changing their name to Seven Acre & Sidcup. Lydd Town came from the Kent County League – Division Two (East) and two newly formed clubs also joined: Ashford United and Erith & Dartford Town.

2011-12

Kent League

Premier Division

Herne Bay	30	21	5	4	73	31	68
Erith & Belvedere	30	19	4	7	77	47	58
VCD Athletic	30	18	4	8	54	26	58
Erith Town	30	17	6	7	56	38	57
Tunbridge Wells	30	17	4	9	66	40	55
Beckenham Town	30	14	11	5	72	36	53
Corinthian	30	13	6	11	54	40	45
Woodstock Sports	30	14	2	14	55	58	44
Canterbury City	30	12	5	13	53	59	41
Fisher	30	10	6	14	51	62	36
Cray Valley Paper Mills	30	9	7	14	34	50	34
Lordswood	30	8	8	14	43	57	32
Holmesdale	30	7	4	19	43	73	25
Sevenoaks Town	30	5	8	17	29	55	23
Deal Town	30	5	8	17	26	70	23
Greenwich Borough	30	5	4	21	29	73	19

Erith & Belvedere had 3 points deducted.
Herne Bay were promoted to the Isthmian League from where Whyteleafe were relegated.
Rochester United joined from the Kent Invicta League, having changed their name from Bly Spartans.

Division One

Herne Bay Reserves	16	12	2	2	50	23	38
Faversham Town Reserves	16	12	1	3	49	12	37
Whitstable Town Reserves	16	11	1	4	46	16	34
Maidstone United Reserves	16	7	5	4	45	24	26
Erith Town Reserves	16	7	3	6	27	21	24
Chatham Town Reserves	16	6	2	8	28	38	20
Margate Reserves	16	3	2	11	26	57	11
Erith & Belvedere Reserves	16	3	0	13	18	51	9
Deal Town Reserves	16	2	2	12	14	61	8

Faversham Town Reserves and Erith & Belvedere Reserves both left.

Division Two

Phoenix Sports Reserves	14	11	1	2	45	14	34
VCD Athletic Reserves	14	11	1	2	40	15	34
Ramsgate Reserves	14	7	2	5	26	21	23
Holmesdale Reserves	14	6	2	6	23	17	20
Welling United Reserves	14	6	2	6	28	23	20
Folkestone Invicta Reserves	14	3	4	7	13	23	13
Lordswood Reserves	14	3	2	9	9	36	11
Woodstock Sports Reserves	14	1	2	11	10	45	5

Welling United Reserves and Folkestone Invicta Reserves left the league.

Division Two merged with Division One.

Kent Invicta League

Bly Spartans	30	17	9	4	75	33	60
Phoenix Sports	30	17	7	6	60	30	58
Hollands & Blair	30	17	4	9	66	30	55
Bridon Ropes	30	16	7	7	57	38	55
Ashford United	30	15	7	8	65	44	52
Sutton Athletic	30	14	6	10	49	42	48
Bearsted	30	11	11	8	40	34	44
Lewisham Borough	30	13	4	13	48	42	43
Woodstock Park	30	12	4	14	54	59	40
Seven Acre & Sidcup	30	10	9	11	47	51	39
Rusthall	30	10	3	17	39	58	33
Lydd Town	30	9	5	16	51	64	32
Erith & Dartford Town	30	9	5	16	38	65	32
Crockenhill	30	9	4	17	43	83	31
Meridian	30	7	6	17	51	85	27
Orpington	30	6	5	19	42	67	23

Bly Spartans were promoted to the Kent League – Premier Division and Eltham Palace joined from the Kent County League. Erith & Dartford merged with Kent Football United youth football club and adopted the Kent Football United name.

2012-13

Kent League

Premier Division

Erith & Belvedere	32	23	7	2	113	45	76
VCD Athletic	32	23	5	4	97	31	74
Erith Town	32	19	4	9	74	40	61
Corinthian	32	17	8	7	74	37	59
Lordswood	32	17	7	8	60	56	58
Whyteleafe	32	16	6	10	67	49	54
Tunbridge Wells	32	15	7	10	82	43	52
Cray Valley Paper Mills	32	13	8	11	63	58	47
Canterbury City	32	12	7	13	52	58	43
Woodstock Sports	32	12	7	13	59	76	43
Beckenham Town	32	11	7	14	63	73	40
Deal Town	32	11	6	15	58	65	39
Rochester United	32	12	2	18	52	70	38
Fisher	32	7	7	18	41	71	28
Greenwich Borough	32	6	5	21	33	93	23
Holmsdale	32	5	6	21	34	83	21
Sevenoaks Town	32	3	1	28	28	102	10

Erith & Belvedere and VCD Athletic were both promoted to the Isthmian League. Phoenix Sports and Ashford United were both promoted from the Kent Invicta League.

Division One

Whitstable Town Reserves	26	19	3	4	86	28	60
Herne Bay Reserves	26	16	5	5	68	40	53
Maidstone United Reserves	26	15	5	6	80	52	50
Chatham Town Reserves	26	13	7	6	55	32	46
Erith Town Reserves	26	13	6	7	56	40	45
Ramsgate Reserves	26	12	4	10	55	54	40
Deal Town Reserves	26	10	4	12	49	55	34
Holmesdale Reserves	26	9	6	11	61	60	33
VCD Athletic Reserves	26	11	0	15	57	60	30
Phoenix Sports Reserves	26	9	2	15	60	66	29
Margate Reserves	26	\8	5	13	47	57	29
Woodstock Sports Reserves	26	8	5	13	41	75	29
Lordswood Reserves	26	6	6	14	40	62	24
Rusthall Reserves	26	4	0	22	26	100	12

Margate Reserves' game with VCD Athletic Reserves was awarded to Margate. VCD Athletic Reserves had 3 points deducted.

Division One closed down as there were insufficient clubs for it to continue but the Premier Division retained its title. Erith Town Reserves and Lordswood Reserves both joined the Suburban League – South, Deal Town Reserves joined the Kent County League – Division Two (East), Phoenix Sports Reserves joined the Kent County League – Division Two (West) and Rushall Reserves joined the Tonbridge & District League.

The Kent League changed their name to Southern Counties East League.

Kent Invicta League

Phoenix Sports	30	25	3	2	108	26	78
Hollands & Blair	30	24	2	4	96	25	74
Ashford United	30	20	6	4	79	32	66
Bearsted	30	18	3	9	82	43	57
Seven Acre & Sidcup	30	15	5	10	59	46	50
Lydd Town	30	15	5	10	63	59	50
Bridon Ropes	30	14	6	10	51	35	48
Sutton Athletic	30	12	5	13	41	41	41
Orpington	30	12	4	14	35	64	40
Eltham Palace	29	10	6	13	49	74	36
Kent Football United	29	8	5	16	43	67	29
Rusthall	30	8	5	17	38	81	29
Crockenhill	30	7	4	19	44	84	25
Woodstock Park	30	6	4	20	33	58	22
Meridian	30	6	3	21	40	80	21
Lewisham Borough	30	5	2	23	38	84	17

Phoenix Sports and Ashford United were both promoted to the Southern Counties East League. Fleet Leisure joined from the Kent County League and Glebe joined as a newly formed club. Woodstock Park moved to the Kent County League – Division Two (East). Meridian changed their name to Meridian VP (VP stands for Valley Park).

2013-14

Southern Counties East League

Premier Division

Whyteleafe	32	26	2	4	111	35	80
Ashford United	32	22	3	7	72	37	69
Erith Town	32	21	4	7	67	43	67
Tunbridge Wells	32	20	5	7	90	47	65
Corinthian	32	16	10	6	60	41	58
Phoenix Sports	32	17	5	10	70	49	56
Cray Valley Paper Mills	32	14	8	10	64	50	50
Beckenham Town	32	15	4	13	76	58	49
Greenwich Borough	32	15	2	15	71	63	47
Holmsdale	32	13	5	14	48	64	44
Lordswood	32	13	3	16	49	79	42
Canterbury City	32	9	5	18	41	63	32
Deal Town	32	9	2	21	46	82	29
Fisher	32	7	7	18	45	77	28
Rochester United	32	7	6	19	43	75	27
Sevenoaks Town	32	5	5	22	44	84	20
Woodstock Sports	32	3	4	25	31	81	13

Whyteleafe were promoted to the Isthmian League from where Erith & Belvedere were relegated. Crowborough Athletic and Lingfield both joined from the Sussex County League and Croydon joined from the Combined Counties League.

Kent Invicta League

Hollands & Blair	28	25	1	2	123	23	76
Lydd Town	28	20	6	2	68	20	66
Sutton Athletic	28	15	7	6	70	29	52
Fleet Leisure	28	17	1	10	71	38	52
Orpington	28	15	7	6	52	30	52
Bearsted	28	16	3	9	75	37	51
Rusthall	28	16	3	9	70	54	51
Bridon Ropes	28	12	4	12	59	52	40
Seven Acre & Sidcup	28	11	4	13	58	64	37
Glebe	28	11	2	15	52	53	35
Kent Football United	28	8	9	11	60	57	33
Eltham Palace	28	6	3	19	26	66	21
Lewisham Borough	28	5	2	21	34	102	17
Meridian VP	28	4	4	20	31	85	16
Crockenhill	28	1	0	27	20	159	3

Sheppey & Sheerness United joined from the Kent County League and changed their name to Sheppey United. Fleet Leisure changed their name to Gravesham Borough.

2014-15

Southern Counties East League

Premier Division

Phoenix Sports	38	28	9	1	94	20	93
Ashford United	38	25	10	3	96	39	85
Erith & Belvedere	38	25	7	6	83	36	82
Greenwich Borough	38	22	8	8	88	49	74
Tunbridge Wells	38	19	9	10	74	51	66
Corinthian	38	19	2	17	78	67	59
Cray Valley Paper Mills	38	16	10	12	77	63	58
Sevenoaks Town	38	15	10	13	68	61	55
Beckenham Town	38	16	5	17	77	63	53
Crowborough Athletic	38	14	7	17	62	78	49
Woodstock Sports	38	14	6	18	45	60	48
Canterbury City	38	14	5	19	50	69	47
Deal Town	38	14	4	20	66	78	46
Holmesdale	38	11	7	20	74	90	40
Lordswood	38	10	9	19	43	77	39
Fisher	38	10	8	20	49	79	38
Lingfield	38	12	2	24	76	129	38
Croydon	38	10	5	23	40	70	35
Erith Town	38	9	7	22	48	84	34
Rochester United	38	9	6	23	57	82	33

Phoenix Sports were promoted to the Isthmian League and Lingfield moved to the Southern Combination. Woodstock Sports disbanded. AFC Croydon Athletic joined from Combined Counties League and Hollands & Blair were promoted from the Kent Invicta League.

Kent Invicta League

Hollands & Blair	30	27	0	3	132	25	81
Bearsted	30	21	4	5	74	34	67
Lydd Town	30	21	3	6	81	37	66
Sutton Athletic	30	20	5	5	68	31	65
Sheppey United	30	18	3	9	75	55	57
Seven Acre & Sidcup	30	16	4	10	56	64	52
Glebe	30	15	6	9	66	36	51
Gravesham Borough	30	11	9	10	66	44	42
Eltham Palace	30	10	7	13	63	62	37
Bridon Ropes	30	10	3	17	40	54	33
Orpington	30	10	2	18	43	53	32
Meridian VP	30	9	4	17	38	63	31
Rusthall	30	7	3	20	49	88	24
Crockenhill	30	6	5	19	33	102	23
Kent Football United	30	5	2	23	31	97	17
Lewisham Borough	30	4	0	26	32	102	12

APM Contrast, FC Elmstead, Forest Hill Park and Phoenix Sports Reserves all joined from the Kent County League. AC London joined, this being their first venture into senior football, having not been playing in a league in 2014-15.

2015-16

Southern Counties East League

Premier Division

Greenwich Borough	36	26	7	3	121	50	85
Hollands & Blair	36	22	7	7	108	40	73
Ashford United	36	23	7	6	95	46	66
Lordswood	36	15	14	7	62	44	59
Sevenoaks Town	36	16	10	10	61	50	58
Corinthian	36	15	11	10	73	61	56
Crowborough Athletic	36	14	9	13	65	77	51
Canterbury City	36	15	5	16	64	59	50
Deal Town	36	15	5	16	76	73	50
Cray Valley Paper Mills	36	14	8	14	57	58	50
AFC Croydon Athletic	36	13	7	16	58	64	46
Beckenham Town	36	11	11	14	68	93	44
Erith Town	36	12	7	17	53	73	43
Tunbridge Wells	36	11	6	19	57	61	39
Rochester United	36	10	9	17	43	77	39
Erith & Belvedere	36	10	8	18	54	66	38
Fisher	36	10	7	19	40	79	37
Croydon	36	9	8	19	46	61	35
Holmesdale	*36*	*4*	*8*	*24*	*45*	*114*	*20*

Ashford United had 10 points deducted after receivers were called in. Greenwich Borough were promoted to the Isthmian League from where Whitstable Town were relegated.

Kent Invicta League

Bearsted	38	29	4	5	91	33	91
Sheppey United	**38**	**27**	**6**	**5**	**107**	**36**	**87**
Glebe	38	26	4	8	107	45	82
Sutton Athletic	38	25	4	9	114	53	79
Bridon Ropes	38	21	7	10	73	49	70
APM Contrast	38	20	9	9	86	44	69
Gravesham Borough	38	21	5	12	118	66	68
Lydd Town	38	21	5	12	90	48	68
Seven Acre & Sidcup	38	20	5	13	91	72	65
AC London	38	15	12	11	77	59	51
FC Elmstead	38	14	8	16	73	74	50
Meridian VP	38	14	7	17	71	92	49
Forest Hill Park	38	13	7	18	46	69	46
Phoenix Sports Reserves	38	12	5	21	46	80	41
Crockenhill	38	11	7	20	57	90	40
Orpington	38	10	6	22	44	68	36
Kent Football United	38	6	6	26	47	119	24
Eltham Palace	38	6	3	29	36	132	21
Rusthall	38	4	8	26	40	97	20
Lewisham Borough	38	2	8	28	29	117	14

AC London had 6 points deducted.
APM Contrast changed their name to K Sports and Seven Acre & Sidcup changed their name to Sporting Club Thamesmead. AC London moved to the Combined Counties League and Snodland Town joined from the Kent County League.

At the end of the season, the Kent Invicta League and the Southern Counties East League merged with the Kent Invicta League becoming Division One of the Southern Counties East League.

2016-17
Southern Counties East League

Premier Division

Ashford United	38	30	2	6	119	39	92
Crowborough Athletic	38	28	6	4	96	36	90
Sevenoaks Town	38	27	3	8	90	35	84
Cray Valley Paper Mills	38	24	3	11	91	57	75
Whitstable Town	38	22	3	13	82	51	69
Sheppey United	38	20	8	10	75	55	68
AFC Croydon Athletic	38	18	11	9	75	62	65
Hollands & Blair	38	18	8	12	68	55	62
Canterbury City	38	17	7	14	66	42	58
Corinthian	38	15	7	16	68	64	52
Croydon	38	15	3	20	66	83	48
Bearsted	38	14	5	19	63	73	47
Deal Town	38	11	13	14	66	74	46
Rochester United	38	9	10	19	47	79	37
Tunbridge Wells	38	10	7	21	41	74	37
Lordswood	38	9	7	22	54	101	34
Erith Town	38	9	4	25	50	116	31
Beckenham Town	38	8	5	25	38	76	29
Fisher	*38*	*7*	*7*	*24*	*50*	*86*	*28*
Erith & Belvedere	*38*	*7*	*5*	*26*	*47*	*94*	*26*

Ashford United were promoted to the Isthmian League from where Chatham Town were relegated.

Division One

Glebe	**36**	**29**	**5**	**2**	**102**	**24**	**92**
Rusthall	**36**	**24**	**8**	**4**	**93**	**34**	**80**
Sutton Athletic	36	23	5	8	122	50	74
Kent Football United	36	24	2	10	85	40	71
K Sports	36	20	8	8	97	63	68
Holmesdale	36	19	6	11	68	53	63
Bridon Ropes	36	15	10	11	60	59	55
Snodland Town	36	16	3	17	59	73	51
Lydd Town	36	14	7	15	68	79	49
Sporting Club Thamesmead	36	12	8	16	60	70	44
FC Elmstead	36	11	10	15	55	64	43
Forest Hill Park	36	12	7	17	50	75	43
Phoenix Sports Reserves	36	13	4	19	65	93	43
Orpington	36	10	10	16	45	58	40
Eltham Palace	36	10	9	17	65	82	39
Gravesham Borough	36	8	8	20	62	84	32
Meridian VP	36	9	2	25	45	78	29
Crockenhill	36	6	8	22	37	91	26
Lewisham Borough	36	4	6	26	45	113	18

Kent Football United had 3 points deducted.

Orpington moved to the Kent County League from where Punjab United joined. Eltham Palace changed their name to Stansfeld.

SUSSEX COUNTY LEAGUE 1920-2017

The Sussex County League was formed in 1920 with 12 founder members. Six of these came from the West Sussex Senior League – Brighton & Hove Amateurs, Chichester, Shoreham, Southwick, Vernon Athletic and Worthing. Three came from the Mid-Sussex League – East Grinstead, Lewes and Newhaven while Rock-A-Nore came from the Hastings & District League. The previous leagues of Eastbourne and Royal Corps of Signals have not been found.

1920-21

Worthing	22	17	3	2	65	17	37
Vernon Athletic	22	16	4	2	71	20	36
Eastbourne	21	13	6	2	63	31	32
Brighton & Hove Amateurs	22	9	6	7	44	40	24
Royal Corps of Signals	22	9	4	9	62	44	22
Rock-A-Nore	22	8	5	9	33	41	21
Chichester	22	9	2	11	35	52	20
Newhaven	22	8	2	12	37	48	18
Shoreham	22	6	5	11	32	35	17
Southwick	21	6	3	12	28	51	15
Lewes	22	4	7	11	29	52	15
East Grinstead	22	1	3	18	23	91	5

One game was not played

Eastbourne moved to the Southern Amateur League and Eastbourne R E Old Comrades joined.
Rock-A-Nore changed their name to Hastings & St. Leonards.

1921-22

Worthing	22	19	1	2	52	13	39
Hastings & St. Leonards	22	16	1	5	64	26	33
Royal Corps of Signals	22	14	4	4	66	20	32
Vernon Athletic	22	13	2	7	47	35	28
Eastbourne R E Old Comrades	22	10	4	8	60	39	24
Lewes	22	11	2	9	46	41	24
Brighton & Hove Amateurs	22	8	3	11	32	37	19
Chichester	22	8	1	13	26	61	17
Southwick	22	7	2	13	33	46	16
Newhaven	22	5	4	13	26	53	12
East Grinstead	22	2	6	14	25	56	10
Shoreham	22	3	2	17	16	54	8

Newhaven had 2 points deducted.

Brighton & Hove Amateurs and East Grinstead both left the league and Hove joined.

1922-23

Vernon Athletic	20	14	3	3	61	28	31
Eastbourne R E Old Comrades	20	12	2	6	45	32	26
Worthing	20	10	4	6	50	26	24
Southwick	20	9	3	8	41	32	21
Royal Corps of Signals	20	8	4	8	42	36	20
Shoreham	20	9	1	10	37	38	19
Newhaven	20	8	3	9	31	48	19
Hastings & St. Leonards	20	9	1	10	29	45	19
Hove	20	7	2	11	36	37	16
Chichester	20	6	1	13	29	48	13
Lewes	20	6	0	14	23	34	12

Allen West joined the league.

1923-24

Royal Corps of Signals	22	14	3	5	68	28	31
Southwick	22	13	4	5	57	33	30
Hastings & St. Leonards	22	12	4	6	53	30	28
Shoreham	22	10	7	5	44	31	27
Allen West	22	12	3	7	42	45	27
Eastbourne R E Old Comrades	22	10	6	6	62	47	26
Worthing	22	11	2	9	43	41	24
Hove	22	9	3	10	44	45	21
Chichester	22	7	3	12	43	52	17
Vernon Athletic	22	6	3	13	42	58	15
Newhaven	22	6	2	14	40	66	14
Lewes	22	2	0	20	28	90	4

Eastbourne R E Old Comrades changed their name to Eastbourne Old Comrades.
East Grinstead joined the league.

1924-25

Royal Corps of Signals	24	18	2	4	55	23	38
Lewes	24	17	2	5	103	47	36
Southwick	24	14	4	6	72	41	32
Hastings & St. Leonards	24	13	5	6	71	39	31
Hove	24	11	7	6	47	37	29
Newhaven	24	11	5	8	56	41	27
Worthing	24	11	4	9	47	40	26
Shoreham	24	9	6	9	60	43	24
Eastbourne Old Comrades	24	11	1	12	51	55	23
Allen West	24	5	7	12	20	55	17
Vernon Athletic	24	5	3	16	38	81	13
Chichester	24	3	2	19	34	86	8
East Grinstead	24	3	2	19	30	100	8

Royal Corps of Signals left the league.

1925-26

Southwick	22	16	3	3	86	33	35
Hastings & St. Leonards	22	16	1	5	83	37	33
Hove	22	11	4	7	80	53	26
Worthing	22	10	5	7	55	37	25
Eastbourne Old Comrades	22	10	5	7	52	43	25
Lewes	22	10	3	9	65	62	23
Chichester	22	8	5	9	57	64	21
Allen West	22	8	3	11	45	60	19
Vernon Athletic	22	8	3	11	33	49	19
Shoreham	22	7	4	11	31	59	18
Newhaven	22	4	5	13	66	88	13
East Grinstead	22	3	1	18	32	100	7

East Grinstead left the league and were replaced by Horsham.

1926-27

Worthing	22	17	2	3	59	19	36
Eastbourne Old Comrades	22	15	2	5	61	37	32
Southwick	22	14	3	5	70	39	31
Lewes	22	14	3	5	68	50	31
Hove	22	10	2	10	70	49	22
Hastings & St. Leonards	22	10	1	11	80	51	21
Horsham	22	7	5	10	68	67	19
Vernon Athletic	22	8	3	11	44	61	19
Chichester	22	8	2	12	59	71	18
Allen West	22	5	6	11	51	61	16
Newhaven	22	5	4	13	45	77	14
Shoreham	22	2	1	19	32	125	5

Hastings & St. Leonards moved to the Southern Amateur League.
Allen West and Shoreham also left the league. Bognor Regis joined from the Brighton, Hove & District League and Haywards Heath and Bexhill also joined.

1927-28

Southwick	22	20	1	1	112	28	41
Worthing	22	18	2	2	79	19	38
Haywards Heath	22	10	3	9	62	62	23
Chichester	22	8	6	8	57	67	22
Horsham	22	10	1	11	69	65	21
Eastbourne Old Comrades	22	9	2	11	61	57	20
Newhaven	22	8	4	10	53	64	20
Bexhill	22	10	0	12	51	72	20
Vernon Athletic	22	8	1	13	54	76	17
Hove	22	6	5	11	38	66	17
Bognor Regis	22	6	4	12	44	68	16
Lewes	22	3	3	16	56	92	9

Eastbourne Old Comrades left to join the Spartan League.
Littlehampton joined the league.

1928-29

Worthing	22	17	2	3	68	26	36
Southwick	22	16	0	6	82	25	32
Horsham	22	10	7	5	84	50	27
Bognor Regis	22	10	4	8	47	53	24
Vernon Athletic	22	10	3	9	63	76	23
Lewes	22	10	2	10	76	74	22
Haywards Heath	22	9	3	10	71	81	21
Chichester	22	8	4	10	67	58	20
Newhaven	22	6	4	12	39	71	16
Littlehampton	22	7	1	14	50	72	15
Hove	22	7	1	14	48	72	15
Bexhill	22	6	1	15	43	80	13

1929-30

Southwick	22	20	1	1	106	18	41
Horsham	22	17	2	3	78	42	36
Haywards Heath	22	15	1	6	60	50	31
Worthing	22	13	2	7	63	40	28
Lewes	22	11	5	6	70	49	27
Newhaven	22	10	3	9	61	54	23
Chichester	22	9	2	11	41	47	20
Bexhill	22	6	6	10	54	78	18
Bognor Regis	22	5	2	15	41	63	12
Hove	22	4	2	16	34	61	10
Vernon Athletic	22	4	2	16	26	81	10
Littlehampton	22	4	0	18	37	88	8

1930-31

	P	W	D	L	F	A	Pts
Worthing	22	18	1	3	88	33	37
Horsham	22	17	0	5	104	53	34
Southwick	22	16	0	6	103	42	32
Haywards Heath	22	14	2	6	70	44	30
Lewes	22	13	3	6	70	45	29
Chichester	22	8	6	8	53	67	22
Hove	22	9	2	11	67	76	20
Newhaven	22	7	1	14	61	82	15
Littlehampton	22	6	3	13	51	91	15
Bexhill	22	4	5	13	46	82	13
Bognor Regis	22	5	1	16	40	80	11
Vernon Athletic	22	2	2	18	34	92	6

1931-32

	P	W	D	L	F	A	Pts
Horsham	22	15	5	2	90	34	35
Worthing	22	15	0	7	83	31	30
Lewes	22	12	5	5	73	45	29
Haywards Heath	22	13	1	8	66	63	27
Southwick	22	10	6	6	60	53	26
Chichester	22	9	3	10	57	52	21
Newhaven	22	9	3	10	56	59	21
Vernon Athletic	22	7	6	9	50	54	20
Hove	22	6	6	10	44	59	18
Bexhill	22	6	5	11	38	60	15
Bognor Regis	22	6	3	13	44	77	15
Littlehampton	22	1	3	18	35	109	5

Bexhill had 2 points deducted.
Shoreham joined the league.

1932-33

	P	W	D	L	F	A	Pts
Horsham	24	20	1	3	111	40	41
Worthing	24	15	4	5	75	37	34
Lewes	24	14	3	7	79	47	31
Southwick	24	13	5	6	48	37	31
Newhaven	24	12	4	8	68	48	28
Chichester	24	10	5	9	62	83	25
Shoreham	24	11	1	12	59	57	23
Hove	24	9	4	11	44	49	22
Vernon Athletic	24	9	2	13	48	59	20
Bognor Regis	24	8	3	13	41	63	19
Littlehampton	24	7	2	15	43	77	16
Bexhill	24	5	3	16	40	74	13
Haywards Heath	24	3	3	18	40	87	9

1933-34

	P	W	D	L	F	A	Pts
Worthing	24	19	1	4	95	35	39
Lewes	24	17	2	5	95	50	36
Shoreham	24	17	1	6	81	73	35
Southwick	24	12	5	7	75	34	29
Vernon Athletic	24	12	5	7	59	41	29
Horsham	24	12	1	11	67	52	25
Littlehampton	24	10	2	12	53	77	22
Newhaven	24	7	6	11	43	54	20
Bexhill	24	7	3	14	41	61	17
Bognor Regis	24	6	5	13	47	86	17
Haywards Heath	24	8	0	16	47	78	16
Hove	24	7	0	17	44	90	14
Chichester	24	5	3	16	34	68	13

1934-35

	P	W	D	L	F	A	Pts
Horsham	24	21	0	3	105	36	42
Shoreham	24	19	2	3	75	44	40
Worthing	24	17	3	4	94	35	37
Chichester	24	12	2	10	58	58	26
Southwick	24	11	3	10	50	43	25
Newhaven	24	11	2	11	53	62	24
Lewes	24	10	3	11	74	67	23
Bexhill	24	7	6	11	44	46	20
Vernon Athletic	24	8	3	13	57	55	19
Bognor Regis	24	8	3	13	49	67	19
Littlehampton	24	8	3	13	47	73	19
Haywards Heath	24	4	1	19	49	102	9
Hove	24	3	3	18	36	103	9

Eastbourne Comrades joined the league.

1935-36

	P	W	D	L	F	A	Pts
Horsham	26	22	2	2	143	42	46
Worthing	26	18	3	5	107	58	39
Hove	26	15	5	6	76	61	35
Lewes	26	13	5	8	102	53	31
Littlehampton	26	13	5	8	68	64	31
Haywards Heath	26	10	6	10	80	82	26
Southwick	26	12	2	12	46	49	26
Bexhill	26	11	4	11	69	77	26
Bognor Regis	26	9	3	14	48	68	21
Chichester	26	8	5	13	62	97	21
Newhaven	26	8	3	15	49	73	19
Shoreham	26	6	6	14	47	73	18
Eastbourne Comrades	26	5	3	18	56	96	13
Vernon Athletic	26	5	2	19	33	93	12

1936-37

	P	W	D	L	F	A	Pts
Horsham	26	21	2	3	145	53	44
Southwick	26	18	3	5	86	42	39
Worthing	26	18	2	6	116	37	38
Haywards Heath	26	17	2	7	114	70	36
Lewes	26	16	3	7	91	65	35
Littlehampton	26	15	2	9	101	65	32
Newhaven	26	13	6	7	73	54	32
Shoreham	26	9	4	13	51	79	22
Hove	26	8	5	13	53	74	21
Bexhill	26	9	2	15	53	71	20
Chichester	26	8	3	15	61	91	19
Eastbourne Comrades	26	8	1	17	47	90	17
Bognor Regis	26	2	2	22	36	117	6
Vernon Athletic	26	1	1	24	27	146	3

Vernon Athletic left the league and East Grinstead joined.

1937-38

	P	W	D	L	F	A	Pts
Horsham	26	20	1	5	88	43	41
Southwick	26	17	4	5	79	38	38
Haywards Heath	26	15	6	5	102	47	36
Worthing	26	14	2	10	69	44	30
East Grinstead	26	14	2	10	56	54	30
Bexhill	26	11	4	11	48	44	26
Newhaven	26	12	2	12	56	56	26
Hove	26	10	4	12	60	56	24
Lewes	26	10	2	14	61	60	22
Eastbourne Comrades	26	9	2	15	46	77	20
Littlehampton	26	9	1	16	49	67	19
Chichester	26	9	1	16	42	78	19
Bognor Regis	26	7	3	16	50	84	17
Shoreham	26	7	2	17	50	84	16

Littlehampton changed their name to Littlehampton Town.

1938-39

Worthing	26	23	1	2	133	38	47
Bognor Regis	26	19	3	4	96	45	41
Southwick	26	19	2	5	97	36	40
Horsham	26	17	0	9	102	42	34
Haywards Heath	26	13	4	9	86	72	30
Lewes	26	12	2	12	93	89	26
Littlehampton Town	26	11	2	13	68	68	24
Newhaven	26	8	6	12	49	69	22
East Grinstead	26	10	2	14	56	81	22
Bexhill	26	8	1	17	64	87	17
Hove	26	6	5	15	60	97	17
Eastbourne Comrades	26	6	3	17	48	102	15
Chichester	26	7	1	18	57	131	15
Shoreham	26	7	0	19	49	101	14

1939-45

The league operated a war-time competition in 1939-40 (won by Worthing, runners-up Southwick) and a League Cup (won by Lewes). In 1940-41, there was just a League Cup, won by Bognor Regis. The league then closed until 1945.

When it restarted, only Eastbourne Comrades and Chichester of the pre-war members did not rejoin immediately while Bexhill rejoined as Bexhill Wanderers. The league was made up to 17 clubs by 5 new members – Brighton & Hove Albion Juniors, Crawley, C A D M & T C (Eastbourne), HMS Peregrine and RAF Tangmere – and then split into two Sections.

1945-46

Eastern Section

Haywards Heath	14	11	0	3	51	13	22
East Grinstead	14	8	4	2	44	20	20
Lewes	14	9	2	3	32	21	20
Newhaven	14	7	3	4	39	40	17
Crawley	14	6	1	7	29	37	13
Bexhill Wanderers	14	3	4	7	26	48	10
Brighton & H.A. Juniors	14	2	2	10	25	59	6
C A D M & T C (Eastbourne)	14	1	2	11	14	20	4

Western Section

Worthing	16	14	1	1	96	15	29
Horsham	16	13	1	2	81	33	27
HMS Peregrine	16	11	1	4	63	41	23
Littlehampton Town	16	9	2	5	66	40	20
Bognor Regis	16	7	1	8	55	72	15
Shoreham	16	5	2	9	36	78	12
Southwick	16	4	1	11	29	60	9
Hove	16	4	0	12	31	89	8
RAF Tangmere	16	0	1	15	15	44	1

Crawley, Brighton & Hove Albion Juniors, C A D M & T C (Eastbourne), HMS Peregrine and RAF Tangmere all left the league. Chichester and Eastbourne Comrades rejoined.
Bexhill Wanderers changed their name to Bexhill Town Athletic.

1946-47

Horsham	26	19	2	5	103	55	40
Littlehampton Town	26	16	4	6	82	49	36
East Grinstead	26	15	3	8	87	54	33
Worthing	26	16	1	9	89	70	33
Newhaven	26	14	3	9	65	69	31
Southwick	26	14	2	10	111	71	30
Lewes	26	13	3	10	60	68	29
Chichester	26	12	4	10	89	91	28
Bognor Regis	26	10	4	12	85	80	24
Haywards Heath	26	8	4	14	64	81	20
Bexhill Town Athletic	26	7	5	14	72	91	19
Shoreham	26	6	4	16	57	92	16
Hove	26	6	2	18	65	108	14
Eastbourne Comrades	26	2	7	17	38	88	11

1947-48

Southwick	26	22	2	2	122	34	46
Horsham	26	20	2	4	98	45	42
Haywards Heath	26	14	6	6	79	52	34
Chichester	26	13	6	7	76	51	32
Worthing	26	14	3	9	72	57	31
Littlehampton Town	26	14	3	9	73	62	31
Hove	26	13	3	10	81	76	29
East Grinstead	26	9	5	12	61	61	23
Bognor Regis	26	9	3	14	49	87	21
Eastbourne Comrades	26	7	2	17	45	85	16
Bexhill Town Athletic	26	5	6	15	46	88	16
Shoreham	26	6	3	17	50	75	15
Newhaven	26	4	6	16	52	87	14
Lewes	26	3	8	15	40	84	14

Worthing left to join the Corinthian League. Lancing Athletic joined from the Brighton, Hove & District League. Chichester changed their name to Chichester City.

1948-49

Bognor Regis	26	20	2	4	85	44	42
Horsham	26	19	3	4	81	32	41
Southwick	26	19	1	6	70	36	39
Bexhill Town Athletic	26	14	4	8	64	42	32
Haywards Heath	26	12	4	10	58	41	28
Littlehampton Town	26	13	2	11	67	55	28
Lancing Athletic	26	13	1	12	70	58	27
Eastbourne Comrades	26	11	4	11	54	62	26
East Grinstead	26	10	0	16	58	77	20
Newhaven	26	8	4	14	54	78	20
Lewes	26	7	4	15	52	84	18
Chichester City	26	8	1	17	42	69	17
Shoreham	26	5	5	16	41	68	15
Hove	26	5	1	20	47	97	11

Hove left to join the Metropolitan League. Arundel joined from the West Sussex League. Bognor Regis changed their name to Bognor Regis Town.

1949-50

Haywards Heath	26	18	3	5	75	36	39
Lancing Athletic	26	16	7	3	75	38	39
Horsham	26	14	5	7	71	51	33
Bexhill Town Athletic	26	12	9	5	56	46	33
Southwick	26	9	8	9	56	47	26
East Grinstead	26	11	4	11	71	67	26
Chichester City	26	11	3	12	74	62	25
Littlehampton Town	26	8	9	9	50	61	25
Bognor Regis Town	26	11	2	13	86	80	24
Shoreham	26	10	4	12	58	65	24
Newhaven	26	6	6	14	48	72	18
Arundel	26	8	2	16	50	86	18
Eastbourne Comrades	26	6	5	15	42	65	17
Lewes	26	7	3	16	51	87	17

1950-51

Haywards Heath	26	19	4	3	75	25	42
Chichester City	26	17	6	3	65	26	40
Horsham	26	16	4	6	83	38	36
Newhaven	26	15	5	6	83	58	35
Arundel	26	13	7	6	48	35	33
East Grinstead	26	13	2	11	60	74	28
Shoreham	26	12	2	12	60	60	26
Lancing Athletic	26	11	2	13	49	54	24
Eastbourne Comrades	26	9	5	12	48	51	23
Southwick	26	8	5	13	50	52	21
Bexhill Town Athletic	26	8	5	13	29	47	21
Bognor Regis Town	26	8	2	16	50	73	18
Lewes	26	3	3	20	38	89	9
Littlehampton Town	26	3	2	21	25	81	8

Horsham left to join the Metropolitan League. Brighton Old Grammarians and Crawley Town both joined the league.
Eastbourne Comrades changed their name to Eastbourne United.

1951-52

Shoreham	28	16	5	7	79	43	37
Bognor Regis Town	28	15	5	8	71	50	35
Brighton Old Grammarians	28	14	5	9	63	50	33
Haywards Heath	28	12	8	8	68	48	32
Southwick	28	13	6	9	70	56	32
Bexhill Town Athletic	28	14	4	10	55	58	32
Lancing Athletic	28	11	8	9	68	56	30
East Grinstead	28	12	5	11	78	73	29
Chichester City	28	13	2	13	76	72	28
Lewes	28	11	5	12	65	76	27
Arundel	28	8	10	10	59	44	26
Eastbourne United	28	9	8	11	51	54	26
Crawley Town	28	7	7	14	57	89	21
Newhaven	28	5	8	15	53	107	18
Littlehampton Town	28	5	4	19	62	109	14

Haywards Heath and Southwick both left to join the Metropolitan League. Whitehawk & Manor Farm Old Boys joined from the Brighton, Hove & District League.

A Second Division was formed containing 12 clubs. Sidley United joined from the East Sussex League and Seaford Town and Three Bridges both joined from the Mid-Sussex League, the previous leagues of the other 9 clubs are unknown.

1952-53

Promoted clubs shown in **bold type**, relegated clubs shown in ***bold italics***.

Division One

Shoreham	26	18	2	6	80	45	38
Brighton Old Grammarians	26	14	7	5	69	48	35
Whitehawk & Manor Farm O.B.	26	15	4	7	72	49	34
Arundel	26	15	3	8	59	34	33
Eastbourne United	26	13	4	9	77	49	30
Newhaven	26	12	4	10	59	43	28
Chichester City	26	12	4	10	62	58	28
Bexhill Town Athletic	26	12	3	11	42	50	27
Lancing Athletic	26	10	6	10	55	53	26
Bognor Regis Town	26	11	4	11	67	68	26
East Grinstead	26	9	6	11	65	66	24
Lewes	26	7	5	14	47	75	19
Littlehampton Town	26	4	4	18	44	78	12
Crawley Town	26	1	2	23	30	112	4

Division Two

Wigmore Athletic	22	19	1	2	107	27	39
Goldstone	22	16	0	6	77	38	32
Rye United	22	11	3	8	59	44	25
Hastings Rangers	22	10	5	7	60	50	25
Cuckfield	22	12	1	9	65	55	25
Sidley United	22	10	3	9	72	61	23
Hove White Rovers	22	9	3	10	53	63	21
Seaford Town	22	7	5	10	48	55	19
Pulborough	22	7	5	10	64	80	19
Three Bridges	22	6	3	13	51	86	15
Moulescoomb Rovers	22	4	3	15	49	80	11
Hastings & St. Leonards	22	3	4	15	36	102	10

Three Bridges changed their name to Three Bridges United.

1953-54

Division One

Newhaven	28	22	3	3	74	27	47
Eastbourne United	28	18	2	8	77	38	38
Shoreham	28	16	3	9	67	49	35
Littlehampton Town	28	14	5	9	72	66	33
East Grinstead	28	15	3	10	58	65	33
Whitehawk & Manor Farm O.B.	28	13	4	11	78	61	30
Bognor Regis Town	28	13	3	12	59	53	29
Arundel	28	13	3	12	51	52	29
Brighton Old Grammarians	28	11	4	13	68	64	26
Lancing Athletic	28	10	5	13	57	59	25
Crawley Town	28	11	2	15	55	70	24
Chichester City	28	9	4	15	47	59	22
Wigmore Athletic	28	10	1	17	61	76	21
Bexhill Town Athletic	28	7	2	19	49	89	16
Lewes	28	4	4	20	53	98	12

Southwick joined from the Metropolitan League.

Division Two

Hove White Rovers	20	16	0	4	69	29	32
Rye United	20	13	3	4	76	33	29
Cuckfield	20	11	5	4	59	44	27
Hastings Rangers	20	11	4	5	63	31	26
Goldstone	20	9	5	6	53	34	23
Three Bridges United	20	9	5	6	58	40	23
Sidley United	20	8	2	10	47	54	18
Pulborough	20	7	3	10	52	77	17
Seaford Town	20	7	1	12	46	59	15
Moulescoomb Rovers	20	4	1	15	38	71	9
Hastings & St. Leonards	20	0	1	19	19	108	1

Pulborough left the league. APV Athletic and Chichester United joined.

1954-55

Division One

Eastbourne United	32	19	9	4	103	49	47
Whitehawk & Manor Farm O.B.	32	22	2	8	106	53	46
East Grinstead	32	18	7	7	95	64	43
Bognor Regis Town	32	17	5	10	71	54	39
Newhaven	32	16	3	13	75	69	35
Chichester City	32	16	1	15	82	83	33
Hove White Rovers	32	13	6	13	66	64	32
Littlehampton Town	32	14	4	14	69	73	32
Brighton Old Grammarians	32	12	8	12	57	63	32
Lewes	32	13	4	15	60	63	30
Shoreham	32	11	5	16	68	82	27
Bexhill Town Athletic	32	11	3	18	66	89	25
Lancing Athletic	32	9	7	16	64	87	25
Southwick	32	8	9	15	49	72	25
Arundel	32	8	9	15	54	83	25
Wigmore Athletic	32	9	6	17	57	71	24
Crawley Town	32	10	4	18	47	70	24

Division Two

Three Bridges United	20	15	1	4	61	28	31
Hastings Rangers	20	11	8	1	69	30	30
Rye United	20	11	5	4	67	48	27
Sidley United	20	11	2	7	50	34	24
Moulescoomb Rovers	20	10	3	7	58	51	23
Cuckfield	20	9	4	7	61	49	22
Chichester United	20	9	4	7	58	49	22
Seaford Town	20	5	4	11	38	62	14
Goldstone	20	6	1	13	44	66	13
APV Athletic	20	2	4	14	31	84	8
Hastings & St. Leonards	20	2	2	16	36	72	6

Battle Rangers, Hailsham and Uckfield Town joined the league.

1955-56

Division One

Eastbourne United	32	23	6	3	114	50	52
Whitehawk & Manor Farm O. B.	32	21	5	6	97	46	47
Bognor Regis Town	32	20	3	9	113	57	43
Lewes	32	19	5	8	89	55	43
Chichester City	32	17	6	9	102	57	40
Arundel	32	15	8	9	84	67	38
Hove White Rovers	32	16	5	11	79	66	37
Southwick	32	14	5	13	66	70	33
Newhaven	32	14	4	14	72	64	32
Littlehampton Town	32	12	8	12	75	68	32
East Grinstead	32	10	7	15	68	96	27
Bexhill Town Athletic	32	11	4	17	67	83	26
Lancing Athletic	32	11	4	17	70	87	26
Brighton Old Grammarians	32	9	7	16	43	77	25
Shoreham	32	7	4	21	59	106	18
Wigmore Athletic	32	6	4	22	42	100	16
Three Bridges United	32	4	1	27	35	126	9

Eastbourne United left to join the Metropolitan League.
Hove White Rovers changed their name to Hove Town

Division Two

Rye United	26	22	1	3	111	45	45
Crawley Town	26	20	2	4	96	28	41
APV Athletic	26	17	2	7	62	43	36
Hastings Rangers	26	16	1	9	73	43	33
Sidley United	26	13	4	9	64	69	30
Hastings & St. Leonards	26	13	2	11	85	78	28
Hailsham	26	11	4	11	72	77	26
Goldstone	26	11	3	12	55	60	25
Uckfield Town	26	10	3	13	60	73	23
Battle Rangers	26	8	3	15	65	74	19
Moulescoomb Rovers	26	7	3	16	57	99	17
Chichester United	26	7	2	17	57	99	16
Seaford Town	26	5	4	17	46	91	14
Cuckfield	26	5	0	21	52	96	10

Crawley Town had 1 point deducted.
Crawley Town left to join the Metropolitan League.
Brighton North End and Old Varndeanians both joined the league.

1956-57

Division One

Bexhill Town Athletic	30	18	7	5	86	52	43
Whitehawk & Manor Farm O. B.	30	18	5	7	89	57	41
Arundel	30	19	3	8	93	66	41
Bognor Regis Town	30	16	7	7	96	71	39
Chichester City	30	17	3	10	87	58	37
Littlehampton Town	30	15	7	8	91	71	37
Southwick	30	14	4	12	60	58	32
Lewes	30	12	5	13	58	59	29
Rye United	30	12	2	16	65	82	26
Hove Town	30	10	6	14	56	81	26
Brighton Old Grammarians	30	10	5	15	72	81	25
Newhaven	30	11	2	17	61	76	24
Shoreham	30	11	1	18	63	68	23
East Grinstead	30	8	5	17	59	91	21
Wigmore Athletic	30	8	4	18	49	80	20
Lancing Athletic	30	8	0	22	48	92	16

Lancing Athletic changed their name to Lancing.

Division Two

APV Athletic	28	23	3	2	131	51	49
Old Varndeanians	28	23	2	3	155	42	48
Sidley United	28	20	2	6	100	56	42
Three Bridges United	28	19	2	7	123	53	40
Hailsham	28	12	7	9	76	74	31
Moulescoomb Rovers	28	13	5	10	79	78	31
Brighton North End	28	12	4	12	80	84	28
Hastings Rangers	28	12	2	14	65	93	26
Battle Rangers	28	10	5	13	55	74	25
Hastings & St. Leonards	28	8	5	15	84	88	21
Goldstone	28	10	1	17	57	69	21
Cuckfield	28	9	3	16	64	97	21
Seaford Town	28	7	1	20	75	116	15
Chichester United	28	5	3	20	50	134	13
Uckfield Town	28	4	1	23	51	136	9

Chichester United left the league and Portslade joined.

1957-58

Division One

Arundel	30	22	5	3	103	49	49
Bexhill Town Athletic	30	21	4	5	76	38	46
APV Athletic	30	19	4	7	93	66	42
Littlehampton Town	30	17	7	6	86	49	41
Whitehawk & Manor Farm O. B.	30	16	6	8	95	66	38
Newhaven	30	14	5	11	63	49	33
Wigmore Athletic	30	12	8	10	88	62	32
Rye United	30	11	8	11	74	72	30
Chichester City	30	12	4	14	80	79	28
Hove Town	30	9	8	13	57	81	26
Bognor Regis Town	30	9	6	15	64	91	24
Shoreham	30	9	5	16	85	92	23
Southwick	30	9	5	16	41	63	23
Lewes	30	7	5	18	59	109	19
East Grinstead	30	5	7	18	47	90	17
Brighton Old Grammarians	30	2	5	23	43	98	9

Division Two

Lancing	28	22	3	3	97	34	47
Old Varndeanians	28	21	2	5	74	33	44
Sidley United	28	17	3	8	69	61	37
Uckfield Town	28	15	4	9	82	65	34
Three Bridges United	28	14	4	10	81	62	32
Hastings Rangers	28	14	3	11	70	67	31
Cuckfield	28	13	2	13	72	62	28
Goldstone	28	10	6	12	53	57	26
Brighton North End	28	11	4	13	53	58	26
Portslade	28	11	3	14	60	60	25
Hailsham	28	11	2	15	58	68	24
Moulescoomb Rovers	28	8	5	15	63	74	21
Battle Rangers	28	7	4	17	58	90	18
Seaford Town	28	7	3	18	46	95	17
Hastings & St. Leonards	28	7	0	21	43	93	14

Burgess Hill joined from the Mid-Sussex League.

1958-59

Division One

Arundel	30	19	3	8	109	59	41
Lewes	30	18	4	8	77	51	40
Chichester City	30	17	2	11	103	81	36
Shoreham	30	14	8	8	65	63	36
Whitehawk & Manor Farm O. B.	30	15	5	10	83	67	35
Bexhill Town Athletic	30	14	7	9	82	82	35
East Grinstead	30	15	3	12	67	55	33
Wigmore Athletic	30	12	7	11	59	61	31
APV Athletic	30	11	8	11	74	77	30
Lancing	30	13	3	14	66	64	29
Newhaven	30	12	5	13	53	54	29
Southwick	30	10	8	12	55	54	28
Rye United	30	10	6	14	76	77	26
Littlehampton Town	30	8	8	14	72	75	24
Bognor Regis Town	30	9	5	16	52	74	22
Hove Town	30	0	4	26	29	128	4

Hove Town left the league.

Division Two

Sidley United	30	26	1	3	160	49	53
Old Varndeanians	30	21	5	4	103	38	47
Brighton North End	30	19	3	8	98	63	41
Portslade	30	19	2	9	98	70	40
Brighton Old Grammarians	30	18	3	9	96	55	39
Uckfield Town	30	16	5	9	105	64	37
Seaford Town	30	15	7	8	100	65	37
Three Bridges United	30	16	3	11	94	61	35
Hastings Rangers	30	14	3	13	102	83	31
Moulescoomb Rovers	30	13	1	16	67	75	27
Hastings & St. Leonards	30	12	2	16	65	99	26
Burgess Hill	30	7	6	17	58	92	20
Cuckfield	30	6	3	21	34	115	15
Hailsham	30	6	2	22	56	143	14
Goldstone	30	5	4	21	39	104	14
Battle Rangers	30	1	4	25	45	144	6

Cuckfield left the league and Horsham YMCA joined from the Mid-Sussex League.

1959-60

Division One

Chichester City	30	23	3	4	108	44	49
Rye United	30	21	2	7	74	40	44
APV Athletic	30	17	6	7	79	48	40
Whitehawk & Manor Farm O. B.	30	16	5	9	72	63	37
Lancing	30	13	8	9	63	53	34
Bexhill Town Athletic	30	15	4	11	75	65	34
Wigmore Athletic	30	13	4	13	58	56	30
Newhaven	30	11	5	14	51	64	27
Arundel	30	10	6	14	62	59	26
Lewes	30	7	10	13	52	77	24
Sidley United	30	9	6	15	51	83	24
East Grinstead	30	9	5	16	51	61	23
Bognor Regis Town	30	7	9	14	43	59	23
Littlehampton Town	30	8	7	15	49	70	23
Shoreham	30	8	5	17	53	69	21
Southwick	*30*	*8*	*5*	*17*	*48*	*78*	*21*

Whitehawk & Manor Farm O. B. changed their name to Whitehawk.

Division Two

Old Varndeanians	28	22	1	5	94	29	45
Hastings & St. Leonards	28	17	5	6	79	39	39
Three Bridges United	28	18	1	9	80	50	37
Seaford Town	28	18	1	9	106	71	37
Battle Rangers	28	15	5	8	72	61	35
Brighton Old Grammarians	28	15	4	9	79	61	34
Hastings Rangers	28	13	5	10	63	72	31
Uckfield Town	28	12	4	12	71	75	28
Brighton North End	28	11	3	14	67	77	25
Moulescoomb Rovers	28	11	3	14	69	84	25
Burgess Hill	28	8	5	15	55	67	21
Horsham YMCA	28	8	4	16	54	78	20
Portslade	28	8	3	17	61	100	19
Hailsham	28	7	2	19	61	101	16
Goldstone	28	1	8	21	44	90	10

L.E.C. Sports joined the league.

1960-61

Division One

Chichester City	30	23	3	4	126	51	49
APV Athletic	30	22	2	6	114	49	46
Lewes	30	16	9	5	86	55	41
Rye United	30	18	4	8	82	47	40
Arundel	30	15	5	10	73	55	35
Bognor Regis Town	30	14	6	10	76	57	34
Littlehampton Town	30	12	4	14	70	86	28
Sidley United	30	10	6	14	51	80	26
Old Varndeanians	30	9	7	14	49	64	25
East Grinstead	30	9	7	14	45	59	25
Wigmore Athletic	30	8	8	14	64	76	24
Lancing	30	10	4	16	59	82	24
Bexhill Town Athletic	30	9	4	17	61	85	22
Whitehawk	30	8	5	17	65	76	21
Newhaven	30	7	6	17	50	96	20
Shoreham	*30*	*8*	*4*	*18*	*50*	*103*	*20*

Haywards Heath joined from the Metropolitan League.

Division Two

Hastings Rangers	30	25	4	1	113	31	54
L.E.C. Sports	30	21	4	5	104	51	46
Southwick	30	19	6	5	90	43	44
Uckfield Town	30	18	6	6	83	56	42
Seaford Town	30	14	4	12	97	79	32
Battle Rangers	30	13	5	12	92	80	31
Three Bridges United	30	11	6	13	78	78	28
Brighton Old Grammarians	30	12	4	14	74	79	28
Hastings & St. Leonards	30	12	4	14	79	85	28
Brighton North End	30	11	5	14	90	87	27
Burgess Hill	30	9	8	13	57	75	26
Goldstone	30	10	3	17	60	79	23
Horsham YMCA	30	9	3	18	57	104	21
Portslade	30	6	6	18	63	98	18
Hailsham	30	7	3	20	54	103	17
Moulescoomb Rovers	30	5	5	20	48	111	15

L.E.C. Sports left the league. Selsey joined from the West Sussex League.

1961-62

Division One

Whitehawk	32	24	3	5	127	49	51
Chichester City	32	23	3	6	132	60	49
Lewes	32	17	8	7	86	53	42
Bognor Regis Town	32	16	8	8	81	54	40
Rye United	32	17	5	10	78	70	39
Newhaven	32	12	10	10	70	88	34
Littlehampton Town	32	13	6	13	66	85	32
Haywards Heath	32	13	5	14	75	78	31
Arundel	32	12	6	14	68	70	30
APV Athletic	32	13	4	15	74	84	30
Wigmore Athletic	32	12	5	15	61	87	29
Lancing	32	11	6	15	77	78	28
East Grinstead	32	11	6	15	65	66	28
Hastings Rangers	32	8	8	16	68	85	24
Bexhill Town Athletic	32	10	1	21	67	94	21
Sidley United	32	8	4	20	52	93	20
Old Varndeanians	*32*	*5*	*6*	*21*	*33*	*84*	*16*

Division Two

Shoreham	30	27	1	2	138	32	55
Selsey	30	25	1	4	123	52	51
Battle Rangers	30	23	3	4	128	43	49
Horsham YMCA	30	19	5	6	85	67	43
Southwick	30	19	3	8	124	58	41
Three Bridges United	30	14	5	11	82	77	33
Burgess Hill	30	14	2	14	72	71	30
Seaford Town	30	13	3	14	81	85	29
Brighton Old Grammarians	30	12	3	15	78	85	27
Goldstone	30	8	9	13	61	84	25
Uckfield Town	30	8	7	15	61	96	23
Brighton North End	30	8	5	17	54	71	21
Hailsham	30	9	3	18	36	76	21
Portslade	30	4	5	21	37	120	13
Hastings & St. Leonards	30	4	4	22	37	102	12
Moulescoomb Rovers	30	1	5	24	45	123	7

Hellingly Hospital Staff joined the league.

1962-63

The league programme was abandoned. An exceptionally severe winter resulted in many postponements and when the weather finally relented, there were too many outstanding games to fit in before the end of the season. The 1962-63 membership was as follows:

Division One: APV Athletic, Arundel, Bexhill Town Athletic, Bognor Regis Town, Chichester City, East Grinstead, Hastings Rangers, Haywards Heath, Lancing, Lewes, Littlehampton Town, Newhaven, Rye United, Shoreham, Sidley United, Whitehawk, Wigmore Athletic.

Division Two: Battle Rangers, Brighton North End, Brighton Old Grammarians, Burgess Hill, Goldstone, Hailsham, Hastings & St. Leonards, Hellingly Hospital Staff, Horsham YMCA, Moulescoomb Rovers, Old Varndeanians, Portslade, Seaford Town, Selsey, Southwick, Three Bridges United, Uckfield Town.

Hailsham resigned during the season while Goldstone, Hellingly Hospital Staff and Portslade left at the end of the season. Portfield joined from the West Sussex League and Ringmer joined from the Brighton, Hove & District League.

1963-64

Division One

Whitehawk	32	26	2	4	101	31	54
Lewes	32	25	1	6	109	42	51
Haywards Heath	32	19	7	6	70	38	45
Littlehampton Town	32	19	2	11	79	54	40
Chichester City	32	17	5	10	78	65	39
Shoreham	32	17	3	12	76	76	37
Hastings Rangers	32	15	6	11	63	64	36
Bexhill Town Athletic	32	13	7	12	75	59	33
Rye United	32	11	7	14	76	72	29
Newhaven	32	12	4	16	58	88	28
Bognor Regis Town	32	12	3	17	61	70	27
Wigmore Athletic	32	10	6	16	61	68	26
Lancing	32	9	7	16	51	70	25
East Grinstead	32	9	6	17	44	67	24
Arundel	32	6	8	18	46	70	20
APV Athletic	*32*	*9*	*1*	*22*	*63*	*104*	*19*
Sidley United	*32*	*5*	*1*	*26*	*47*	*120*	*11*

Division Two

Selsey	28	26	0	2	145	33	52
Seaford Town	28	24	3	1	140	38	51
Ringmer	28	21	3	4	106	36	45
Southwick	28	17	5	6	91	41	39
Horsham YMCA	28	16	5	7	84	63	37
Brighton North End	28	13	2	13	74	69	28
Hastings & St. Leonards	28	12	3	13	51	76	27
Old Varndeanians	28	9	5	14	45	55	23
Uckfield Town	28	11	0	17	49	101	22
Battle Rangers	28	9	3	16	65	92	21
Three Bridges United	28	8	3	17	58	86	19
Burgess Hill	28	5	7	16	52	82	17
Portfield	28	6	3	19	47	96	15
Moulescoomb Rovers	28	6	1	21	60	118	13
Brighton Old Grammarians	28	3	2	21	38	119	11

Moulescoomb Rovers left the league. Wick joined from the West Sussex League. Ferring, Steyning and Wadhurst also joined.
Three Bridge United changed their name to Three Bridges.

1964-65

Division One

Lewes	31	27	4	0	102	22	58
Lancing	32	21	5	6	75	44	47
Rye United	32	17	4	11	92	67	38
Bognor Regis Town	32	15	7	10	60	56	37
Littlehampton Town	31	16	4	11	71	48	36
Haywards Heath	32	15	6	11	58	46	36
Chichester City	32	14	8	10	79	65	36
Selsey	32	15	5	12	84	69	35
Seaford Town	32	11	9	12	65	68	31
Whitehawk	32	13	4	15	67	82	30
Wigmore Athletic	32	11	5	16	57	68	27
Bexhill Town Athletic	32	10	4	18	52	85	24
East Grinstead	32	10	3	19	69	100	23
Arundel	32	8	7	17	42	62	23
Shoreham	32	9	4	19	76	94	22
Hastings Rangers	*32*	*8*	*5*	*19*	*53*	*82*	*21*
Newhaven	*32*	*7*	*4*	*21*	*49*	*93*	*18*

One game not played.
Lewes left to join the Athenian League.

Division Two

Sidley United	**34**	**28**	**1**	**5**	**129**	**39**	**57**
Southwick	**34**	**27**	**2**	**5**	**139**	**26**	**56**
Ringmer	34	26	4	4	114	41	56
Wadhurst	34	19	8	7	86	67	46
Wick	34	15	8	11	77	55	38
APV Athletic	34	15	6	13	86	76	36
Horsham YMCA	34	16	4	14	83	78	36
Portfield	34	13	8	13	75	81	34
Brighton North End	34	15	3	16	86	94	33
Three Bridges	34	14	4	16	76	82	32
Steyning	34	12	6	16	54	85	30
Old Varndeanians	34	11	7	16	52	65	29
Battle Rangers	34	13	3	18	78	100	29
Brighton Old Grammarians	34	9	9	16	77	92	27
Hastings & St. Leonards	34	11	2	21	59	81	24
Burgess Hill	34	8	6	20	45	77	22
Ferring	34	6	9	19	43	93	21
Uckfield Town	34	2	2	30	49	176	6

1965-66

Division One

Bexhill Town Athletic	30	18	10	2	81	41	46
Chichester City	30	20	6	4	92	47	46
Sidley United	30	18	7	5	87	49	43
Seaford Town	30	15	6	9	73	57	36
Southwick	30	14	7	9	78	56	35
Rye United	30	14	5	11	69	57	33
Lancing	30	15	2	13	61	48	32
Selsey	30	13	6	11	78	76	32
East Grinstead	30	11	7	12	61	68	29
Whitehawk	30	10	8	12	67	80	28
Haywards Heath	30	12	2	16	57	55	26
Littlehampton Town	30	7	11	12	52	69	25
Shoreham	30	9	4	17	56	68	22
Bognor Regis Town	30	7	5	18	51	78	19
Arundel	*30*	*6*	*5*	*19*	*45*	*91*	*17*
Wigmore Athletic	*30*	*4*	*3*	*23*	*36*	*104*	*11*

Division Two

Horsham YMCA	**34**	**31**	**2**	**1**	**141**	**30**	**64**
Newhaven	**34**	**30**	**2**	**2**	**142**	**34**	**62**
Ringmer	34	24	2	8	155	68	50
Wadhurst	34	22	2	10	102	66	46
Hastings & St. Leonards	34	17	6	11	99	77	40
Ferring	34	18	3	13	100	76	39
APV Athletic	34	17	3	14	95	79	37
Old Varndeanians	34	14	6	14	83	67	34
Wick	34	17	0	17	96	90	34
Hastings Rangers	34	15	3	16	91	92	33
Three Bridges	34	11	10	13	78	82	32
Brighton Old Grammarians	34	14	3	17	74	85	31
Brighton North End	34	12	6	16	94	126	30
Burgess Hill	34	11	3	20	57	82	25
Steyning	34	10	4	20	68	94	24
Portfield	34	6	4	24	55	123	16
Uckfield Town	34	3	2	29	58	180	8
Battle Rangers	34	3	1	30	57	194	7

Uckfield Town left the league.

1966-67

Division One

Bexhill Town Athletic	30	20	6	4	80	36	46
Chichester City	30	17	8	5	97	49	42
Sidley United	30	16	5	9	54	37	37
Southwick	30	10	14	6	64	51	34
Littlehampton Town	30	12	8	10	64	65	32
Horsham YMCA	30	10	9	11	72	56	29
Selsey	30	11	7	12	65	73	29
East Grinstead	30	9	11	10	49	57	29
Haywards Heath	30	9	10	11	50	49	28
Rye United	30	10	8	12	54	67	28
Bognor Regis Town	30	10	7	13	51	50	27
Newhaven	30	10	7	13	55	62	27
Lancing	30	10	7	13	56	87	27
Seaford Town	30	8	9	13	45	63	25
Whitehawk	*30*	*8*	*8*	*14*	*51*	*63*	*24*
Shoreham	*30*	*5*	*6*	*19*	*32*	*74*	*16*

Division Two

Wadhurst	**32**	**22**	**6**	**4**	**99**	**36**	**50**
Arundel	**32**	**18**	**9**	**5**	**103**	**58**	**45**
APV Athletic	32	18	7	7	107	48	43
Hastings & St. Leonards	32	16	9	7	84	54	41
Wigmore Athletic	32	19	3	10	97	69	41
Ringmer	32	17	3	12	80	58	37
Burgess Hill	32	14	9	9	62	47	37
Portfield	32	13	10	9	68	62	36
Hastings Rangers	32	14	6	12	65	74	34
Old Varndeanians	32	12	9	11	55	61	33
Steyning	32	12	6	14	67	46	30
Three Bridges	32	12	4	16	65	71	28
Wick	32	10	6	16	64	63	26
Brighton Old Grammarians	32	11	1	20	67	84	23
Ferring	32	7	5	20	49	91	19
Brighton North End	32	6	6	20	61	103	16
Battle Rangers	32	1	1	30	33	201	3

Brighton North End had 2 points deducted
Battle Rangers and Brighton North End both left the league.

1967-68

Division One

Chichester City	30	17	10	3	78	38	44
Bexhill Town Athletic	30	19	6	5	68	38	44
Southwick	30	17	5	8	72	36	39
Haywards Heath	30	16	7	7	53	34	39
Seaford Town	30	15	6	9	55	50	36
Rye United	30	14	7	9	68	40	35
Horsham YMCA	30	13	9	8	56	42	35
Sidley United	30	11	6	13	49	49	28
Bognor Regis Town	30	11	6	13	44	52	28
Arundel	30	12	4	14	48	60	28
East Grinstead	30	12	3	15	61	69	27
Littlehampton Town	30	10	4	16	43	57	24
Wadhurst	30	9	5	16	59	76	23
Selsey	30	10	1	19	45	78	21
Lancing	*30*	*6*	*5*	*19*	*40*	*64*	*17*
Newhaven	*30*	*4*	*4*	*22*	*28*	*84*	*12*

Division Two

Whitehawk	28	22	3	3	75	31	47
Wigmore Athletic	28	14	8	6	58	46	36
Portfield	28	16	3	9	72	41	35
Hastings & St. Leonards	28	16	1	11	72	57	33
Shoreham	28	14	5	9	49	39	33
Three Bridges	28	12	6	10	50	46	29
Hastings Rangers	28	11	5	12	65	60	27
Ferring	28	11	5	12	39	50	27
APV Athletic	28	8	10	10	45	54	26
Ringmer	28	10	5	13	57	55	25
Burgess Hill	28	9	4	15	58	73	22
Old Varndeanians	28	10	2	16	52	72	22
Wick	28	8	4	16	44	58	20
Steyning	28	7	6	15	41	62	20
Brighton Old Grammarians	28	5	5	18	36	69	15

Three Bridges had 1 point deducted.

1968-69

Division One

Southwick	30	25	2	3	91	23	52
Arundel	30	19	4	7	78	51	42
Chichester City	30	17	7	6	78	35	41
Bexhill Town Athletic	30	16	5	9	57	44	37
Littlehampton Town	30	15	5	10	47	37	35
Rye United	30	12	9	9	42	35	33
Horsham YMCA	30	14	3	13	60	54	31
Whitehawk	30	13	5	12	44	51	31
East Grinstead	30	13	3	14	63	60	29
Haywards Heath	30	11	6	13	48	45	28
Seaford Town	30	9	7	14	44	59	25
Wadhurst	30	9	5	16	48	66	23
Sidley United	30	8	7	15	41	60	23
Bognor Regis Town	30	8	4	18	53	74	20
Selsey	*30*	*6*	*4*	*20*	*44*	*85*	*16*
Wigmore Athletic	*30*	*4*	*6*	*20*	*29*	*88*	*14*

Bexhill Town Athletic changed their name to Bexhill Town.

Division Two

Ringmer	28	20	4	4	74	35	44
Three Bridges	28	20	3	5	74	25	43
Lancing	28	17	9	2	75	28	43
Newhaven	28	15	6	7	81	47	36
Portfield	28	15	5	8	61	37	35
Shoreham	28	12	8	8	51	42	32
Steyning	28	10	11	7	38	34	31
Ferring	28	10	5	13	47	59	25
Hastings Rangers	28	8	6	14	59	82	22
Old Varndeanians	28	9	3	16	50	58	21
Hastings & St. Leonards	28	8	5	15	42	58	21
APV Athletic	28	9	3	16	47	72	21
Burgess Hill	28	8	4	16	43	59	20
Brighton Old Grammarians	28	6	6	16	36	66	18
Wick	28	3	2	23	32	108	8

Brighton Old Grammarians left the league. Peacehaven & Telscombe joined from the Brighton, Hove & District League. Burgess Hill changed their name to Burgess Hill Town.

1969-70

Division One

Haywards Heath	30	21	5	4	65	25	47
Chichester City	30	19	4	7	74	35	42
Southwick	30	16	8	6	55	32	40
Littlehampton Town	30	17	6	7	61	47	40
Rye United	30	14	8	8	58	40	36
Ringmer	30	14	7	9	58	40	35
East Grinstead	30	10	12	8	47	40	32
Bexhill Town	30	12	6	12	51	42	30
Horsham YMCA	30	10	8	12	44	51	28
Sidley United	30	10	7	13	44	42	27
Whitehawk	30	9	7	14	48	56	25
Seaford Town	30	7	11	12	47	70	25
Arundel	30	8	7	15	62	61	23
Three Bridges	30	9	5	16	45	62	23
Bognor Regis Town	*30*	*7*	*7*	*16*	*34*	*52*	*21*
Wadhurst	*30*	*1*	*4*	*25*	*26*	*124*	*6*

Division Two

Lancing	28	19	4	5	71	24	42
APV Athletic	28	18	6	4	61	32	42
Burgess Hill Town	28	15	10	3	61	29	40
Newhaven	28	14	5	9	56	37	33
Wigmore Athletic	28	12	8	8	53	53	32
Selsey	28	12	6	10	57	58	30
Wick	28	11	5	12	48	46	27
Hastings & St. Leonards	28	11	4	13	49	57	26
Peacehaven & Telscombe	28	11	3	14	41	54	25
Shoreham	28	10	5	13	40	53	25
Steyning	28	11	2	15	48	50	24
Hastings Rangers	28	8	6	14	32	57	22
Ferring	28	6	8	14	43	44	20
Old Varndeanians	28	7	2	19	42	65	16
Portfield	28	5	6	17	38	81	16

Pagham joined from the West Sussex League.

1970-71

Division One

Ringmer	30	21	3	6	73	29	45
Southwick	30	20	5	5	64	37	45
Haywards Heath	30	16	6	8	60	39	38
Littlehampton Town	30	14	8	8	61	49	36
Chichester City	30	15	4	11	70	48	34
Arundel	30	16	2	12	75	66	34
East Grinstead	30	15	4	11	62	60	34
Bexhill Town	30	14	4	12	45	34	32
Whitehawk	30	12	6	12	58	52	30
Rye United	30	9	9	12	41	50	27
Lancing	30	10	4	16	31	47	24
APV Athletic	30	9	4	17	40	62	22
Horsham YMCA	30	7	8	15	44	63	21
Three Bridges	30	8	4	18	33	55	20
Sidley United	*30*	*7*	*5*	*18*	*28*	*58*	*19*
Seaford Town	*30*	*7*	*4*	*19*	*35*	*71*	*18*

Horsham YMCA had 1 point deducted.

Division Two

Bognor Regis Town	30	23	5	2	99	27	51
Burgess Hill Town	30	21	7	2	72	22	49
Pagham	30	20	4	6	84	34	44
Shoreham	30	19	5	6	52	27	43
Portfield	30	18	5	7	77	45	41
Newhaven	30	16	4	10	71	50	36
Wadhurst	30	10	8	12	52	59	28
Peacehaven & Telscombe	30	11	6	13	41	51	28
Wick	30	8	9	13	38	52	25
Selsey	30	9	6	15	66	79	24
Hastings & St. Leonards	30	10	3	17	45	63	23
Old Varndeanians	30	7	8	15	43	63	22
Steyning	30	8	5	17	46	69	21
Wigmore Athletic	30	6	6	18	41	89	18
Ferring	30	7	2	21	29	61	16
Hastings Rangers	30	3	6	21	34	99	12

1971-72

Division One

Bognor Regis Town	30	24	1	5	73	22	49
Littlehampton Town	30	21	6	3	72	31	48
Chichester City	30	19	6	5	81	47	44
Southwick	30	15	5	10	52	36	35
Arundel	30	14	6	10	50	41	34
Haywards Heath	30	12	6	12	41	44	30
Ringmer	30	11	7	12	51	50	29
Burgess Hill Town	30	9	10	11	37	47	28
Whitehawk	30	10	7	13	47	59	27
Bexhill Town	30	10	5	15	44	42	25
Three Bridges	30	8	9	13	43	54	24
Horsham YMCA	30	9	6	15	47	74	24
Rye United	30	9	5	16	58	74	23
East Grinstead	30	9	4	17	44	64	22
APV Athletic	30	7	6	17	48	58	20
Lancing	*30*	*8*	*1*	*21*	*35*	*80*	*17*

Three Bridges had 1 point deducted.
Bognor Regis Town left to join the Southern League and APV Athletic also left the league.

Division Two

Newhaven	30	21	8	1	76	21	50
Sidley United	30	22	3	5	81	26	47
Pagham	30	17	9	4	84	38	43
Portfield	30	18	4	8	66	42	40
Peacehaven & Telscombe	30	16	6	8	64	32	38
Shoreham	30	14	10	6	66	36	38
Old Varndeanians	30	14	8	8	66	47	36
Selsey	30	13	8	9	73	48	34
Wick	30	9	8	13	39	50	26
Steyning	30	8	9	13	62	77	25
Wadhurst	30	9	5	16	42	54	23
Wigmore Athletic	30	8	7	15	48	68	23
Seaford Town	30	7	3	20	42	98	17
Hastings & St. Leonards	30	3	9	18	35	71	15
Ferring	30	4	5	21	30	75	13
Hastings Rangers	30	5	2	23	32	123	12

Ferring and Wadhurst both left the league.

1972-73

Division One

Chichester City	28	17	7	4	63	33	41
Ringmer	28	15	8	5	34	20	38
East Grinstead	28	12	10	6	34	21	34
Haywards Heath	28	15	2	11	45	34	32
Bexhill Town	28	10	8	10	40	34	28
Southwick	28	9	10	9	35	42	28
Littlehampton Town	28	9	9	10	40	38	27
Whitehawk	28	10	7	11	33	35	27
Newhaven	28	10	6	12	41	40	26
Sidley United	28	7	11	10	40	42	25
Rye United	28	9	7	12	34	45	25
Arundel	28	6	12	10	33	35	24
Horsham YMCA	28	9	6	13	38	50	24
Burgess Hill Town	*28*	*7*	*9*	*12*	*26*	*46*	*23*
Three Bridges	*28*	*5*	*8*	*15*	*30*	*51*	*18*

Division Two

Portfield	24	20	3	1	86	22	43
Shoreham	24	17	2	5	52	29	36
Pagham	24	12	7	5	44	28	31
Peacehaven & Telscombe	24	12	4	8	48	35	28
Old Varndeanians	24	11	5	8	46	42	27
Wick	24	11	4	9	35	23	26
Hastings & St. Leonards	24	10	6	8	37	34	26
Seaford Town	24	10	5	9	37	34	25
Hastings Rangers	24	6	5	13	35	72	17
Lancing	24	6	5	13	21	45	17
Selsey	24	6	4	14	27	45	16
Steyning	24	5	4	15	30	51	14
Wigmore Athletic	24	2	2	20	24	62	6

Hastings Rangers and Old Varndeanians both left the league.

1973-74

Division One

Newhaven	28	18	7	3	50	24	43
Littlehampton Town	28	19	3	6	53	24	41
Southwick	28	17	6	5	49	24	40
Sidley United	28	14	7	7	48	34	35
Haywards Heath	28	11	8	9	41	34	30
Whitehawk	28	12	5	11	43	42	29
Bexhill Town	28	11	5	12	42	46	27
Portfield	28	10	6	12	40	40	26
East Grinstead	28	10	5	13	36	44	25
Arundel	28	9	7	12	34	43	25
Chichester City	28	9	6	13	34	42	24
Horsham YMCA	28	8	6	14	37	51	22
Ringmer	28	9	4	15	32	46	22
Shoreham	*28*	*5*	*8*	*15*	*35*	*57*	*18*
Rye United	*28*	*4*	*5*	*19*	*23*	*46*	*13*

Division Two

Wigmore Athletic	**20**	**11**	**7**	**2**	**46**	**27**	**29**
Three Bridges	**20**	**12**	**4**	**4**	**41**	**23**	**28**
Seaford Town	20	9	6	5	38	23	24
Peacehaven & Telscombe	20	11	2	7	36	42	24
Burgess Hill Town	20	8	7	5	28	21	23
Hastings & St. Leonards	20	9	4	7	37	30	22
Wick	20	6	4	10	29	30	16
Pagham	20	4	8	8	31	33	16
Lancing	20	7	1	12	26	39	15
Selsey	20	5	2	13	28	51	12
Steyning	20	2	7	11	21	42	11

Crowborough Athletic joined from the Brighton, Hove & District League.

1974-75

Division One

Southwick	28	18	5	5	58	24	41
Haywards Heath	28	16	7	5	48	20	39
Wigmore Athletic	28	13	10	5	38	24	36
Ringmer	28	13	4	11	45	38	30
Littlehampton Town	28	12	5	11	36	33	29
East Grinstead	28	10	7	11	30	30	27
Horsham YMCA	28	11	5	12	38	44	27
Arundel	28	10	7	11	31	37	27
Newhaven	28	10	5	13	36	40	25
Whitehawk	28	11	3	14	37	44	25
Bexhill Town	28	10	5	13	30	38	25
Chichester City	28	9	7	12	27	41	25
Three Bridges	28	7	9	12	32	36	23
Sidley United	*28*	*9*	*6*	*13*	*32*	*41*	*22*
Portfield	*28*	*6*	*5*	*17*	*36*	*64*	*17*

Sidley United had 2 points deducted.

Division Two

Burgess Hill Town	**22**	**16**	**5**	**1**	**49**	**14**	**37**
Rye United	**22**	**15**	**5**	**2**	**48**	**16**	**35**
Shoreham	22	11	4	7	34	25	26
Crowborough Athletic	22	9	7	6	38	36	25
Hastings & St. Leonards	22	8	6	8	33	34	22
Peacehaven & Telscombe	22	9	3	10	40	38	21
Steyning	22	5	10	7	28	32	20
Lancing	22	5	7	10	25	34	17
Seaford Town	22	5	7	10	25	34	16
Selsey	22	7	2	13	29	45	16
Pagham	22	6	3	13	25	26	15
Wick	22	4	5	13	20	40	13

Seaford Town had 1 point deducted.
Hailsham Town joined from the Southern Counties Combination.

1975-76

Division One

Burgess Hill Town	28	18	8	2	70	27	44
Littlehampton Town	28	17	4	7	60	29	38
Bexhill Town	28	16	6	6	59	33	38
Southwick	28	14	8	6	54	34	36
Haywards Heath	28	13	5	10	51	34	31
Wigmore Athletic	28	13	3	12	56	47	29
Whitehawk	28	10	9	9	39	36	29
Horsham YMCA	28	10	8	10	40	40	28
Ringmer	28	12	3	13	35	37	27
East Grinstead	28	9	8	11	26	34	26
Three Bridges	28	10	4	14	34	49	24
Rye United	28	8	6	14	32	46	22
Chichester City	28	6	8	14	29	47	20
Arundel	*28*	*4*	*6*	*18*	*27*	*62*	*14*
Newhaven	*28*	*4*	*6*	*18*	*32*	*89*	*14*

Eastbourne Town joined from the Athenian League.

Division Two

Selsey	**24**	**19**	**3**	**2**	**60**	**22**	**41**
Peacehaven & Telscombe	**24**	**16**	**5**	**3**	**60**	**25**	**37**
Portfield	24	14	4	6	53	31	32
Sidley United	24	11	6	7	41	33	28
Shoreham	24	12	3	9	38	47	27
Hailsham Town	24	10	4	10	57	48	24
Steyning	24	8	7	9	38	36	23
Hastings & St. Leonards	24	8	4	12	40	47	20
Wick	24	7	6	11	23	28	20
Crowborough Athletic	24	7	5	12	42	48	19
Lancing	24	5	5	14	23	42	15
Pagham	24	6	3	15	31	61	15
Seaford Town	24	4	3	17	21	59	11

Storrington joined from the West Sussex League.
Hastings & St. Leonards changed their name to Hastings Town.

1976-77

Division One

Eastbourne Town	30	18	8	4	51	21	44
Southwick	30	17	7	6	45	25	41
Burgess Hill Town	30	15	7	8	57	28	37
Horsham YMCA	30	14	6	10	47	35	34
Peacehaven & Telscombe	30	15	4	11	58	49	34
Haywards Heath	30	13	8	9	45	40	34
Ringmer	30	13	5	12	41	40	31
Littlehampton Town	30	11	9	10	43	42	31
Bexhill Town	30	13	3	14	40	46	29
Wigmore Athletic	30	10	8	12	48	56	28
Rye United	30	7	12	11	39	44	26
East Grinstead	30	8	10	12	42	49	26
Chichester City	30	11	4	15	40	47	26
Selsey	30	9	7	14	34	57	25
Three Bridges	*30*	*5*	*8*	*17*	*32*	*55*	*18*
Whitehawk	*30*	*6*	*4*	*20*	*40*	*68*	*16*

Division Two

Shoreham	**26**	**19**	**2**	**5**	**62**	**30**	**40**
Arundel	**26**	**18**	**3**	**5**	**49**	**23**	**39**
Steyning	26	16	5	5	65	32	37
Hailsham Town	26	13	5	8	60	43	31
Storrington	26	11	6	9	39	36	28
Newhaven	26	10	7	9	43	42	27
Sidley United	26	10	6	10	44	39	26
Lancing	26	11	3	12	32	33	25
Pagham	26	9	6	11	42	44	24
Portfield	26	10	4	12	31	38	24
Wick	26	5	10	11	31	41	20
Hastings Town	26	6	5	15	35	47	15
Crowborough Athletic	26	5	4	17	22	67	14
Seaford Town	26	3	6	17	27	67	10

Hastings Town and Seaford Town each had 2 points deducted.
Albion United joined from the East Sussex League.

1977-78
Division One

Shoreham	30	21	5	4	77	25	47
Peacehaven & Telscombe	30	21	4	5	59	26	46
Horsham YMCA	30	17	8	5	55	32	42
Burgess Hill Town	30	15	10	5	58	28	40
Southwick	30	17	6	7	64	40	40
Bexhill Town	30	16	5	9	63	37	37
Littlehampton Town	30	15	7	8	57	37	37
Eastbourne Town	30	13	5	12	56	44	31
Arundel	30	10	9	11	40	41	29
Rye United	30	10	6	14	46	53	26
Chichester City	30	9	7	14	41	58	25
East Grinstead	30	8	7	15	40	50	23
Haywards Heath	30	8	6	16	38	45	22
Ringmer	30	6	9	15	39	47	21
Selsey	*30*	*3*	*3*	*24*	*15*	*95*	*9*
Wigmore Athletic	*30*	*2*	*1*	*27*	*22*	*112*	*5*

Division Two

Steyning	**28**	**20**	**5**	**3**	**84**	**21**	**45**
Sidley United	**28**	**18**	**4**	**6**	**69**	**40**	**40**
Pagham	28	16	6	6	66	27	38
Three Bridges	28	16	4	8	50	30	36
Albion United	28	14	5	9	47	35	33
Hastings Town	28	14	5	9	53	43	33
Portfield	28	13	6	9	46	43	32
Hailsham Town	28	11	6	11	47	52	28
Storrington	28	11	5	12	51	52	27
Whitehawk	28	11	4	13	42	53	26
Lancing	28	9	6	13	35	37	24
Crowborough Athletic	28	7	8	13	33	39	22
Wick	28	8	5	15	33	40	21
Seaford Town	28	4	2	22	22	81	10
Newhaven	28	2	1	25	19	103	5

Seaford Town left the league.

From the following season, goal difference replaced goal average to decide positions when teams ended on equal points.

1978-79
Division One

Peacehaven & Telscombe	30	18	9	3	61	28	45
Southwick	30	16	9	5	60	33	41
Horsham YMCA	30	18	5	7	58	33	41
Steyning	30	15	7	8	56	45	37
Littlehampton Town	30	14	7	9	54	34	35
Ringmer	30	13	8	9	41	44	34
Arundel	30	13	7	10	44	37	33
Shoreham	30	10	10	10	43	40	30
Haywards Heath	30	9	12	9	44	47	30
Bexhill Town	30	11	5	14	56	56	27
Eastbourne Town	30	10	6	14	47	51	26
Chichester City	30	10	5	15	51	64	25
Burgess Hill Town	30	8	6	16	34	56	22
Rye United	30	8	5	17	31	42	21
East Grinstead	*30*	*5*	*8*	*17*	*40*	*65*	*18*
Sidley United	*30*	*5*	*5*	*20*	*22*	*67*	*15*

Steyning changed their name to Steyning Town.

Division Two

Pagham	**26**	**20**	**4**	**2**	**58**	**16**	**44**
Portfield	**26**	**16**	**6**	**4**	**43**	**22**	**38**
Three Bridges	26	14	6	6	52	30	34
Hastings Town	26	15	3	8	43	33	33
Hailsham Town	26	14	3	9	47	42	31
Wick	26	10	7	9	33	29	27
Storrington	26	8	9	9	42	36	25
Newhaven	26	9	7	10	32	36	25
Albion United	26	8	8	10	43	40	24
Lancing	26	8	7	11	37	36	23
Crowborough Athletic	26	6	6	14	28	49	18
Wigmore Athletic	26	6	4	16	36	53	16
Whitehawk	26	6	4	16	24	50	16
Selsey	26	2	6	18	24	70	10

1979-80
Division One

Chichester City	30	21	5	4	66	30	47
Southwick	30	19	7	4	63	25	45
Burgess Hill Town	30	18	6	6	65	37	42
Pagham	30	15	9	6	52	31	39
Eastbourne Town	30	13	9	8	50	37	35
Littlehampton Town	30	13	8	9	39	34	34
Steyning Town	30	12	8	10	59	41	32
Shoreham	30	13	8	9	48	37	32
Horsham YMCA	30	13	5	12	46	38	31
Ringmer	30	13	4	13	51	36	30
Arundel	30	9	10	11	42	41	28
Peacehaven & Telscombe	30	10	7	13	40	54	27
Bexhill Town	30	7	4	19	30	76	18
Portfield	30	6	4	20	37	69	16
Haywards Heath	*30*	*4*	*7*	*19*	*24*	*54*	*15*
Rye United	*30*	*2*	*3*	*25*	*22*	*94*	*7*

Shoreham had 2 points deducted.

Division Two

Hastings Town	**26**	**18**	**4**	**4**	**68**	**22**	**40**
Three Bridges	**26**	**17**	**5**	**4**	**59**	**16**	**39**
Hailsham Town	26	16	7	3	52	27	39
Wick	26	14	4	8	44	27	32
Newhaven	26	11	7	8	39	34	29
Crowborough Athletic	26	10	7	9	39	35	27
East Grinstead	26	11	4	11	34	39	26
Whitehawk	26	8	9	9	37	40	25
Storrington	26	11	3	12	41	48	25
Lancing	26	8	5	13	34	38	21
Sidley United	26	7	4	15	38	69	18
Albion United	26	5	7	14	19	43	17
Selsey	26	4	6	16	22	54	14
Wigmore Athletic	26	4	4	18	27	61	12

1980-81
Division One

Pagham	30	18	9	3	52	22	45
Peacehaven & Telscombe	30	16	10	4	53	28	42
Steyning Town	30	15	10	5	61	37	40
Hastings Town	30	14	8	8	64	35	36
Southwick	30	10	13	7	42	35	33
Burgess Hill Town	30	9	14	7	37	29	32
Three Bridges	30	12	7	11	44	39	31
Arundel	30	11	7	12	34	27	29
Shoreham	30	9	10	11	40	50	28
Chichester City	30	8	11	11	47	47	27
Littlehampton Town	30	10	7	13	42	43	27
Ringmer	30	9	9	12	45	54	27
Eastbourne Town	30	10	6	14	36	41	26
Horsham YMCA	30	8	9	13	35	55	25
Portfield	*30*	*5*	*9*	*16*	*29*	*68*	*19*
Bexhill Town	*30*	*5*	*3*	*22*	*23*	*74*	*13*

Division Two

Whitehawk	**26**	**19**	**3**	**4**	**57**	**22**	**41**
Hailsham Town	**26**	**17**	**5**	**4**	**56**	**21**	**39**
Wick	26	17	3	6	69	32	37
Haywards Heath	26	11	7	8	40	28	29
East Grinstead	26	11	7	8	34	35	29
Wigmore Athletic	26	8	9	9	47	47	25
Sidley United	26	9	6	11	33	30	24
Storrington	26	10	4	12	31	36	24
Newhaven	26	9	4	13	44	56	22
Lancing	26	8	6	12	28	48	22
Rye United	26	6	9	11	26	37	21
Crowborough Athletic	26	8	4	14	35	50	20
Selsey	26	5	6	15	22	41	16
Albion United	26	5	5	16	25	64	15

Hassocks and Midhurst & Easebourne both joined from the Southern
Counties Combination.

1981-82

Division One

Peacehaven & Telscombe	30	22	6	2	66	20	48
Littlehampton Town	30	17	8	5	67	32	42
Burgess Hill Town	30	14	10	6	58	48	38
Steyning Town	30	16	5	9	65	37	37
Pagham	30	13	9	8	49	36	35
Three Bridges	30	13	9	8	40	38	35
Arundel	30	10	11	9	40	36	31
Hastings Town	30	11	6	13	39	40	28
Chichester City	30	8	12	10	40	47	28
Hailsham Town	30	8	11	11	45	58	27
Ringmer	30	11	5	14	36	52	27
Southwick	30	9	10	11	39	37	26
Eastbourne Town	30	11	3	16	38	43	25
Whitehawk	30	7	8	15	38	54	22
Horsham YMCA	*30*	*3*	*10*	*17*	*19*	*50*	*16*
Shoreham	*30*	*2*	*7*	*21*	*37*	*88*	*11*

Peacehaven & Telscombe and Southwick each had 2 points deducted.

Division Two

Wick	**30**	**25**	**3**	**2**	**94**	**15**	**53**
Midhurst & Easebourne	**30**	**18**	**8**	**4**	**60**	**37**	**44**
Portfield	30	18	5	7	48	25	41
Bexhill Town	30	17	6	7	46	32	40
Sidley United	30	15	10	5	46	36	40
Haywards Heath	30	10	13	7	47	32	33
Rye United	30	12	8	10	41	37	32
East Grinstead	30	9	12	9	41	34	30
Lancing	30	11	6	13	54	44	28
Newhaven	30	10	7	13	37	53	27
Crowborough Athletic	30	11	4	15	32	44	26
Hassocks	30	9	5	16	47	58	23
Storrington	30	6	8	16	32	52	20
Wigmore Athletic	30	6	7	17	33	60	19
Selsey	30	7	0	23	33	71	14
Albion United	30	2	6	22	21	82	10

1982-83

Division One

Peacehaven & Telscombe	30	22	6	2	61	19	50
Southwick	30	17	9	4	67	32	43
Hastings Town	30	18	6	6	86	39	42
Steyning Town	30	18	5	7	52	29	41
Whitehawk	30	15	9	6	49	30	39
Littlehampton Town	30	13	10	7	59	47	36
Wick	30	12	6	12	63	52	30
Three Bridges	30	11	8	11	33	33	30
Eastbourne Town	30	9	10	11	36	51	28
Hailsham Town	30	11	5	14	55	58	27
Burgess Hill Town	30	9	6	15	42	50	24
Pagham	30	8	7	15	46	61	23
Ringmer	30	8	6	16	32	42	22
Midhurst & Easebourne	30	5	11	14	42	68	21
Arundel	*30*	*6*	*4*	*20*	*32*	*68*	*16*
Chichester City	*30*	*3*	*2*	*25*	*22*	*98*	*8*

Division Two

Horsham YMCA	**30**	**21**	**6**	**3**	**74**	**30**	**48**
Lancing	**30**	**20**	**6**	**4**	**57**	**26**	**46**
Haywards Heath	30	18	2	10	70	40	38
Hassocks	30	16	6	8	69	54	38
East Grinstead	30	15	7	8	46	30	37
Bexhill Town	30	15	7	8	56	41	37
Portfield	30	15	6	9	70	45	36
Rye United	30	14	4	12	49	45	32
Shoreham	30	13	5	12	54	49	31
Selsey	30	11	6	13	43	53	28
Wigmore Athletic	30	8	6	16	41	57	22
Sidley United	30	7	5	18	43	59	19
Albion United	30	6	7	17	37	67	19
Newhaven	30	5	7	18	30	65	17
Crowborough Athletic	30	8	1	21	37	81	17
Storrington	30	6	3	21	36	70	15

Rye United left the league and Lingfield joined from the Combined
Counties League.

A new Division Three was formed with 13 members. The 13 member were
(previous league in brackets where known): Bosham (West Sussex
League), Broadbridge Heath (Southern Counties Combination), East
Preston (West Sussex League), Eastbourne Rangers (Eastbourne & Hastings
League), Ferring (West Sussex League), Franklands Village (Southern
Counties Combination), Hurstpierpoint, Langney Sports (Eastbourne &
Hastings League), Lower Bevenden, Midway, Seaford Town (Brighton, Hove
& District League), St. Francis Hospital and Westdene.

Three points awarded for a win instead of two from the next season.

1983-84

Division One

Whitehawk	30	23	5	2	77	19	74
Littlehampton Town	30	22	5	3	92	32	71
Steyning Town	30	20	6	4	62	27	66
Southwick	30	18	9	3	67	22	63
Three Bridges	30	16	4	10	59	45	52
Hastings Town	30	13	7	10	52	34	46
Peacehaven & Telscombe	30	12	7	11	50	37	43
Ringmer	30	10	5	15	38	52	35
Hailsham Town	30	10	3	17	35	66	33
Eastbourne Town	30	8	8	14	33	43	32
Horsham YMCA	30	10	2	18	43	65	32
Midhurst & Easebourne	30	8	8	14	36	77	32
Lancing	30	8	6	16	41	61	30
Wick	30	6	8	16	31	57	26
Burgess Hill Town	30	4	9	17	29	56	21
Pagham	*30*	*4*	*4*	*22*	*26*	*78*	*16*

Southwick left to join the Combined Counties League.

Division Two

Portfield	30	23	6	1	71	21	75
Arundel	30	20	6	4	72	27	66
Hassocks	30	18	5	7	66	38	59
Wigmore Athletic	30	17	8	5	57	33	59
Bexhill Town	30	17	7	6	65	31	58
Chichester City	30	15	4	11	54	39	49
Haywards Heath	30	12	12	6	53	33	48
East Grinstead	30	10	9	11	39	41	39
Lingfield	30	10	8	12	47	42	38
Sidley United	30	9	6	15	52	58	33
Albion United	30	9	6	15	47	68	33
Selsey	30	6	10	14	41	56	28
Storrington	30	6	10	14	39	54	28
Newhaven	30	7	5	18	31	58	26
Shoreham	30	2	8	20	23	88	14
Crowborough Athletic	*30*	*1*	*6*	*23*	*22*	*92*	*9*

Division Two

Shoreham	30	23	4	3	58	22	73
7Chichester City	30	23	3	4	71	19	72
Pagham	30	19	4	7	61	32	61
Storrington	30	15	6	9	52	36	51
Hassocks	30	13	8	9	48	34	47
East Grinstead	30	14	3	13	56	46	45
Haywards Heath	30	12	8	10	64	41	44
Ferring	30	14	2	14	43	48	44
Sidley United	30	12	7	11	46	55	43
Franklands Village	30	10	10	10	55	48	40
Selsey	30	10	6	14	27	42	36
Lingfield	30	9	8	13	46	46	35
Albion United	30	9	4	17	39	66	31
Wigmore Athletic	30	7	4	19	40	68	25
Newhaven	30	4	4	22	18	64	16
Bexhill Town	*30*	*1*	*9*	*20*	*27*	*84*	*12*

Division Three

East Preston	24	15	6	3	38	15	51
Franklands Village	24	13	11	0	48	19	50
Ferring	24	13	8	3	53	15	47
Bosham	24	11	5	8	50	38	38
Langney Sports	24	10	8	6	43	36	38
Westdene	24	10	4	10	42	32	34
Broadbridge Heath	24	9	7	8	36	31	34
Seaford Town	24	9	5	10	32	40	32
Midway	24	10	1	13	40	35	31
Hurstpierpoint	24	6	7	11	27	46	25
Eastbourne Rangers	24	7	2	15	31	52	23
Lower Bevenden	24	3	5	16	24	61	14
St. Francis Hospital	24	3	5	16	19	63	14

Lower Bevenden left the league. Oakwood joined from the Southern Counties Combination, Ifield joined from the Crawley & District League and Saltdean United joined from the Brighton, Hove & District League. Cooksbridge also joined.

Division Three

Oakwood	28	21	4	3	85	28	67
Bosham	28	18	7	3	80	36	61
Saltdean United	28	16	8	4	68	31	56
Midway	28	14	3	11	50	45	45
Langney Sports	28	12	6	10	52	41	42
Seaford Town	28	13	3	12	44	43	42
Crowborough Athletic	28	10	8	10	43	42	38
Broadbridge Heath	28	11	5	12	38	41	38
Westdene	28	11	4	13	50	56	37
East Preston	28	11	3	14	31	43	36
Cooksbridge	28	10	4	14	56	51	34
Eastbourne Rangers	28	10	4	14	39	53	30
Ifield	28	7	6	15	27	57	27
Hurstpierpoint	28	6	4	18	24	60	22
St. Francis Hospital	28	4	3	21	32	87	15

Eastbourne Rangers had 4 points deducted.
St. Francis Hospital left the league. APV Athletic and Leftovers Sports Club both joined from the Crawley & District League and Patcham joined from the Southern Counties Combination.

1984-85

Division One

Steyning Town	30	23	3	4	74	26	72
Littlehampton Town	30	21	3	6	65	26	66
Eastbourne Town	30	19	6	5	66	26	63
Whitehawk	30	18	7	5	69	34	61
Arundel	30	17	7	6	77	38	58
Three Bridges	30	14	6	10	65	38	48
Portfield	30	12	5	13	36	38	41
Burgess Hill Town	30	8	14	8	48	49	38
Hastings Town	30	8	8	14	45	64	32
Peacehaven & Telscombe	30	9	5	16	44	64	32
Horsham YMCA	30	7	8	15	37	57	29
Lancing	30	7	7	16	41	59	28
Ringmer	30	5	13	12	22	47	28
Hailsham Town	30	6	10	14	32	70	28
Midhurst & Easebourne	30	7	5	18	39	56	26
Wick	*30*	*3*	*5*	*22*	*25*	*93*	*14*

Hastings Town left to join the Southern League.

1985-86

Division One

Steyning Town	30	22	6	2	61	16	72
Three Bridges	30	19	6	5	58	24	63
Eastbourne Town	30	18	7	5	71	23	61
Whitehawk	30	13	11	6	46	30	50
Peacehaven & Telscombe	30	15	4	11	55	44	49
Littlehampton Town	30	13	7	10	44	29	46
Burgess Hill Town	30	13	6	11	47	41	45
Portfield	30	13	6	11	40	48	45
Arundel	30	12	8	10	55	37	44
Lancing	30	11	7	12	42	52	40
Hailsham Town	30	9	7	14	45	49	34
Shoreham	30	10	4	16	42	57	34
Chichester City	30	7	6	17	35	64	27
Midhurst & Easebourne	30	5	7	18	33	65	22
Horsham YMCA	30	5	4	21	33	90	19
Ringmer	*30*	*4*	*6*	*20*	*19*	*57*	*18*

Steyning Town left to join the Wessex League.

56 Sussex County League 1986-1988

Division Two

Wick	30	22	6	2	94	35	72
Haywards Heath	30	22	5	3	72	26	71
Pagham	30	21	6	3	70	18	69
Sidley United	30	15	8	7	52	36	53
East Grinstead	30	15	5	10	44	30	50
Albion United	30	13	6	11	49	48	45
Bosham	30	12	7	11	56	53	43
Ferring	30	12	6	12	47	51	42
Storrington	30	10	10	10	48	41	40
Oakwood	30	10	7	13	31	50	37
Hassocks	30	8	9	13	38	38	33
Newhaven	30	8	5	17	32	57	29
Selsey	30	7	5	18	35	67	26
Wigmore Athletic	30	7	3	20	44	71	24
Franklands Village	30	6	4	20	36	74	22
Lingfield	30	5	2	23	35	88	17

Albion United changed their name to Little Common Albion.

Division Two

Pagham	30	22	6	2	63	11	72
Selsey	30	21	2	7	68	28	65
Bexhill Town	30	15	7	8	54	39	52
East Grinstead	30	14	10	6	46	33	52
Oakwood	30	14	5	11	40	37	47
Little Common Albion	30	13	7	10	57	42	46
Ferring	30	12	6	12	34	35	42
Bosham	30	12	6	12	48	55	42
Seaford Town	30	11	7	12	37	35	40
Newhaven	30	10	6	14	36	48	36
Hassocks	30	10	6	14	32	53	36
Wigmore Athletic	30	9	6	15	48	56	33
Storrington	30	8	6	16	32	43	30
Ringmer	30	6	11	13	35	48	29
Franklands Village	30	7	6	17	31	59	27
Sidley United	30	4	7	19	33	72	19

Hassocks were relegated as their facilities were deemed inadequate for membership of Division Two.

Division Three

Seaford Town	28	18	5	5	64	31	59
Bexhill Town	28	17	7	4	72	31	58
East Preston	28	15	5	8	54	32	50
Langney Sports	28	14	4	10	53	39	46
Saltdean United	28	13	6	9	58	41	45
Ifield	28	13	3	12	56	66	42
APV Athletic	28	12	5	11	50	72	41
Eastbourne Rangers	28	11	6	11	55	63	39
Crowborough Athletic	28	10	6	12	49	56	36
Westdene	28	9	7	12	44	49	34
Hurstpierpoint	28	8	8	12	43	56	32
Midway	28	6	9	13	44	51	27
Cooksbridge	28	6	8	14	50	57	26
Broadbridge Heath	28	5	10	13	35	50	25
Leftovers Sports Club	28	6	5	17	33	66	23

Patcham withdrew from the league during the season and their record was deleted.

Division Three

Langney Sports	26	21	3	2	101	19	66
Crowborough Athletic	26	18	4	4	60	25	58
Midway	26	14	6	6	52	23	48
Cooksbridge	26	14	5	7	56	34	47
Ifield	26	13	4	9	49	44	43
East Preston	26	12	4	10	47	52	40
Westdene	26	12	3	11	60	56	39
Broadbridge Heath	26	10	7	9	38	34	37
Saltdean United	26	10	3	13	36	47	33
APV Athletic	26	9	4	13	51	54	31
Eastbourne Rangers	26	9	2	15	41	65	29
Hurstpierpoint	26	6	5	15	31	63	23
Leftovers Sports Club	26	6	2	18	31	71	20
Lingfield	26	1	2	23	14	80	5

Eastbourne Rangers and Westdene both left the league. Mile Oak joined.

1986-87

Division One

Arundel	30	20	5	5	83	39	65
Whitehawk	30	19	6	5	56	24	63
Haywards Heath	30	18	5	7	63	39	59
Three Bridges	30	18	4	8	67	41	58
Eastbourne Town	30	15	11	4	56	23	56
Littlehampton Town	30	14	7	9	49	33	49
Peacehaven & Telscombe	30	13	7	10	49	61	46
Shoreham	30	12	8	10	41	42	44
Wick	30	11	9	10	61	57	42
Lancing	30	11	5	14	55	48	38
Burgess Hill Town	30	8	6	16	32	40	30
Portfield	30	7	7	16	32	46	28
Horsham YMCA	30	7	5	18	38	54	26
Hailsham Town	30	5	10	15	31	62	25
Chichester City	30	4	7	19	23	75	19
Midhurst & Easebourne	30	4	6	20	26	78	18

1987-88

Division One

Pagham	30	20	7	3	60	22	67
Three Bridges	30	18	7	5	59	26	61
Wick	30	18	4	8	52	40	58
Eastbourne Town	30	17	4	9	63	41	55
Whitehawk	30	15	3	12	47	31	48
Hailsham Town	30	14	6	10	46	33	48
Haywards Heath	30	11	6	13	53	51	39
Peacehaven & Telscombe	30	10	8	12	49	55	38
Burgess Hill Town	30	10	8	12	33	40	38
Shoreham	30	9	10	11	51	54	37
Selsey	30	9	9	12	36	49	36
Arundel	30	9	6	15	39	53	33
Lancing	30	7	10	13	32	45	31
Littlehampton Town	30	8	6	16	31	46	30
Portfield	30	7	7	16	25	51	28
Horsham YMCA	30	5	5	20	28	67	20

Redhill joined from the Spartan League.

Division Two

Langney Sports	28	20	6	2	65	19	66
Bexhill Town	28	17	4	7	52	29	55
Oakwood	**28**	**15**	**7**	**6**	**56**	**33**	**52**
Chichester City	28	12	9	7	61	36	45
Ringmer	28	12	7	9	50	38	43
Little Common Albion	28	11	8	9	43	33	41
Storrington	28	11	7	10	47	42	40
Midhurst & Easebourne	28	12	4	12	39	47	40
Seaford Town	28	11	5	12	43	50	38
Ferring	28	8	9	11	29	36	33
East Grinstead	28	9	4	15	41	48	31
Crowborough Athletic	28	9	4	15	32	46	31
Newhaven	28	9	4	15	39	62	31
Bosham	28	5	6	17	36	68	21
Wigmore Athletic	*28*	*5*	*4*	*19*	*28*	*74*	*19*

Wigmore Athletic changed their name to Worthing United.

Division Three

Midway	26	20	3	3	58	11	63
Ifield	26	18	2	6	60	26	56
Broadbridge Heath	**26**	**17**	**4**	**5**	**56**	**24**	**55**
Mile Oak	26	15	7	4	57	27	52
Hurstpierpoint	26	11	5	10	58	45	38
Cooksbridge	26	12	2	12	48	45	38
APV Athletic	26	12	2	12	51	59	38
Franklands Village	26	10	6	10	46	42	36
Hassocks	26	9	6	11	39	35	33
Leftovers Sports Club	26	7	7	12	23	47	28
Saltdean United	26	8	3	15	44	66	27
East Preston	26	5	7	14	47	59	22
Sidley United	26	4	6	16	33	69	18
Lingfield	26	2	4	20	14	79	10

APV Athletic left the league. Stamco joined from the Southern Counties Combination and Forest joined from the Mid-Sussex League. AFC Falcons also joined.

Division Two

Seaford Town	**26**	**15**	**7**	**4**	**50**	**30**	**52**
Ringmer	**26**	**16**	**3**	**7**	**45**	**14**	**51**
Midhurst & Easebourne	26	14	6	6	49	34	48
Storrington	26	14	5	7	42	31	47
Chichester City	26	12	8	6	41	30	44
Bexhill Town	26	12	7	7	47	37	43
Newhaven	26	8	14	4	46	35	38
Horsham YMCA	26	7	7	12	56	49	28
Broadbridge Heath	26	7	6	13	37	47	27
Ferring	26	8	3	15	35	52	27
Bosham	26	7	6	13	32	60	27
Little Common Albion	26	7	5	14	31	51	26
Crowborough Athletic	26	7	3	16	25	52	24
East Grinstead	*26*	*6*	*4*	*16*	*21*	*35*	*22*

Division Three

Saltdean United	**30**	**20**	**5**	**5**	**52**	**21**	**65**
Stamco	30	19	5	6	58	29	62
Franklands Village	**30**	**17**	**8**	**5**	**54**	**29**	**59**
Sidley United	30	17	2	11	60	44	53
AFC Falcons	30	13	11	6	35	25	50
Forest	30	15	3	12	61	55	48
Worthing United	30	13	8	9	56	37	47
Hassocks	30	13	7	10	48	29	46
Hurstpierpoint	30	12	8	10	53	41	44
Mile Oak	30	11	8	11	56	47	41
Ifield	30	11	4	15	53	53	37
Cooksbridge	30	9	6	15	45	59	33
East Preston	30	9	5	16	41	57	32
Leftovers Sports Club	30	4	10	16	26	58	22
Midway	30	5	2	23	24	81	17
Lingfield	30	4	4	22	32	89	16

AFC Falcons and Midway both moved to the Brighton, Hove & District League, Lingfield moved to the Mid-Sussex League and Cooksbridge also left. Buxted joined from the Mid-Sussex League, Town Mead joined from the Crawley & District League and Withdean joined from the Brighton, Hove & District League. Rottingdean '89 joined as a newly formed club.

1988-89

Division One

Pagham	34	25	6	3	83	33	81
Three Bridges	34	19	9	6	70	29	66
Whitehawk	34	19	8	7	55	32	65
Hailsham Town	34	16	10	8	55	33	58
Burgess Hill Town	34	17	5	12	54	41	56
Wick	34	13	11	10	50	40	50
Littlehampton Town	34	14	8	12	43	33	50
Peacehaven & Telscombe	34	14	8	12	48	41	50
Selsey	34	15	5	14	55	63	50
Langney Sports	34	12	13	9	54	46	49
Redhill	34	13	3	18	49	56	42
Lancing	34	10	9	15	41	51	39
Haywards Heath	34	11	4	19	48	64	37
Shoreham	34	10	7	17	49	76	37
Eastbourne Town	34	9	9	16	46	58	36
Arundel	34	7	11	16	33	66	32
Oakwood	*34*	*6*	*11*	*17*	*39*	*65*	*29*
Portfield	*34*	*5*	*5*	*24*	*33*	*78*	*20*

Haywards Heath changed their name to Haywards Heath Town.

1989-90

Division One

Wick	34	25	4	5	88	30	79
Littlehampton Town	34	24	4	6	65	22	76
Langney Sports	34	20	6	8	63	33	66
Burgess Hill Town	34	18	8	8	68	38	62
Peacehaven & Telscombe	34	15	8	11	44	33	53
Whitehawk	34	16	4	14	45	41	52
Three Bridges	34	13	12	9	61	38	51
Pagham	34	15	6	13	53	46	51
Shoreham	34	14	5	15	58	65	47
Ringmer	34	11	8	15	48	64	41
Seaford Town	34	12	4	18	43	58	40
Haywards Heath Town	34	11	7	16	47	69	40
Hailsham Town	34	9	11	14	41	54	38
Selsey	34	9	9	16	45	63	36
Eastbourne Town	34	9	8	17	42	58	35
Arundel	34	9	7	18	33	56	34
Lancing	*34*	*8*	*9*	*17*	*43*	*68*	*33*
ITRedhill	*34*	*6*	*4*	*24*	*24*	*75*	*22*

Division Two

Bexhill Town	30	22	3	5	76	20	69
Oakwood	30	20	3	7	74	27	60
Chichester City	30	18	3	9	57	26	57
Portfield	30	17	5	8	49	36	56
Horsham YMCA	30	16	3	11	42	31	51
Stamco	30	15	4	11	60	38	49
Crowborough Athletic	30	15	4	11	38	36	49
Saltdean United	30	13	7	10	42	45	46
Broadbridge Heath	30	13	4	13	55	53	43
Franklands Village	30	10	8	12	52	52	38
Newhaven	30	9	8	13	36	40	35
Midhurst & Easebourne	30	9	6	15	42	45	33
Bosham	30	7	8	15	33	59	29
Little Common Albion	30	7	8	15	34	62	29
Ferring	*30*	*4*	*6*	*20*	*32*	*80*	*18*
Storrington	*30*	*2*	*6*	*22*	*19*	*91*	*12*

Oakwood had 3 points and 2 goals deducted.

Division Two

Newhaven	30	20	4	6	60	30	64
Chichester City	30	18	8	4	56	24	62
Horsham YMCA	30	17	7	6	45	23	58
Redhill	30	15	8	7	53	38	53
Portfield	30	14	7	9	60	38	49
Worthing United	30	14	6	10	53	42	48
Lancing	30	14	6	10	39	33	48
Broadbridge Heath	30	14	4	12	57	47	46
Bosham	30	12	6	12	50	53	42
Stamco	30	11	5	14	42	37	38
Little Common Albion	30	10	7	13	39	53	37
Midhurst & Easebourne	30	8	7	15	40	58	31
Crowborough Athletic	30	5	10	15	35	61	25
Saltdean United	30	5	9	16	31	60	24
Sidley United	30	5	8	17	42	70	23
Franklands Village	*30*	*4*	*6*	*20*	*22*	*57*	*18*

Division Three

Worthing United	26	20	4	2	82	29	64
Sidley United	26	15	3	8	62	36	48
Mile Oak	26	13	8	5	69	49	47
Hassocks	26	12	8	6	43	26	44
East Grinstead	26	11	7	8	33	31	40
Hurstpierpoint	26	11	6	9	44	39	39
Rottingdean '89	26	9	7	10	50	45	34
East Preston	26	9	5	12	45	48	32
Forest	26	7	11	8	36	40	32
Leftovers Sports Club	26	7	7	12	29	51	28
Town Mead	26	6	8	12	24	46	26
Buxted	26	5	9	12	41	55	24
Ifield	26	5	7	14	24	63	22
Withdean	26	4	6	16	25	49	18

Town Mead withdrew from the league just before the start of the new season. They played in the Crawley & District League in 1991-92.

Division Three

Ifield	24	13	8	3	46	24	47
East Preston	24	14	4	6	51	36	46
East Grinstead	24	13	6	5	45	23	45
Withdean	24	13	5	6	45	34	44
Mile Oak	24	10	9	5	52	40	39
Hassocks	24	10	4	10	37	35	34
Forest	24	8	7	9	49	48	31
Rottingdean '89	24	8	7	9	36	42	31
Ferring	24	6	7	11	36	41	25
Storrington	24	5	9	10	27	39	24
Leftovers Sports Club	24	6	5	13	18	42	23
Buxted	24	5	6	13	29	42	21
Hurstpierpoint	24	5	3	16	33	58	18

Lindfield Rangers joined from the Mid-Sussex League and Sidlesham joined from the West Sussex League.

1990-91

Division One

Littlehampton Town	34	24	5	5	89	30	77
Peacehaven & Telscombe	34	24	5	5	70	31	77
Langney Sports	34	23	5	6	89	42	74
Pagham	34	20	7	7	85	44	67
Wick	34	18	5	11	61	49	59
Burgess Hill Town	34	17	7	10	66	43	58
Three Bridges	34	15	9	10	65	47	54
Arundel	34	14	12	8	54	46	54
Oakwood	34	14	5	15	53	60	47
Whitehawk	34	12	9	13	39	36	45
Shoreham	34	11	7	16	53	77	40
Ringmer	34	9	10	15	51	66	37
Hailsham Town	34	10	6	18	55	75	36
Haywards Heath Town	34	9	8	17	52	61	35
Bexhill Town	34	8	8	18	46	77	32
Eastbourne Town	34	7	7	20	32	54	28
Seaford Town	*34*	*5*	*8*	*21*	*34*	*79*	*23*
Selsey	*34*	*3*	*3*	*28*	*28*	*105*	*12*

1991-92

Division One

Peacehaven & Telscombe	34	29	4	1	115	24	91
Langney Sports	34	22	10	2	96	36	76
Littlehampton Town	34	23	7	4	95	42	76
Pagham	34	18	9	7	85	53	63
Wick	34	16	11	7	61	50	59
Burgess Hill Town	34	16	7	11	64	46	55
Three Bridges	34	14	11	9	66	51	53
Hailsham Town	34	14	8	12	73	63	50
Ringmer	34	13	7	14	57	60	46
Newhaven	34	13	6	15	63	73	45
Arundel	34	10	10	14	43	49	40
Eastbourne Town	34	12	4	18	33	63	40
Whitehawk	34	9	7	18	36	56	34
Oakwood	34	7	9	18	50	70	30
Chichester City	34	7	5	22	37	96	26
Bexhill Town	34	5	10	19	33	71	25
Shoreham	*34*	*5*	*9*	*20*	*34*	*71*	*24*
Haywards Heath Town	*34*	*2*	*8*	*24*	*29*	*96*	*14*

Division Two

Portfield	32	22	8	2	73	27	74
Midhurst & Easebourne	32	21	3	8	88	53	66
Stamco	32	18	7	7	76	46	61
Redhill	32	18	6	8	70	40	60
Worthing United	32	18	5	9	73	49	59
Horsham YMCA	32	17	7	8	72	44	58
Selsey	32	16	5	11	63	48	53
Seaford Town	32	15	6	11	68	53	51
Crowborough Athletic	32	14	4	14	58	56	46
Sidley United	32	12	3	17	60	80	39
Broadbridge Heath	32	10	5	17	50	63	35
Little Common Albion	32	10	5	17	52	66	35
Saltdean United	32	9	4	19	40	68	31
East Grinstead	32	7	7	18	43	69	28
Lancing	32	7	6	19	46	58	27
Bosham	32	7	5	20	41	106	26
East Preston	32	4	8	20	39	86	20

Eastbourne United and Southwick joined from the Isthmian League.

Division Two

Crowborough Athletic	36	26	6	4	98	34	84
Stamco	36	26	4	6	94	36	82
East Grinstead	36	21	10	5	78	40	73
Lancing	36	18	10	8	73	37	64
Worthing United	36	19	6	11	70	60	63
Horsham YMCA	36	18	8	10	71	46	62
Shoreham	36	16	11	9	74	56	59
Hassocks	36	16	7	13	61	49	55
Mile Oak	36	14	10	12	69	65	52
Southwick	36	14	10	12	59	56	52
Selsey	36	12	3	21	55	65	39
Redhill	36	10	9	17	55	71	39
Little Common Albion	36	10	8	18	42	77	38
Sidley United	36	9	8	19	57	80	35
Broadbridge Heath	36	9	8	19	43	84	35
Eastbourne United	36	9	6	21	48	76	33
Saltdean United	36	9	6	21	44	76	33
Seaford Town	36	8	5	23	38	79	29
Haywards Heath Town	36	7	7	22	49	91	28

Steyning Town joined from the Combined Counties League.

Division Three

Hassocks	26	22	1	3	72	14	67
Mile Oak	26	17	6	3	61	25	57
Sidlesham	26	13	8	5	48	36	47
Ifield	26	13	6	7	49	32	45
Withdean	26	12	6	8	50	40	42
Hurstpierpoint	26	10	6	10	45	48	36
Lindfield Rangers	26	10	4	12	48	50	34
Ferring	26	10	4	12	44	53	34
Storrington	26	9	6	11	36	40	33
Franklands Village	26	7	7	12	33	42	28
Buxted	26	7	5	14	43	64	26
Forest	26	5	7	14	31	45	22
Rottingdean '89	26	5	5	16	33	70	20
Leftovers Sports Club	26	3	7	16	19	53	16

Leftovers Sports Club left to join the Mid-Sussex League and Rottingdean left to join the Brighton, Hove & District League. Shinewater Association joined from the East Sussex League and St. Francis Hospital joined from the Mid-Sussex League.

Division Three

Withdean	26	18	5	3	69	21	59
Storrington	26	16	4	6	62	27	52
Bosham	26	15	4	7	52	51	49
Sidlesham	26	12	7	7	51	49	43
Forest	26	11	8	7	51	40	41
Hurstpierpoint	26	9	10	7	45	42	37
Ifield	26	10	7	9	44	43	37
St. Francis Hospital	26	9	8	9	42	40	35
Lindfield Rangers	26	9	6	11	38	43	33
Franklands Village	26	7	6	13	22	45	27
Shinewater Association	26	6	7	13	39	49	25
East Preston	26	6	7	13	34	49	25
Buxted	26	6	6	14	45	66	24
Ferring	26	3	5	18	27	56	14

Ferring moved to the West Sussex League. Edwards Sports joined from the Crawley & District League, Lingfield joined from the Mid-Sussex League and Sunallon joined from the West Sussex League.

1992-93

Division One

Peacehaven & Telscombe	34	27	6	1	89	23	87
Pagham	34	25	5	4	103	32	80
Wick	34	25	3	6	81	35	78
Langney Sports	34	20	5	9	77	42	65
Whitehawk	34	18	9	7	55	32	63
Newhaven	34	16	5	13	63	51	53
Littlehampton Town	34	15	7	12	64	58	52
Oakwood	34	14	9	11	55	52	51
Three Bridges	34	14	6	14	50	50	48
Hailsham Town	34	13	6	15	64	53	45
Bexhill Town	34	10	6	18	43	61	36
Arundel	34	10	6	18	42	75	36
Portfield	34	8	10	16	39	60	34
Burgess Hill Town	34	7	8	19	39	59	29
Ringmer	34	8	5	21	44	73	29
Chichester City	34	8	5	21	41	85	29
Eastbourne Town	34	8	4	22	35	78	28
Midhurst & Easebourne	34	5	5	24	26	91	20

1993-94

Division One

Wick	38	31	4	3	111	30	97
Whitehawk	38	25	6	7	74	43	81
Langney Sports	38	22	7	9	84	59	73
Peacehaven & Telscombe	38	16	15	7	71	37	63
Pagham	38	18	9	11	77	51	63
Hailsham Town	38	18	8	12	72	61	62
Burgess Hill Town	38	17	9	12	75	55	60
Newhaven	38	17	9	12	79	67	60
Stamco	38	16	7	15	77	59	55
Arundel	38	15	9	14	66	57	54
Oakwood	38	14	7	17	56	64	49
Three Bridges	38	12	9	17	68	84	45
Littlehampton Town	38	11	11	16	58	62	44
Portfield	38	12	7	19	60	90	43
East Grinstead	38	10	13	15	39	69	43
Crowborough Athletic	38	10	7	21	62	88	37
Eastbourne Town	38	10	7	21	41	73	37
Ringmer	38	11	3	24	50	93	36
Bexhill Town	38	9	6	23	53	82	33
Chichester City	38	5	9	24	47	96	24

Division Two

	P	W	D	L	F	A	Pts
Shoreham	34	25	4	5	68	28	79
Southwick	34	22	8	4	74	26	74
Hassocks	34	20	6	8	78	38	66
Redhill	34	20	5	9	89	51	65
Lancing	34	18	9	7	63	37	63
Horsham YMCA	34	17	7	10	65	42	58
Selsey	34	15	9	10	66	51	54
Mile Oak	34	14	6	14	70	63	48
Sidley United	34	14	6	14	72	77	48
Worthing United	34	13	7	14	55	59	46
Eastbourne United	34	12	8	14	58	64	44
Saltdean United	34	13	5	16	55	67	44
Withdean	34	11	5	18	50	72	38
Steyning Town	34	8	5	21	47	84	29
Broadbridge Heath	34	7	7	20	45	70	28
Storrington	34	6	8	20	45	72	26
Midhurst & Easebourne	34	8	2	24	40	94	26
Little Common Albion	34	6	7	21	29	74	25

Division Two

	P	W	D	L	F	A	Pts
Mile Oak	34	23	5	6	77	38	74
Hassocks	34	21	9	4	89	35	72
Horsham YMCA	34	21	7	6	73	31	70
Selsey	34	21	6	7	62	38	69
Redhill	34	18	3	13	70	45	57
Saltdean United	34	15	10	9	72	47	55
Bosham	34	15	7	12	71	57	52
Broadbridge Heath	34	14	9	11	52	54	51
Lancing	34	13	9	12	61	46	48
Sidley United	34	12	9	13	60	57	45
Withdean	34	13	5	16	57	66	44
Steyning Town	34	11	9	14	62	63	42
Worthing United	34	11	9	14	42	60	42
Bexhill Town	34	7	10	17	38	59	31
Chichester City	34	9	4	21	47	86	31
Eastbourne United	34	7	8	19	40	74	29
Storrington	34	6	5	23	31	79	23
Lingfield	34	5	4	25	42	111	19

Division Three

	P	W	D	L	F	A	Pts
Bosham	30	19	5	6	69	33	62
Lingfield	30	18	5	7	62	43	59
East Preston	30	14	6	10	60	46	48
Ifield	30	13	8	9	68	48	47
Sunallon	30	12	8	10	58	48	44
Seaford Town	30	13	4	13	36	37	43
Hurstpierpoint	30	12	6	12	55	51	42
Forest	30	12	6	12	51	62	42
St. Francis Hospital	30	10	7	13	40	44	37
Buxted	30	10	6	14	51	67	36
Sidlesham	30	9	9	12	49	66	36
Lindfield Rangers	30	9	8	13	45	43	35
Haywards Heath Town	30	10	5	15	39	54	35
Edwards Sports	30	7	13	10	46	60	34
Shinewater Association	30	9	6	15	39	53	33
Franklands Village	30	7	10	13	40	53	31

Division Three

	P	W	D	L	F	A	Pts
Midhurst & Easebourne	30	22	1	7	84	37	67
East Preston	30	18	5	7	61	28	59
Franklands Village	30	15	10	5	60	39	55
Lindfield Rangers	30	16	6	8	72	55	54
Seaford Town	30	16	3	11	56	54	51
Haywards Heath Town	30	14	3	13	44	57	45
Sidlesham	30	11	11	8	57	46	44
Forest	30	12	5	13	46	45	41
Hurstpierpoint	30	11	8	11	51	51	41
Sunallon	30	11	8	11	40	47	41
Shinewater Association	30	12	2	16	44	59	38
Ifield	30	10	4	16	57	71	34
St. Francis Hospital	30	9	4	17	54	66	31
Buxted	30	8	6	16	36	56	30
Little Common Albion	30	7	5	18	39	59	26
Edwards Sports	30	4	7	19	38	69	19

Sunallon changed their name to Sun Alliance.
Edwards Sports and Little Common Albion both left the league. Crawley Down Village joined from the Mid-Sussex League and Thomson Athletic also joined.

1994-95

Division One

	P	W	D	L	F	A	Pts
Peacehaven & Telscombe	38	29	2	7	134	38	89
Stamco	38	25	9	4	109	39	84
Wick	38	26	6	6	80	45	84
Shoreham	38	24	8	6	92	42	80
Hailsham Town	38	20	11	7	78	48	71
Ringmer	38	21	7	10	71	37	70
Pagham	38	21	4	13	84	62	67
Burgess Hill Town	38	17	7	14	60	48	58
Portfield	38	14	10	14	62	63	52
Whitehawk	38	14	9	15	51	54	51
Langney Sports	38	13	11	14	61	58	50
Three Bridges	38	12	9	17	54	70	45
Eastbourne Town	38	10	10	18	50	79	40
Crowborough Athletic	38	11	7	20	59	94	40
Oakwood	38	10	10	18	56	93	40
Southwick	38	11	6	21	56	72	39
Arundel	38	8	10	20	45	67	34
Newhaven	38	7	6	25	42	103	27
Littlehampton Town	38	5	11	22	47	102	26
East Grinstead	38	2	7	29	37	114	13

1995-96

Division One

	P	W	D	L	F	A	Pts
Peacehaven & Telscombe	38	32	5	1	133	23	101
Stamco	38	29	3	6	130	38	90
Shoreham	38	25	8	5	91	37	83
Wick	38	23	6	9	95	52	75
Hailsham Town	38	21	10	7	84	48	73
Pagham	38	20	3	15	59	59	63
Arundel	38	19	4	15	80	61	61
Hassocks	38	18	7	13	71	62	61
Langney Sports	38	17	9	12	70	52	60
Ringmer	38	16	6	16	70	59	54
Burgess Hill Town	38	14	10	14	66	66	52
Horsham YMCA	38	15	7	16	56	75	52
Portfield	38	15	5	18	65	81	50
Eastbourne Town	38	12	4	22	51	89	40
Southwick	38	10	9	19	38	75	39
Whitehawk	38	10	6	22	49	71	36
Mile Oak	38	9	6	23	48	93	33
Three Bridges	38	6	6	26	46	101	24
Oakwood	38	5	2	31	30	113	17
Crowborough Athletic	38	4	4	30	40	117	16

Stamco changed their name to St. Leonards Stamcroft and were promoted to the Southern League.

Division Two

Saltdean United	34	25	6	3	87	40	81
Selsey	34	24	6	4	113	33	78
Chichester City	34	19	8	7	71	35	65
East Grinstead	34	19	8	7	76	53	65
Redhill	34	15	6	13	67	54	51
Newhaven	34	16	3	15	63	62	51
East Preston	34	13	10	11	63	55	49
Lancing	34	11	10	13	62	70	43
Worthing United	34	10	12	12	67	61	42
Steyning Town	34	11	9	14	61	76	42
Sidley United	34	10	10	14	45	56	40
Bexhill Town	34	11	6	17	65	59	39
Midhurst & Easebourne	34	11	6	17	55	69	39
Withdean	34	11	6	17	57	81	39
Littlehampton Town	34	8	14	12	48	58	38
Broadbridge Heath	34	10	7	17	55	82	37
Bosham	34	10	4	20	65	103	34
Eastbourne United	34	3	7	24	33	106	16

Division Two

Littlehampton Town	34	24	4	6	95	31	76
Chichester City	34	22	3	9	69	35	69
Redhill	34	20	7	7	88	42	67
Sidley United	34	18	10	6	80	38	64
Eastbourne United	34	18	9	7	75	43	63
East Preston	34	18	5	11	79	48	59
Withdean	34	17	8	9	70	46	59
Worthing United	34	16	10	8	83	51	58
East Grinstead	34	16	2	16	49	56	50
Crawley Down Village	34	14	7	13	63	63	49
Bexhill Town	34	14	5	15	65	72	47
Newhaven	34	13	7	14	67	62	46
Midhurst & Easebourne	34	10	6	18	57	91	36
Crowborough Athletic	34	10	5	19	46	81	35
Lancing	34	8	6	20	45	73	30
Broadbridge Heath	34	8	3	23	46	98	27
Bosham	*34*	*6*	*2*	*26*	*46*	*107*	*20*
Steyning Town	*34*	*3*	*3*	*28*	*32*	*118*	*12*

East Grinstead changed their name to East Grinstead Town.

Division Three

Ifield	30	22	6	2	77	37	72
Crawley Down Village	*30*	*22*	*3*	*5*	*83*	*31*	*69*
Shinewater Association	30	21	5	4	89	35	68
Sidlesham	30	18	6	6	73	34	60
Franklands Village	30	17	8	5	60	37	59
Lindfield Rangers	30	15	3	12	64	59	48
Forest	30	11	10	9	43	42	43
Hurstpierpoint	30	12	5	13	48	55	41
Haywards Heath Town	30	9	8	13	37	50	35
Thomson Athletic	30	9	6	15	44	53	33
Buxted	30	9	5	16	38	57	32
Storrington	30	8	4	18	36	54	28
Seaford Town	30	7	5	18	50	75	26
St. Francis Hospital	30	8	1	21	37	74	25
Sun Alliance	30	5	6	19	35	68	21
Lingfield	30	5	3	22	30	83	18

Lindfield Rangers moved to the Mid-Sussex League.
Ansty Rangers and Uckfield Town both joined the league.

Division Three

Sidlesham	*30*	*23*	*5*	*2*	*91*	*24*	*74*
Shinewater Association	*30*	*22*	*6*	*2*	*77*	*24*	*72*
Franklands Village	30	17	6	7	69	43	57
Ansty Rangers	30	12	11	7	55	47	47
Hurstpierpoint	30	14	5	11	57	51	47
Lingfield	30	13	7	10	57	37	46
Sun Alliance	30	13	4	13	55	66	43
Buxted	30	12	6	12	42	41	42
Storrington	30	11	7	12	47	57	40
St. Francis Hospital	30	10	7	13	50	59	37
Uckfield Town	30	11	4	15	55	65	37
Thomson Athletic	30	9	7	14	46	58	34
Ifield	30	9	4	17	44	64	31
Forest	30	6	8	16	31	54	26
Haywards Heath Town	30	7	5	18	34	65	26
Seaford Town	30	1	8	21	25	80	11

Sun Alliance changed their name to Royal & Sun Alliance. Seaford Town moved to the East Sussex League and Thomson Athletic also left. Oving Social Club joined from the West Sussex League and Westfield joined from the East Sussex League.

1996-97

Division One

Burgess Hill Town	38	28	4	6	105	46	88
Wick	38	23	7	8	102	44	76
Peacehaven & Telscombe	38	22	8	8	75	41	74
Saltdean United	38	20	6	12	66	42	66
Ringmer	38	19	5	14	62	53	62
Langney Sports	38	16	10	12	72	56	58
Eastbourne Town	38	17	6	15	59	51	57
Horsham YMCA	38	14	9	15	58	53	51
Hassocks	38	14	8	16	45	53	50
Pagham	38	14	7	17	59	67	49
Shoreham	38	14	6	18	62	64	48
Arundel	38	12	11	15	66	78	47
Hailsham Town	38	11	13	14	66	67	46
Portfield	38	13	6	19	61	81	45
Selsey	38	13	6	19	49	70	45
Mile Oak	38	12	9	17	47	74	45
Whitehawk	38	14	3	21	46	80	45
Three Bridges	*38*	*12*	*8*	*18*	*53*	*69*	*44*
Oakwood	*38*	*11*	*9*	*18*	*48*	*69*	*42*
Southwick	*38*	*7*	*7*	*24*	*44*	*87*	*28*

1997-98

Division One

Burgess Hill Town	38	29	5	4	105	34	92
Littlehampton Town	38	27	6	5	102	45	87
Wick	38	23	7	8	81	39	76
Langney Sports	38	23	5	10	77	46	74
Redhill	38	21	5	12	85	38	68
Saltdean United	38	20	6	12	76	67	66
Ringmer	38	16	10	12	67	59	58
Selsey	38	14	12	12	60	51	54
Pagham	38	14	12	12	41	42	54
Shoreham	38	16	6	16	55	58	54
Whitehawk	38	12	12	14	50	54	48
Hassocks	38	11	11	16	53	62	44
Horsham YMCA	38	13	5	20	72	83	44
Eastbourne Town	38	12	7	19	54	73	43
Portfield	38	11	8	19	58	85	41
Chichester City	38	10	9	19	62	76	39
Hailsham Town	38	12	1	25	60	96	37
Mile Oak	*38*	*8*	*10*	*20*	*45*	*71*	*34*
Peacehaven & Telscombe	*38*	*7*	*8*	*23*	*40*	*88*	*29*
Arundel	*38*	*6*	*5*	*27*	*44*	*120*	*23*

Division Two

East Preston	34	25	5	4	113	42	80
Eastbourne United	34	21	6	7	82	36	69
Broadbridge Heath	34	20	3	11	72	46	63
Sidley United	34	18	9	7	68	42	63
Sidlesham	34	17	9	8	72	49	60
Shinewater Association	34	17	5	12	62	50	56
Three Bridges	34	16	6	12	63	52	54
Southwick	34	16	6	12	70	64	54
Worthing United	34	13	7	14	68	68	46
East Grinstead Town	34	13	6	15	51	51	45
Crawley Down Village	34	12	8	14	56	68	44
Crowborough Athletic	34	12	6	16	53	65	42
Lancing	34	12	4	18	57	84	40
Oakwood	34	10	9	15	70	60	39
Withdean	34	9	8	17	52	75	35
Newhaven	34	7	9	18	40	80	30
Midhurst & Easebourne	*34*	*8*	*4*	*22*	*47*	*115*	*28*
Bexhill Town	*34*	*4*	*2*	*28*	*42*	*91*	*14*

Division Three

Lingfield	30	19	8	3	70	24	65
Storrington	30	19	7	4	70	32	64
Oving Social Club	30	18	7	5	75	41	61
Westfield	30	14	8	8	75	55	50
St. Francis Hospital	30	14	6	10	59	52	48
Uckfield Town	30	13	7	10	54	35	46
Franklands Village	30	12	8	10	59	51	44
Hurstpierpoint	30	11	11	8	53	50	44
Ifield	30	11	9	10	58	49	42
Ansty Rangers	30	12	6	12	61	60	42
Buxted	30	11	4	15	39	54	37
Royal & Sun Alliance	30	8	7	15	54	72	31
Steyning Town	30	9	4	17	36	58	31
Haywards Heath Town	30	5	8	17	36	64	23
Forest	30	4	10	16	25	59	22
Bosham	30	2	6	22	27	95	12

Bosham moved to the West Sussex League and Wealden joined from the Mid-Sussex League.

1998-99

Division One

Burgess Hill Town	38	28	5	5	106	24	89
Saltdean United	38	26	8	4	100	35	86
Horsham YMCA	38	24	7	7	97	50	79
Langney Sports	38	20	6	12	69	43	66
Shoreham	38	19	8	11	80	57	65
Wick	38	18	7	13	65	49	61
East Preston	38	18	6	14	69	57	60
Eastbourne United	38	17	8	13	59	51	59
Pagham	38	16	11	11	42	39	59
Eastbourne Town	38	14	12	12	61	62	54
Redhill	38	14	11	13	79	60	53
Portfield	38	12	13	13	62	66	49
Hassocks	38	13	7	18	51	51	46
Whitehawk	38	11	10	17	50	61	43
Chichester City	38	10	11	17	44	66	41
Littlehampton Town	38	10	7	21	38	87	37
Ringmer	38	8	11	19	35	64	35
Selsey	38	7	8	23	42	93	29
Hailsham Town	*38*	*7*	*4*	*27*	*40*	*101*	*25*
Broadbridge Heath	*38*	*4*	*8*	*26*	*32*	*105*	*20*

Division Two

Sidley United	34	26	4	4	72	23	82
Three Bridges	34	23	4	7	74	35	73
Crawley Down Village	34	22	7	5	66	35	73
Southwick	34	18	9	7	84	34	63
Mile Oak	34	18	8	8	63	49	62
Storrington	34	18	6	10	54	30	60
Sidlesham	34	17	6	11	70	38	57
Arundel	34	16	9	9	57	43	57
Lancing	34	10	11	13	50	55	41
Lingfield	34	10	9	15	54	56	39
Shinewater Association	34	10	9	15	47	58	39
Peacehaven & Telscombe	34	8	12	14	50	67	36
East Grinstead Town	34	10	5	19	50	78	35
Worthing United	34	8	9	17	48	73	33
Oakwood	34	10	3	21	37	72	33
Withdean	34	5	12	17	43	67	27
Crowborough Athletic	*34*	*7*	*6*	*21*	*45*	*80*	*27*
Newhaven	*34*	*2*	*7*	*25*	*26*	*97*	*13*

Division Three

Oving Social Club	30	25	2	3	72	20	74
Westfield	30	22	4	4	75	26	70
St. Francis Hospital	30	21	4	5	59	26	67
Wealden	30	14	9	7	46	35	51
Uckfield Town	30	15	3	12	60	43	48
Franklands Village	30	11	9	10	47	38	42
Ifield	30	12	4	14	61	78	40
Steyning Town	30	11	4	15	49	54	37
Hurstpierpoint	30	10	4	16	43	51	37
Bexhill Town	30	11	4	15	43	66	37
Ansty Rangers	30	9	9	12	52	46	36
Forest	30	10	6	14	46	57	36
Royal & Sun Alliance	30	7	8	15	52	81	29
Haywards Heath Town	30	6	8	16	35	53	26
Buxted	30	4	10	16	32	60	22
Midhurst & Easebourne	30	6	4	20	45	83	22

Hurstpierpoint had 3 additional points awarded.
Oving Social Club had 3 points deducted.
St. Francis Hospital changed their name to St. Francis and Oving Social Club changed their name to Oving. Midhurst & Easebourne moved to the West Sussex League and Buxted also left the league. Bosham joined from the West Sussex League and Seaford Town joined from East Sussex League.

1999-2000

Division One

Langney Sports	38	31	6	1	101	25	99
Burgess Hill Town	38	26	7	5	78	37	85
Saltdean United	38	24	7	7	97	45	79
East Preston	38	21	5	12	83	52	68
Horsham YMCA	38	18	10	10	78	53	64
Sidley United	38	17	10	11	63	54	61
Hassocks	38	18	5	15	56	45	59
Littlehampton Town	38	17	6	15	53	55	57
Eastbourne Town	38	14	14	10	73	49	56
Selsey	38	16	7	15	80	67	55
Whitehawk	38	16	7	15	58	59	55
Redhill	38	12	12	14	63	58	48
Portfield	38	14	3	21	64	105	45
Three Bridges	38	11	9	18	53	76	42
Eastbourne United	38	11	8	19	62	80	41
Pagham	38	10	9	19	46	68	39
Chichester City	38	9	7	22	64	77	34
Wick	38	9	4	25	49	102	31
Ringmer	38	7	5	26	47	95	26
Shoreham	*38*	*7*	*3*	*28*	*43*	*109*	*24*

Chichester City and Portfield merged to form Chichester City United, using Portfield's ground in Church Road. Chichester City's Oaklands Park ground was to be redeveloped using money from the sale of the Church Road ground for housing, when the club would move in to Oaklands Park. Langney Sports were promoted to the Southern League.

Division Two

Sidlesham	34	25	6	3	85	29	81
Arundel	34	23	5	6	89	37	74
Lancing	34	17	10	7	64	43	63
Crawley Down Village	34	18	8	8	54	33	62
Oving	34	15	6	13	59	43	51
East Grinstead Town	34	13	8	13	71	57	47
Hailsham Town	34	12	11	11	59	48	47
Southwick	34	13	8	13	75	76	47
Westfield	34	13	8	13	45	47	47
Storrington	34	12	8	14	52	57	44
Mile Oak	34	12	8	14	63	61	43
Broadbridge Heath	34	11	9	14	62	67	42
Oakwood	34	11	7	16	52	77	40
Peacehaven & Telscombe	34	9	10	15	52	70	37
Worthing United	34	10	7	17	46	80	37
Withdean	34	8	6	20	40	64	30
Shinewater Association	34	8	6	20	40	77	30
Lingfield	34	8	5	21	42	84	29

Lancing had an additional 2 points awarded.
Mile Oak had 1 point deducted.
Withdean moved to the Combined Counties League but did not play in it until 2001-02.

Division Three

Bosham	30	24	3	3	109	36	75
Wealden	30	22	2	6	78	38	68
Ansty Rangers	30	21	3	6	80	33	66
Crowborough Athletic	30	17	7	6	65	44	58
Haywards Heath Town	30	17	6	7	74	38	57
Uckfield Town	30	16	3	11	55	48	51
Bexhill Town	30	15	4	11	62	60	49
Seaford Town	30	14	3	13	65	60	45
Forest	30	13	6	11	42	48	45
St. Francis	30	10	6	14	42	50	36
Franklands Village	30	9	5	16	39	52	32
Steyning Town	30	9	3	18	55	76	30
Ifield	30	5	6	19	43	69	21
Hurstpierpoint	30	5	5	20	44	81	20
Newhaven	30	5	2	23	34	104	17
Royal & Sun Alliance	30	4	4	22	33	83	16

Rye United joined from the Kent County League and TSC joined from the Crawley & District League.

Division Two

Southwick	34	23	3	8	76	32	72
Peacehaven & Telscombe	34	22	5	7	66	36	71
Hailsham Town	34	20	6	8	81	43	66
East Grinstead Town	34	19	6	9	58	37	63
Broadbridge Heath	34	18	7	9	80	43	61
Worthing United	34	18	6	10	77	46	60
Oving	34	16	6	12	64	50	54
Westfield	34	13	9	12	49	52	48
Oakwood	34	12	10	12	55	50	46
Bosham	34	13	6	15	48	73	45
Wealden	34	12	8	14	61	59	44
Storrington	34	12	5	17	54	75	41
Shoreham	34	12	4	18	67	84	40
Shinewater Association	34	12	4	18	57	78	40
Mile Oak	34	11	6	17	66	69	39
Crawley Down Village	34	10	7	17	50	68	37
Crowborough Athletic	*34*	*6*	*7*	*21*	*49*	*79*	*25*
Lingfield	*34*	*3*	*3*	*28*	*26*	*110*	*12*

Division Three

Rye United	28	21	3	4	89	38	66
Seaford Town	28	20	2	6	70	33	62
Haywards Heath Town	28	19	5	4	62	30	62
Steyning Town	28	15	5	8	51	43	50
Franklands Village	28	12	7	9	62	38	43
Ifield	28	12	5	11	58	57	41
TSC	28	10	8	10	58	53	38
St. Francis	28	9	9	10	49	53	36
Uckfield Town	28	10	2	16	45	60	35
Ansty Rangers	28	10	4	14	51	63	34
Bexhill Town	28	8	5	15	37	51	29
Forest	28	6	10	12	39	45	28
Hurstpierpoint	28	7	6	15	37	64	24
Newhaven	28	7	3	18	39	69	24
Royal & Sun Alliance	28	4	6	18	26	76	18

Uckfield Town had an additional 3 points awarded.
Hurstpierpoint had 3 points deducted.
Rye United merged with Iden of the Kent County League – Division One (East) to form Rye & Iden United. The first team continued to play in the Sussex County League, playing at the Sydney Allnut Pavilion, The Salts in Fishmarket Road in Rye while the Reserves took over Iden's place in the Kent County League, playing at Iden's ground on the Iden Playing Fields. Royal & Sun Alliance moved to the West Sussex League. Upper Beeding joined from the West Sussex League and Pease Pottage Village joined from the Mid-Sussex League.

2000-01

Division One

Sidley United	38	25	8	5	65	31	83
Burgess Hill Town	38	23	9	6	77	46	78
Wick	38	19	10	9	78	51	67
Selsey	38	20	5	13	68	48	65
Horsham YMCA	38	19	6	13	74	54	63
Pagham	38	17	11	10	78	56	62
Chichester City United	38	17	6	15	82	67	57
Three Bridges	38	16	9	13	61	59	57
Sidlesham	38	17	6	15	64	64	57
Ringmer	38	17	5	16	55	67	56
Eastbourne United	38	14	10	14	60	53	52
Hassocks	38	15	5	18	57	58	50
Arundel	38	14	8	16	52	68	50
Redhill	38	13	8	17	62	66	47
Littlehampton Town	38	11	10	17	57	61	43
Saltdean United	38	11	8	19	54	73	41
Whitehawk	38	9	11	18	53	73	38
Lancing	*38*	*9*	*10*	*19*	*58*	*77*	*37*
Eastbourne Town	*38*	*9*	*8*	*21*	*47*	*66*	*35*
East Preston	*38*	*7*	*3*	*28*	*41*	*105*	*24*

2001-02

Division One

Burgess Hill Town	38	28	6	4	100	33	90
Ringmer	38	23	5	10	86	46	74
Chichester City United	38	21	4	13	72	66	67
Selsey	38	19	9	10	69	54	66
Sidley United	38	18	11	9	70	36	65
Hailsham Town	38	20	2	16	62	55	62
Three Bridges	38	18	7	13	82	61	61
Pagham	38	18	8	13	80	67	59
Arundel	38	16	6	16	51	64	57
Horsham YMCA	38	16	6	16	74	58	54
Hassocks	38	15	8	15	57	65	53
Peacehaven & Telscombe	38	15	7	16	58	63	52
Whitehawk	38	14	9	15	69	55	51
Wick	38	15	3	20	56	64	48
Redhill	38	12	5	21	65	83	41
Littlehampton Town	38	11	7	20	64	84	40
Sidlesham	38	12	7	19	56	77	40
Southwick	38	10	9	19	44	76	39
Eastbourne United	*38*	*9*	*10*	*19*	*48*	*67*	*37*
Saltdean United	*38*	*3*	*7*	*28*	*40*	*129*	*16*

Arundel had an additional 3 points awarded.
Sidlesham had 3 points deducted.

Division Two

	P	W	D	L	F	A	Pts
Rye & Iden United	34	26	3	5	102	33	81
Shoreham	34	22	7	5	74	32	73
East Preston	34	20	9	5	89	48	69
Eastbourne Town	34	20	5	9	84	39	65
East Grinstead Town	34	18	10	6	70	40	64
Lancing	34	13	10	11	58	48	49
Broadbridge Heath	34	14	7	13	63	54	49
Westfield	34	14	6	14	65	57	48
Worthing United	34	13	9	12	65	63	48
Seaford Town	34	13	8	13	65	63	47
Crawley Down Village	34	12	9	13	58	50	45
Oakwood	34	12	8	14	45	55	44
Wealden	34	13	4	17	55	68	43
Mile Oak	34	11	4	19	42	70	37
Oving	34	10	5	19	40	78	35
Shinewater Association	34	9	6	19	51	91	33
Storrington	*34*	*4*	*6*	*24*	*31*	*74*	*15*
Bosham	*34*	*2*	*4*	*28*	*31*	*125*	*13*

Bosham had an additional 3 points awarded.
Storrington had 3 points deducted.

Division Three

	P	W	D	L	F	A	Pts
Pease Pottage Village	30	22	6	2	88	35	72
Steyning Town	30	21	4	5	79	21	69
Forest	30	17	7	6	44	27	58
Crowborough Athletic	30	17	3	10	67	48	54
Franklands Village	30	16	5	9	51	31	53
Haywards Heath Town	30	14	5	11	46	47	47
Newhaven	30	12	7	11	53	43	43
Upper Beeding	30	11	9	10	59	48	42
TSC	30	9	8	13	61	58	35
Ifield	30	7	13	10	43	57	33
Uckfield Town	30	8	9	13	36	61	33
Hurstpierpoint	30	8	6	16	49	63	30
Bexhill Town	30	8	4	18	32	65	28
Ansty Rangers	30	7	5	18	48	75	26
St. Francis	30	7	4	19	43	83	25
Lingfield	30	6	5	19	39	76	23

Steyning Town had 2 additional points awarded.
Ifield had 1 point deducted.
Bexhill Town merged with Bexhill AAC (Amateur Athletic Club) of the East Sussex League to form Bexhill United. The merged club continued to play at Bexhill Town's ground, The Polegrove. St. Francis and Ansty Rangers merged to form St. Francis Rangers. The merged club continued to play at St. Francis' ground at St. Francis Hospital, Colwell Lane, Haywards Heath. TSC left and Midhurst & Easebourne joined from the West Sussex League.

2002-03
Division One

	P	W	D	L	F	A	Pts
Burgess Hill Town	38	29	4	5	97	27	91
Whitehawk	38	22	4	12	79	41	70
Horsham YMCA	38	21	6	11	101	51	69
Chichester City United	38	20	9	9	79	51	69
Sidlesham	38	20	6	12	65	62	66
Southwick	38	18	6	14	67	50	60
Ringmer	38	17	9	12	55	56	60
Hassocks	38	16	8	14	67	65	56
Pagham	38	16	7	15	69	52	55
East Preston	38	16	6	16	63	66	54
Selsey	38	14	11	13	59	44	53
Redhill	38	16	5	17	53	62	53
Sidley United	38	15	6	17	55	51	51
Three Bridges	38	14	7	17	88	83	49
Hailsham Town	38	13	8	17	54	60	47
Shoreham	38	13	6	19	54	69	45
Arundel	38	11	11	16	50	65	44
Peacehaven & Telscombe	*38*	*9*	*5*	*24*	*43*	*95*	*32*
Wick	*38*	*7*	*5*	*26*	*51*	*123*	*26*
Littlehampton Town	*38*	*4*	*9*	*25*	*34*	*110*	*21*

Burgess Hill Town were promoted to the Southern League and St. Leonards joined after relegation from the Southern League.

Division Two

	P	W	D	L	F	A	Pts
Rye & Iden United	34	27	4	3	77	35	85
Eastbourne Town	34	25	7	2	97	28	82
East Grinstead Town	34	17	12	5	67	39	63
Oakwood	34	17	5	12	70	55	56
Saltdean United	34	15	6	13	70	55	51
Westfield	34	13	10	11	54	53	49
Wealden	34	14	6	14	64	60	48
Eastbourne United	34	14	6	14	63	60	48
Lancing	34	12	11	11	47	49	47
Steyning Town	34	13	7	14	47	43	46
Shinewater Association	34	13	7	14	46	59	46
Seaford Town	34	11	7	16	51	51	40
Broadbridge Heath	34	11	5	18	54	74	38
Worthing United	34	11	5	18	41	64	38
Crawley Down Village	34	9	10	15	43	51	37
Mile Oak	34	9	6	19	47	74	33
Pease Pottage Village	34	9	4	21	38	79	31
Oving	34	5	4	25	37	84	19

Crawley Down Village changed their name to Crawley Down. Eastbourne United and Shinewater Association merged to form Eastbourne United Association, playing at Eastbourne United's ground, The Oval in Channel View Road. Shinewater Association's ground in Shinewater Lane was later used by Langney Wanderers. Oving disbanded because their clubhouse did not meet new regulations and they were unable to fund the required changes. Without the clubhouse, the club was no longer viable.

Division Three

	P	W	D	L	F	A	Pts
Midhurst & Easebourne	28	20	4	4	80	26	64
Haywards Heath Town	28	17	9	2	76	31	60
Crowborough Athletic	28	18	4	6	87	32	58
Franklands Village	28	14	8	6	48	30	50
Ifield	28	13	5	10	47	50	44
St. Francis Rangers	28	12	7	9	60	52	43
Newhaven	28	12	5	11	58	54	41
Forest	28	10	6	12	56	55	36
Lingfield	28	11	3	14	38	65	36
Bexhill United	28	10	5	13	53	56	35
Hurstpierpoint	28	8	8	12	37	44	32
Storrington	28	9	4	15	53	59	31
Upper Beeding	28	5	8	15	31	61	23
Bosham	28	6	3	19	30	102	21
Uckfield Town	28	5	1	22	39	76	16

Ifield merged with Edwards Sports of the Crawley & District League to form Ifield Edwards. The merged club played at the Edwards Sports & Social Club, a short distance along Rusper Road from Ifield's home on the Rusper Road Playing Field that was not able to be enclosed as it was on common land. Wadhurst United joined from the East Sussex League.

2003-04   Division One

	P	W	D	L	F	A	Pts
Chichester City United	36	23	8	5	87	40	77
Rye & Iden United	36	20	11	5	75	37	71
East Preston	36	22	5	9	72	36	71
Three Bridges	36	20	10	6	63	34	70
Eastbourne Town	36	21	3	12	85	53	66
Arundel	36	18	7	11	77	61	61
Hassocks	36	16	11	9	74	54	59
Whitehawk	36	17	8	11	59	48	59
East Grinstead Town	36	17	4	15	64	60	55
Ringmer	36	14	11	11	54	54	53
Redhill	36	13	7	16	53	50	46
Hailsham Town	36	13	7	16	55	58	46
Horsham YMCA	36	11	9	16	55	62	42
Southwick	36	10	11	15	39	51	41
Sidlesham	36	10	8	18	50	71	38
Sidley United	36	10	8	18	42	63	38
Pagham	36	6	10	20	30	55	28
Selsey	*36*	*5*	*5*	*26*	*35*	*94*	*20*
Shoreham	*36*	*2*	*5*	*29*	*30*	*118*	*11*

St. Leonard's resigned from the league and disbanded during the season because of financial problems and their record was deleted when it stood as follows: 21   7   4   10   32   35   25

Division Two

Littlehampton Town	34	23	7	4	89	29	76
Worthing United	34	21	6	7	74	32	69
Eastbourne United Association	34	18	12	4	78	39	66
Wick	34	17	8	9	57	38	59
Oakwood	34	18	4	12	77	50	58
Midhurst & Easebourne	34	18	4	12	75	50	58
Mile Oak	34	17	6	11	56	49	57
Steyning Town	34	16	9	9	39	35	57
Westfield	34	16	5	13	70	63	53
Broadbridge Heath	34	15	5	14	51	54	50
Crawley Down	34	14	5	15	51	48	47
Peacehaven & Telscombe	34	14	4	16	54	52	46
Saltdean United	34	11	7	16	52	56	40
Wealden	34	12	4	18	43	64	40
Seaford Town	34	10	8	16	55	51	38
Pease Pottage Village	34	5	5	24	43	121	20
Lancing	34	4	4	26	26	89	16
Haywards Heath Town	*34*	*3*	*5*	*26*	*23*	*93*	*14*

Division Two

Crowborough Athletic	34	23	7	4	76	42	76
Wick	34	21	5	8	58	31	68
Shoreham	34	20	7	7	80	49	67
St. Francis Rangers	34	20	3	11	61	35	63
Wealden	34	19	3	12	82	47	60
Seaford Town	34	15	9	10	70	59	54
Westfield	34	16	6	12	51	47	54
Oakwood	34	15	4	15	66	63	49
Midhurst & Easebourne	34	14	7	13	57	60	49
Crawley Down	34	15	2	17	41	52	47
Mile Oak	34	13	7	14	57	61	46
Broadbridge Heath	34	14	4	16	55	61	46
Lancing	34	14	2	18	56	71	44
Selsey	34	12	6	16	59	61	42
Saltdean United	34	9	7	18	43	68	34
Steyning Town	34	7	12	15	46	60	33
Peacehaven & Telscombe	*34*	*5*	*4*	*25*	*48*	*93*	*19*
Pease Pottage Village	*34*	*5*	*3*	*26*	*37*	*83*	*18*

Division Three

Crowborough Athletic	26	21	1	4	91	27	64
St. Francis Rangers	26	17	2	7	69	41	53
Ifield Edwards	26	16	4	6	71	39	52
Wadhurst United	26	15	5	6	58	35	50
Storrington	26	14	5	7	55	37	47
Franklands Village	26	12	5	9	50	30	41
Uckfield Town	26	12	2	12	47	53	38
Lingfield	26	10	5	11	46	43	35
Hurstpierpoint	26	9	5	12	42	52	32
Bosham	26	10	2	14	43	55	32
Forest	26	9	2	15	41	56	29
Bexhill United	26	8	4	14	38	54	28
Newhaven	26	6	2	18	40	60	20
Upper Beeding	26	0	2	24	11	120	2

Franklands Village moved to the Mid-Sussex League – Division One (second tier) and Rustington joined from the West Sussex League.

Division Three

Storrington	24	16	6	2	58	21	54
Bexhill United	24	16	3	5	64	33	51
Lingfield	24	13	4	7	55	47	43
Uckfield Town	24	12	3	9	47	47	39
Wadhurst United	24	11	5	8	52	33	38
Ifield Edwards	24	11	3	10	49	43	36
Bosham	24	10	6	8	45	39	36
Rustington	24	9	7	8	40	43	34
Hurstpierpoint	24	9	4	11	39	40	31
Forest	24	7	5	12	25	36	26
Newhaven	24	6	3	15	29	50	21
Haywards Heath Town	24	5	6	13	35	61	21
Upper Beeding	24	1	5	18	31	76	8

Little Common joined from the East Sussex League.

2004-05

Division One

Horsham YMCA	38	28	5	5	87	33	89
Rye & Iden United	38	23	5	10	80	47	74
Whitehawk	38	21	10	7	71	40	73
Littlehampton Town	38	21	2	15	60	53	65
Eastbourne United Association	38	18	8	12	74	61	62
Ringmer	38	16	12	10	55	38	60
Three Bridges	38	15	11	12	71	51	56
Hassocks	38	14	10	14	69	61	54
Arundel	38	15	8	15	69	57	52
Eastbourne Town	38	14	10	14	56	57	52
East Preston	38	13	11	14	70	59	50
Hailsham Town	38	14	8	16	58	76	50
Redhill	38	12	11	15	55	65	47
Worthing United	38	11	11	16	59	61	44
Sidley United	38	12	8	18	63	76	44
Chichester City United	38	9	16	13	63	62	43
Southwick	38	11	9	18	46	63	42
East Grinstead Town	*38*	*11*	*8*	*19*	*48*	*68*	*41*
Pagham	*38*	*8*	*10*	*20*	*45*	*98*	*34*
Sidlesham	*38*	*6*	*3*	*29*	*43*	*116*	*21*

Hassocks had 2 additional points awarded.
Arundel had 1 point deducted.

2005-06

Division One

Horsham YMCA	38	27	7	4	83	31	88
Ringmer	38	24	7	7	68	34	79
Whitehawk	38	20	7	11	66	36	67
Littlehampton Town	38	20	7	11	63	44	67
Eastbourne Town	38	19	8	11	69	44	65
Crowborough Athletic	38	19	8	11	68	45	65
Arundel	38	16	15	7	61	43	63
Chichester City United	38	17	9	12	61	55	60
Hassocks	38	15	12	11	63	48	57
Hailsham Town	38	13	13	12	43	46	52
Sidley United	38	16	4	18	65	80	52
Wick	38	14	9	15	56	49	51
Shoreham	38	15	6	17	58	59	51
Eastbourne United Association	38	12	8	18	48	62	44
Three Bridges	38	10	12	16	46	50	42
East Preston	38	8	15	15	41	60	39
Worthing United	38	9	12	17	41	60	39
Redhill	38	10	4	24	39	78	34
Rye & Iden United	38	4	8	26	38	83	20
Southwick	*38*	*2*	*9*	*27*	*28*	*98*	*15*

Rye & Iden United changed their name to Rye United.
Horsham YMCA were promoted to the Isthmian League.

Division Two

Oakwood	34	25	5	4	87	25	80
Selsey	34	23	6	5	80	28	75
St. Francis Rangers	34	20	8	6	85	42	71
Westfield	34	18	4	12	67	52	58
Crawley Down	34	15	10	9	61	43	55
Wealden	34	16	7	11	64	62	55
East Grinstead Town	34	17	3	14	70	61	54
Mile Oak	34	15	7	12	61	53	49
Seaford Town	34	12	6	16	57	64	42
Sidlesham	34	10	11	13	53	56	41
Broadbridge Heath	34	12	5	17	53	69	41
Lancing	34	11	7	16	42	53	40
Pagham	34	9	12	13	65	63	39
Storrington	34	11	6	17	47	63	39
Steyning Town	34	10	8	16	50	69	38
Saltdean United	34	11	3	20	45	75	36
Midhurst & Easebourne	34	8	7	19	42	70	31
Bexhill United	34	3	5	26	28	109	14

St. Francis Rangers had 3 additional points awarded.
Mile Oak had 3 points deducted.

Division Three

Peacehaven & Telscombe	26	20	2	4	81	31	62
Lingfield	26	19	3	4	73	29	60
Rustington	26	17	4	5	65	31	55
Newhaven	26	15	5	6	61	31	50
Forest	26	13	7	6	51	37	46
Ifield Edwards	26	13	1	12	68	52	40
Hurstpierpoint	26	11	5	10	47	49	38
Haywards Heath Town	26	10	7	9	57	41	37
Little Common	26	10	3	13	43	50	33
Bosham	26	9	5	12	44	58	29
Uckfield Town	26	8	3	15	30	46	27
Pease Pottage Village	26	7	5	14	39	51	26
Wadhurst United	26	3	3	20	33	78	12
Upper Beeding	26	0	1	25	14	122	4

Upper Beeding had 3 additional points awarded.
Bosham had 3 points deducted.
Upper Beeding moved to the West Sussex League and Wadhurst United withdrew, taking their reserves' place in the East Sussex League – Division Two (third tier). Loxwood joined from the West Sussex League and Rottingdean Village joined from the Brighton, Hove & District League.

2006-07

Division One

Eastbourne Town	38	27	6	5	97	42	87
Whitehawk	38	25	11	2	70	17	86
Arundel	38	23	6	9	82	39	75
Crowborough Athletic	38	22	9	7	73	40	75
Hassocks	38	20	8	10	80	45	68
Hailsham Town	38	17	15	6	52	29	66
Eastbourne United Association	38	16	9	13	66	51	57
Selsey	38	14	14	10	46	46	56
Ringmer	38	13	11	14	59	66	52
East Preston	38	16	3	19	47	49	51
Chichester City United	38	14	7	17	59	58	49
Three Bridges	38	11	12	15	59	60	45
Shoreham	38	11	10	17	61	71	43
Sidley United	38	11	9	18	47	76	42
Redhill	38	11	8	19	61	65	41
Wick	38	11	7	20	51	69	39
Oakwood	38	11	6	21	42	79	39
Worthing United	38	7	10	21	55	100	31
Rye United	38	6	9	23	33	73	27
Littlehampton Town	38	5	8	25	30	95	23

Ringmer had 2 additional points awarded.
Wick had 1 point deducted.
Eastbourne Town were promoted to the Isthmian League.

Division Two

Pagham	34	22	4	8	68	35	70
St. Francis Rangers	34	18	4	12	64	46	60
Westfield	34	17	8	9	59	42	59
Wealden	34	18	4	12	76	49	58
Peacehaven & Telscombe	34	17	7	10	60	61	58
Seaford Town	34	16	7	11	54	46	55
Midhurst & Easebourne	34	15	7	12	82	65	52
Steyning Town	34	16	4	14	60	53	52
Mile Oak	34	15	5	14	59	60	50
Lingfield	34	14	3	17	43	49	45
East Grinstead Town	34	12	8	14	48	47	44
Sidlesham	34	11	10	13	56	63	43
Southwick	34	10	11	13	43	56	41
Lancing	34	10	8	16	40	57	38
Storrington	34	11	5	18	43	63	38
Crawley Down	34	10	7	17	49	57	37
Broadbridge Heath	34	8	10	16	34	53	33
Saltdean United	34	7	6	21	41	77	27

St. Francis Rangers had 2 additional points awarded.
Broadbridge Heath had 1 point deducted.

Division Three

Rustington	24	18	3	3	65	21	57
Pease Pottage Village	24	13	5	6	46	31	44
Little Common	24	13	4	7	46	39	43
Rottingdean Village	24	12	5	7	39	34	41
Forest	24	11	4	9	42	41	37
Haywards Heath Town	24	11	3	10	34	30	36
Loxwood	24	10	4	10	37	38	34
Ifield Edwards	24	10	2	12	33	38	32
Newhaven	24	9	5	10	38	45	32
Uckfield Town	24	9	4	11	47	48	31
Bexhill United	24	7	3	14	49	55	24
Hurstpierpoint	24	7	3	14	28	43	24
Bosham	24	2	3	19	29	70	9

Dorking Wanderers joined from the West Sussex League.

2007-08

Division One

Crowborough Athletic	38	30	5	3	99	33	95
Whitehawk	38	21	12	5	61	34	75
Arundel	38	21	10	7	90	49	70
East Preston	38	19	10	9	48	40	67
Wick	38	19	7	12	77	55	64
Three Bridges	38	17	9	12	74	60	60
Hassocks	38	15	13	10	57	46	58
Redhill	38	16	8	14	59	56	56
Pagham	38	15	8	15	60	55	53
Ringmer	38	14	9	15	81	73	51
Eastbourne United Association	38	14	8	16	67	62	50
Shoreham	38	12	14	12	54	50	50
Hailsham Town	38	13	11	14	54	58	50
St. Francis Rangers	38	13	7	18	56	62	45
Selsey	38	10	12	16	67	72	42
Chichester City United	38	11	4	23	66	100	43
Worthing United	38	8	8	22	53	84	35
Oakwood	38	7	12	19	52	85	33
Rye United	38	8	6	24	46	86	30
Sidley United	38	8	5	25	39	100	29

Chichester City United had 2 additional points awarded and Worthing United had 3 additional points awarded.
Arundel had 3 points deducted, St. Francis Rangers had 1 point deducted.
Crowborough Athletic were promoted to the Isthmian League and Horsham YMCA rejoined following relegation from the Isthmian League.

Division Two

East Grinstead Town	34	26	6	2	89	41	84
Lingfield	34	21	6	7	73	40	66
Rustington	34	19	8	7	70	29	65
Peacehaven & Telscombe	34	20	5	9	93	59	65
Mile Oak	34	17	8	9	79	56	59
Crawley Down	34	19	1	14	59	60	58
Westfield	34	18	3	13	71	64	57
Littlehampton Town	34	16	5	13	66	54	53
Wealden	34	14	7	13	69	56	49
Midhurst & Easebourne	34	15	4	15	52	67	49
Steyning Town	34	12	6	16	51	53	42
Lancing	34	10	8	16	64	61	38
Sidlesham	34	11	5	18	61	65	38
Southwick	34	11	5	18	44	62	38
Seaford Town	34	12	1	21	61	79	37
Storrington	34	9	7	18	48	67	34
Broadbridge Heath	*34*	*7*	*5*	*22*	*45*	*75*	*29*
Pease Pottage Village	*34*	*3*	*2*	*29*	*39*	*146*	*11*

Broadbridge Heath had 3 additional points awarded.
Lingfield had 3 points deducted.

Division Three

Loxwood	24	15	4	5	51	26	51
Bexhill United	24	15	6	3	60	35	48
Haywards Heath Town	24	12	7	5	45	26	46
Dorking Wanderers	24	12	7	5	58	47	42
Newhaven	24	10	7	7	52	42	37
Little Common	24	10	7	7	52	49	37
Rottingdean Village	24	9	5	10	36	36	32
Ifield Edwards	24	8	6	10	42	53	30
Saltdean United	24	9	3	12	32	45	30
Bosham	24	7	2	15	35	45	23
Forest	24	6	5	13	26	39	23
Uckfield Town	24	6	3	15	28	37	21
Hurstpierpoint	24	4	4	16	25	62	16

Loxwood had 2 additional points awarded and Haywards Heath Town had 3 additional points awarded.
Bexhill United had 3 points deducted and Dorking Wanderers had 1 point deducted.
Clymping joined from the West Sussex League.

Division Two

Peacehaven & Telscombe	34	25	5	4	104	31	80
Mile Oak	34	24	3	7	92	35	75
Crawley Down	34	19	10	5	77	33	67
Rustington	34	20	4	10	66	39	64
Westfield	34	17	8	9	57	46	59
Rye United	34	16	8	10	66	45	56
* Seaford Town	34	16	5	13	61	56	56
Sidley United	34	12	9	13	49	57	45
Lancing	34	12	6	16	55	65	42
Loxwood	34	11	8	15	44	49	41
Southwick	34	12	5	17	58	71	41
Storrington	34	12	5	17	43	58	41
Steyning Town	34	12	6	16	42	67	39
Littlehampton Town	34	9	10	15	65	82	37
Wealden	34	10	6	18	57	69	36
Midhurst & Easebourne	34	9	6	19	46	74	33
Bexhill United	*34*	*8*	*6*	*20*	*45*	*67*	*30*
Sidlesham	*34*	*3*	*8*	*23*	*27*	*110*	*17*

Seaford Town had 3 additional points awarded.
Steyning Town had 3 points deducted.

Division Three

Clymping	26	19	3	4	70	29	60
Little Common	26	18	3	5	66	37	57
Haywards Heath Town	26	17	4	5	57	20	55
Newhaven	26	15	6	5	64	39	51
Dorking Wanderers	26	15	2	9	70	45	47
Forest	26	11	7	8	40	33	40
Saltdean United	26	10	6	10	32	42	36
Uckfield Town	26	10	4	12	47	48	34
Broadbridge Heath	26	8	3	15	41	57	27
Bosham	26	7	5	14	35	53	26
Rottingdean Village	26	5	10	11	31	48	25
Ifield Edwards	26	6	6	14	39	54	24
Hurstpierpoint	26	4	4	18	34	75	16
Pease Pottage Village	26	4	3	19	30	76	15

TD Shipley joined from the West Sussex League.

2008-09

Division One

Eastbourne United Association	38	23	6	9	79	37	75
Arundel	38	21	10	7	96	53	73
Horsham YMCA	38	23	4	11	72	53	73
Wick	38	21	8	9	77	60	71
Three Bridges	38	20	7	11	75	51	67
Shoreham	38	18	11	9	63	45	65
Chichester City United	38	19	5	14	74	70	62
Redhill	38	16	13	9	70	43	61
Lingfield	38	14	15	9	62	51	57
Ringmer	38	19	5	14	86	60	52
Selsey	38	14	9	15	59	48	51
Pagham	38	13	9	16	51	59	48
St. Francis Rangers	38	13	8	17	64	65	47
Whitehawk	38	13	8	17	62	64	47
Hailsham Town	38	12	7	19	54	92	43
Hassocks	38	10	10	18	49	61	40
East Grinstead Town	38	8	9	21	54	84	33
East Preston	*38*	*9*	*5*	*24*	*53*	*85*	*32*
Oakwood	*38*	*8*	*5*	*25*	*43*	*97*	*29*
Worthing United	*38*	*4*	*10*	*24*	*42*	*107*	*22*

Ringmer had 10 points deducted
Horsham YMCA were promoted to the Isthmian League and Crowborough Athletic joined following relegation from the Isthmian League.
Chichester City United changed their name to Chichester City.

2009-10

Division One

Whitehawk	38	26	7	5	85	36	85
Peacehaven & Telscombe	38	23	9	6	83	42	78
Chichester City	38	21	6	11	87	51	69
Wick	38	19	10	9	80	58	67
Redhill	38	18	11	9	65	49	65
Eastbourne United Association	38	16	9	13	70	63	57
Three Bridges	38	16	7	15	78	56	55
Crawley Down	38	14	12	12	71	76	54
Shoreham	38	15	8	15	63	59	53
Lingfield	38	12	16	10	69	67	52
Selsey	38	13	12	13	70	70	51
Arundel	38	12	13	13	74	71	49
Ringmer	38	12	14	12	68	71	49
Hassocks	38	12	12	14	51	59	48
East Grinstead Town	38	11	7	20	62	74	40
St. Francis Rangers	38	11	7	20	55	76	40
Pagham	38	10	10	18	46	76	40
Crowborough Athletic	38	11	4	23	51	101	37
Hailsham Town	38	9	4	25	50	78	31
Mile Oak	*38*	*6*	*8*	*24*	*36*	*81*	*26*

Ringmer had 1 point deducted.
Whitehawk were promoted to the Isthmian League.

Division Two

Team	P	W	D	L	F	A	Pts
Rye United	34	25	1	8	89	41	76
Worthing United	34	22	8	4	73	26	74
Sidley United	34	22	7	5	80	35	73
Little Common	34	22	5	7	88	49	71
Loxwood	34	18	7	9	74	37	61
Clymping	34	16	8	10	77	50	56
Storrington	34	17	1	16	55	65	52
Wealden	34	15	5	14	56	56	50
Oakwood	34	15	4	15	65	68	46
Seaford Town	34	14	4	16	61	65	46
Lancing	34	14	3	17	61	82	45
Littlehampton Town	34	12	7	15	61	60	43
Rustington	34	11	9	14	53	64	42
East Preston	34	12	5	17	55	69	41
Westfield	34	11	4	19	46	69	37
Southwick	34	5	7	22	48	72	22
Steyning Town	34	4	7	23	36	86	19
Midhurst & Easebourne	34	4	2	28	31	115	14

Oakwood had 3 points deducted.
Wealden changed their name to AFC Uckfield.

Division Two

Team	P	W	D	L	F	A	Pts
AFC Uckfield	34	24	7	3	107	47	79
Lancing	34	24	6	4	103	30	78
Worthing United	34	22	7	5	84	38	73
Bexhill United	34	17	9	8	71	47	60
Seaford Town	34	16	10	8	69	42	58
Loxwood	34	18	4	12	71	51	58
Mile Oak	34	18	4	12	71	52	58
Storrington	34	15	4	15	64	57	49
Rustington	34	14	7	13	51	46	49
Westfield	34	14	7	13	67	70	49
Littlehampton Town	34	12	9	13	71	72	45
Southwick	34	13	6	15	55	59	45
Little Common	34	12	7	15	55	61	43
East Preston	34	9	7	18	57	84	34
Midhurst & Easebourne	34	7	6	21	40	74	27
Steyning Town	34	6	7	21	52	103	25
Oakwood	34	3	7	24	42	100	16
Clymping	34	3	4	27	33	130	13

Division Three

Team	P	W	D	L	F	A	Pts
Bosham	28	20	4	4	64	25	64
Bexhill United	28	19	4	5	69	31	61
Haywards Heath Town	28	19	2	7	79	36	59
Dorking Wanderers	28	15	6	7	78	44	51
Ifield Edwards	28	14	5	9	61	43	47
Uckfield Town	28	13	6	9	48	36	45
TD Shipley	28	14	3	11	57	54	45
Saltdean United	28	13	4	11	39	47	43
Newhaven	28	11	3	14	55	50	36
Rottingdean Village	28	10	4	14	44	56	34
Sidlesham	28	10	3	15	38	54	33
Forest	28	8	2	18	38	74	26
Pease Pottage Village	28	7	2	19	30	74	23
Broadbridge Heath	28	6	3	19	31	63	21
Hurstpierpoint	28	3	5	20	34	78	14

Barnham joined from the West Sussex League and Ferring joined from the Worthing & District League.

Division Three

Team	P	W	D	L	F	A	Pts
Dorking Wanderers	30	24	2	4	93	35	74
Hurstpierpoint	30	18	4	8	61	37	58
Barnham	30	16	7	7	60	39	55
Bosham	30	17	4	9	73	55	55
Saltdean United	30	15	6	9	71	49	51
Broadbridge Heath	30	15	4	11	61	45	49
Newhaven	30	15	1	14	73	64	46
Haywards Heath Town	30	12	6	12	52	56	42
Pease Pottage Village	30	12	5	13	66	62	41
Rottingdean Village	30	11	6	13	41	49	39
TD Shipley	30	9	7	14	58	71	34
Ferring	30	9	6	15	56	67	33
Ifield Edwards	30	8	6	16	48	76	30
Uckfield Town	30	8	5	17	49	76	29
Forest	30	6	8	16	40	68	26
Sidlesham	30	4	5	21	39	92	17

Sidlesham moved to the West Sussex League and Roffey joined from the Mid-Sussex League.

2010-11

Division One

Team	P	W	D	L	F	A	Pts
Crawley Down	38	28	7	3	100	35	91
Rye United	38	23	7	8	76	37	76
Peacehaven & Telscombe	38	22	10	6	74	38	76
Pagham	38	23	2	13	91	53	71
Three Bridges	38	23	1	14	69	49	70
Hassocks	38	19	11	8	64	38	68
East Grinstead Town	38	20	6	12	88	50	66
Redhill	38	16	8	14	77	68	56
Arundel	38	15	9	14	81	68	54
Ringmer	38	16	4	18	67	72	52
Lingfield	38	13	10	15	71	83	49
Crowborough Athletic	38	14	6	18	59	67	48
Sidley United	38	13	9	16	46	59	48
Chichester City	38	14	6	18	57	62	45
Wick	38	13	6	19	54	74	45
Hailsham Town	38	13	5	20	66	71	44
Selsey	38	13	5	20	49	78	44
Shoreham	38	8	7	23	46	89	31
St. Francis Rangers	38	8	5	25	35	81	29
Eastbourne United Association	38	2	4	32	26	124	10

Chichester City had 3 points deducted.
Crawley Down were promoted to the Isthmian League and Horsham YMCA rejoined following relegation from the Isthmian League.

2011-12

Division One

Team	P	W	D	L	F	A	Pts
Three Bridges	38	28	5	5	75	37	89
Lancing	38	26	8	4	88	37	86
Rye United	38	26	6	6	99	44	84
Hassocks	38	22	6	10	89	58	72
Peacehaven & Telscombe	38	21	8	9	83	51	71
Pagham	38	21	8	9	83	54	71
Lingfield	38	20	8	10	90	56	65
AFC Uckfield	38	16	7	15	71	72	55
East Grinstead Town	38	17	4	17	71	77	55
Redhill	38	16	6	16	85	68	54
Sidley United	38	15	5	18	45	60	50
Selsey	38	13	5	20	62	75	44
Crowborough Athletic	38	12	7	19	69	82	43
Worthing United	38	10	12	16	63	91	42
Ringmer	38	11	7	20	50	62	40
Horsham YMCA	38	12	3	23	53	79	39
Arundel	38	10	8	20	59	88	38
Shoreham	38	9	9	20	65	93	36
St. Francis Rangers	38	2	13	23	40	87	19
Chichester City	38	4	3	31	36	105	15

Lingfield had 3 points deducted.
Three Bridges were promoted to the Isthmian League.

Division Two

East Preston	34	29	3	2	124	34	90
Hailsham Town	34	24	6	4	86	34	78
Dorking Wanderers	34	21	6	7	80	48	69
Littlehampton Town	34	15	12	7	67	39	57
Loxwood	34	17	4	13	65	68	55
Eastbourne United Association	34	15	8	11	54	49	53
Bexhill United	34	16	5	13	60	64	53
Southwick	34	12	12	10	44	40	48
Storrington	34	11	8	15	62	59	41
Mile Oak	34	12	4	18	55	65	40
Rustington	34	10	10	14	52	68	40
Westfield	34	9	10	15	58	73	37
Steyning Town	34	9	8	17	54	74	35
Wick	34	9	6	19	40	70	33
Midhurst & Easebourne	34	10	4	20	62	102	33
Little Common	34	8	8	18	53	69	32
Seaford Town	34	9	4	21	47	64	31
Oakwood	34	5	12	17	44	87	27

Midhurst & Easebourne had 1 point deducted.

Division Three

Newhaven	30	22	4	4	94	32	70
Saltdean United	30	21	7	2	88	26	70
Pease Pottage Village	30	22	1	7	94	44	67
Barnham	30	19	3	8	91	44	60
Broadbridge Heath	30	17	5	8	67	43	56
Forest	30	15	6	9	63	50	51
Ferring	30	14	4	12	51	56	46
Rottingdean Village	30	14	3	13	53	71	45
Uckfield Town	30	10	10	10	60	61	40
Ifield Edwards	30	10	5	15	50	60	35
Bosham	30	9	6	15	45	58	33
Hurstpierpoint	30	9	6	15	45	61	33
TD Shipley	30	10	1	19	49	70	31
Clymping	30	5	3	22	31	96	18
Haywards Heath Town	30	3	7	20	29	69	16
Roffey	30	2	5	23	33	102	11

Forest resigned from the league as their landlords only offered a 1-year lease on their ground, the Roffey Sports & Social Club in Spooners Road. Their reserves continued to play in the West Sussex League – Division Three (North), in effect becoming the first team. Bosham moved to the West Sussex League and Pease Pottage Village disbanded. Billingshurst and Sidlesham both joined from the West Sussex League. Ifield Edwards changed their name to Ifield.

2012-13

Division One

Peacehaven & Telscombe	42	28	10	4	114	35	94
Redhill	42	29	6	7	95	42	93
East Preston	42	25	10	7	97	50	85
Rye United	42	24	11	7	117	57	83
Pagham	42	26	5	11	90	52	83
Lingfield	42	23	7	12	102	78	76
Hassocks	42	21	7	14	97	69	70
East Grinstead Town	42	21	6	15	97	65	69
Ringmer	42	20	9	13	76	68	69
Horsham YMCA	42	19	7	16	97	71	64
St. Francis Rangers	42	17	8	17	76	73	59
Hailsham Town	42	17	2	23	77	90	53
Lancing	42	14	10	18	80	75	52
Arundel	42	14	8	20	61	86	50
Crowborough Athletic	42	15	5	22	68	99	50
Sidley United	42	13	7	22	67	87	46
Shoreham	42	14	4	24	69	106	46
Selsey	42	11	12	19	53	76	45
Chichester City	42	12	6	24	63	107	42
Dorking Wanderers	42	10	11	21	62	80	41
AFC Uckfield	42	5	4	33	53	141	19
Worthing United	42	3	7	32	43	147	16

Peacehaven & Telscombe and Redhill were both promoted to the Isthmian League. Sidley United disbanded.

Division Two

Littlehampton Town	34	26	4	4	91	27	82
Newhaven	34	22	4	8	90	52	70
Little Common	34	21	5	8	94	43	68
Eastbourne United Association	34	20	5	9	97	64	65
Westfield	34	17	7	10	67	56	58
Broadbridge Heath	34	17	4	13	82	62	55
Mile Oak	34	15	8	11	65	57	53
Midhurst & Easebourne	34	14	9	11	80	73	51
Loxwood	34	14	7	13	57	60	49
Steyning Town	34	14	6	14	73	61	48
Bexhill United	34	12	10	12	67	71	46
Seaford Town	34	12	8	14	64	64	44
Storrington	34	12	7	15	50	67	43
Southwick	34	9	4	21	58	75	31
Oakwood	34	8	7	19	62	88	31
Wick	34	8	7	19	44	74	31
Rustington	34	7	8	19	53	81	29
Saltdean United	34	2	2	30	37	156	8

Wick merged with Barnham of Division Three to form Wick & Barnham United. The merged club continued at Wick's ground, Crabtree Park, Coomes Way in Wick.

Division Three

Sidlesham	22	17	3	2	71	23	54
Haywards Heath Town	22	16	5	1	59	13	53
Barnham	22	14	3	5	73	30	45
Billingshurst	22	10	5	7	45	37	35
Clymping	22	9	5	8	35	29	32
Uckfield Town	22	9	5	8	41	43	32
Ferring	22	9	7	6	51	45	31
Roffey	22	6	4	12	33	50	22
Hurstpierpoint	22	6	4	12	24	42	22
Ifield	22	4	5	13	34	52	17
Rottingdean Village	22	4	2	16	28	76	14
TD Shipley	22	3	2	17	15	69	11

Ferring had 3 points deducted.
Langney Wanderers joined from the East Sussex League. TD Shipley disbanded.

2013-14

Division One

East Preston	38	30	6	2	92	23	96
East Grinstead Town	38	24	7	7	84	39	79
Littlehampton Town	38	24	5	9	85	41	77
Horsham YMCA	38	22	10	6	110	45	76
Crowborough Athletic	38	21	7	10	69	41	70
Hassocks	38	17	9	12	72	65	60
Pagham	38	16	10	12	66	57	58
Dorking Wanderers	38	16	7	15	68	63	55
Ringmer	38	16	5	17	61	64	53
St. Francis Rangers	38	15	6	17	66	68	51
Chichester City	38	14	9	15	53	65	51
Arundel	38	15	5	18	58	68	50
Newhaven	38	13	10	15	67	63	49
Shoreham	38	12	8	18	65	82	44
Lingfield	38	12	6	20	70	88	42
Hailsham Town	38	13	3	22	63	91	42
Selsey	38	12	5	21	45	76	41
Lancing	38	12	8	18	55	80	38
Rye United	38	6	8	24	38	45	26
Worthing United	38	2	2	34	22	145	8

Lancing had 6 points deducted.
Rye United resigned and disbanded on 21st March 2014 when their record stood as follows: 23 | 6 | 8 | 9 | 38 | 45 | 26
Their 15 outstanding games were all awarded as wins for their opponents.

East Grinstead Town were promoted to the Isthmian League and Crawley Down Gatwick and Eastbourne Town both joined following relegation from the Isthmian League. Lingfield and Crowborough Athletic both moved to the Southern Counties East League.

Division Two

Eastbourne United Association	32	23	5	4	99	34	74
Broadbridge Heath	32	21	9	2	85	21	72
Loxwood	32	22	4	6	98	52	70
Little Common	32	19	4	9	86	61	61
Haywards Heath Town	32	15	11	6	73	55	56
Wick & Barnham United	32	15	7	10	64	47	52
Mile Oak	32	14	10	8	55	44	51
Bexhill United	32	12	9	11	57	43	45
Westfield	32	12	5	15	55	50	38
AFC Uckfield	32	10	8	14	55	62	38
Steyning Town	32	10	8	14	53	68	38
Oakwood	32	11	5	16	57	82	38
Saltdean United	32	10	3	19	53	101	33
Midhurst & Easebourne	32	9	1	22	35	81	28
Storrington	32	7	5	20	50	74	26
Rustington	32	7	3	22	40	76	24
Seaford Town	32	4	5	23	31	95	17

Mile Oak had 1 point deducted.
Westfield had 3 points deducted.
AFC Uckfield merged with Uckfield Town of Division Three to form AFC Uckfield Town. The merged club continued to play at AFC Uckfield's ground, The Oaks in Old Eastbourne Road.

Division Three

Langney Wanderers	20	16	2	2	64	20	50
Ferring	20	12	5	3	44	20	41
Roffey	20	10	3	7	37	30	33
Uckfield Town	20	10	3	7	35	30	33
Sidlesham	20	9	3	8	35	31	30
Ifield	20	9	2	9	45	47	29
Hurstpierpoint	20	9	1	10	29	42	28
Clymping	20	6	4	10	23	33	22
Southwick	20	6	2	12	31	42	20
Rottingdean Village	20	4	3	13	28	49	15
Billingshurst	20	4	2	14	29	56	14

Hurstpierpoint merged with Burgess Hill Albion of the Mid-Sussex League to form Burgess Hill & Hurst Albion. The merged club continued to play at Hurstpierpoint's ground, the Fairfield Recreation Ground, Cuckfield Road, Hurstpierpoint. Bosham joined from the West Sussex League.

2014-15

Division One

Littlehampton Town	38	25	9	4	122	51	84
Dorking Wanderers	38	26	5	7	101	51	83
Pagham	38	24	7	7	77	41	79
Eastbourne Town	38	21	9	8	96	44	72
Horsham YMCA	38	21	5	12	100	57	68
Loxwood	38	18	14	6	82	52	68
Newhaven	38	18	10	10	84	56	64
Lancing	38	15	10	13	68	69	55
Broadbridge Heath	38	15	7	16	63	60	52
Arundel	38	15	10	13	59	59	52
East Preston	38	14	10	14	59	68	52
Eastbourne United Association	38	13	12	13	67	53	51
St. Francis Rangers	38	13	8	17	67	70	47
Chichester City	38	11	12	15	42	61	45
Hassocks	38	11	11	16	68	78	44
Shoreham	38	12	7	19	58	68	43
Hailsham Town	38	11	4	23	82	108	37
Ringmer	*38*	*9*	*7*	*22*	*58*	*120*	*34*
Crawley Down Gatwick	*38*	*3*	*4*	*31*	*34*	*110*	*13*
Selsey	*38*	*2*	*5*	*31*	*42*	*153*	*11*

Arundel had 3 points deducted.
Dorking Wanderers were promoted to the Isthmian League and Horsham joined following relegation from the Isthmian League.

Division Two

Worthing United	28	24	0	4	86	28	72
AFC Uckfield Town	28	17	7	4	58	26	58
Wick & Barnham United	28	17	7	4	62	35	58
Oakwood	28	16	4	8	78	46	52
Mile Oak	28	15	6	7	53	28	51
Bexhill United	28	14	7	7	47	34	49
Little Common	28	14	3	11	54	50	45
Midhurst & Easebourne	28	11	5	12	53	68	38
Haywards Heath Town	28	11	3	14	38	53	36
Steyning Town	28	10	3	15	44	48	33
Rustington	*28*	*9*	*3*	*16*	*47*	*62*	*30*
Westfield	*28*	*7*	*8*	*13*	*48*	*61*	*29*
Saltdean United	28	8	4	16	36	60	28
Storrington	28	4	5	19	41	80	17
Seaford Town	28	0	1	27	16	82	1

Lingfield joined from the Southern Counties East League.

Division Three

Southwick	20	15	2	3	46	16	47
Sidlesham	20	14	4	2	53	17	46
Langney Wanderers	20	14	1	5	63	28	43
Bosham	20	12	2	6	51	24	35
Ifield	20	11	1	8	51	38	31
Billingshurst	20	9	2	9	58	46	29
Rottingdean Village	20	8	2	10	39	37	26
Roffey	20	6	5	9	39	37	23
Burgess Hill & Hurst Albion	20	5	4	11	26	44	19
Ferring	20	2	3	15	24	75	9
Clymping	20	1	0	19	16	104	3

Bosham and Ifield each had 3 points deducted.
Alfold, AFC Roffey Club, Cowfold and Upper Beeding all joined from the West Sussex League while AFC Varndeanians and Montpelier Villa both joined from the Mid-Sussex League. Burgess Hill and Hurst Albion demerged and the two clubs (who had merged just a year earlier), reverted to their former identities. Hurstpierpoint resumed in Division Three while Burgess Hill Albion rejoined the Mid-Sussex League. Ifield changed their name to Ifield Galaxy.

The league changed its name to Southern Combination and renamed its divisions to the Premier Division, Division One and Division Two.

SOUTHERN COMBINATION

2015-16

Premier Division

Horsham	38	31	4	3	131	22	97
Eastbourne Town	38	27	5	6	107	42	86
Newhaven	38	25	3	10	120	39	78
Lancing	38	24	5	9	98	46	77
Chichester City	38	23	5	10	99	46	74
Pagham	38	23	4	11	94	49	73
Horsham YMCA	38	22	5	11	105	62	71
Loxwood	38	22	5	11	95	60	71
Broadbridge Heath	38	19	6	13	75	57	63
Eastbourne United Association	38	19	6	13	81	72	63
Littlehampton Town	38	19	3	16	103	76	60
Arundel	38	16	8	14	88	68	56
Hassocks	38	13	9	16	59	66	47
Worthing United	38	12	6	20	68	83	42
AFC Uckfield Town	38	8	9	21	62	91	33
Wick & Barnham United	38	10	2	26	55	105	32
Shoreham	38	8	5	25	53	94	29
Hailsham Town	38	4	6	28	47	149	18
East Preston	*38*	*3*	*3*	*32*	*35*	*144*	*12*
St. Francis Rangers	*38*	*1*	*3*	*34*	*10*	*214*	*6*

Hassocks had 1 point deducted.
Horsham were promoted to the Isthmian League and Peacehaven & Telscombe joined following relegation from the Isthmian League. Wick & Barnham United changed their name to Wick.

Division One

Haywards Heath Town	32	30	0	2	123	23	90
Crawley Down Gatwick	32	24	2	6	88	50	74
Oakwood	32	19	3	10	89	64	60
Storrington	32	18	4	10	68	45	58
Southwick	32	17	5	10	75	54	56
Mile Oak	32	17	4	11	61	52	55
Little Common	32	16	2	14	75	61	50
Lingfield	32	15	3	14	76	66	48
Langney Wanderers	32	14	5	13	73	55	47
Steyning Town	32	14	3	15	56	63	45
Sidlesham	*32*	*14*	*1*	*17*	*54*	*72*	*43*
Ringmer	32	10	7	15	47	68	37
Selsey	32	9	4	19	53	88	31
Bexhill United	32	8	5	19	48	74	29
Midhurst & Easebourne	32	7	7	18	37	64	28
Seaford Town	32	5	4	23	22	67	19
Saltdean United	32	2	7	23	30	109	13

Division Two

AFC Varndeanians	30	22	4	4	91	26	70
Roffey	30	20	4	6	101	37	64
Cowfold	30	19	6	5	81	34	63
Rottingdean Village	30	19	6	5	71	32	63
Billingshurst	**30**	**19**	**5**	**6**	**73**	**35**	**62**
Bosham	30	18	5	7	70	27	59
Upper Beeding	30	14	10	6	70	39	52
Montpelier Villa	30	15	2	13	70	61	47
Rustington	30	11	7	12	68	64	40
Westfield	30	11	5	14	58	69	38
Ferring	30	9	4	17	54	77	31
Clymping	30	7	4	19	57	96	25
Alfold	30	5	8	17	41	75	23
Ifield Galaxy	30	7	1	22	41	108	22
AFC Roffey Club	30	3	4	23	34	95	13
Hurstpierpoint	30	2	3	25	24	129	9

Hurstpierpoint moved to the Mid-Sussex League and Ifield Galaxy withdrew from senior football. Jarvis Brook joined from the Mid-Sussex League, Lancing United joined from the West Sussex League and Worthing Town Leisure joined from the Brighton, Worthing & District League.

Division One

Saltdean United	34	24	7	3	87	33	79
Little Common	34	23	6	5	103	49	75
East Preston	**34**	**23**	**6**	**5**	**85**	**33**	**75**
Mile Oak	34	21	6	7	84	48	69
Lingfield	34	20	3	11	87	65	63
Steyning Town	34	18	6	10	81	64	60
Selsey	34	15	8	11	82	69	53
Langney Wanderers	34	16	3	15	92	87	51
Midhurst & Easebourne	34	12	8	14	66	72	44
Bexhill United	34	13	5	16	60	68	44
Southwick	34	12	7	15	65	67	42
Storrington	34	9	10	15	52	70	36
Seaford Town	34	8	7	19	47	68	31
Oakwood	34	8	7	19	41	78	31
Billingshurst	34	7	7	20	55	86	28
Ringmer	34	7	7	20	47	86	28
St. Francis Rangers	34	6	6	22	43	85	24
AFC Varndeanians	34	4	11	19	45	94	23

Southwick and Storrington each had 3 points deducted.

Division Two

Bosham	28	21	4	3	102	24	67
Jarvis Brook	28	19	7	2	108	42	64
Sidlesham	28	18	6	4	83	28	60
Lancing United	28	17	4	7	88	45	55
Upper Beeding	28	13	8	7	86	39	47
Westfield	28	14	4	10	80	48	46
Roffey	28	11	8	9	73	37	41
Cowfold	28	12	5	11	82	54	41
Rottingdean Village	28	11	4	13	55	71	37
Montpelier Villa	28	9	5	14	64	52	32
Rustington	28	9	5	14	40	56	32
Clymping	28	8	6	14	63	75	30
Worthing Town Leisure	28	8	2	18	63	72	26
Alfold	28	5	2	21	48	106	17
Ferring	28	0	0	28	14	300	0

AFC Roffey Club resigned from the league and their record was deleted.

2016-17

Premier Division

Shoreham	38	30	2	6	110	30	92
Haywards Heath Town	38	31	3	4	114	28	87
Chichester City	38	26	6	6	94	47	84
Pagham	38	22	6	10	93	45	72
Eastbourne Town	38	21	7	10	85	60	70
Loxwood	38	18	7	13	75	59	61
Eastbourne United Association	38	19	2	17	64	67	59
Broadbridge Heath	38	18	3	17	71	63	57
Newhaven	38	15	10	13	85	70	55
Horsham YMCA	38	15	9	14	67	67	54
Crawley Down Gatwick	38	15	7	16	95	86	52
Lancing	38	15	5	18	74	83	50
Hassocks	38	15	3	20	70	68	48
Peacehaven & Telscombe	38	14	6	18	69	78	48
Arundel	38	12	6	20	57	84	42
Littlehampton Town	38	12	4	22	61	87	40
Worthing United	38	11	4	23	52	104	37
AFC Uckfield Town	38	11	2	25	49	95	35
Wick	*38*	*8*	*6*	*24*	*53*	*91*	*30*
Hailsham Town	*38*	*2*	*2*	*34*	*32*	*158*	*8*

Haywards Heath Town had 9 points deducted.
Shoreham were promoted to the Isthmian League and Three Bridges rejoined following relegation from the Isthmian League.

ESSEX COUNTY LEAGUE 1937-1938

The first attempt to form a county league to cover the whole of Essex came in 1937 by the 5 clubs from the county who two years earlier, had been founder members of the Eastern Counties League. Although this competition had been a great success in terms of attracting crowds, the time needed to travel to places such as Lowestoft and Kings Lynn was far more than the Essex clubs had been used to previously. The ECL's Essex clubs – Chelmsford, Clacton Town, Colchester Town, Crittall Athletic and Harwich & Parkeston – therefore decided to form their own competition, the Essex County League.

It is thought that these 5 clubs hoped that they would be joined in their new venture by Essex clubs such as Barking, Ilford, Leyton, Leytonstone or Walthamstow Avenue who were playing in one of the established amateur leagues but the only additional entry they attracted was from Dagenham Town of the London League.

With just 6 members, the clubs had to play each other four times to make up a full programme and fans soon tired of the repetitive nature of the fixture list. Things got worse in December 1937 when Colchester Town folded, after their best players and most of their crowd were drawn to the newly formed professional club, Colchester United, with whom they shared the Layer Road ground. This spelled doom for the Essex County League which, with just five clubs remaining, closed down at the end of the season.

1937-38

Harwich & Parkeston	16	12	1	3	51	18	25
Crittall Athletic	16	9	3	4	38	20	21
Chelmsford	16	6	2	8	37	38	14
Dagenham Town	16	3	4	9	28	53	10
Clacton Town	16	4	2	10	15	40	10

Colchester Town withdrew from the league and disbanded in December 1937 and their record was deleted.
At the end of the season, Harwich & Parkeston, Crittall Athletic and Clacton Town returned to the Eastern Counties League and Dagenham Town returned to the London League. Chelmsford were replaced by a new professional club called Chelmsford City who joined the Southern League.

ESSEX SENIOR LEAGUE 1971-2017

More than 30 years later, another attempt was made to form a county league for Essex and this time, it was successful. Nine clubs competed in the Essex Senior League in its first season of 1971-72 and the league has now been operating for 46 years. In that time, it has produced three Wembley F.A. Vase winners, Billericay Town in 1975-76 and 1976-77, and Stansted in 1983-84. The league changed their name to the Essex League for the 1986-87 season as not all members were senior clubs but that situation lasted for just two years and so in 1988, the league reverted to its original title which it has retained ever since.

A separate division for member clubs' reserve sides and also for reserve sides of other Essex clubs was introduced in 1972. Woodford Town played its first team in this division in 1975-76, a first step back for the club which had dropped into junior football after a poor season in the Southern League in 1971-72. Woodford moved up to the Senior League in 1976-77 while their reserves took the first team's place in the Reserve Division. In 1984, Loughton Athletic became the second club to field its first team in the Reserve Division and over the next few years, a handful of other clubs did the same and so the division changed their name to Division One as a result. The last first team left in 1988 and the division reverted to being called the Reserve Division in 1991.

There were 9 clubs who formed the league in 1971:

Basildon United and Pegasus Athletic who both joined from the Greater London League – Reserve Section Division One, Billericay Town joined from the Essex Olympian League, Heybridge Swifts, Tiptree United and Witham Town all joined from the Essex & Suffolk Border League, Saffron Walden Town and Stansted both joined from Hertfordshire County League, Southend United re-formed their "A" team which also entered the league.

1971-72

Witham Town	16	11	3	2	38	11	25
Billericay Town	16	11	2	3	30	13	24
Pegasus Athletic	16	8	5	3	39	16	21
Tiptree United	16	9	1	6	21	19	19
Saffron Walden Town	16	8	0	8	27	25	16
Basildon United	16	7	2	7	22	21	16
Heybridge Swifts	16	5	6	5	26	27	16
Southend United "A"	16	1	3	12	18	45	5
Stansted	16	1	0	15	11	55	2

Southend United "A" left the league.
Brightlingsea United and Coggeshall Town joined from the Essex & Suffolk
Border League and Maldon Town joined from the Eastern Counties League.

1972-73

Billericay Town	18	13	5	0	38	12	31
Basildon United	18	11	4	3	37	19	26
Stansted	18	7	7	4	20	17	21
Brightlingsea United	18	7	6	5	30	27	20
Witham Town	18	6	6	6	20	17	18
Coggeshall Town	18	5	7	6	28	27	17
Tiptree United	18	5	4	9	26	34	14
Heybridge Swifts	18	6	2	10	21	34	14
Saffron Walden Town	18	4	2	12	20	35	10
Maldon Town	18	3	3	12	16	34	9

Pegasus Athletic played one game, an 11-1 defeat at Tiptree United. They
then resigned from the league and that result was deleted from the table.

1973-74

Saffron Walden Town	18	15	1	2	46	13	31
Billericay Town	18	14	1	3	40	10	29
Coggeshall Town	18	13	1	4	40	13	27
Tiptree United	18	11	2	5	33	21	24
Basildon United	18	6	6	6	27	23	18
Witham Town	18	7	3	8	34	25	17
Maldon Town	18	4	6	8	21	24	14
Brightlingsea United	18	3	3	12	15	51	9
Stansted	18	2	4	12	11	46	8
Heybridge Swifts	18	1	1	16	9	50	3

Saffron Walden Town moved to the Eastern Counties League. Bowers
United and Brentwood joined from the Essex Olympian League, Ford
United joined from the Metropolitan-London League and Romford
Reserves joined, not having played in a league in 1973-74. Southend
United "A" and Colchester United "A" also joined.

1974-75

Billericay Town	28	21	3	4	63	16	45
Basildon United	28	17	5	6	54	24	39
Coggeshall Town	28	14	9	5	49	29	37
Colchester United "A"	28	14	8	6	57	42	36
Bowers United	28	14	6	8	49	28	34
Witham Town	28	15	4	9	55	39	34
Tiptree United	28	13	4	11	43	50	30
Romford Reserves	28	10	6	12	55	53	26
Maldon Town	28	8	9	11	31	39	25
Southend United "A"	28	9	5	14	32	35	23
Ford United	28	8	7	13	31	36	23
Brentwood	28	7	8	13	32	52	22
Heybridge Swifts	28	7	5	16	34	60	19
Stansted	28	5	5	18	29	66	15
Brightlingsea United	28	4	4	20	24	69	12

Colchester United "A" and Romford Reserves both left the league.
Canvey Island and Eton Manor joined from the Metropolitan-London
League.

1975-76

Billericay Town	28	23	3	2	84	23	49
Tiptree United	28	18	6	4	56	32	42
Basildon United	28	17	7	4	55	20	41
Bowers United	28	16	6	6	52	31	38
Witham Town	28	17	2	9	63	36	36
Brightlingsea United	28	11	9	8	45	35	31
Eton Manor	28	13	4	11	46	37	30
Ford United	28	12	6	10	45	42	30
Brentwood	28	10	6	12	48	44	26
Maldon Town	28	12	1	15	42	44	25
Canvey Island	28	8	5	15	30	45	21
Heybridge Swifts	28	8	2	18	42	59	18
Southend United "A"	28	6	1	21	25	75	13
Coggeshall Town	28	4	3	21	30	77	11
Stansted	28	3	3	22	27	90	9

Southend United ceased to run their "A" team for financial reasons.
Sawbridgeworth Town joined from the Essex Olympian League and
Chelmsford City Reserves and Woodford Town also joined. Woodford were
champions of the Essex Senior League's Reserve Division in 1975-76 when
their record was as follows: 28 23 3 2 97 22 49
Woodford had dropped into junior football after finishing bottom of the
Southern League – Division One (South) in 1971-72 and the Reserve
Division was their first step back into senior football. The other 14
members of this division consisted of 12 reserve teams of Essex Senior
League clubs, plus the reserve teams of Clacton Town and of Saffron
Walden, both of whose first teams were playing in the Eastern Counties
League.

From the next season goal difference was used to decide final position
when teams were on level points, instead of goal average.

1976-77

Basildon United	32	26	3	3	75	16	55
Brentwood	32	24	5	3	77	35	53
Billericay Town	32	23	5	4	88	23	51
Brightlingsea United	32	18	8	6	56	36	44
Bowers United	32	16	9	7	52	32	41
Eton Manor	32	12	9	11	45	42	33
Woodford Town	32	13	6	13	50	50	32
Maldon Town	32	11	8	13	42	51	30
Tiptree United	32	10	9	13	46	58	29
Canvey Island	32	9	9	14	39	47	27
Heybridge Swifts	32	10	7	15	44	57	27
Sawbridgeworth Town	32	8	6	18	34	56	22
Chelmsford City Reserves	32	7	8	17	42	65	22
Ford United	32	6	10	16	29	56	22
Witham Town	32	6	7	19	39	65	19
Stansted	32	6	7	19	42	71	19
Coggeshall Town	32	4	10	18	30	70	18

Billericay Town moved to the Athenian League.

1977-78

Basildon United	30	25	4	1	71	15	54
Tiptree United	30	22	5	3	82	29	49
Ford United	30	15	9	6	47	29	39
Brentwood	30	14	8	8	50	38	36
Witham Town	30	15	6	9	36	33	36
Canvey Island	30	14	6	10	43	34	34
Heybridge Swifts	30	13	7	10	40	32	33
Bowers United	30	10	10	10	37	40	30
Eton Manor	30	13	3	14	44	42	29
Woodford Town	30	9	9	12	40	48	27
Brightlingsea United	30	10	4	16	47	50	24
Stansted	30	6	8	16	36	63	20
Chelmsford City Reserves	30	7	5	18	39	64	19
Coggeshall Town	30	7	4	19	30	64	18
Maldon Town	30	6	5	19	29	56	17
Sawbridgeworth Town	30	5	5	20	29	63	15

East Ham United joined from the London-Spartan League.

1978-79

Basildon United	32	26	5	1	86	14	57
Canvey Island	32	22	8	2	73	21	52
Eton Manor	32	19	6	7	68	37	44
Heybridge Swifts	32	17	9	6	50	32	43
Brentwood	32	15	9	8	64	49	39
East Ham United	32	16	6	10	57	42	38
Witham Town	32	14	7	11	47	43	35
Tiptree United	32	11	11	10	42	32	33
Brightlingsea United	32	12	9	11	53	51	33
Bowers United	32	12	8	12	41	47	32
Chelmsford City Reserves	32	11	6	15	41	47	28
Maldon Town	32	7	14	11	43	60	28
Woodford Town	32	10	7	15	46	62	27
Ford United	32	4	9	19	28	47	17
Stansted	32	7	2	23	34	72	16
Coggeshall Town	32	2	10	20	40	82	14
Sawbridgeworth Town	32	3	2	27	29	104	8

Tiptree United moved to the Eastern Counties League, Woodford Town moved to the Athenian League and Chelmsford City Reserves also left the league. East Thurrock United joined from the London-Spartan League and Wivenhoe Town joined from the Essex & Suffolk Border League.

1979-80

Basildon United	30	25	3	2	65	8	53
Wivenhoe Town	30	16	9	5	53	31	41
Canvey Island	30	17	5	8	57	34	39
Witham Town	30	16	6	8	55	33	38
East Ham United	30	14	9	7	44	30	37
Eton Manor	30	14	7	9	45	38	35
Sawbridgeworth Town	30	10	13	7	33	22	33
Brentwood	30	14	5	11	45	41	33
Bowers United	30	13	6	11	38	37	32
Heybridge Swifts	30	12	7	11	44	30	31
Coggeshall Town	30	9	6	15	37	43	24
East Thurrock United	30	9	6	15	28	39	24
Maldon Town	30	8	8	14	28	42	24
Ford United	30	6	7	17	32	53	19
Brightlingsea United	30	2	6	22	27	75	10
Stansted	30	2	3	25	18	93	7

Basildon United moved to the Athenian League. Halstead Town joined from the Essex & Suffolk Border League and Chelmsford City Reserves also joined.

1980-81

Bowers United	32	22	8	2	73	31	52
Heybridge Swifts	32	20	7	5	69	27	47
Wivenhoe Town	32	20	5	7	67	34	45
Canvey Island	32	14	13	5	53	35	41
Witham Town	32	13	12	7	54	30	38
Brentwood	32	15	7	10	52	43	37
Maldon Town	32	13	7	12	48	47	33
Sawbridgeworth Town	32	10	11	11	45	41	31
Stansted	32	10	10	12	43	46	30
Ford United	32	10	10	12	47	55	30
East Ham United	32	8	11	13	33	48	27
East Thurrock United	32	9	9	14	34	50	27
Brightlingsea United	32	10	4	18	33	52	24
Coggeshall Town	32	9	5	18	44	71	23
Chelmsford City Reserves	32	7	8	17	38	59	22
Halstead Town	32	6	7	19	42	82	19
Eton Manor	32	6	6	20	32	56	18

1981-82

Heybridge Swifts	32	26	4	2	74	21	56
Wivenhoe Town	32	20	4	8	66	35	44
Brentwood	32	19	5	8	61	32	43
Bowers United	32	16	8	8	56	33	40
Witham Town	32	16	6	10	49	27	38
Canvey Island	32	15	7	10	42	38	37
Sawbridgeworth Town	32	16	4	12	55	35	36
Stansted	32	12	9	11	42	41	33
Brightlingsea United	32	12	9	11	34	44	33
Halstead Town	32	13	4	15	52	49	30
Chelmsford City Reserves	32	8	10	14	36	53	26
Coggeshall Town	32	9	8	15	39	57	26
Ford United	32	11	3	18	36	70	25
East Thurrock United	32	6	10	16	25	47	22
Maldon Town	32	6	9	17	36	59	21
Eton Manor	32	7	7	18	26	60	20
East Ham United	32	3	7	22	29	57	13

Eton Manor had 1 point deducted.

1982-83

Heybridge Swifts	32	25	3	4	90	21	53
Stansted	32	22	7	3	64	30	51
Halstead Town	32	24	2	6	87	32	50
Bowers United	32	19	4	9	76	40	42
Canvey Island	31	17	7	7	61	39	41
Witham Town	32	15	9	8	54	36	39
Wivenhoe Town	32	12	9	11	48	50	33
Chelmsford City Reserves	32	10	9	13	41	53	29
Coggeshall Town	32	12	3	17	49	71	27
Maldon Town	32	8	9	15	54	74	25
Brentwood	32	9	7	16	37	57	25
Ford United	32	10	4	18	47	58	24
Sawbridgeworth Town	32	8	8	16	51	65	24
Brightlingsea United	32	9	6	17	38	56	24
East Ham United	32	6	7	19	48	84	19
Eton Manor	31	7	5	19	33	75	19
East Thurrock United	32	4	9	19	29	66	17

Canvey Island vs Eton Manor was not played.

1983-84

Heybridge Swifts	32	27	3	2	65	21	57
Bowers United	32	17	10	5	56	25	44
Witham Town	32	18	6	8	61	32	42
Stansted	31	18	4	9	62	29	40
Chelmsford City Reserves	32	17	4	11	62	37	38
Brentwood	32	14	7	11	50	45	35
Sawbridgeworth Town	31	14	5	12	56	40	33
Canvey Island	32	11	9	12	48	44	31
Wivenhoe Town	32	10	11	11	45	43	31
Ford United	32	13	5	14	49	55	31
Eton Manor	32	10	10	12	56	47	30
East Thurrock United	32	11	6	15	25	44	28
Maldon Town	32	11	3	18	40	53	25
East Ham United	32	7	9	16	41	60	23
Halstead Town	32	5	13	14	34	56	23
Brightlingsea United	32	4	14	14	41	63	22
Coggeshall Town	32	1	7	24	19	116	9

Stansted vs Sawbridgeworth Town was not played.
Heybridge Swifts moved to the Isthmian League.

Three points were awarded for a win instead of two from the next season.

1984-85

Maldon Town	30	20	4	6	71	29	64
Witham Town	30	20	4	6	59	27	64
Stansted	30	19	5	6	80	29	62
Wivenhoe Town	30	16	10	4	54	27	58
Brentwood	30	18	3	9	73	46	57
Chelmsford City Reserves	30	14	8	8	61	37	50
Canvey Island	30	14	8	8	53	40	50
Ford United	30	13	7	10	47	33	46
Bowers United	30	12	10	8	48	39	46
Eton Manor	30	11	8	11	49	46	41
Halstead Town	30	9	4	17	51	67	31
Brightlingsea United	30	8	6	16	42	60	30
East Thurrock United	30	7	8	15	30	44	29
Sawbridgeworth Town	30	4	8	18	23	55	20
East Ham United	30	4	5	21	37	83	17
Coggeshall Town	30	2	0	28	8	124	6

Burnham Ramblers joined from the Essex Olympian League.

Loughton Athletic had joined the Reserve Division in 1984 as a newly formed club and were the only non-reserve side playing in that division. They were champions of the division during the 1984-85 season when their record was:

	26	22	4	0	81	17	70

At the end of the 1984-85 season, they merged with Woodford Town and continued in the Reserve Division as Woodford Town Reserves. The Reserve Division admitted 3 more non-reserve sides for 1985-86 and changed its name to Division One. The 3 non-reserve sides were Purfleet, who joined as a newly formed club and Southend Manor and Stambridge who both joined from the Southend Alliance.

Promoted clubs in **bold type**, relegated clubs in ***bold italics***.

1985-86

Senior Division

Witham Town	32	24	5	3	73	23	77
Wivenhoe Town	32	19	5	8	82	47	62
Ford United	32	19	4	9	65	41	61
Maldon Town	32	17	9	6	48	24	60
East Thurrock United	32	16	9	7	64	41	57
Brentwood	32	18	0	14	71	47	54
Chelmsford City Reserves	32	15	7	10	48	38	52
Bowers United	32	13	7	12	54	49	46
Canvey Island	32	10	11	11	53	45	41
Eton Manor	32	11	6	15	52	80	39
Brightlingsea United	32	10	8	14	46	52	38
Burnham Ramblers	32	10	7	15	45	54	37
Stansted	32	10	4	18	37	51	34
Sawbridgeworth Town	32	9	6	17	53	72	33
Halstead Town	32	8	6	18	47	67	30
East Ham United	32	7	9	16	41	74	30
Coggeshall Town	*32*	*2*	*5*	*25*	*31*	*105*	*11*

Wivenhoe Town moved to the Isthmian League.

Division One

Woodford Town Reserves	36	30	5	1	118	19	95
Southend Manor	36	28	4	4	111	27	88
Purfleet	36	26	7	3	104	34	85
Stambridge	36	24	5	7	118	42	77
Brentwood Reserves	36	24	4	8	87	49	76
Witham Town Reserves	36	19	4	13	78	63	61
Bowers United Reserves	36	17	9	10	77	46	60
Wivenhoe Town Reserves	36	17	3	16	88	72	54
Burnham Ramblers Reserves	36	15	4	17	62	70	49
East Thurrock United Reserves	36	12	8	16	59	65	44
Canvey Island Reserves	36	11	6	19	56	76	39
Stansted Reserves	36	12	3	21	56	86	39
Eton Manor Reserves	36	10	9	17	43	74	39
Maldon Town Reserves	36	11	5	20	43	74	38
Halstead Town Reserves	36	10	5	21	58	100	35
East Ham United Reserves	36	9	6	21	49	92	33
Sawbridgeworth Town Reserves	36	7	6	23	43	96	27
Brightlingsea United Reserves	36	5	9	22	30	77	24
Coggeshall Town Reserves	36	1	6	29	24	142	9

Purfleet Reserves joined the league.

Division One was split into two sections, North and South.

ESSEX LEAGUE

1986-87

Senior Division

Canvey Island	32	22	4	6	62	32	70
Witham Town	32	19	6	7	58	22	63
Purfleet	32	18	7	7	83	40	61
Bowers United	32	17	7	8	62	33	58
East Thurrock United	32	15	10	7	62	45	55
Burnham Ramblers	32	14	9	9	49	36	51
Woodford Town Reserves	*32*	*14*	*9*	*9*	*50*	*38*	*51*
Sawbridgeworth Town	32	14	5	13	53	57	47
Chelmsford City Reserves	32	13	7	12	51	42	46
Brentwood	32	12	10	10	50	48	46
Halstead Town	32	12	9	11	41	37	45
Ford United	32	7	13	12	40	43	33
Eton Manor	32	7	8	17	36	59	29
Stansted	32	6	6	20	30	81	24
Maldon Town	32	5	8	19	34	66	23
East Ham United	32	5	8	19	40	86	23
Brightlingsea United	32	2	14	16	27	63	20

Ford United had 1 point deducted for fielding an ineligible player. Witham Town moved to the Isthmian League. Woodford Town joined from the Southern League and so Woodford Town Reserves moved down to Division One.

Division One – North

Wivenhoe Town Reserves	16	11	3	2	46	14	36
Maldon Town Reserves	16	9	5	2	38	30	32
Sawbridgeworth Town Reserves	16	9	3	4	40	31	30
Stansted Reserves	16	6	4	6	19	19	22
Halstead Town Reserves	16	5	6	5	19	22	21
Witham Town Reserves	16	5	3	8	21	27	18
Burnham Ramblers Reserves	16	4	4	8	22	29	16
Brightlingsea United Reserves	16	4	1	11	25	42	13
Coggeshall Town	*16*	*3*	*3*	*10*	*20*	*36*	*12*

Wivenhoe Town Reserves and Witham Town Reserves left the league. Coggeshall Town moved up to the Senior Division.

Division One – South

Southend Manor	15	12	2	1	36	6	38
East Ham United Reserves	14	9	2	3	32	21	29
Stambridge	14	8	1	5	39	21	25
Purfleet Reserves	14	7	2	5	21	21	23
East Thurrock United Reserves	14	6	3	5	31	22	21
Canvey Island Reserves	15	6	3	6	23	27	21
Eton Manor Reserves	16	3	5	8	23	35	14
Bowers United Reserves	16	3	1	12	22	45	10
Brentwood Reserves	16	3	1	12	23	52	10

5 games were left unplayed.

Divisional Play-off Final

Southend Manor vs Wivenhoe Town Reserves   1-2, 1-0
Aggregate 2-2. The Championship was shared.

East Ham United Reserves left the league. St. Osyth and Coggeshall Town Reserves both joined.

The two sections of Division One were combined into a single division.

1987-88

Senior Division

Purfleet	32	23	4	5	76	24	73
Brentwood	32	22	5	5	84	36	71
Halstead Town	32	19	6	7	79	38	63
Woodford Town	32	19	6	7	61	27	63
East Thurrock United	32	17	7	8	73	39	58
Ford United	32	16	4	12	45	42	52
Stansted	32	15	6	11	58	45	51
Sawbridgeworth Town	32	14	7	11	67	51	49
Eton Manor	32	14	5	13	52	48	47
Canvey Island	32	12	8	12	53	53	44
Brightlingsea United	32	11	9	12	58	57	42
Chelmsford City Reserves	32	13	3	16	47	53	42
Burnham Ramblers	32	9	8	15	52	60	35
Bowers United	32	9	7	16	30	53	34
East Ham United	32	9	4	19	44	80	31
Maldon Town	32	2	1	29	24	98	7
Coggeshall Town	32	1	4	27	22	121	7

Purfleet moved to the Isthmian League and Halstead Town moved to the Eastern Counties League.

Division One

Southend Manor	**32**	**25**	**5**	**2**	**105**	**29**	**80**
Stambridge	**32**	**22**	**8**	**2**	**69**	**23**	**74**
Burnham Ramblers Reserves	32	21	8	3	58	24	71
Canvey Island Reserves	32	19	3	10	60	55	60
East Thurrock United Reserves	32	16	5	11	53	45	53
Purfleet Reserves	32	13	10	9	79	47	49
Woodford Town Reserves	32	14	6	12	59	45	48
Halstead Town Reserves	32	15	3	14	63	67	48
St. Osyth	32	12	7	13	41	45	43
Brentwood Reserves	32	11	7	14	62	62	40
Eton Manor Reserves	32	10	5	17	43	58	35
Brightlingsea United Reserves	32	8	10	14	30	49	34
Sawbridgeworth Town Reserves	32	9	7	16	46	74	34
Bowers United Reserves	32	8	5	19	41	55	29
Stansted Reserves	32	7	6	19	43	71	27
Maldon Town Reserves	32	7	3	22	47	74	24
Coggeshall Town Reserves	32	4	4	24	38	114	16

St. Osyth moved to the Essex Intermediate League and from this point, Division One contained only Reserve sides. Its title reverted to the Reserve Division in 1991.

The league reverted to its original title of Essex Senior League.

ESSEX SENIOR LEAGUE

1988-89

Brightlingsea United	32	21	5	6	68	28	68
East Thurrock United	32	19	8	5	70	38	65
Ford United	32	18	7	7	56	31	61
Burnham Ramblers	32	17	8	7	65	43	59
Stansted	32	15	5	12	53	52	50
Canvey Island	32	14	7	11	62	52	49
Southend Manor	32	13	10	9	46	39	49
Eton Manor	32	12	9	11	46	43	45
Brentwood	32	12	8	12	45	52	44
Woodford Town	32	12	7	13	40	37	43
Sawbridgeworth Town	32	11	7	14	43	43	40
Stambridge	32	10	8	14	45	56	38
Chelmsford City Reserves	32	7	11	14	41	55	32
Coggeshall Town	32	8	8	16	42	57	32
Bowers United	32	7	10	15	36	55	31
East Ham United	32	7	7	18	42	75	28
Maldon Town	32	3	7	22	28	72	16

Coggeshall Town resigned from the league for financial reasons and joined the Essex & Suffolk Border League in 1990.

1989-90

Brightlingsea United	30	21	5	4	70	22	68
Woodford Town	30	19	7	4	64	35	64
East Thurrock United	30	16	8	6	64	29	56
Canvey Island	30	15	10	5	76	34	55
Sawbridgeworth Town	30	15	7	8	67	46	52
Stambridge	30	14	8	8	66	37	50
Brentwood	30	14	7	9	55	40	49
Burnham Ramblers	30	12	8	10	62	45	44
Ford United	30	13	5	12	48	50	44
Southend Manor	30	12	6	12	52	42	42
Bowers United	30	12	5	13	42	40	41
Eton Manor	30	8	4	18	34	56	28
Stansted	30	8	3	19	31	77	27
Chelmsford City Reserves	30	7	5	18	38	57	26
Maldon Town	30	6	4	20	32	84	22
East Ham United	30	1	2	27	17	124	5

Brightlingsea United moved to the Eastern Counties League and Chelmsford City Reserves moved to the Essex & Herts. Border Combination. Hullbridge Sports joined from the Essex Intermediate League, formerly known as the Essex Olympian League.

1990-91

Southend Manor	28	20	4	4	52	20	64
Brentwood	28	18	6	4	66	30	60
Burnham Ramblers	28	17	8	3	57	30	59
Sawbridgeworth Town	28	15	5	8	47	26	50
Bowers United	28	14	7	7	50	32	49
Stambridge	28	13	5	10	50	38	44
Ford United	28	13	4	11	47	33	43
East Thurrock United	28	11	9	8	46	38	42
Canvey Island	28	9	7	12	34	47	34
Stansted	28	7	8	13	40	42	29
Eton Manor	28	6	9	13	35	45	27
Hullbridge Sports	28	5	8	15	16	38	23
Maldon Town	28	6	5	17	27	57	23
East Ham United	28	5	4	19	35	95	19
Woodford Town	28	5	3	20	33	64	18

Basildon United joined from the Isthmian League and Concord Rangers joined from the Essex Intermediate League.

1991-92

Ford United	32	20	6	6	64	18	66
Brentwood	32	20	6	6	77	37	66
East Thurrock United	32	19	9	4	62	24	66
Sawbridgeworth Town	32	19	8	5	67	43	65
Canvey Island	32	19	6	7	49	24	63
Basildon United	32	17	5	10	65	39	56
Bowers United	32	15	9	8	49	31	54
Southend Manor	32	14	6	12	62	40	48
Stambridge	32	12	8	12	60	49	44
Woodford Town	32	12	7	13	46	44	43
Concord Rangers	32	10	10	12	39	52	40
Stansted	32	11	6	15	40	50	39
Burnham Ramblers	32	10	4	18	48	71	34
Hullbridge Sports	32	7	7	18	25	63	28
East Ham United	32	7	5	20	35	72	26
Eton Manor	32	5	3	24	24	71	18
Maldon Town	32	1	3	28	20	104	6

East Thurrock United moved to the Isthmian League and Stambridge moved to the Essex Intermediate League. Great Wakering Rovers joined from the Essex Intermediate League and Romford joined as a newly formed club.

1992-93

Canvey Island	32	23	7	2	66	20	76
Sawbridgeworth Town	32	19	7	6	82	41	64
Bowers United	32	18	9	5	56	27	63
Burnham Ramblers	32	17	6	9	80	53	57
Basildon United	32	16	7	9	65	37	55
Brentwood	32	13	9	10	58	49	48
Great Wakering Rovers	32	13	8	11	50	43	47
Ford United	32	14	10	8	47	26	46
Romford	32	12	9	11	48	42	45
Southend Manor	32	13	4	15	49	45	43
Concord Rangers	32	9	9	14	41	51	36
Maldon Town	32	8	10	14	45	59	34
East Ham United	32	10	4	18	46	67	34
Woodford Town	32	7	9	16	46	84	30
Eton Manor	32	7	8	17	32	75	29
Hullbridge Sports	32	7	6	19	38	70	27
Stansted	32	2	6	24	27	87	12

Ford United had 6 points deducted for fielding ineligible and unregistered players.
Woodford Town moved to the Spartan League.

1993-94

Basildon United	30	21	7	2	64	18	70
Ford United	30	20	6	4	64	16	66
Canvey Island	30	19	5	6	50	22	62
Romford	30	16	6	8	52	37	54
Great Wakering Rovers	30	16	5	9	69	40	53
Bowers United	30	14	6	10	40	44	48
Brentwood	30	13	6	11	49	43	45
Sawbridgeworth Town	30	13	6	11	46	40	45
Concord Rangers	30	11	7	12	50	41	40
East Ham United	30	10	8	12	46	54	38
Maldon Town	30	11	3	16	38	46	36
Eton Manor	30	8	2	20	37	74	26
Southend Manor	30	6	7	17	42	65	25
Burnham Ramblers	30	7	4	19	32	55	25
Hullbridge Sports	30	5	7	18	30	74	22
Stansted	30	4	7	19	28	68	19

Canvey Island moved to the Isthmian League.

1994-95

Great Wakering Rovers	28	23	2	3	82	14	71
Sawbridgeworth Town	28	23	2	3	73	20	71
Romford	28	18	7	3	54	30	61
Maldon Town	28	16	6	6	58	33	54
Ford United	28	13	6	9	48	30	45
Bowers United	28	12	3	13	41	45	39
Burnham Ramblers	28	12	3	13	42	47	39
Basildon United	28	10	8	10	57	35	38
East Ham United	28	9	9	10	28	32	36
Brentwood	28	7	11	10	39	37	32
Concord Rangers	28	9	5	14	32	42	32
Stansted	28	8	7	13	40	57	31
Southend Manor	28	3	8	17	32	80	17
Hullbridge Sports	28	4	1	23	17	67	13
Eton Manor	28	2	4	22	19	93	10

1995-96

Romford	28	23	2	3	91	27	71
Great Wakering Rovers	28	20	4	4	67	28	64
Concord Rangers	28	20	3	5	67	31	63
Maldon Town	28	16	4	8	87	47	52
Ford United	28	14	6	8	59	53	48
Sawbridgeworth Town	28	13	5	10	59	43	44
Stansted	28	12	8	8	47	34	44
Southend Manor	28	12	7	9	50	49	43
Burnham Ramblers	28	13	3	12	63	48	42
Brentwood	28	13	2	13	56	53	41
Basildon United	28	5	8	15	31	52	23
Bowers United	28	5	6	17	28	57	21
Eton Manor	28	4	6	18	32	72	18
Hullbridge Sports	28	4	5	19	30	88	17
East Ham United	28	0	3	25	18	103	3

Bowers United had 3 points deducted.
Romford merged with Collier Row of the Isthmian League to form Collier Row & Romford who continued to play in the Isthmian League at Collier Row's ground, Sungate in Collier Row Road, Romford. Romford had been playing at Hornchurch's ground in Upminster. Maldon Town moved to the Eastern Counties League. Saffron Walden Town joined from the Isthmian League and Ilford joined as a newly re-formed senior club.

1996-97

Team	P	W	D	L	F	A	Pts
Ford United	28	21	6	1	91	24	69
Great Wakering Rovers	28	20	6	2	67	19	66
Concord Rangers	28	19	5	4	106	31	62
Stansted	28	19	2	7	53	37	59
Burnham Ramblers	28	13	6	9	62	40	45
Brentwood	28	11	10	7	46	34	43
Hullbridge Sports	28	13	4	11	52	42	43
Ilford	28	11	3	14	36	40	36
Basildon United	28	11	5	12	39	52	35
Saffron Walden Town	28	8	8	12	40	39	32
Southend Manor	28	8	5	15	32	42	29
Bowers United	28	8	4	16	32	77	28
East Ham United	28	7	3	18	29	61	24
Sawbridgeworth Town	28	3	3	22	17	69	12
Eton Manor	28	1	4	23	13	108	7

Basildon United had 3 points deducted.
Ford United moved to the Isthmian League.

1997-98

Team	P	W	D	L	F	A	Pts
Concord Rangers	26	23	2	1	74	20	71
Basildon United	26	22	3	1	75	15	69
Bowers United	26	19	2	5	65	25	59
Stansted	26	15	3	8	71	43	48
Burnham Ramblers	26	13	5	8	52	33	44
Hullbridge Sports	26	11	5	10	44	37	38
Great Wakering Rovers	26	10	5	11	39	42	35
Brentwood	26	9	4	13	34	44	31
East Ham United	26	9	3	14	41	61	30
Sawbridgeworth Town	26	8	3	15	32	57	27
Ilford	26	7	5	14	38	48	26
Southend Manor	26	4	6	16	27	66	18
Eton Manor	26	3	4	19	34	59	13
Saffron Walden Town	26	3	2	21	24	100	11

1998-99

Team	P	W	D	L	F	A	Pts
Bowers United	26	21	3	2	78	16	66
Great Wakering Rovers	26	20	2	4	73	26	62
Saffron Walden Town	26	16	8	2	49	20	56
Burnham Ramblers	26	14	6	6	61	25	48
Southend Manor	26	11	9	6	49	40	42
Ilford	26	13	3	10	49	44	42
Basildon United	26	13	5	8	46	35	41
Hullbridge Sports	26	8	3	15	42	38	27
Concord Rangers	26	8	7	11	33	48	27
Brentwood	26	5	6	15	30	60	21
Stansted	26	6	3	17	40	88	21
East Ham United	26	5	5	16	33	88	20
Sawbridgeworth Town	26	4	6	16	19	47	18
Eton Manor	26	3	4	19	36	63	13

Basildon United had 3 points deducted.
Concord Rangers had 4 points deducted.
Great Wakering Rovers moved to the Isthmian League. Leyton joined from the Essex Intermediate league, Woodford Town joined from the London Intermediate League and Bury Academy joined as a newly formed club.

1999-2000

Team	P	W	D	L	F	A	Pts
Saffron Walden Town	28	19	5	4	85	33	62
Southend Manor	28	19	5	4	81	33	62
Burnham Ramblers	28	19	5	4	68	32	62
Ilford	28	18	4	6	70	34	58
Brentwood	28	17	2	9	49	40	53
Bowers United	28	14	6	8	51	42	48
Sawbridgeworth Town	28	11	10	7	65	48	43
Concord Rangers	28	11	9	8	46	41	42
Leyton	28	9	5	14	45	55	32
Hullbridge Sports	28	8	3	17	44	63	27
East Ham United	28	5	8	15	30	65	23
Eton Manor	28	6	8	14	41	61	22
Basildon United	28	6	6	16	37	61	22
Woodford Town	28	5	3	20	46	99	18
Stansted	28	2	3	23	35	86	9

Bury Academy withdrew and their record (P5, L5, F2, A18, P0) was deleted.
Eton Manor had 4 points deducted.
Basildon United had 2 points deducted.
Barkingside joined from the Essex & Herts. Border Combination.

2000-01

Team	P	W	D	L	F	A	Pts
Brentwood	30	21	3	6	68	26	66
Saffron Walden Town	30	18	3	9	53	24	57
Barkingside	30	17	5	8	55	34	56
Southend Manor	30	17	4	9	71	40	55
Concord Rangers	30	17	3	10	57	38	54
Ilford	30	15	5	10	64	48	50
Bowers United	30	13	8	9	53	47	47
Basildon United	30	13	6	11	66	48	45
Stansted	30	12	8	10	45	47	44
Leyton	30	12	7	11	50	43	43
East Ham United	30	12	3	15	52	73	39
Hullbridge Sports	30	11	4	15	60	59	37
Sawbridgeworth Town	30	10	6	14	41	46	36
Burnham Ramblers	30	8	6	16	47	59	30
Eton Manor	30	3	5	22	38	92	14
Woodford Town	30	2	2	26	23	119	8

East Ham United merged with Barking of the Isthmian League to form Barking & East Ham United. The merged club continued to play in the Isthmian League, playing at Barking's Mayesbrook Park ground. East Ham had lost their Manorway home and were ground-sharing at Barking in 2000-01. Enfield Town joined as a newly formed club.

2001-02

Team	P	W	D	L	F	A	Pts
Leyton	**30**	**24**	**3**	**3**	**75**	**23**	**75**
Enfield Town	30	22	3	5	83	28	69
Burnham Ramblers	30	17	2	11	57	42	53
Concord Rangers	30	16	2	12	65	51	50
Southend Manor	30	14	7	9	57	42	49
Bowers United	30	13	9	8	70	51	46
Sawbridgeworth Town	30	13	7	10	59	54	46
Stansted	30	12	6	12	55	54	42
Ilford	30	11	5	14	51	49	38
Basildon United	30	10	7	13	58	64	37
Saffron Walden Town	30	10	6	14	40	62	36
Hullbridge Sports	30	9	6	15	44	76	33
Barkingside	30	8	8	14	44	50	32
Brentwood	30	8	6	16	45	53	30
Eton Manor	30	4	7	19	40	72	19
Woodford Town	30	5	4	21	29	101	19

Bowers United had 2 points deducted.
Leyton moved to the Isthmian League. Romford joined from the Isthmian League and Waltham Abbey joined from the Essex & Herts. Border Combination.

2002-03

Enfield Town	32	23	6	3	77	28	75
Concord Rangers	32	23	2	7	83	46	71
Ilford	32	21	4	7	87	40	67
Southend Manor	32	20	7	5	73	43	67
Romford	32	21	4	7	63	34	67
Sawbridgeworth Town	32	18	7	7	57	30	61
Bowers United	32	16	6	10	58	49	54
Burnham Ramblers	32	14	4	14	45	43	46
Barkingside	32	14	3	15	66	55	45
Waltham Abbey	32	12	6	14	45	41	42
Brentwood	32	12	5	15	44	62	41
Saffron Walden Town	32	10	4	18	49	57	34
Basildon United	32	9	4	19	54	71	31
Stansted	32	8	4	20	36	64	28
Hullbridge Sports	32	5	3	24	35	90	18
Eton Manor	32	3	8	21	44	98	17
Woodford Town	32	3	3	26	22	87	12

Saffron Walden Town were refused permission to make a cross-pyramid move to the Eastern Counties League but left the Essex Senior League anyway and played only friendlies in 2003-04. They joined the Eastern Counties League in 2004. Woodford Town resigned from the league and disbanded. London APSA joined from the London Intermediate League.

2003-04

Concord Rangers	30	22	4	4	75	26	70
Ilford	30	19	8	3	66	23	65
Sawbridgeworth Town	30	19	6	5	60	29	63
Enfield Town	30	18	9	3	60	35	63
Romford	30	18	4	8	66	39	58
Waltham Abbey	30	16	6	8	50	37	54
Basildon United	30	15	4	11	67	42	49
Bowers United	30	13	4	13	41	51	43
Eton Manor	30	9	8	13	43	52	35
Southend Manor	30	9	7	14	42	50	34
Barkingside	30	9	6	15	46	62	33
Burnham Ramblers	30	7	10	13	42	58	31
Stansted	30	7	5	18	33	72	26
Brentwood	30	5	5	20	31	60	20
London APSA	30	5	5	20	34	76	20
Hullbridge Sports	30	2	3	25	28	72	9

Ilford moved to the Isthmian League. Bowers United changed their name to Bowers & Pitsea and Brentwood changed their name to Brentwood Town.

2004-05

Enfield Town	28	20	6	2	62	21	66
Burnham Ramblers	28	21	2	5	63	34	65
Waltham Abbey	28	19	2	7	61	29	58
Barkingside	28	16	7	5	62	31	55
Romford	28	16	5	7	56	40	53
Southend Manor	28	14	5	9	51	44	47
Basildon United	28	14	4	10	42	31	46
Sawbridgeworth Town	28	11	9	8	47	36	42
Concord Rangers	28	12	3	13	50	44	39
Bowers & Pitsea	28	9	7	12	53	53	34
Stansted	28	7	4	17	41	74	25
Eton Manor	28	6	3	19	34	62	21
London APSA	28	5	4	19	33	72	19
Brentwood Town	28	3	7	18	30	66	16
Hullbridge Sports	28	1	4	23	22	70	7

Waltham Abbey had 1 point deducted.
Enfield Town moved to the Southern League. Tilbury joined from the Southern League and AFC Hornchurch joined as a newly formed club, replacing Hornchurch FC who had resigned from the Football Conference and disbanded. The Hornchurch Stadium ground was taken over by the new club.

2005-06

AFC Hornchurch	30	25	3	2	71	21	78
Waltham Abbey	30	18	6	6	64	28	60
Tilbury	30	16	7	7	63	37	55
Barkingside	30	15	10	5	44	30	55
Burnham Ramblers	30	15	9	6	72	44	54
Sawbridgeworth Town	30	12	11	7	47	28	47
Concord Rangers	30	14	5	11	36	32	47
Brentwood Town	30	11	7	12	46	41	40
London APSA	30	7	11	12	36	52	32
Southend Manor	30	9	5	16	37	57	32
Basildon United	30	8	8	14	47	76	31
Romford	30	6	11	13	38	54	29
Eton Manor	30	6	8	16	35	57	26
Hullbridge Sports	30	6	7	17	38	60	25
Bowers & Pitsea	30	7	4	19	36	65	25
Stansted	30	5	8	17	31	59	23

Basildon United had 1 point deducted.
AFC Hornchurch, Waltham Abbey and Tilbury all moved to the Isthmian League. Clapton joined from the Isthmian League, Beaumont Athletic joined from the Essex Business House League and Barking also joined as a newly formed club, following the disbanding of Barking & East Ham United who had been playing in the Southern League. Barking took over the folded club's ground at Mayesbrook Park.

2006-07

Brentwood Town	30	27	6	2	74	21	72
Romford	30	20	6	4	75	32	66
Barkingside	30	17	7	6	61	28	58
Bowers & Pitsea	30	16	7	7	65	33	55
Burnham Ramblers	30	17	4	9	59	29	55
Barking	30	16	7	7	65	43	55
Concord Rangers	30	16	6	8	67	42	54
Sawbridgeworth Town	30	14	6	10	60	35	48
Southend Manor	30	13	7	10	45	35	46
Basildon United	30	11	9	10	44	40	42
Eton Manor	30	9	7	14	52	57	34
Hullbridge Sports	30	5	8	17	27	61	23
London APSA	30	5	6	19	29	69	21
Clapton	30	5	5	20	34	56	20
Beaumont Athletic	30	4	3	23	41	132	15
Stansted	30	1	4	25	20	105	7

Brentwood Town moved to the Isthmian League. Enfield 1893 joined as a newly formed club after Enfield resigned from the Isthmian League and disbanded. Mauritius Sports Association also joined as a new club formed by a merger of Mauritius Sports (CMB) and Walthamstow Avenue & Pennant, both of the Middlesex County League. The merged club left their previous homes and moved in with Aveley.

2007-08

Concord Rangers	32	25	2	5	94	26	77
Enfield 1893	32	24	5	3	88	29	77
Barkingside	32	24	2	6	79	25	74
Eton Manor	32	20	5	7	81	44	65
Romford	32	19	7	6	75	41	64
Southend Manor	32	18	4	10	50	31	58
Bowers & Pitsea	32	17	5	10	57	41	56
Burnham Ramblers	32	15	7	10	69	45	52
Barking	32	14	6	12	54	43	48
Stansted	32	10	8	14	50	50	38
Clapton	32	8	9	15	38	57	33
Sawbridgeworth Town	32	8	4	20	34	69	28
Mauritius Sports Association	32	7	5	20	41	70	26
Hullbridge Sports	32	4	12	16	35	66	24
Beaumont Athletic	32	6	3	23	36	113	21
Basildon United	32	3	8	21	26	82	17
London APSA	32	2	4	26	24	99	10

Concord Rangers moved to the Isthmian League and Beaumont Athletic moved to the Essex Olympian League. Takeley joined from the Essex Olympian League.

2008-09

Romford	30	21	8	1	79	25	71
Enfield 1893	30	21	1	8	62	29	64
Takeley	30	19	4	7	59	37	61
Southend Manor	30	16	7	7	65	41	55
Barkingside	30	13	7	10	48	51	46
Eton Manor	30	12	8	10	52	40	44
Burnham Ramblers	30	12	7	11	62	50	43
Basildon United	30	14	3	13	53	50	42
Hullbridge Sports	30	11	8	11	44	46	41
Stansted	30	12	4	14	57	50	40
Bowers & Pitsea	30	11	7	12	35	35	37
Barking	30	8	7	15	45	62	31
Sawbridgeworth Town	30	8	5	17	43	70	29
London APSA	30	7	5	18	34	67	25
Mauritius Sports Association	30	4	8	18	42	76	20
Clapton	30	5	3	22	40	91	18

Basildon United and Bowers & Pitsea each had 3 points deducted.
London APSA had 1 point deducted.
Romford moved to the Isthmian League. Bethnal Green United joined from the Middlesex County League, Tiptree United joined from the Eastern Counties League and Witham Town joined from the Isthmian League.

2009-10

Stansted	34	22	8	4	99	35	74
Witham Town	34	22	5	7	81	44	68
Burnham Ramblers	34	20	7	7	86	44	67
Enfield 1893	34	19	7	8	63	38	63
Bethnal Green United	34	17	10	7	73	38	61
Takeley	34	16	7	11	55	40	55
Southend Manor	34	15	9	10	66	47	54
Barking	34	16	6	12	49	33	54
Barkingside	34	15	10	9	62	51	52
Sawbridgeworth Town	34	13	6	15	44	75	45
Hullbridge Sports	34	10	10	14	50	54	40
Basildon United	34	12	6	16	47	69	39
London APSA	34	10	7	17	38	55	37
Tiptree United	34	11	1	22	49	82	34
Eton Manor	34	8	9	17	57	71	33
Clapton	34	9	3	22	38	86	30
Bowers & Pitsea	34	8	5	21	48	77	29
Mauritius Sports Association	34	3	4	27	31	97	13

Enfield 1893 had 1 point deducted
Barkingside, Basildon United and Witham Town each had 3 points deducted.
Tiptree United merged with Maldon Town of the Isthmian League to form Maldon & Tiptree. The merged club continued to play in the Isthmian League at Maldon Town's Wallace Binder Ground. Tiptree's Chapel Road ground succumbed to building works.

2010-11

Enfield 1893	32	23	4	5	83	27	73
Stansted	32	22	9	1	81	25	72
Witham Town	32	20	8	4	82	40	67
Bethnal Green United	32	17	6	9	59	35	57
Southend Manor	32	16	5	11	58	47	53
Barking	32	15	4	13	52	44	49
Burnham Ramblers	32	14	6	12	67	50	48
Eton Manor	32	11	10	11	59	56	43
Hullbridge Sports	32	10	10	12	48	53	40
London APSA	32	12	4	16	27	42	40
Mauritius Sports Association	32	11	5	16	53	62	38
Basildon United	32	10	4	18	45	66	34
Takeley	32	9	7	16	48	73	34
Bowers & Pitsea	32	8	8	16	41	72	32
Barkingside	32	9	4	19	51	78	31
Sawbridgeworth Town	32	10	1	21	38	75	31
Clapton	32	3	9	20	37	84	18

Stansted had 3 points deducted.
Witham Town had 1 point deducted.

Mauritius Sports Association changed their name to Haringey & Waltham Development. Sporting Bengal United joined from the Kent League.

2011-12

Witham Town	34	25	7	2	117	24	82
Southend Manor	34	23	6	5	72	32	75
Takeley	34	21	5	8	68	40	68
Burnham Ramblers	34	19	7	8	75	42	64
Barking	34	19	3	12	81	53	60
Sawbridgeworth Town	34	16	8	10	69	54	56
Enfield 1893	34	15	9	10	52	36	54
Barkingside	34	16	6	12	56	45	54
Bethnal Green United	34	15	6	13	53	53	51
Sporting Bengal United	34	13	8	13	49	62	44
Hullbridge Sports	34	11	10	13	63	65	43
Haringey & Waltham Development	34	9	9	16	58	69	35
London APSA	34	8	6	20	46	87	30
Eton Manor	34	10	6	18	43	85	27
Bowers & Pitsea	34	6	9	19	47	77	26
Stansted	34	7	8	19	50	82	26
Clapton	34	6	8	20	35	78	23
Basildon United	34	3	7	24	42	92	16

Haringey & Waltham Development and Bowers & Pitsea each had 1 point deducted.
Sporting Bengal United, Stansted and Clapton each had 3 points deducted. Eton Manor had 9 points deducted.
Witham Town were promoted to the Isthmian League and Great Wakering Rovers joined after relegation from the Isthmian League. Bari joined from the Essex Sunday Corinthian League and changed their name to London Bari.

2012-13

Burnham Ramblers	36	25	7	4	92	46	82
Barkingside	36	22	7	7	72	40	73
Takeley	36	22	7	7	85	49	70
Great Wakering Rovers	36	19	8	9	97	54	65
Eton Manor	36	20	5	11	86	61	65
Barking	36	17	9	10	68	49	60
Southend Manor	36	15	11	10	78	50	56
Haringey & Waltham Development	36	15	8	13	70	65	53
Enfield 1893	36	14	9	13	66	59	51
London Bari	36	13	12	11	63	60	51
Sporting Bengal United	36	11	11	14	79	95	44
Bethnal Green United	36	11	10	15	61	73	43
Basildon United	36	12	5	19	52	79	41
Sawbridgeworth Town	36	10	9	17	67	87	39
Hullbridge Sports	36	9	8	19	53	70	35
London APSA	36	8	11	17	44	70	35
Stansted	36	7	13	16	48	69	34
Clapton	36	3	12	21	37	76	21
Bowers & Pitsea	36	4	8	24	42	110	20

Takeley had 3 points deducted.
Barkingside and Burnham Ramblers were both promoted to the Isthmian League and Ilford joined after relegation from the Isthmian League.
F.C. Romania joined from the Middlesex County League and Haringey Borough joined from the Spartan South Midlands League. Haringey & Waltham Development changed their name to Greenhouse London and Bethnal Green United changed their name to Tower Hamlets.

2013-14

Great Wakering Rovers	38	29	5	4	112	40	92
Haringey Borough	38	29	4	5	103	31	91
Enfield 1893	38	28	5	5	102	39	89
Tower Hamlets	38	24	7	7	73	48	79
FC Romania	38	21	9	8	82	56	72
Sawbridgeworth Town	38	22	5	11	87	59	71
Takeley	38	17	5	16	64	72	56
Basildon United	38	16	7	15	85	69	55
Hullbridge Sports	38	15	8	15	51	51	53
Clapton	38	14	8	16	54	54	50
Eton Manor	38	12	12	14	56	72	48
Barking	38	13	7	18	61	60	46
Sporting Bengal United	38	12	8	18	74	99	44
Bowers & Pitsea	38	11	10	17	60	72	43
London APSA	38	10	8	20	53	70	38
Ilford	38	9	7	22	50	86	34
Stansted	38	8	8	22	50	87	32
Greenhouse London	38	6	12	20	43	85	30
Southend Manor	38	6	9	23	38	81	27
London Bari	38	3	6	29	29	96	15

Greenhouse London vs Basildon United was not played and the match was awarded as a win to Greenhouse London. London APSA changed their name to Newham.
Great Wakering Rovers were promoted to the Isthmian League and Waltham Forest joined following relegation from the Isthmian League.

2014-15

Haringey Borough	38	34	1	3	129	30	103
Bowers & Pitsea	38	29	5	4	124	25	92
Barking	38	28	5	5	80	31	89
Hullbridge Sports	38	23	5	10	76	44	74
Sawbridgeworth Town	38	21	3	14	102	71	66
FC Romania	38	21	2	15	88	72	65
Stansted	38	18	6	14	68	63	60
Clapton	38	17	6	15	71	65	57
Waltham Forest	38	15	9	14	85	79	54
Ilford	38	16	6	16	63	72	54
Takeley	38	16	6	16	71	85	54
Basildon United	38	12	8	18	70	75	44
Newham	38	13	4	21	59	100	43
Eton Manor	38	10	9	19	56	86	39
London Bari	38	10	8	20	66	81	38
Enfield 1893	38	10	6	22	49	79	36
Tower Hamlets	38	9	8	21	38	81	35
Southend Manor	38	8	7	23	55	99	31
Greenhouse London	38	9	2	27	47	92	29
Sporting Bengal United	38	5	6	27	44	111	16

Sporting Bengal United had 5 points deducted.
Haringey Borough were promoted to the Isthmian League and Burnham Ramblers joined following relegation from the Isthmian League.
Wadham Lodge joined from the Essex Olympian League.
Greenhouse London changed their name to Greenhouse Sports.

2015-16

Bowers & Pitsea	40	31	3	6	118	34	96
Basildon United	40	30	4	6	109	45	94
FC Romania	40	27	8	5	114	43	89
Barking	40	23	10	7	101	50	79
Ilford	40	21	9	10	86	51	71
Wadham Lodge	40	19	10	11	85	56	67
Clapton	40	19	10	11	86	67	67
London Bari	40	17	12	11	60	52	63
Stansted	40	18	7	15	76	75	61
Sawbridgeworth Town	40	19	8	13	68	70	61
Hullbridge Sports	40	13	13	14	73	74	52
Sporting Bengal United	40	11	13	16	53	65	46
Eton Manor	40	13	6	21	73	96	45
Burnham Ramblers	40	12	8	20	62	87	44
Greenhouse Sports	40	13	4	23	58	94	43
Southend Manor	40	12	5	23	56	80	41
Tower Hamlets	40	10	6	24	49	90	36
Takeley	40	8	11	21	47	81	35
Waltham Forest	40	9	4	27	60	98	31
Enfield 1893	40	9	4	27	70	125	31
Newham	40	4	9	27	40	111	21

Ilford had 1 point deducted.
Sawbridgeworth Town had 4 points deducted.
Bowers & Pitsea were promoted to the Isthmian League and Redbridge and Barkingside both joined following relegation from the Isthmian League. Newham moved to the Essex Olympian League.
West Essex joined from the Middlesex County League.
Greenhouse Sports changed their name to Haringey & Waltham.

2016-17

Barking	42	32	4	6	125	46	100
Clapton	42	29	5	8	89	46	92
FC Romania	42	27	7	8	125	56	88
Takeley	42	25	8	9	93	51	83
Sawbridgeworth Town	42	25	8	9	98	67	83
Ilford	42	22	9	11	85	56	75
Southend Manor	42	22	5	15	76	56	71
Stansted	42	20	10	12	82	50	70
Basildon United	42	18	7	17	81	72	61
Barkingside	42	19	9	14	81	74	60
Hullbridge Sports	42	16	12	14	72	66	60
Waltham Forest	42	17	8	17	67	67	59
West Essex	42	17	7	18	77	79	58
Redbridge	42	16	7	19	93	87	55
Wadham Lodge	42	13	10	19	56	75	49
Eton Manor	42	14	4	24	74	98	46
London Bari	42	12	8	22	59	88	44
Enfield 1893	42	12	6	24	69	114	42
Sporting Bengal United	42	11	6	25	65	95	39
Tower Hamlets	42	6	6	30	47	100	24
Burnham Ramblers	42	5	6	31	45	130	21
Haringey & Waltham	42	4	8	30	38	124	20

Barkingside had 6 points deducted.
Barking were promoted to the Isthmian League and Great Wakering Rovers rejoined following relegation from the Isthmian League. London Bari merged with Hackney Wick of the Middlesex County League. The merged club continued to play in the Essex Senior League as Hackney Wick, playing at London Bari's ground, the Old Spotted Dog Ground in Forest Gate, London. Hackney Wick had been playing at Mabley Green in Hackney. Eton Manor ceased playing activity.

GREAT WESTERN SUBURBAN LEAGUE 1904-1931

The Great Western Suburban League was formed in 1904 and it broadly covered an area served by the Great Western Railway's suburban passenger services operating from Paddington station, i.e. Middlesex, Berkshire, Buckinghamshire and the surrounding area. The league's 9 founder members were: 2nd Grenadier Guards (quartered at the Victoria Barracks, Windsor), Hounslow, Kensington Town, Maidenhead, Maidenhead Norfolkians, Staines, Uxbridge, Willesden Town and Windsor & Eton.

Maidenhead, Maidenhead Norfolkians and Windsor & Eton had previously been playing in the West Berkshire League while both Maidenhead clubs had also been playing in the Berks. & Bucks. Senior League. Hounslow had been playing in the West Middlesex League Apart from joining the league, Willesden Town also fielded two teams in the London League in 1904-05.

1904-05

2nd Grenadier Guards	16	11	2	3	33	18	24
Maidenhead Norfolkians	16	9	4	3	43	17	22
Hounslow	15	9	2	4	40	23	20
Willesden Town	16	9	0	7	47	36	18
Uxbridge	16	7	2	7	28	34	16
Maidenhead	16	6	1	9	32	37	11
Staines	15	3	4	8	19	23	10
Windsor & Eton	16	4	2	10	19	40	10
Kensington Town	14	3	1	10	20	53	7

Maidenhead had 2 points deducted.
Two games were not played.
Kensington Town and Willesden Town both left the league. Hanwell and Brentford Reserves both joined from the London League, Brentford Reserves also continuing to play in the London League. Slough joined from the Berks & Bucks Senior League.

1905-06

Hounslow	18	15	2	1	52	14	32
Brentford Reserves	18	10	2	6	49	25	22
Maidenhead Norfolkians	18	9	4	5	48	26	22
Windsor & Eton	18	4	8	6	27	32	16
Hanwell	18	6	4	8	31	60	16
Slough	18	6	3	9	46	33	15
Uxbridge	18	6	3	9	35	39	15
Maidenhead	18	4	6	8	34	45	14
Staines	18	6	2	10	21	36	14
2nd Grenadier Guards	18	6	2	10	27	60	14

2nd Grenadier Guards were replaced by 3rd Grenadier Guards. Shepherds Bush joined the league.

1906-07

Shepherds Bush	20	17	1	2	82	11	35
Brentford Reserves	20	16	0	4	69	18	32
Hounslow	20	12	3	5	37	28	27
Maidenhead Norfolkians	20	12	2	6	63	28	26
Slough	20	10	3	7	51	41	23
Uxbridge	20	7	4	9	36	47	18
Windsor & Eton	20	7	1	12	32	47	15
3rd Grenadier Guards	20	5	3	12	31	53	13
Hanwell	20	5	1	14	29	72	11
Maidenhead	20	4	2	14	31	69	10
Staines	20	4	2	14	19	66	10

3rd Grenadier Guards replaced by 1st Grenadier Guards. Shepherds Bush moved to the Spartan League. Southall joined having regained senior status after leaving the Southern League and ceasing activity in 1905 because of financial problems.

1907-08

Brentford Reserves	20	17	1	2	78	25	35
1st Grenadier Guards	20	14	3	3	53	25	31
Windsor & Eton	20	13	2	5	40	30	28
Southall	20	11	1	8	53	35	23
Maidenhead Norfolkians	20	9	2	9	45	50	20
Hounslow	20	7	4	9	34	40	18
Uxbridge	20	6	4	10	36	38	16
Maidenhead	20	5	6	9	35	45	16
Staines	20	7	2	11	28	51	16
Hanwell	20	4	4	12	28	47	12
Slough	20	1	4	15	15	59	6

1st Grenadier Guards replaced by 1st Irish Guards. Reading Reserves joined from the Southern League – Division Two and Wycombe Wanderers joined while continuing in the Southern League – Division Two.

1908-09

Brentford Reserves	24	17	5	2	70	28	39
Reading Reserves	24	17	3	4	108	22	37
Wycombe Wanderers	24	14	6	4	46	30	34
Hounslow	24	11	7	6	36	31	29
Windsor & Eton	24	9	8	7	35	38	26
Maidenhead	24	11	3	10	47	47	25
Maidenhead Norfolkians	24	9	5	10	43	52	23
Southall	24	9	3	12	48	52	21
Hanwell	24	8	5	11	40	55	21
1st Irish Guards	24	8	3	13	49	62	19
Uxbridge	24	6	5	13	40	59	17
Staines	24	4	4	16	24	64	12
Slough	24	3	3	18	19	65	9

1st Irish Guards replaced by 2nd Scots Guards. Hounslow resigned from the league and disbanded.

1909-10

Reading Reserves	22	19	2	1	110	21	38
Brentford Reserves	22	18	1	3	95	21	37
Wycombe Wanderers	22	14	1	7	65	33	29
Windsor & Eton	22	14	1	7	46	33	29
Southall	22	10	3	9	37	38	23
Maidenhead	22	10	3	9	45	48	23
Uxbridge	22	8	4	10	53	44	20
2nd Scots Guards	22	8	1	13	44	57	17
Hanwell	22	6	3	13	30	79	15
Maidenhead Norfolkians	22	4	2	16	28	80	10
Staines	22	4	4	14	26	86	10
Slough	22	3	3	16	24	63	9

Reading Reserves and Staines each had 2 points deducted.
2nd Scots Guards left the league. 1st Coldstream Guards and Royal Horse Guards both joined.

1910-11

Brentford Reserves	24	22	2	0	103	15	46
Uxbridge	24	15	7	2	52	21	37
Southall	24	15	4	5	80	32	34
1st Coldstream Guards	23	14	3	6	56	27	31
Wycombe Wanderers	24	11	3	10	62	43	25
Windsor & Eton	24	9	3	12	40	47	21
Maidenhead Norfolkians	24	8	4	12	38	51	20
Maidenhead	24	9	4	11	40	57	20
Hanwell	24	8	3	13	43	65	19
Staines	24	7	4	13	44	53	18
Reading Reserves	24	12	1	11	48	42	13
Slough	24	1	5	18	17	77	5
Royal Horse Guards	23	2	1	20	21	114	5

Maidenhead and Slough each had 2 points deducted.
Reading Reserves had 12 points deducted.
1st Coldstream Guards and Royal Horse Guards both left the league and were replaced by 2nd Grenadier Guards. The league banned professional teams from membership so Reading Reserves moved to the South-Eastern League while Brentford Reserves left but continued to play in the London League. Marlow joined, having resigned from the Spartan League during the 1910-11 season.

1911-12

2nd Grenadier Guards	20	17	2	1	79	21	36
Staines	20	12	3	5	43	30	27
Wycombe Wanderers	20	11	3	6	56	39	25
Maidenhead	20	10	2	8	52	45	22
Windsor & Eton	20	10	2	8	39	34	22
Maidenhead Norfolkians	20	9	1	10	49	36	19
Southall	20	7	3	10	43	50	17
Uxbridge	20	7	3	10	32	42	17
Slough	20	5	5	10	25	41	15
Marlow	20	6	3	11	22	46	13
Hanwell	20	2	1	17	27	83	5

Marlow had 2 points deducted.
2nd Grenadier Guards left the league and 19th Royal Hussars and 3rd Coldstream Guards both joined. Hanwell also left the league.

1912-13

Southall	20	14	3	3	53	22	31
19th Royal Hussars	20	11	4	5	49	37	26
Windsor & Eton	20	11	3	6	55	35	25
Uxbridge	20	10	4	6	40	29	24
3rd Coldstream Guards	20	11	1	8	60	49	23
Slough	20	6	8	6	33	38	20
Wycombe Wanderers	20	7	2	11	44	43	16
Maidenhead Norfolkians	20	6	3	11	30	60	15
Staines	20	6	2	12	25	36	14
Maidenhead	20	5	2	13	32	47	12
Marlow	20	6	2	12	23	48	12

Marlow had 2 points deducted.
Staines left the league.

1913-14

19th Royal Hussars	18	13	1	4	46	20	27
Maidenhead Norfolkians	18	12	2	4	34	19	26
Southall	18	10	5	3	47	16	25
Wycombe Wanderers	18	9	3	6	49	34	21
Maidenhead	18	8	4	6	42	32	20
3rd Coldstream Guards	18	5	6	7	30	44	16
Windsor & Eton	18	6	3	9	29	37	15
Marlow	18	3	5	10	25	48	11
Slough	18	4	2	12	21	36	10
Uxbridge	18	3	3	12	18	55	7

Uxbridge had 2 points deducted.

1914-19

The league closed down during the First World War and did not resume playing until 1919. 19th Royal Hussars and 3rd Coldstream Guards did not rejoin but were replaced by 1st Scots Guards. Maidenhead merged with Maidenhead Norfolkians to form Maidenhead Town. Southall and Uxbridge both moved to the Athenian League and Wycombe Wanderers moved to the Spartan League. Uxbridge and Wycombe Wanderers were replaced by their reserves.

New members to join in 1919 were Botwell Mission, Chesham United Reserves, Newbury Town, Reading United and Yiewsley.

1919-20

Maidenhead United	22	14	7	1	76	14	35
Botwell Mission	22	15	2	5	75	32	32
Slough	22	14	4	4	85	37	32
Windsor & Eton	22	11	5	6	52	38	27
Reading United	22	11	2	9	47	40	24
Yiewsley	22	10	3	9	49	50	23
Wycombe Wanderers Reserves	22	7	7	8	57	47	21
Chesham United Reserves	22	8	5	9	42	48	21
Marlow	22	7	2	13	40	70	16
Newbury Town	22	5	3	14	34	74	13
Uxbridge Town Reserves	22	4	2	16	31	72	10
1st Scots Guards	22	4	2	16	29	95	10

1st Scots Guards left the league and were replaced by 2nd Scots Guards and 1st Grenadier Guards. Slough moved to the Spartan League and Chesham United Reserves and Wycombe Wanderers Reserves also left. Uxbridge Town joined from the Athenian League, replacing their reserves, and R.A.F. Uxbridge and Slough Trading Company both also joined. Maidenhead Town changed their name to Maidenhead United.

1920-21

Botwell Mission	22	19	3	0	95	14	41
Maidenhead United	22	16	4	2	65	25	36
Windsor & Eton	22	11	8	3	43	25	30
Reading United	22	12	3	7	65	45	27
Slough Trading Company	22	11	3	8	48	25	25
R.A.F. Uxbridge	22	10	3	9	46	44	23
Uxbridge Town	22	8	5	9	44	38	21
Yiewsley	22	3	9	10	29	49	15
2nd Scots Guards	22	4	5	13	29	61	13
Marlow	22	5	3	14	30	70	13
Newbury Town	22	4	4	14	34	63	12
1st Grenadier Guards	22	2	4	16	17	86	8

2nd Scots Guards and 1st Grenadier Guards both left the league and Reading United were replaced by Reading Amateurs. Hounslow joined, having just re-formed after 12 years of inactivity. Hanwell Athletic and Staines Lagonda also joined the league.

1921-22

Botwell Mission	24	18	4	2	79	25	40
Windsor & Eton	24	18	3	3	68	29	39
Uxbridge Town	24	10	9	5	45	35	29
Hounslow	24	11	7	6	51	44	29
Staines Lagonda	24	12	3	9	58	36	27
Hanwell Athletic	24	10	5	9	35	44	25
Maidenhead United	24	9	4	11	34	45	22
Yiewsley	24	8	5	11	53	51	21
Slough Trading Company	24	8	5	11	38	44	21
Marlow	24	8	5	11	43	50	21
R.A.F. Uxbridge	24	6	4	14	40	46	16
Newbury Town	24	5	1	18	39	90	11
Reading Amateurs	24	3	5	16	29	73	11

Windsor & Eton moved to the Athenian League and were replaced by their reserves. Maidenhead United moved to the Spartan League while Reading Amateurs and Slough Trading Company also left the league.

1922-23

Botwell Mission	18	10	5	3	59	21	25
Staines Lagonda	18	11	3	4	44	23	25
Hounslow	18	11	2	5	49	29	24
Hanwell Athletic	18	7	5	6	51	36	19
Uxbridge Town	18	7	5	6	30	25	19
Newbury Town	18	9	1	8	35	43	19
Windsor & Eton Reserves	18	7	2	9	31	54	16
Yiewsley	18	5	2	11	30	41	12
R.A.F. Uxbridge	18	4	4	10	29	62	12
Marlow	18	3	3	12	20	44	9

R.A.F. Uxbridge left the league.
Chiswick Generals, Cowley and Harrow Weald all joined.

1923-24

Botwell Mission	22	18	3	1	88	11	39
Staines Lagonda	22	16	1	5	81	27	33
Cowley	22	14	3	5	57	29	31
Uxbridge Town	22	14	1	7	63	33	29
Newbury Town	22	10	2	10	49	46	22
Hounslow	22	8	4	10	33	32	20
Yiewsley	22	9	2	11	44	45	20
Hanwell Athletic	22	7	5	10	26	43	19
Windsor & Eton Reserves	22	9	1	12	38	62	19
Harrow Weald	22	7	3	12	39	65	17
Marlow	22	2	6	14	25	71	10
Chiswick Generals	22	1	3	18	9	88	5

Botwell Mission moved to the Spartan League and were replaced by their
reserves. Staines Lagonda also moved to the Spartan League while
Uxbridge Town moved to the Athenian League and Marlow moved to the
Reading & District League. Chiswick Generals and Hanwell Athletic also left
the league. Leavesden Mental Hospital joined from the Spartan League
while Ashford (Middlesex), Savoy Hotel, Watford Old Boys and Bush Hill
Park Reserves also joined.

1924-25

Hounslow	22	15	3	4	63	24	33
Yiewsley	22	12	5	5	53	22	29
Newbury Town	22	13	3	6	44	28	29
Cowley	22	9	9	4	48	31	27
Leavesden Mental Hospital	22	12	2	8	32	25	26
Harrow Weald	22	11	3	8	51	39	25
Botwell Mission Reserves	22	11	3	8	44	36	25
Watford Old Boys	22	9	3	10	39	39	21
Savoy Hotel	22	10	0	12	39	50	20
Windsor & Eton Reserves	22	5	3	14	36	66	13
Ashford (Middlesex)	22	4	2	16	24	65	10
Bush Hill Park Reserves	22	1	4	17	18	66	6

Savoy Hotel, Bush Hill Park Reserves and Windsor & Eton Reserves all left
the league and Berkhamsted Town Reserves joined.

1925-26

Newbury Town	18	13	2	3	70	25	28
Watford Old Boys	18	14	0	4	80	29	28
Yiewsley	18	12	3	3	54	23	27
Leavesden Mental Hospital	18	9	3	6	43	31	21
Berkhamsted Town Reserves	18	7	4	7	37	45	18
Hounslow	18	7	1	10	42	61	15
Cowley	18	5	3	10	37	44	13
Botwell Mission Reserves	18	5	1	12	44	78	11
Harrow Weald	18	5	1	12	32	61	11
Ashford (Middlesex)	18	3	2	13	26	68	8

Watford Old Boys moved to the Spartan League and were replaced by their
reserves. Yiewsley also moved to the Spartan League while Harrow Weald
and Botwell Mission Reserves both left the league. Leyland Motors joined
from the Surrey Senior League.

1926-27

The teams played each other 4 times.

Leyland Motors	28	20	3	5	72	29	43
Newbury Town	27	18	1	8	66	43	37
Watford Old Boys Reserves	26	16	4	6	48	33	36
Cowley	27	13	6	8	60	46	32
Leavesden Mental Hospital	28	11	1	16	42	44	23
Ashford (Middlesex)	26	8	2	16	15	68	18
Hounslow	26	6	3	17	46	67	15
Berkhamsted Town Reserves	28	6	0	22	24	43	12

4 games were not played.
Leavesden Mental Hospital and Berkhamsted Town Reserves both moved
to the Hertfordshire League, Leyland Motors moved to the Surrey Senior
League and Hounslow moved to the London League. Ashford (Middlesex),
Cowley, Newbury Town and Watford Old Boys all also left, leaving the
league without any members. It therefore had to reform with an entirely
new membership of 13 clubs: Ealing Celtic, Feltham Sports, Great Western
Railway Reserves, Hanwell Guild, Harmondsworth St. Mary's, Harrow &
Greenhill, Holland Athletic Reserves, Hounslow Rangers, Lyons Club
Reserves, Napier, Roweth & Harrow Old Boys, W.E.R.S.A.C. and Western
United.

1927-28

Napier	24	21	1	2	124	26	43
Holland Athletic Reserves	24	17	4	3	99	28	38
Hounslow Rangers	24	17	2	5	72	41	36
Roxeth & Harrow Old Boys	24	12	6	6	68	57	30
Western United	24	11	6	7	72	58	28
Lyons Club Reserves	24	12	1	11	72	56	25
Harrow & Greenhill	24	10	1	13	60	83	21
Ealing Celtic	24	7	5	12	58	59	19
Hanwell Guild	24	8	3	13	54	89	19
Harmondsworth St. Mary's	24	6	6	12	57	83	18
W.E.R.S.A.C.	24	7	4	13	64	103	18
Feltham Sports	24	7	3	14	74	95	17
Great Western Railway Reserves	24	2	0	22	40	134	4

Great Western Railway Reserves, Harmondsworth St. Mary's, Harrow &
Greenhill, Hounslow Rangers and W.E.R.S.A.C. all left the league and
Paddington joined.

1928-29

Napier	16	15	1	0	85	9	31
Roxeth & Harrow Old Boys	16	11	1	4	58	26	23
Holland Athletic Reserves	16	10	0	6	47	45	20
Feltham Sports	15	9	0	6	59	44	18
Ealing Celtic	15	8	2	5	37	31	18
Western United	15	7	1	7	36	35	15
Lyons Club Reserves	16	7	0	9	36	37	14
Hanwell Guild	15	1	1	13	21	59	3
Paddington	15	1	0	14	17	75	2

Some games were not completed.
Hanwell Guild, Holland Athletic Reserves, Lyons Club Reserves, Paddington
and Western United all left the league. Firestones, Fourstores, Hayesco,
Minters Athletic, Park Royal Reserves, Southall United, Uxbridge Unity and
Yiewsley Juniors all joined.

1929-30

Napier	22	15	4	3	93	36	34
Ealing Celtic	22	13	5	4	69	40	31
Minters Athletic	22	13	2	7	59	39	28
Uxbridge Unity	22	12	4	6	46	39	28
Southall United	22	11	4	7	75	55	26
Roxeth & Harrow Old Boys	22	10	2	10	54	77	22
Feltham Sports	22	9	3	10	43	37	21
Park Royal Reserves	22	6	7	9	65	58	19
Yiewsley Juniors	22	6	4	12	50	56	16
Firestones	22	6	4	12	31	49	16
Hayesco	22	5	4	13	35	70	14
Fourstores	22	3	3	16	31	95	9

Fourstores, Hayesco, Park Royal Reserves, Roxeth & Harrow Old Boys and Yiewsley Juniors all left the league.

1930-31

The teams played each other 3 times.

Napier	18	13	4	1	66	37	30
Feltham Sports	18	11	3	4	81	60	25
Ealing Celtic	18	11	1	6	70	41	23
Southall United	16	7	4	5	59	42	18
Minters Athletic	15	4	1	10	39	45	9
Firestones	18	3	1	14	25	67	7
Uxbridge Unity	13	2	0	11	8	56	4

Southall United had 2 points deducted.
Uxbridge Unity failed to play 5 games.

The Great Western Suburban League closed at the end of the 1930-31 season.

ATHENIAN LEAGUE 1912-1984

The Athenian League was formed at a meeting held at Norwich House, Southampton Street, Holborn, London on Friday 21st June 1912. The league was to be called the Corinthian League but, when the F.A. sanctioned the league, it was on condition that a different name was used. The first suggestion was the Home Counties League but it was the title Athenian League that was finally agreed upon. The 10 founder members were:

Barking who had been playing in the both the London League and South Essex League and continued to play in both.

Barnet & Alston who moved from the London League.

Catford Southend who had been playing in the London League and also continued to play in it.

Chelmsford who had been playing in the South Essex League and also continued to play in it.

Chesham Town who moved from the Southern League – Division Two.

Enfield who had been playing in the London League and also continued to play in it.

Finchley who moved from the London League.

Grays Athletic who had been playing in the South Essex League and also continued to play in it.

Romford Town who had been playing in the South Essex League and also continued to play in it.

Tufnell Park who had been playing in both the London League and the Spartan League but did not continue in either.

1912-13

Catford Southend	16	11	3	2	50	15	25
Barnet & Alston	16	9	3	4	36	17	21
Tufnell Park	16	8	5	3	25	13	21
Finchley	16	8	4	4	19	11	20
Grays Athletic	16	4	6	6	18	23	14
Chelmsford	16	5	3	8	21	36	13
Enfield	16	3	6	7	18	28	12
Chesham Town	16	3	4	9	21	42	10
Romford Town	16	2	4	10	17	40	8

Barking withdrew from the league and their record at the time was deleted:

	2	0	0	2	1	9	0

Barking had been fined £5 for contravention of Rule 8e which states that "Each club shall play its recognised first eleven team in all League matches." in relation to their away game with Catford Southend on 7th September which they lost 6-0. Barking resigned on 30th October but at a meeting on 6th November, the league initially refused to accept their resignation and ordered them to fulfil their fixture at Romford on 9th November. Barking, however, did not turn up and were fined a further £1-10 s. by the league which then had to accept their resignation.

Luton Clarence joined from the Northamptonshire League, Metrogas joined from the Kent League and St. Leonards Amateurs joined from the East Sussex League, changing their name to Hastings & St. Leonards.

1913-14

Tufnell Park	22	15	3	4	61	24	33
Luton Clarence	22	15	2	5	64	34	32
Grays Athletic	22	13	3	6	43	27	29
Metrogas	22	11	3	8	62	52	25
Enfield	22	10	3	9	52	37	23
Barnet & Alston	22	9	4	9	32	28	22
Catford Southend	22	7	7	8	35	41	21
Romford Town	22	8	5	9	47	65	21
Finchley	22	8	3	11	53	47	19
Hastings & St. Leonards	22	7	2	13	38	59	16
Chelmsford	22	6	1	15	32	68	13
Chesham Town	22	4	2	16	24	61	10

June 1914

Grays Athletic and Romford Town both moved to the London League.

Hastings & St. Leonards resigned because they were about to lose their Brisco Recreation Ground home to the Hastings town improvement scheme. They were unable to find a new ground and ceased activity after the declaration of war. They did not resume when the war ended but in 1920, the Pilot Field in Hastings was made available for football and so a pre-war junior club called Rock-a-Nore moved in and joined the Sussex County League. In 1921, they changed their name to Hastings & St. Leonards.

Chesham Town moved to the Great Western Suburban League but in 1917, they merged with Chesham Generals of the Spartan League to form Chesham United who replaced Chesham Generals in the Spartan League.

Old Kingstonians, Summerstown and Tooting Graveney all joined from the Southern Suburban League and Townley Park joined from the Southern Amateur League, getting one more vote in the ballot on 5th June than Hampstead Town, also of the Southern Amateur League. However, they resigned their place on 15th June because of ground problems and Hampstead accepted an invitation to replace them. Townley Park did not resume after the war.

August 1914

When war was declared, the league closed down but the London League did not and Catford Southend and Finchley both joined the London League. Catford Southend continued to play in the London League after the war but Finchley did not reform until 1921 when they joined the Spartan League.

After the war in 1919

Tooting Graveney returned to the Southern Suburban League instead of taking up their place in the Athenian League, having changed their name to Tooting Town. Enfield joined the Middlesex League instead of returning to the Athenian League, and Tufnell Park moved to the Isthmian League. Southall and Uxbridge Town both joined from the Great Western Suburban League, Cheshunt joined from the Southern Amateur League, Bromley joined from the Kent League and Wimbledon joined from the Southern Suburban League. Wimbledon were in the Mid-Surrey League in 1914-15. Old Kingstonians merged with Kingston Town of the Southern Suburban League and took up their Athenian League place as Kingstonian. Barnet & Alston changed their name to Barnet.

1919-20

Luton Clarence	22	16	5	1	71	14	37
Metrogas	22	12	5	5	63	43	29
Barnet	22	11	4	7	53	31	26
Hampstead Town	22	10	6	6	43	37	26
Bromley	22	10	4	8	41	35	24
Summerstown	22	9	6	7	31	29	24
Wimbledon	22	8	5	9	44	43	21
Kingstonian	22	7	4	11	49	53	18
Chelmsford	22	7	3	12	38	51	17
Southall	22	7	1	14	28	51	15
Uxbridge Town	22	7	1	14	24	69	15
Cheshunt	22	4	4	14	42	71	12

Cheshunt moved to the Southern Amateur League and Uxbridge Town moved to the Great Western Suburban League. St. Albans City joined from the Spartan League and West London Old Boys also joined. They had been playing in the London League in 1913-14 and joined the Spartan League for the 1914-15 season. However, war was declared before they could play in that league and the club did not resume until 1920 when they joined the Athenian League.

1920-21

St. Albans City	22	14	5	3	53	29	33
Wimbledon	22	14	3	5	41	22	31
Hampstead Town	22	12	4	6	46	41	28
Metrogas	22	11	4	7	46	31	26
Luton Clarence	22	11	2	9	57	40	24
Barnet	22	11	2	9	49	35	24
Bromley	22	8	4	10	38	42	20
Summerstown	22	9	2	11	38	42	20
Chelmsford	22	8	3	11	39	42	19
Southall	22	6	6	10	31	48	18
Kingstonian	22	6	4	12	30	49	16
West London Old Boys	22	1	3	18	14	61	5

Wimbledon moved to the Isthmian League and West London Old Boys disbanded. Guildford and Sutton United both joined from the Southern Suburban League, Cheshunt joined from the Southern Amateur League and Enfield joined from the London League

1921-22

St. Albans City	26	18	5	3	71	23	41
Metrogas	26	14	8	4	55	36	36
Summerstown	26	12	7	7	40	35	31
Hampstead Town	26	12	5	9	40	38	29
Southall	26	11	5	10	46	49	27
Bromley	26	11	5	10	31	35	27
Cheshunt	26	11	4	11	47	52	26
Sutton United	26	11	3	12	57	56	25
Enfield	26	8	7	11	48	48	23
Luton Clarence	26	8	5	13	50	53	21
Guildford	26	6	9	11	39	52	21
Barnet	26	6	8	12	29	45	20
Chelmsford	26	6	7	13	26	44	19
Kingstonian	26	6	6	14	34	47	18

Chelmsford moved to the Middlesex League and Windsor & Eton joined from the Great Western Suburban League. Metrogas resigned just before the start of the 1922-23 season after their players and officials were banned by the F.A. for administrative irregularities. They joined the London League for the 1923-24 season.

1922-23

Bromley	24	18	4	2	64	25	40
St. Albans City	24	15	4	5	69	31	34
Southall	24	13	6	5	48	31	32
Kingstonian	24	13	3	8	60	42	29
Enfield	24	12	5	7	38	35	29
Barnet	24	11	5	8	43	40	27
Sutton United	24	10	6	8	46	39	26
Hampstead Town	24	9	2	13	48	53	20
Summerstown	24	7	5	12	37	43	19
Windsor & Eton	24	6	6	12	36	53	18
Luton Clarence	24	6	4	14	37	68	16
Cheshunt	24	4	4	16	37	64	12
Guildford	24	4	2	18	32	71	10

St. Albans City moved to the Isthmian League and Guildford moved to the Surrey Senior League. Barking Town and Redhill both joined from the London League.

1923-24

Kingstonian	24	17	2	5	63	32	36
Redhill	24	14	5	5	63	39	33
Southall	24	12	7	5	52	28	31
Barnet	24	11	6	7	48	29	28
Hampstead Town	24	10	6	8	49	37	26
Summerstown	24	9	7	8	46	40	25
Bromley	24	11	2	11	60	44	24
Barking Town	24	8	8	8	43	40	24
Windsor & Eton	24	8	5	11	43	51	21
Sutton United	24	9	3	12	32	48	21
Cheshunt	24	7	5	12	33	51	19
Enfield	24	6	2	16	38	63	14
Luton Clarence	24	4	2	18	31	99	10

Luton Clarence moved their first team to the Bedfordshire County League, replacing their reserves. Uxbridge Town joined from the Great Western Suburban League and West Norwood joined from the London League.

1924-25

Redhill	26	19	3	4	90	35	41
Barking Town	26	15	5	6	58	35	35
Kingstonian	26	15	4	7	48	34	34
Southall	26	16	1	9	62	29	33
Hampstead Town	26	10	11	5	55	34	31
Barnet	26	10	7	9	35	38	27
Enfield	26	8	9	9	46	42	25
Summerstown	26	9	7	10	41	42	25
Cheshunt	26	8	7	11	43	57	23
Uxbridge Town	26	8	6	12	43	70	22
Bromley	26	7	4	15	47	50	18
Windsor & Eton	26	4	10	12	47	77	18
Sutton United	26	5	8	13	37	64	18
West Norwood	26	5	4	17	30	75	14

1925-26

Kingstonian	26	22	0	4	80	40	44
Redhill	26	18	2	6	91	46	38
Barking Town	26	17	2	7	94	53	36
Hampstead Town	26	15	1	10	66	46	31
Uxbridge Town	26	13	3	10	75	64	29
Barnet	26	12	4	10	74	57	28
Bromley	26	10	5	11	66	65	25
Southall	26	10	4	12	49	49	24
Windsor & Eton	26	10	4	12	66	70	24
Cheshunt	26	10	2	14	73	83	22
West Norwood	26	7	5	14	44	69	19
Enfield	26	8	3	15	49	77	19
Summerstown	26	6	5	15	41	70	17
Sutton United	26	3	2	21	37	116	8

Hampstead Town changed their name to Hampstead.

1926-27

Southall	26	18	3	5	76	40	39
Kingstonian	26	16	2	8	85	54	34
Barking Town	26	14	5	7	76	61	33
Enfield	26	14	2	10	86	68	30
Cheshunt	26	13	3	10	82	74	29
Uxbridge Town	26	10	6	10	70	58	26
Barnet	26	10	6	10	48	40	26
Redhill	26	11	3	12	79	70	25
Windsor & Eton	26	11	3	12	63	85	25
Bromley	26	8	8	10	56	60	24
Sutton United	26	10	4	12	54	65	24
Summerstown	26	9	3	14	57	66	21
Hampstead	26	7	2	17	59	78	16
West Norwood	26	3	6	17	38	110	12

West Norwood moved to the Surrey Senior League and Leyton joined from the London League.

1927-28

Sutton United	26	20	3	3	83	35	43
Redhill	26	19	3	4	76	43	41
Barking Town	26	17	2	7	90	44	36
Leyton	26	17	1	8	77	40	35
Kingstonian	26	13	5	8	80	61	31
Enfield	26	13	3	10	70	61	29
Southall	26	11	5	10	55	50	27
Barnet	26	11	5	10	68	63	27
Bromley	26	10	2	14	60	85	22
Summerstown	26	7	7	12	51	64	21
Hampstead	26	6	4	16	44	76	16
Windsor & Eton	26	6	3	17	52	93	15
Uxbridge Town	26	5	2	19	59	99	12
Cheshunt	26	3	3	20	51	102	9

Summerstown disbanded and Wealdstone joined from the Spartan League.

1928-29

Leyton	26	19	5	2	78	33	43
Hampstead	26	16	3	7	64	39	35
Sutton United	26	13	7	6	73	50	33
Southall	26	12	5	9	66	47	29
Enfield	26	11	7	8	47	51	29
Bromley	26	11	6	9	68	63	28
Barnet	26	12	3	11	67	55	27
Wealdstone	26	11	3	12	81	63	25
Redhill	26	9	6	11	70	59	24
Barking Town	26	11	2	13	52	55	24
Kingstonian	26	10	1	15	61	71	21
Uxbridge Town	26	7	3	16	59	71	17
Windsor & Eton	26	5	6	15	33	94	16
Cheshunt	26	4	5	17	52	120	13

Kingstonian moved to the Isthmian League and Windsor & Eton moved to the Spartan League.
Finchley joined from the London League and Walthamstow Avenue joined from the Spartan League.

1929-30

Walthamstow Avenue	26	19	3	4	94	39	41
Barnet	26	17	3	6	75	35	37
Leyton	26	15	7	4	58	35	37
Barking Town	26	14	3	9	66	60	31
Wealdstone	26	12	5	9	59	50	29
Enfield	26	11	5	10	53	50	27
Redhill	26	11	3	12	72	67	25
Sutton United	26	9	6	11	49	51	24
Uxbridge Town	26	11	2	13	60	65	24
Bromley	26	11	1	14	65	68	23
Hampstead	26	9	5	12	46	51	23
Finchley	26	7	5	14	53	74	19
Southall	26	5	4	17	45	74	14
Cheshunt	26	4	2	20	42	118	10

Finchley moved to the London League and Hayes joined from the Spartan League.

1930-31

Barnet	26	22	2	2	103	30	46
Walthamstow Avenue	26	14	6	6	73	47	34
Leyton	26	15	4	7	62	44	34
Enfield	26	12	5	9	75	52	29
Wealdstone	26	12	5	9	79	60	29
Southall	26	13	2	11	59	51	28
Hayes	26	12	4	10	66	58	28
Hampstead	26	11	6	9	68	60	28
Bromley	26	11	4	11	57	73	26
Barking Town	26	10	5	11	69	60	25
Sutton United	26	9	4	13	45	57	22
Uxbridge Town	26	6	4	16	53	88	16
Redhill	26	5	5	16	53	89	15
Cheshunt	26	1	2	23	32	125	4

Cheshunt disbanded because of financial difficulties and the loss of their ground. Romford joined from the London League.

1931-32

Barnet	26	17	5	4	90	56	39
Hayes	26	16	4	6	74	50	36
Leyton	26	15	4	7	74	46	34
Hampstead	26	14	4	8	72	52	32
Barking Town	26	13	6	7	71	54	32
Wealdstone	26	12	3	11	65	70	27
Enfield	26	12	2	12	81	65	26
Romford	26	10	6	10	64	61	26
Sutton United	26	9	7	10	65	56	25
Walthamstow Avenue	26	10	5	11	57	65	25
Southall	26	8	4	14	52	72	20
Redhill	26	7	3	16	59	83	17
Bromley	26	7	2	17	65	91	16
Uxbridge Town	26	4	1	21	29	97	9

Barking Town changed their name to Barking.

1932-33

Walthamstow Avenue	26	16	6	4	80	29	38
Hampstead	26	15	6	5	82	35	36
Barnet	26	15	4	7	74	48	34
Barking	26	14	6	6	54	48	34
Leyton	26	8	11	7	58	54	27
Sutton United	26	10	5	11	54	66	25
Romford	26	8	8	10	50	66	24
Enfield	26	10	3	13	55	51	23
Redhill	26	9	5	12	53	66	23
Wealdstone	26	9	4	13	38	56	22
Southall	26	7	7	12	53	75	21
Hayes	26	7	6	13	53	57	20
Uxbridge Town	26	8	3	15	46	80	19
Bromley	26	7	4	15	68	87	18

Hampstead changed their name to Golders Green.

1933-34

Walthamstow Avenue	26	20	1	5	80	34	41
Romford	26	16	4	6	61	39	36
Golders Green	26	16	2	8	80	37	34
Enfield	26	12	5	9	56	51	29
Barnet	26	13	2	11	66	55	28
Sutton United	26	12	2	12	58	56	26
Barking	26	12	2	12	59	64	26
Hayes	26	11	3	12	66	69	25
Leyton	26	10	4	12	55	60	24
Uxbridge Town	26	10	3	13	55	56	23
Southall	26	9	4	13	50	69	22
Redhill	26	9	3	14	55	71	21
Wealdstone	26	5	6	15	54	78	16
Bromley	26	4	5	17	42	98	13

1934-35

Barking	26	15	5	6	57	40	35
Enfield	26	15	3	8	51	33	33
Leyton	26	13	7	6	57	39	33
Walthamstow Avenue	26	13	5	8	50	38	31
Romford	26	11	7	8	62	46	29
Golders Green	26	12	5	9	70	56	29
Bromley	26	12	4	10	44	50	28
Southall	26	10	5	11	43	57	25
Sutton United	26	10	3	13	69	63	23
Barnet	26	9	3	14	41	53	21
Hayes	26	8	5	13	45	59	21
Uxbridge Town	26	7	6	13	54	66	20
Redhill	26	7	5	14	51	69	19
Wealdstone	26	5	7	14	47	72	17

1935-36

Romford	26	15	8	3	79	36	38
Bromley	26	16	5	5	52	26	37
Walthamstow Avenue	26	16	4	6	81	41	36
Enfield	26	13	6	7	49	42	32
Golders Green	26	13	5	8	73	60	31
Southall	26	13	3	10	57	60	29
Redhill	26	11	5	10	48	47	27
Leyton	26	10	6	10	45	49	26
Barking	26	8	7	11	65	48	23
Sutton United	26	9	5	12	40	61	23
Hayes	26	7	7	12	45	61	21
Barnet	26	6	3	17	53	83	15
Wealdstone	26	6	2	18	48	80	14
Uxbridge Town	26	3	6	17	45	86	12

Southall merged with Park Royal of the London League, continuing to play in the Athenian League as Southall.

1936-37

Romford	26	24	1	1	102	35	49
Walthamstow Avenue	26	17	5	4	101	45	39
Wealdstone	26	17	3	6	66	44	37
Sutton United	26	11	5	10	47	45	27
Bromley	26	12	3	11	51	63	27
Barnet	26	11	3	12	66	82	25
Leyton	26	10	4	12	56	51	24
Redhill	26	7	9	10	56	66	23
Hayes	26	7	9	10	49	58	23
Golders Green	26	8	5	13	58	56	21
Barking	26	9	2	15	56	64	20
Southall	26	8	4	14	54	76	20
Enfield	26	8	2	16	57	68	18
Uxbridge Town	26	3	5	18	31	97	11

Uxbridge Town moved to the Spartan League and Tooting & Mitcham United joined from the London League.

1937-38

Walthamstow Avenue	26	19	4	3	96	32	42
Barnet	26	15	3	8	62	46	33
Romford	26	13	5	8	73	49	31
Wealdstone	26	11	7	8	58	45	29
Golders Green	26	11	6	9	61	56	28
Sutton United	26	10	6	10	56	63	26
Leyton	26	12	1	13	49	46	25
Bromley	26	10	4	12	38	49	24
Barking	26	8	7	11	39	41	23
Hayes	26	10	3	13	45	55	23
Redhill	26	9	4	13	50	67	22
Tooting & Mitcham United	26	9	4	13	44	63	22
Enfield	26	5	8	13	38	62	18
Southall	26	7	4	15	40	75	18

1938-39

Walthamstow Avenue	26	19	4	3	79	28	42
Romford	26	18	1	7	81	35	37
Wealdstone	26	15	5	6	70	49	35
Hayes	26	14	6	6	63	36	34
Barnet	26	10	5	11	62	68	25
Barking	26	11	2	13	53	48	24
Bromley	26	8	8	10	50	49	24
Golders Green	26	9	6	11	42	57	24
Leyton	26	10	3	13	44	50	23
Sutton United	26	9	4	13	45	57	22
Tooting & Mitcham United	26	8	3	15	38	50	19
Southall	26	7	5	14	31	66	19
Redhill	26	6	6	14	48	83	18
Enfield	26	6	6	14	33	63	18

Walthamstow Avenue and Romford both moved to the Isthmian League.
Finchley joined from the London League and Hitchin Town joined from the
Spartan League.

1939-40

War was declared on 3rd September 1939 and the league closed down
immediately. 13 games had been played and when the league closed
down, the table stood as follows:

Hitchin Town	2	2	0	0	14	2	4
Bromley	2	2	0	0	4	1	4
Sutton United	2	1	1	0	6	1	3
Golders Green	2	1	1	0	6	4	3
Tooting & Mitcham United	1	1	0	0	3	1	2
Barking	2	1	0	1	4	2	2
Enfield	2	1	0	1	5	4	2
Hayes	2	1	0	1	4	4	2
Redhill	3	1	0	2	4	6	2
Leyton	3	0	1	2	2	11	1
Southall	3	0	1	2	2	14	1
Barnet	1	0	0	1	4	6	0
Finchley	1	0	0	1	1	3	0
Wealdstone	0	0	0	0	0	0	0

When the league resumed at the end of the war in 1945, it was able to do
so with the same membership as in 1939-40.

1945-46

Sutton United	26	17	6	3	100	44	40
Leyton	26	17	5	4	80	35	39
Tooting & Mitcham United	26	17	2	7	103	53	36
Hayes	26	16	4	6	68	45	36
Bromley	26	16	1	9	92	55	33
Wealdstone	26	10	9	7	64	55	29
Southall	26	12	3	11	62	60	27
Barnet	26	10	5	11	73	70	25
Finchley	26	8	6	12	59	71	22
Hitchin Town	26	10	1	15	61	68	21
Enfield	27	7	4	15	55	84	18
Golders Green	26	7	3	16	56	84	17
Barking	26	5	3	18	40	93	13
Redhill	26	2	4	20	39	135	8

Golders Green changed their name to Hendon.

1946-47

Barnet	26	15	4	7	88	45	34
Sutton United	26	15	4	7	59	37	34
Bromley	26	13	4	9	79	54	30
Wealdstone	26	12	6	8	58	46	30
Southall	26	13	4	9	66	62	30
Hitchin Town	26	11	5	10	64	63	27
Tooting & Mitcham United	26	12	3	11	72	78	27
Hendon	26	12	2	12	62	59	26
Hayes	26	11	3	12	48	63	25
Redhill	26	11	1	14	59	69	23
Finchley	26	9	4	13	59	67	22
Barking	26	8	6	12	42	52	22
Enfield	26	8	3	15	52	77	19
Leyton	26	6	3	17	36	72	15

1947-48

Barnet	26	18	2	6	86	38	38
Hendon	26	14	5	7	45	30	33
Bromley	26	12	6	8	60	50	30
Tooting & Mitcham United	26	12	4	10	46	41	28
Wealdstone	26	9	8	9	44	36	26
Enfield	26	10	6	10	55	60	26
Hayes	26	9	7	10	43	43	25
Sutton United	26	9	7	10	32	38	25
Leyton	26	10	5	11	48	59	25
Finchley	26	10	5	11	38	52	25
Hitchin Town	26	10	4	12	43	61	24
Redhill	26	8	5	13	32	39	21
Barking	26	6	9	11	27	37	21
Southall	26	6	5	15	37	52	17

1948-49

Bromley	26	18	5	3	88	35	41
Hendon	26	15	7	4	55	33	37
Tooting & Mitcham United	26	14	4	7	64	42	34
Wealdstone	26	12	5	9	56	54	29
Sutton United	26	9	8	9	32	33	26
Finchley	26	9	8	9	47	50	26
Hitchin Town	26	9	7	10	44	46	25
Hayes	26	9	7	10	48	52	25
Barnet	26	10	3	13	46	53	23
Barking	26	7	7	12	46	48	21
Redhill	26	9	2	15	51	64	20
Enfield	26	7	6	13	32	52	20
Southall	26	6	7	13	46	63	19
Leyton	26	7	4	15	37	67	18

1949-50

Tooting & Mitcham United	26	16	7	3	51	26	39
Hayes	26	15	4	7	51	29	34
Bromley	26	12	9	5	59	39	33
Barking	26	14	5	7	51	46	33
Wealdstone	26	11	7	8	55	42	29
Hitchin Town	26	12	5	9	44	50	29
Hendon	26	13	2	11	54	48	28
Barnet	26	10	2	14	53	56	22
Finchley	26	8	6	12	40	49	22
Southall	26	7	8	11	36	51	22
Enfield	26	8	5	13	43	47	21
Sutton United	26	9	2	15	37	48	20
Redhill	26	6	4	16	39	56	16
Leyton	26	5	6	15	29	55	16

Cambridge City joined from the Spartan League and Walton & Hersham
joined from the Corinthian League.

1950-51

Bromley	30	24	1	5	90	34	49
Walton & Hersham	30	21	3	6	77	42	45
Hayes	30	17	10	3	88	38	44
Hendon	30	15	6	9	45	40	36
Sutton United	30	15	5	10	63	51	35
Redhill	30	14	7	9	56	60	35
Tooting & Mitcham United	30	14	2	14	59	57	30
Barnet	30	13	3	14	82	69	29
Wealdstone	30	11	5	14	52	52	27
Finchley	30	12	3	15	68	82	27
Southall	30	10	6	14	41	53	26
Barking	30	10	4	16	54	65	24
Cambridge City	30	8	7	15	49	72	23
Enfield	30	8	4	18	36	64	20
Hitchin Town	30	6	6	18	47	75	18
Leyton	30	4	4	22	36	89	12

1951-52

Wealdstone	30	23	4	3	81	29	50
Hendon	30	20	8	2	84	32	48
Bromley	30	15	8	7	74	53	38
Sutton United	30	15	8	7	70	53	38
Hayes	30	15	7	8	65	40	37
Southall	30	12	11	7	71	49	35
Walton & Hersham	30	14	4	12	56	51	32
Finchley	30	12	6	12	64	62	30
Redhill	30	12	6	12	55	63	30
Barking	30	11	4	15	56	86	26
Leyton	30	8	7	15	51	52	23
Barnet	30	7	8	15	53	72	22
Tooting & Mitcham United	30	6	9	15	64	71	21
Cambridge City	30	6	8	16	44	70	20
Enfield	30	6	7	17	47	77	19
Hitchin Town	30	5	1	24	36	111	11

Bromley and Barking both moved to the Isthmian League.

1952-53

Hendon	26	18	6	2	68	21	42
Wealdstone	26	17	3	6	58	35	37
Southall	26	17	2	7	55	28	36
Tooting & Mitcham United	26	11	6	9	42	34	28
Leyton	26	12	4	10	59	58	28
Finchley	26	12	2	12	52	57	26
Walton & Hersham	26	11	3	12	42	36	25
Cambridge City	26	11	2	13	38	38	24
Barnet	26	10	3	13	39	46	23
Hayes	26	9	4	13	41	51	22
Hitchin Town	26	8	4	14	37	56	20
Enfield	26	7	5	14	51	65	19
Sutton United	26	7	4	15	44	60	18
Redhill	26	6	4	16	41	82	16

1953-54

Finchley	26	17	4	5	61	37	38
Hitchin Town	26	16	3	7	58	32	35
Southall	26	15	3	8	56	40	33
Tooting & Mitcham United	26	12	5	9	49	35	29
Hendon	26	12	5	9	40	32	29
Hayes	26	9	10	7	49	42	28
Cambridge City	26	11	6	9	45	49	28
Sutton United	26	8	7	11	35	42	23
Redhill	26	9	4	13	44	40	22
Walton & Hersham	26	9	4	13	32	55	22
Leyton	26	9	3	14	38	56	21
Wealdstone	26	8	4	14	51	60	20
Barnet	26	8	4	14	36	54	20
Enfield	26	4	8	14	40	60	16

1954-55

Tooting & Mitcham United	26	15	8	3	65	32	38
Southall	26	16	5	5	64	39	37
Enfield	26	12	9	5	51	39	33
Sutton United	26	11	8	7	57	45	30
Hendon	26	8	11	7	51	45	27
Finchley	26	11	5	10	47	44	27
Hayes	26	9	7	10	47	43	25
Redhill	26	8	8	10	45	52	24
Leyton	26	10	4	12	36	47	24
Walton & Hersham	26	8	7	11	51	53	23
Barnet	26	6	11	9	39	48	23
Hitchin Town	26	6	9	11	44	60	21
Cambridge City	26	9	1	16	37	53	19
Wealdstone	26	4	5	17	36	70	13

Hounslow Town joined from the Corinthian League.

1955-56

Hendon	28	18	5	5	63	35	41
Hounslow Town	28	15	8	5	67	42	38
Enfield	28	16	5	7	60	39	37
Tooting & Mitcham United	28	17	2	9	60	47	36
Redhill	28	12	5	11	45	37	29
Walton & Hersham	28	13	3	12	59	68	29
Barnet	28	11	6	11	53	58	28
Finchley	28	8	12	8	52	62	28
Southall	28	10	7	11	50	46	27
Wealdstone	28	11	3	14	64	60	25
Hayes	28	8	6	14	55	56	22
Sutton United	28	9	4	15	56	64	22
Leyton	28	8	6	14	46	67	22
Cambridge City	28	7	4	17	39	61	18
Hitchin Town	28	7	4	17	47	74	18

Tooting & Mitcham United moved to the Isthmian League and Carshalton Athletic joined from the Corinthian League.

1956-57

Hayes	28	18	4	6	73	38	40
Finchley	28	18	4	6	75	43	40
Hounslow Town	28	17	4	7	78	49	38
Hendon	28	15	4	9	85	51	34
Leyton	28	13	6	9	59	47	32
Southall	28	14	1	13	57	54	29
Enfield	28	9	9	10	46	58	27
Carshalton Athletic	28	9	8	11	53	59	26
Cambridge City	28	11	4	13	48	62	26
Hitchin Town	28	10	5	13	67	73	25
Sutton United	28	10	5	13	40	51	25
Redhill	28	7	9	12	46	65	23
Wealdstone	28	10	1	17	61	69	21
Walton & Hersham	28	8	3	17	43	74	19
Barnet	28	4	7	17	41	79	15

Maidstone United joined from the Corinthian League.

1957-58

Sutton United	30	18	7	5	64	37	43
Maidstone United	30	19	4	7	63	45	42
Hendon	30	15	7	8	73	40	37
Barnet	30	16	5	9	78	52	37
Hounslow Town	30	16	4	10	60	55	36
Finchley	30	13	9	8	64	46	35
Hayes	30	14	3	13	76	70	31
Wealdstone	30	11	8	11	64	65	30
Hitchin Town	30	12	6	12	52	65	30
Southall	30	13	3	14	66	55	29
Enfield	30	10	8	12	47	49	28
Carshalton Athletic	30	9	6	15	48	67	24
Leyton	30	9	6	15	59	80	24
Redhill	30	6	7	17	53	71	19
Cambridge City	30	7	5	18	47	82	19
Walton & Hersham	30	5	6	19	45	80	16

Cambridge City moved to the Southern League and Grays Athletic joined from the Corinthian League.

1958-59

Barnet	30	20	4	6	85	44	44
Wealdstone	30	19	6	5	74	39	44
Maidstone United	30	16	6	8	53	37	38
Hendon	30	15	6	9	69	56	36
Grays Athletic	30	11	11	8	67	52	33
Hounslow Town	30	13	7	10	62	49	33
Hayes	30	13	7	10	61	58	33
Finchley	30	13	3	14	61	70	29
Enfield	30	10	7	13	63	55	27
Sutton United	30	10	6	14	49	60	26
Carshalton Athletic	30	8	10	12	41	61	26
Southall	30	8	9	13	50	56	25
Leyton	30	10	4	16	49	65	24
Hitchin Town	30	8	8	14	37	52	24
Walton & Hersham	30	9	4	17	39	61	22
Redhill	30	5	6	19	35	80	16

Maidstone United moved to the Isthmian League and Hornchurch & Upminster joined from the Delphian League.

1959-60

Hounslow Town	30	21	4	5	80	43	46
Barnet	30	17	9	4	79	35	43
Enfield	30	14	7	9	65	46	35
Wealdstone	30	16	3	11	64	51	35
Hornchurch & Upminster	30	15	5	10	56	47	35
Sutton United	30	16	1	13	66	60	33
Southall	30	12	7	11	58	49	31
Hendon	30	9	12	9	48	39	30
Hayes	30	11	7	12	52	51	29
Hitchin Town	30	11	6	13	55	57	28
Grays Athletic	30	10	5	15	59	64	25
Redhill	30	9	6	15	45	66	24
Finchley	30	8	6	16	50	69	22
Walton & Hersham	30	8	6	16	49	75	22
Leyton	30	8	5	17	39	75	21
Carshalton Athletic	30	7	7	16	37	75	21

1960-61

Hendon	30	18	6	6	72	38	42
Wealdstone	30	18	5	7	78	44	41
Barnet	30	17	5	8	69	43	39
Sutton United	30	17	3	10	71	55	37
Hitchin Town	30	15	6	9	81	52	36
Enfield	30	14	6	10	76	49	34
Hounslow Town	30	16	2	12	73	66	34
Hornchurch & Upminster	30	13	6	11	65	57	32
Walton & Hersham	30	11	8	11	66	57	30
Hayes	30	13	3	14	63	65	29
Southall	30	9	11	10	48	64	29
Leyton	30	8	6	16	45	79	22
Redhill	30	8	4	18	46	85	20
Grays Athletic	30	7	5	18	46	74	19
Finchley	30	8	3	19	43	81	19
Carshalton Athletic	30	8	1	21	50	83	17

Hornchurch & Upminster changed their name to Hornchurch.

1961-62

Enfield	30	25	2	3	97	36	52
Barnet	30	23	3	4	85	30	49
Wealdstone	30	16	5	9	76	52	37
Hayes	30	16	4	10	58	63	36
Walton & Hersham	30	14	6	10	70	55	34
Hitchin Town	30	15	4	11	85	71	34
Hendon	30	13	5	12	54	56	31
Grays Athletic	30	13	3	14	56	65	29
Sutton United	30	13	2	15	70	69	28
Hounslow Town	30	11	6	13	56	62	28
Finchley	30	10	7	13	49	46	27
Leyton	30	9	9	12	60	79	27
Redhill	30	7	4	19	51	75	18
Carshalton Athletic	30	6	5	19	45	71	17
Hornchurch	30	4	9	17	37	77	17
Southall	30	6	4	20	41	83	16

1962-63

Enfield	30	26	2	2	130	28	54
Barnet	30	22	3	5	90	39	47
Wealdstone	30	19	4	7	62	39	42
Sutton United	30	16	4	10	75	47	36
Hitchin Town	30	16	3	11	74	61	35
Walton & Hersham	30	15	4	11	66	49	34
Hendon	30	12	5	13	60	60	29
Finchley	30	13	2	15	55	46	28
Hayes	30	13	2	15	52	62	28
Hounslow Town	30	10	7	13	49	63	27
Hornchurch	30	12	3	15	59	77	27
Southall	30	9	6	15	48	53	24
Grays Athletic	30	9	3	18	54	88	21
Carshalton Athletic	30	7	3	20	34	95	17
Leyton	30	7	2	21	34	82	16
Redhill	30	6	3	21	36	89	15

The league expanded to three divisions by absorbing the Corinthian League and the Delphian League, both of which then closed down. The existing league became the Premier Division and new First and Second Divisions were created.

Enfield, Sutton United, Hitchin Town and Hendon all moved to the Isthmian League.

The new Premier Division was formed by 14 clubs, consisting of the remaining 12 clubs who were already members plus Dagenham and Maidenhead United from the Corinthian League.

The new First Division was formed by the 14 remaining members of the Corinthian League:
Chesham United, Dorking, Eastbourne, Edgware Town, Epsom & Ewell, Erith & Belvedere, Horsham, Leatherhead, Letchworth Town, Slough Town, Uxbridge, Wembley, Wokingham Town and Worthing.

The new Second Division was formed by 15 of the 16 clubs from the Delphian League:
Aveley, Aylesbury United, Berkhamsted Town, Bishop's Stortford, Brentwood & Warley, Edmonton, Harlow Town, Harrow Town, Hemel Hempstead Town, Hertford Town, Histon, Tilbury, Ware, Windsor & Eton and Wingate.

The only one of the Delphian League clubs not to join the Athenian League was Stevenage Town who turned professional and joined the Southern League.

1963-64

Promoted clubs in **bold type**, relegated clubs in ***bold italics***

Premier Division

Barnet	26	17	4	5	82	34	38
Finchley	26	14	6	6	61	39	34
Carshalton Athletic	26	15	4	7	42	28	34
Hayes	26	9	12	5	50	39	30
Wealdstone	26	12	5	9	54	47	29
Dagenham	26	12	4	10	57	42	28
Walton & Hersham	26	13	2	11	52	54	28
Redhill	26	9	9	8	39	40	27
Maidenhead United	26	12	2	12	54	48	26
Hornchurch	26	7	8	11	35	49	22
Grays Athletic	26	9	4	13	27	43	22
Leyton	26	4	9	13	33	62	17
Hounslow Town	26	7	1	18	38	76	15
Southall	26	5	4	17	36	59	14

Wealdstone moved to the Isthmian League.

First Division

Leatherhead	**26**	**18**	**3**	**5**	**86**	**45**	**39**
Worthing	**26**	**18**	**2**	**6**	**76**	**40**	**38**
Edgware Town	**26**	**17**	**4**	**5**	**72**	**40**	**38**
Erith & Belvedere	26	12	8	6	46	30	32
Slough Town	26	15	2	9	54	37	32
Letchworth Town	26	12	6	8	80	52	30
Chesham United	26	14	2	10	75	57	30
Uxbridge	26	11	5	10	45	42	27
Wokingham Town	26	11	3	12	42	54	25
Wembley	26	8	4	14	48	67	20
Eastbourne	26	7	3	16	44	75	17
Dorking	26	7	2	17	44	74	16
Horsham	26	4	3	19	27	67	11
Epsom & Ewell	26	4	1	21	45	104	9

Second Division

Tilbury	**28**	**18**	**6**	**4**	**90**	**44**	**42**
Harrow Town	**28**	**20**	**2**	**6**	**85**	**42**	**42**
Harlow Town	**28**	**17**	**6**	**5**	**74**	**34**	**40**
Hertford Town	**28**	**15**	**7**	**6**	**72**	**42**	**37**
Hemel Hempstead Town	**28**	**15**	**4**	**9**	**63**	**43**	**34**
Aveley	28	14	5	9	70	40	33
Bishop's Stortford	28	14	3	11	67	40	31
Windsor & Eton	28	12	4	12	61	61	28
Ware	28	11	5	12	62	59	27
Brentwood & Warley	28	10	5	13	49	59	25
Berkhamsted Town	28	9	6	13	52	67	24
Edmonton	28	7	6	15	53	65	20
Aylesbury United	28	8	1	19	45	87	17
Wingate	28	5	5	18	36	79	15
Histon	28	2	1	25	25	142	5

Cheshunt and Croydon Amateurs both joined from the Spartan League, Eastbourne United and Rainham Town both joined from the Metropolitan League, Harwich & Parkeston joined from the Eastern Counties League and Herne Bay joined from the Aetolian League.

1964-65

Premier Division

Barnet	30	23	4	3	107	29	50
Leyton	30	19	3	8	67	41	41
Finchley	30	19	1	10	67	45	39
Worthing	30	15	8	7	70	65	38
Walton & Hersham	30	16	3	11	69	55	35
Hayes	30	14	5	11	71	56	33
Hounslow Town	30	14	5	11	69	61	33
Carshalton Athletic	30	13	4	13	62	54	30
Maidenhead United	30	12	6	12	60	53	30
Leatherhead	30	13	3	14	51	54	29
Hornchurch	30	11	6	13	61	67	28
Dagenham	30	8	8	14	40	57	24
Edgware Town	30	8	5	17	33	78	21
Grays Athletic	30	8	4	18	48	75	20
Southall	30	7	5	18	37	67	19
Redhill	***30***	***4***	***2***	***24***	***32***	***87***	***10***

Barnet moved to the Southern League.

First Division

Slough Town	**30**	**21**	**6**	**3**	**81**	**23**	**48**
Hemel Hempstead Town	**30**	**21**	**4**	**5**	**77**	**32**	**46**
Chesham United	30	21	3	6	64	38	45
Horsham	30	17	3	10	74	47	37
Harrow Town	30	16	5	9	79	56	37
Hertford Town	30	16	3	11	51	41	35
Letchworth Town	30	16	3	11	68	60	35
Erith & Belvedere	30	14	5	11	48	49	33
Tilbury	30	13	4	13	56	49	30
Eastbourne	30	9	9	12	53	67	27
Wokingham Town	30	8	6	16	50	62	22
Uxbridge	30	6	9	15	48	59	21
Harlow Town	30	6	6	18	37	66	18
Wembley	29	5	5	19	31	66	15
Dorking	30	5	5	20	31	92	15
Epsom & Ewell	***30***	***6***	***3***	***21***	***52***	***93***	***13***

Epsom & Ewell had 2 points deducted.

Division Two

Harwich & Parkeston	**30**	**24**	**2**	**4**	**95**	**33**	**50**
Bishop's Stortford	**30**	**20**	**8**	**2**	**71**	**35**	**48**
Ware	30	21	5	4	81	42	47
Aveley	30	18	6	6	62	32	42
Windsor & Eton	30	17	4	9	80	45	38
Herne Bay	30	18	2	10	80	53	38
Croydon Amateurs	30	16	4	10	63	38	36
Eastbourne United	30	13	8	9	70	43	34
Cheshunt	30	13	7	10	60	41	33
Edmonton	30	10	4	16	40	64	24
Berkhamsted Town	30	8	5	17	44	79	21
Rainham Town	30	7	5	18	41	67	19
Aylesbury United	30	6	5	19	41	73	17
Wingate	30	6	2	22	39	77	14
Brentwood & Warley	30	4	5	21	32	79	13
Histon	30	2	2	26	27	125	6

Histon moved to the Eastern Counties League and Brentwood & Warley disbanded. Marlow and Ruislip Manor both joined from the Spartan League and Lewes joined from the Sussex County League.

1965-66

Premier Division

Leyton	30	21	6	3	76	28	48
Finchley	30	22	4	4	83	39	48
Maidenhead United	30	21	3	6	63	29	45
Leatherhead	30	14	9	7	41	34	37
Hounslow Town	30	15	4	11	66	60	34
Dagenham	30	14	4	12	61	49	32
Southall	30	13	4	13	38	57	30
Slough Town	30	12	5	13	69	50	29
Hemel Hempstead Town	30	11	6	13	57	51	28
Grays Athletic	30	8	10	12	41	54	26
Walton & Hersham	30	9	6	15	56	66	24
Worthing	30	10	4	16	51	66	24
Hayes	30	9	5	16	50	55	23
Edgware Town	30	8	7	15	37	62	23
Carshalton Athletic	*30*	*7*	*2*	*21*	*48*	*93*	*16*
Hornchurch	*30*	*3*	*7*	*20*	*34*	*78*	*13*

First Division

Bishop's Stortford	**30**	**24**	**3**	**3**	**84**	**33**	**51**
Harwich & Parkeston	**30**	**23**	**0**	**7**	**66**	**36**	**46**
Hertford Town	30	17	7	6	58	26	41
Letchworth Town	30	17	7	6	80	49	41
Wembley	30	15	7	8	56	48	37
Chesham United	30	15	4	11	74	52	34
Erith & Belvedere	30	13	8	9	55	44	34
Redhill	30	16	0	14	56	44	32
Harlow Town	30	11	7	12	53	55	29
Tilbury	30	10	4	16	58	66	24
Dorking	30	11	1	18	50	75	23
Uxbridge	30	7	6	17	49	65	20
Wokingham Town	30	7	5	18	37	74	19
Harrow Town	30	7	5	18	32	71	19
Horsham	*30*	*5*	*5*	*20*	*50*	*84*	*15*
Eastbourne	*30*	*6*	*3*	*21*	*45*	*81*	*15*

Division Two

Croydon Amateurs	**30**	**21**	**5**	**4**	**85**	**37**	**47**
Cheshunt	**30**	**22**	**3**	**5**	**82**	**38**	**47**
Eastbourne United	30	19	3	8	83	46	41
Lewes	30	17	6	7	66	42	40
Herne Bay	30	18	3	9	74	45	39
Windsor & Eton	30	16	4	10	79	49	36
Aveley	30	15	6	9	68	44	36
Ware	30	15	5	10	77	71	35
Epsom & Ewell	30	12	7	11	57	49	31
Rainham Town	30	10	7	13	58	65	27
Edmonton	30	8	6	16	43	71	22
Berkhamsted Town	30	7	4	19	51	80	18
Marlow	30	5	7	18	41	79	17
Wingate	30	6	4	20	47	84	16
Aylesbury United	30	5	5	20	45	89	15
Ruislip Manor	30	5	3	22	37	104	13

Berkhamsted Town moved to the Spartan League and Boreham Wood joined from the Spartan League.

1966-67

Premier Division

Leyton	30	18	7	5	73	32	43
Bishop's Stortford	30	19	5	6	56	33	43
Finchley	30	16	6	8	72	38	38
Leatherhead	30	17	3	10	53	42	37
Harwich & Parkeston	30	15	5	10	64	42	35
Hounslow Town	30	14	6	10	62	49	34
Slough Town	30	14	5	11	52	38	33
Dagenham	30	13	7	10	48	40	33
Hayes	30	13	6	11	51	45	32
Grays Athletic	30	11	7	12	45	50	29
Hemel Hempstead Town	30	8	11	11	39	42	27
Southall	30	8	9	13	43	47	25
Walton & Hersham	30	10	5	15	46	58	25
Maidenhead United	30	7	10	13	49	65	24
Worthing	*30*	*5*	*4*	*21*	*32*	*85*	*14*
Edgware Town	*30*	*2*	*4*	*24*	*19*	*98*	*8*

Division One

Hornchurch	**30**	**20**	**6**	**4**	**51**	**24**	**46**
Redhill	**30**	**19**	**7**	**4**	**71**	**32**	**45**
Chesham United	30	17	5	8	57	34	39
Wembley	30	15	5	10	49	40	35
Croydon Amateurs	30	17	0	13	71	48	34
Erith & Belvedere	30	12	6	12	54	41	30
Hertford Town	30	13	4	13	41	42	30
Letchworth Town	30	12	5	13	70	64	29
Harlow Town	30	10	8	12	39	42	28
Carshalton Athletic	30	11	6	13	43	49	28
Tilbury	30	11	5	14	63	64	27
Cheshunt	30	9	7	14	41	45	25
Dorking	30	10	5	15	42	60	25
Wokingham Town	30	10	3	17	47	66	23
Uxbridge	*30*	*9*	*5*	*16*	*35*	*72*	*23*
Harrow Town	*30*	*5*	*3*	*22*	*37*	*88*	*13*

Harrow Town changed their name to Harrow Borough.

Division Two

Eastbourne United	**30**	**22**	**6**	**2**	**83**	**25**	**50**
Ware	**30**	**19**	**8**	**3**	**79**	**33**	**46**
Horsham	30	20	3	7	59	32	43
Marlow	30	16	5	9	57	58	37
Lewes	30	14	8	8	62	37	36
Aveley	30	14	4	12	49	51	32
Windsor & Eton	30	11	7	12	47	54	29
Herne Bay	30	12	4	14	64	57	28
Boreham Wood	30	8	9	13	56	59	25
Aylesbury United	30	11	3	16	46	59	25
Rainham Town	30	7	10	13	48	59	24
Epsom & Ewell	30	9	6	15	65	91	24
Eastbourne	30	9	5	16	51	61	23
Ruislip Manor	30	9	4	17	48	71	22
Edmonton	30	6	9	15	25	48	21
Wingate	30	5	5	20	34	74	15

1967-68

Premier Division

Slough Town	30	23	5	2	93	23	51
Dagenham	30	20	4	6	73	34	44
Bishop's Stortford	30	18	3	9	75	38	39
Hayes	30	15	5	10	57	40	35
Leatherhead	30	15	4	11	55	44	34
Maidenhead United	30	15	4	11	50	48	34
Hounslow	30	13	6	11	50	50	32
Walton & Hersham	30	13	5	12	51	39	31
Hornchurch	30	10	9	11	42	46	29
Redhill	30	11	7	12	43	48	29
Grays Athletic	30	11	6	13	45	54	28
Southall	30	9	8	13	34	65	26
Finchley	30	6	9	15	42	53	21
Harwich & Parkeston	30	7	5	18	36	60	19
Leyton	*30*	*5*	*6*	*19*	*22*	*63*	*16*
Hemel Hempstead Town	*30*	*4*	*4*	*22*	*23*	*86*	*12*

Division One

Cheshunt	**30**	**18**	**6**	**6**	**59**	**30**	**42**
Wembley	**30**	**16**	**8**	**6**	**67**	**37**	**40**
Tilbury	30	16	6	8	58	35	38
Erith & Belvedere	30	14	9	7	55	41	37
Hertford Town	30	15	7	8	49	38	37
Croydon Amateurs	30	11	14	5	47	27	36
Carshalton Athletic	30	15	6	9	54	38	36
Dorking	30	13	6	11	37	31	32
Ware	30	12	6	12	42	49	30
Eastbourne United	30	11	6	13	44	47	28
Chesham United	30	8	12	10	33	38	28
Wokingham Town	30	11	5	14	53	70	27
Letchworth Town	30	11	3	16	50	52	25
Harlow Town	30	6	7	17	33	59	19
Worthing	*30*	*6*	*5*	*19*	*35*	*58*	*17*
Edgware Town	*30*	*1*	*6*	*23*	*11*	*77*	*8*

Division Two

Lewes	**30**	**21**	**4**	**5**	**89**	**22**	**46**
Aylesbury United	**30**	**18**	**6**	**6**	**62**	**35**	**42**
Horsham	30	16	6	8	61	36	38
Edmonton	30	17	2	11	73	49	36
Boreham Wood	30	15	4	11	63	38	34
Windsor & Eton	30	14	6	10	46	38	34
Rainham Town	30	12	7	11	55	54	31
Marlow	30	14	2	14	54	54	30
Ruislip Manor	30	11	8	11	41	50	30
Harrow Borough	30	12	6	12	41	49	30
Aveley	30	12	5	13	54	53	29
Herne Bay	30	13	2	15	49	50	28
Uxbridge	30	9	5	16	41	60	23
Epsom & Ewell	30	10	3	17	44	66	23
Eastbourne	30	5	3	22	37	94	13
Wingate	30	5	3	22	23	85	13

1968-69

Premier Division

Walton & Hersham	30	24	4	2	79	22	52
Slough Town	30	21	6	3	65	30	48
Southall	30	18	3	9	55	31	39
Leatherhead	30	16	6	8	48	32	38
Dagenham	30	15	7	8	51	34	37
Bishop's Stortford	30	14	6	10	57	44	34
Maidenhead United	30	10	11	9	42	35	31
Cheshunt	30	10	9	11	33	39	29
Wembley	30	11	7	12	35	45	29
Harwich & Parkeston	30	9	7	14	33	47	25
Redhill	30	10	5	15	31	51	25
Hayes	30	7	10	13	31	45	24
Grays Athletic	30	7	7	16	34	48	21
Finchley	30	5	10	15	19	39	20
Hornchurch	*30*	*3*	*10*	*17*	*23*	*53*	*16*
Hounslow	*30*	*5*	*2*	*23*	*26*	*67*	*12*

Division One

Tilbury	**30**	**20**	**5**	**5**	**65**	**28**	**45**
Eastbourne United	**30**	**19**	**6**	**5**	**70**	**40**	**44**
Lewes	30	15	9	6	57	39	39
Hertford Town	30	16	6	8	48	28	38
Wokingham Town	30	12	11	7	44	28	35
Dorking	30	13	7	10	54	51	33
Erith & Belvedere	30	9	13	8	48	48	31
Carshalton Athletic	30	11	8	11	47	40	30
Harlow Town	30	12	4	14	47	49	28
Croydon Amateurs	30	7	12	11	39	45	26
Aylesbury United	30	8	10	12	45	64	26
Chesham United	30	8	9	13	44	42	25
Letchworth Town	30	8	8	14	41	56	24
Ware	30	8	6	16	44	69	22
Hemel Hempstead Town	*30*	*6*	*6*	*18*	*32*	*67*	*18*
Leyton	*30*	*5*	*6*	*19*	*37*	*68*	*16*

Division Two

Boreham Wood	**30**	**20**	**6**	**4**	**68**	**25**	**46**
Aveley	**30**	**20**	**6**	**4**	**77**	**32**	**46**
Eastbourne	30	17	8	5	60	33	42
Herne Bay	30	15	10	5	60	34	40
Horsham	30	17	4	9	63	38	38
Edmonton	30	16	2	12	48	42	34
Worthing	30	15	4	11	51	51	34
Marlow	30	11	11	8	45	36	33
Wingate	30	12	5	13	45	41	29
Windsor & Eton	30	11	7	12	35	46	29
Uxbridge	30	10	7	13	45	58	27
Ruislip Manor	30	6	6	18	40	65	18
Edgware Town	30	7	4	19	30	61	18
Epsom & Ewell	30	5	7	18	25	63	17
Rainham Town	30	5	6	19	37	64	16
Harrow Borough	30	5	3	22	45	85	13

1969-70

Premier Division

Bishop's Stortford	30	20	5	5	72	33	45
Walton & Hersham	30	16	8	6	56	32	40
Dagenham	30	15	9	6	62	22	39
Slough Town	30	15	9	6	52	21	39
Leatherhead	30	15	9	6	51	29	39
Redhill	30	17	5	8	48	36	39
Hayes	30	11	9	10	47	45	31
Tilbury	30	10	9	11	48	43	29
Cheshunt	30	9	9	12	33	30	27
Harwich & Parkeston	30	7	12	11	44	43	26
Southall	30	10	6	14	32	47	26
Grays Athletic	30	9	8	13	26	40	26
Wembley	30	9	7	14	34	46	25
Maidenhead United	30	6	9	15	29	54	21
Finchley	*30*	*7*	*5*	*18*	*30*	*73*	*19*
Eastbourne United	*30*	*3*	*3*	*24*	*27*	*97*	*9*

Division One

Lewes	**30**	**20**	**5**	**5**	**59**	**20**	**45**
Boreham Wood	**30**	**20**	**5**	**5**	**66**	**27**	**45**
Erith & Belvedere	30	15	9	6	59	33	39
Aveley	30	16	5	9	65	44	37
Hertford Town	30	14	6	10	43	31	34
Harlow Town	30	15	4	11	53	47	34
Chesham United	30	11	10	9	53	43	32
Dorking	30	10	10	10	39	37	30
Carshalton Athletic	30	11	7	12	39	39	29
Hounslow	30	11	5	14	37	43	27
Aylesbury United	30	9	8	13	38	50	26
Hornchurch	30	8	9	13	30	36	25
Wokingham Town	30	9	7	14	34	51	25
Letchworth Town	30	8	5	17	41	74	21
Ware	*30*	*4*	*9*	*17*	*35*	*81*	*17*
Croydon Amateurs	*30*	*5*	*4*	*21*	*28*	*63*	*14*

Division Two

Horsham	**30**	**19**	**9**	**2**	**68**	**30**	**47**
Edmonton	**30**	**20**	**4**	**6**	**85**	**34**	**44**
Herne Bay	30	18	5	7	69	34	41
Eastbourne	30	17	7	6	48	26	41
Marlow	30	13	9	8	51	39	35
Uxbridge	30	13	8	9	49	40	34
Rainham Town	30	11	11	8	47	39	33
Edgware Town	30	10	10	10	38	38	30
Leyton	30	12	5	13	50	64	29
Worthing	30	9	9	12	39	44	27
Windsor & Eton	30	7	13	10	34	40	27
Hemel Hempstead Town	30	10	4	16	36	50	24
Wingate	30	7	8	15	36	56	22
Harrow Borough	30	4	8	18	33	67	16
Epsom & Ewell	30	5	6	19	22	55	16
Ruislip Manor	30	4	6	20	33	82	14

1970-71

Premier Division

Dagenham	30	23	5	2	54	19	51
Walton & Hersham	30	20	7	3	56	21	47
Slough Town	30	17	7	6	48	21	41
Cheshunt	30	18	3	9	48	34	39
Maidenhead United	30	14	8	8	53	29	36
Leatherhead	30	14	6	10	45	31	34
Tilbury	30	13	4	13	48	44	30
Hayes	30	11	7	12	43	41	29
Lewes	30	11	6	13	42	42	28
Boreham Wood	30	9	9	12	39	41	27
Redhill	30	10	7	13	36	48	27
Bishop's Stortford	30	11	4	15	45	61	26
Harwich & Parkeston	30	8	6	16	43	62	22
Wembley	30	4	8	18	33	62	16
Grays Athletic	30	7	2	21	27	68	16
Southall	30	4	3	23	17	53	11

Bishop's Stortford, Hayes and Walton & Hersham all moved to the Isthmian League.

Division One

Aveley	**30**	**18**	**8**	**4**	**59**	**24**	**44**
Erith & Belvedere	**30**	**19**	**6**	**5**	**67**	**34**	**44**
Hornchurch	**30**	**18**	**5**	**7**	**54**	**30**	**41**
Horsham	30	16	6	8	62	36	38
Carshalton Athletic	30	15	6	9	51	35	36
Hertford Town	30	12	10	8	55	42	34
Wokingham Town	30	13	8	9	39	32	34
Edmonton	30	15	3	12	50	54	33
Dorking	30	11	9	10	36	40	31
Aylesbury United	30	11	7	12	45	47	29
Finchley	30	8	12	10	29	33	28
Harlow Town	30	6	9	15	35	54	21
Chesham United	30	7	5	18	37	57	19
Letchworth Town	30	7	4	19	30	62	18
Eastbourne United	30	5	6	19	26	57	16
Hounslow	30	4	6	20	25	63	14

Division Two

Herne Bay	**30**	**22**	**3**	**5**	**76**	**38**	**47**
Croydon Amateurs	**30**	**20**	**4**	**6**	**78**	**24**	**44**
Marlow	**30**	**18**	**7**	**5**	**54**	**29**	**43**
Windsor & Eton	30	14	7	9	52	39	35
Worthing	30	14	6	10	49	35	34
Ware	30	13	6	11	53	46	32
Uxbridge	30	14	4	12	54	50	32
Eastbourne	30	12	5	13	41	42	29
Rainham Town	30	9	8	13	39	46	26
Ruislip Manor	30	10	6	14	29	37	26
Edgware Town	30	9	8	13	44	58	26
Harrow Borough	30	8	9	13	32	39	25
Hemel Hempstead Town	30	9	7	14	45	56	25
Wingate	30	9	6	15	36	57	24
Leyton	30	9	4	17	40	61	22
Epsom & Ewell	30	3	4	23	23	86	10

Addlestone, Hampton and Staines Town all joined from the Spartan League. Eastbourne changed their name to Eastbourne Town.

1971-72

Premier Division

Slough Town	30	22	4	4	60	17	48
Dagenham	30	19	5	6	61	27	43
Leatherhead	30	16	8	6	56	29	40
Tilbury	30	15	9	6	62	46	39
Harwich & Parkeston	30	14	9	7	47	40	37
Maidenhead United	30	13	8	9	38	31	34
Redhill	30	11	10	9	51	35	32
Cheshunt	30	10	11	9	43	37	31
Aveley	30	12	6	12	46	37	30
Hornchurch	30	10	8	12	39	38	28
Boreham Wood	30	11	6	13	40	45	28
Lewes	30	10	8	12	48	52	28
Erith & Belvedere	30	9	8	13	39	54	26
Southall	30	5	9	16	25	49	19
Wembley	30	3	5	22	26	58	11
Grays Athletic	*30*	*1*	*4*	*25*	*25*	*111*	*6*

Leatherhead moved to the Isthmian League.

Division One

Harlow Town	**30**	**22**	**5**	**3**	**96**	**40**	**49**
Croydon Amateurs	**30**	**20**	**6**	**4**	**77**	**25**	**46**
Horsham	30	17	6	7	59	34	40
Carshalton Athletic	30	16	7	7	57	37	39
Marlow	30	12	11	7	53	41	35
Hertford Town	30	16	3	11	58	49	35
Finchley	30	12	9	9	43	43	33
Chesham United	30	12	8	10	45	33	32
Eastbourne United	30	10	8	12	48	51	28
Herne Bay	30	10	8	12	43	51	28
Dorking	30	10	6	14	48	62	26
Edmonton	30	9	7	14	47	61	25
Wokingham Town	30	7	6	17	30	51	20
Letchworth Town	30	5	6	19	34	61	16
Aylesbury United	30	4	8	18	42	90	16
Hounslow	30	3	6	21	33	84	12

Hertford Town moved to the Eastern Counties League.

Division Two

Staines Town	**30**	**22**	**7**	**1**	**76**	**24**	**51**
Worthing	**30**	**18**	**5**	**7**	**54**	**29**	**41**
Hampton	30	17	6	7	57	32	40
Windsor & Eton	30	17	5	8	51	35	39
Addlestone	30	17	4	9	47	35	38
Ware	30	16	2	12	45	41	34
Hemel Hempstead Town	30	14	5	11	40	37	33
Edgware Town	30	13	5	12	56	46	31
Leyton	30	12	7	11	46	46	31
Uxbridge	30	10	8	12	34	36	28
Ruislip Manor	30	9	4	17	41	51	22
Eastbourne Town	30	5	12	13	24	42	22
Harrow Borough	30	7	6	17	27	47	20
Wingate	30	8	3	19	33	72	19
Rainham Town	30	5	7	18	34	60	17
Epsom & Ewell	30	5	4	21	26	58	14

Hemel Hempstead Town merged with Hemel Hempstead United of the South Midlands League to form Hemel Hempstead. The merged club took Town's place in the Athenian League and played at United's former ground in Vauxhall Road, leaving Town's ground in Crabtree Lane.
Edgware Town changed their name to Edgware.

1972-73

Premier Division

Slough Town	30	22	4	4	74	23	48
Dagenham	30	17	9	4	47	18	43
Tilbury	30	17	9	4	57	35	43
Harlow Town	30	18	5	7	54	31	41
Erith & Belvedere	30	14	8	8	35	28	36
Harwich & Parkeston	30	11	10	9	44	38	32
Aveley	30	11	10	9	34	34	32
Cheshunt	30	13	6	11	36	36	32
Maidenhead United	30	12	6	12	43	41	30
Southall	30	12	5	13	30	38	29
Boreham Wood	30	9	7	14	30	34	25
Lewes	30	5	11	14	28	45	21
Croydon Amateurs	30	5	11	14	21	37	21
Hornchurch	30	6	6	18	23	45	18
Redhill	30	3	9	18	20	49	15
Wembley	30	4	6	20	26	70	14

Croydon Amateurs changed their name to Croydon.

Division One

Horsham	30	24	3	3	74	24	51
Staines Town	30	20	3	7	54	32	43
Grays Athletic	30	16	5	9	33	27	37
Hounslow	30	13	7	10	49	36	33
Wokingham Town	30	11	7	12	51	47	29
Carshalton Athletic	30	11	7	12	41	42	29
Eastbourne United	30	11	7	12	32	38	29
Letchworth Town	30	10	9	11	32	43	29
Marlow	30	11	6	13	40	38	28
Chesham United	30	11	5	14	41	41	27
Edmonton	30	9	9	12	41	45	27
Finchley	30	10	6	14	43	46	26
Herne Bay	30	10	6	14	45	62	26
Worthing	30	7	10	13	29	42	24
Aylesbury United	30	8	6	16	38	58	22
Dorking	30	6	8	16	26	48	20

Edmonton merged with Haringey Borough of the Metropolitan-London League – Reserve Division to form Edmonton & Haringey. The merged club took Edmonton's place in the Athenian League but left Edmonton's Barrass Stadium and played at Haringey Borough's ground at Coles Park.

Division Two

Ruislip Manor	26	18	6	2	51	20	42
Hampton	26	14	8	4	39	20	36
Ware	26	14	8	4	61	38	36
Leyton	26	14	7	5	52	22	35
Edgware	26	11	10	5	32	20	32
Rainham Town	26	10	11	5	46	36	31
Uxbridge	26	13	4	9	42	27	30
Addlestone	26	11	7	8	42	28	29
Harrow Borough	26	12	5	9	43	30	29
Hemel Hempstead	26	5	7	14	26	53	17
Windsor & Eton	26	5	4	17	29	54	14
Eastbourne Town	26	6	2	18	24	51	14
Epsom & Ewell	26	4	6	16	24	54	14
Wingate	26	2	1	23	21	79	5

Epsom & Ewell moved to the Surrey Senior League.

The Isthmian League added a new Division Two with its existing members forming Division One. The new Division Two was formed by 16 clubs, 15 of which came from the Athenian League. There were 8 from the Premier Division – Aveley, Dagenham, Harlow Town, Harwich & Parkeston, Maidenhead United, Slough Town, Southall and Tilbury; 6 from Division One – Carshalton Athletic, Chesham United, Finchley, Horsham, Staines Town and Wokingham Town; and Hampton from Division Two.

The Athenian League was then re-organised into two divisions, One and Two. The new Division One consisted of the 8 remaining Premier Division club plus 8 clubs from the old Division One – Eastbourne United, Edmonton & Haringey, Grays Athletic, Herne Bay, Hounslow, Letchworth Town, Marlow and Worthing; and also Ruislip Manor and Ware from the old Division Two.

The new Division Two consisted of Aylesbury United and Dorking from the old Division One, plus the 10 remaining clubs from the old Division Two. The division was made up to 16 clubs by 4 new clubs: Alton Town who joined from the Hampshire League, Faversham Town who joined from the Metropolitan-London League and Feltham and Molesey who both joined from the Spartan League.

1973-74

Division One

Boreham Wood	34	25	6	3	68	20	56
Cheshunt	34	18	11	5	58	24	47
Ruislip Manor	34	18	10	6	61	29	46
Ware	34	16	8	10	55	47	40
Hornchurch	34	15	9	10	48	44	39
Croydon	34	14	12	8	49	34	40
Erith & Belvedere	34	14	9	11	41	32	37
Edmonton & Haringey	34	12	12	10	40	35	36
Hounslow	34	13	9	12	55	46	35
Worthing	34	14	7	13	47	51	35
Lewes	34	11	12	11	50	43	34
Redhill	34	13	8	13	46	45	34
Grays Athletic	34	8	12	14	34	40	28
Wembley	34	11	6	17	42	55	28
Eastbourne United	34	8	9	17	34	60	25
Marlow	34	8	6	20	23	48	22
Letchworth Town	34	7	7	20	28	56	21
Herne Bay	34	1	7	26	16	86	9

Boreham Wood and Croydon both moved to the Isthmian League and Herne Bay moved to the Kent League.

Division Two

Alton Town	**30**	**19**	**7**	**4**	**54**	**23**	**45**
Rainham Town	**30**	**17**	**7**	**6**	**48**	**33**	**41**
Leyton	**30**	**14**	**11**	**5**	**55**	**30**	**39**
Uxbridge	30	14	11	5	36	23	39
Faversham Town	30	14	7	9	47	31	35
Wingate	30	15	5	10	42	37	35
Molesey	30	15	5	10	36	33	35
Harrow Borough	30	11	9	10	44	37	31
Addlestone	30	12	5	13	41	38	29
Aylesbury United	30	8	10	12	42	45	26
Hemel Hempstead	30	8	9	13	37	41	25
Edgware	30	9	6	15	33	54	24
Eastbourne Town	30	8	7	15	31	46	23
Feltham	30	7	5	18	29	50	19
Dorking	30	5	7	18	38	67	17
Windsor & Eton	30	6	5	19	25	50	17

Dorking merged with Guildford City of the Southern League to form Guildford & Dorking United. The merged club took Guildford's place in the Southern League but left Guildford's Joseph's Road ground and played at Dorking's Meadowbank ground in Mill Lane. Egham Town joined from the Spartan League and Epping Town and Willesden both joined from the Metropolitan London League.

1974-75

Division One

Letchworth Town	34	21	7	6	63	32	49
Wembley	34	18	12	4	57	26	48
Grays Athletic	34	20	7	7	68	35	47
Cheshunt	34	16	10	8	57	43	42
Lewes	34	15	11	8	60	39	41
Alton Town	34	15	10	9	59	42	40
Hornchurch	34	14	11	9	48	39	39
Ruislip Manor	34	13	9	12	42	43	35
Erith & Belvedere	34	11	11	12	55	38	33
Redhill	34	11	10	13	45	44	32
Edmonton & Haringey	34	11	10	13	51	53	32
Ware	34	12	8	14	59	68	32
Marlow	34	9	12	13	33	50	30
Rainham Town	34	10	9	15	39	47	29
Hounslow	34	12	4	18	52	75	28
Worthing	34	10	7	17	46	64	27
Leyton	34	7	6	21	30	53	20
Eastbourne United	*34*	*2*	*4*	*28*	*21*	*94*	*8*

Leyton of Division One merged with Wingate of Division Two to form Leyton-Wingate. The merged club continued in Leyton's place in Division One, playing at Leyton's Hare & Hounds ground in Lea Bridge Road, Leyton. Wingate's ground in Hall Lane, Hendon had been demolished in 1972 to make way for an extension of the M1 and they had been ground-sharing at Finchley's Summer's Lane ground until 1975. Hornchurch, Ware and Wembley all moved to the Isthmian League.

Division Two

Egham Town	**28**	**18**	**5**	**5**	**51**	**22**	**41**
Addlestone	**28**	**18**	**4**	**6**	**54**	**23**	**40**
Wingate	28	17	4	7	43	22	38
Willesden	28	13	10	5	43	20	36
Eastbourne Town	28	14	8	6	38	25	36
Molesey	28	14	5	9	39	27	33
Epping Town	28	12	4	12	43	38	28
Uxbridge	28	8	11	9	31	31	27
Harrow Borough	28	11	5	12	35	37	27
Hemel Hempstead	28	8	7	13	29	36	23
Aylesbury United	28	7	7	14	33	49	21
Windsor & Eton	28	8	4	16	31	57	20
Edgware	28	9	1	18	33	44	19
Faversham Town	28	7	5	16	27	56	19
Feltham	28	2	8	18	19	62	12

Harrow Borough moved to the Isthmian League. Camberley Town, Harefield United and Tring Town all joined from the Spartan League and Epsom & Ewell joined from the Surrey Senior League.

1975-76

Division One

Cheshunt	30	18	5	7	66	31	41
Egham Town	30	16	7	7	46	28	39
Addlestone	30	15	7	8	40	30	37
Grays Athletic	30	15	6	9	39	29	36
Rainham Town	30	15	3	12	52	37	33
Erith & Belvedere	30	11	10	9	29	28	32
Alton Town	30	14	4	12	37	42	32
Worthing	30	12	7	11	42	35	31
Hounslow	30	11	7	12	50	43	29
Lewes	30	9	11	10	45	45	29
Letchworth Town	30	10	9	11	31	38	29
Redhill	30	10	7	13	31	34	27
Ruislip Manor	30	9	8	13	39	41	26
Leyton-Wingate	30	8	8	14	37	41	24
Marlow	30	6	6	18	27	61	18
Edmonton & Haringey	30	5	7	18	31	79	17

Letchworth Town changed their name to Letchworth Garden City and Edmonton & Haringey changed their name to Haringey Borough.

Division Two

Epping Town	**30**	**16**	**10**	**4**	**47**	**21**	**42**
Epsom & Ewell	**30**	**16**	**8**	**6**	**58**	**25**	**40**
Edgware	30	14	10	6	36	29	38
Hemel Hempstead	30	15	6	9	46	36	36
Windsor & Eton	30	13	7	10	42	26	33
Tring Town	30	12	9	9	31	31	33
Eastbourne Town	30	11	9	10	45	42	31
Feltham	30	11	8	11	39	42	30
Aylesbury United	30	8	12	10	36	40	28
Willesden	30	10	10	10	22	34	28
Molesey	30	10	7	13	36	39	27
Camberley Town	30	7	11	12	31	43	25
Uxbridge	30	7	10	13	22	31	24
Eastbourne United	30	7	8	15	29	41	22
Harefield United	30	6	10	14	29	43	22
Faversham Town	30	8	3	19	28	54	19

Willesden had 2 points deducted.
Aylesbury United moved to the Southern League, Eastbourne Town moved to the Sussex County League and Faversham Town moved to the Kent League. Chalfont St. Peter, Chertsey Town, Farnborough Town and Kingsbury Town all joined from the London-Spartan League.

1976-77

Division One

Leyton-Wingate	34	22	6	6	65	26	50
Letchworth Garden City	34	21	7	6	66	33	49
Addlestone	34	19	10	5	58	24	48
Lewes	34	18	8	8	63	43	44
Cheshunt	34	18	8	8	57	39	44
Epping Town	34	17	8	9	54	37	42
Alton Town	34	14	10	10	46	39	38
Rainham Town	34	12	13	9	63	56	37
Egham Town	34	14	7	13	46	45	35
Epsom & Ewell	34	12	9	13	46	42	33
Redhill	34	12	9	13	43	43	33
Haringey Borough	34	11	8	15	42	47	30
Worthing	34	9	9	16	47	59	27
Hounslow	34	10	7	17	37	56	27
Erith & Belvedere	34	4	14	16	27	44	22
Grays Athletic	34	6	10	18	38	63	22
Marlow	34	5	8	21	42	90	18
Ruislip Manor	34	4	5	25	33	87	13

Addlestone and Hounslow both moved to the Southern League.

Division Two

Farnborough Town	28	19	5	4	65	33	43
Tring Town	28	16	8	4	49	30	40
Molesey	28	12	10	6	50	35	34
Hemel Hempstead	28	14	5	9	48	29	33
Chalfont St. Peter	28	13	7	8	41	28	33
Harefield United	28	8	13	7	45	35	29
Uxbridge	28	11	7	10	32	25	29
Feltham	28	11	7	10	34	40	27
Edgware	28	11	5	12	29	36	25
Eastbourne United	28	8	7	13	41	42	23
Kingsbury Town	28	9	5	14	28	38	23
Camberley Town	28	6	11	11	25	34	23
Windsor & Eton	28	5	11	12	34	42	19
Willesden	28	6	7	15	23	49	19
Chertsey Town	28	3	8	17	22	70	14

Feltham. Edgware and Windsor & Eton each had 2 points deducted.

The Isthmian League renamed its Division One the Premier Division and Division Two as Division One. A new Division Two of 17 clubs was also formed, 16 of which came from the Athenian League, 8 from each of the two divisions. The 8 Division One clubs who moved were Cheshunt, Egham Town, Epping Town, Epsom & Ewell, Letchworth Garden City, Lewes, Rainham Town and Worthing. The 8 Division Two clubs who moved were Camberley Town, Eastbourne United, Farnborough Town, Feltham, Hemel Hempstead, Molesey, Tring Town and Willesden.

The Athenian League was then reduced to a single division of 18 clubs, consisting of the remaining 15 clubs plus Billericay Town who joined from the Essex Senior League, Burnham who joined from the Hellenic League and Hoddesdon Town who joined from the London Spartan League.

1977-78

Billericay Town	34	23	7	4	80	21	53
Leyton-Wingate	34	21	8	5	73	42	50
Grays Athletic	34	20	8	6	72	31	48
Burnham	34	20	8	6	69	33	48
Chalfont St. Peter	34	20	5	9	59	31	45
Edgware	34	14	14	6	54	29	42
Alton Town	34	13	12	9	50	33	38
Marlow	34	14	7	13	61	59	35
Windsor & Eton	34	13	8	13	47	44	34
Harefield United	34	10	13	11	37	50	33
Haringey Borough	34	9	12	13	49	48	30
Uxbridge	34	10	9	15	30	37	29
Hoddesdon Town	34	8	12	14	41	54	28
Ruislip Manor	34	10	8	16	44	58	28
Chertsey Town	34	8	8	18	47	77	24
Kingsbury Town	34	6	9	19	33	60	21
Erith & Belvedere	34	6	6	22	34	82	18
Redhill	34	2	4	28	19	110	8

Erith & Belvedere moved to the Kent League and Kingsbury Town moved to the London-Spartan League. Dorking Town joined from the Surrey Senior League, Fleet Town joined from the Hampshire League and Welling United joined from the London-Spartan League.

1978-79

Billericay Town	36	26	5	5	86	29	57
Burnham	36	22	10	4	86	37	54
Edgware	36	19	11	6	83	34	49
Windsor & Eton	36	21	6	9	62	30	48
Haringey Borough	36	16	15	5	60	42	47
Uxbridge	36	17	12	7	45	22	46
Welling United	36	17	9	10	60	46	43
Leyton-Wingate	36	16	10	10	67	48	42
Grays Athletic	36	17	8	11	55	46	42
Alton Town	36	15	9	12	51	45	39
Hoddesdon Town	36	13	7	16	63	60	33
Chalfont St. Peter	36	12	8	16	41	58	32
Harefield United	36	11	7	18	53	70	29
Dorking Town	36	10	7	19	39	64	27
Marlow	36	9	4	23	48	92	22
Ruislip Manor	36	8	4	24	35	71	20
Fleet Town	36	6	7	23	37	73	19
Redhill	36	6	7	23	29	79	19
Chertsey Town	36	4	8	24	36	90	16

Billericay Town moved to the Isthmian League. Banstead Athletic joined from the London-Spartan League and Woodford Town joined from the Essex Senior League.

1979-80

Windsor & Eton	38	26	6	6	72	26	58
Burnham	38	24	8	6	73	28	56
Leyton-Wingate	38	22	8	8	86	48	52
Dorking Town	38	20	8	10	61	41	48
Welling United	38	20	7	11	86	46	47
Uxbridge	38	20	7	11	49	41	47
Grays Athletic	38	20	2	16	69	48	42
Ruislip Manor	38	16	10	12	55	46	42
Marlow	38	16	10	12	66	58	42
Edgware	38	15	11	12	62	63	41
Redhill	38	15	9	14	55	46	39
Banstead Athletic	38	15	9	14	57	54	39
Woodford Town	38	13	9	16	57	60	35
Hoddesdon Town	38	12	7	19	56	55	31
Chalfont St. Peter	38	10	10	18	50	67	30
Harefield United	38	10	8	20	41	60	28
Fleet Town	38	10	6	22	43	80	26
Haringey Borough	38	9	7	22	41	83	25
Alton Town	38	8	5	25	43	101	21
Chertsey Town	38	4	3	31	33	104	11

Dorking Town moved to the Isthmian League. Basildon United joined from the Essex Senior League.

1980-81

Windsor & Eton	38	27	6	5	100	32	60
Basildon United	38	24	11	3	71	24	59
Banstead Athletic	38	23	10	5	73	32	56
Grays Athletic	38	23	7	8	81	42	53
Edgware	38	20	8	10	77	38	48
Leyton-Wingate	38	18	12	8	72	46	48
Welling United	38	19	8	11	62	48	46
Woodford Town	38	18	9	11	84	53	45
Burnham	38	20	4	14	62	45	44
Harefield United	38	16	10	12	67	51	42
Ruislip Manor	38	14	13	11	49	51	41
Uxbridge	38	11	13	14	38	39	35
Fleet Town	38	8	13	17	50	65	29
Haringey Borough	38	9	10	19	41	68	28
Redhill	38	8	11	19	45	59	27
Hoddesdon Town	38	10	6	22	53	80	26
Chertsey Town	38	9	7	22	30	84	25
Marlow	38	7	10	21	43	85	24
Chalfont St. Peter	38	5	5	28	39	89	15
Alton Town	38	2	5	31	33	139	9

Basildon United and Windsor & Eton both moved to the Isthmian League,

Welling United moved to the Southern League and Alton Town moved to the Combined Counties League. Horley Town, Kingsbury Town and Whyteleafe all joined from the London-Spartan League.

1981-82

Leyton-Wingate	36	28	8	0	87	19	64
Edgware	36	20	10	6	76	52	50
Uxbridge	36	20	9	7	56	27	49
Burnham	36	19	7	10	64	44	45
Redhill	36	14	13	9	43	38	41
Harefield United	36	14	12	10	52	47	40
Ruislip Manor	36	15	9	12	58	55	39
Banstead Athletic	36	13	12	11	51	39	38
Chertsey Town	36	11	14	11	43	44	36
Woodford Town	36	13	8	15	48	45	34
Marlow	36	12	8	16	40	46	32
Kingsbury Town	36	11	10	15	43	52	32
Whyteleafe	36	8	15	13	30	41	31
Horley Town	36	10	10	16	40	45	30
Hoddesdon Town	36	11	7	18	50	57	29
Grays Athletic	36	10	8	18	41	62	28
Chalfont St. Peter	36	8	10	18	42	50	26
Fleet Town	36	7	9	20	38	76	23
Haringey Borough	36	4	9	23	77	90	17

Leyton-Wingate and Uxbridge both moved to the Isthmian League and Woodford Town moved to the Southern League. Flackwell Heath, Newbury Town and Thatcham Town all joined from the Hellenic League and Camberley Town joined from the Isthmian League.

1982-83

Newbury Town	38	27	5	6	97	42	59
Grays Athletic	38	25	3	10	79	27	53
Redhill	38	22	9	7	68	38	53
Marlow	38	21	8	9	67	40	50
Chalfont St. Peter	38	18	12	8	64	40	48
Burnham	38	17	13	8	80	46	47
Banstead Athletic	38	16	10	12	62	50	42
Whyteleafe	38	15	12	11	46	39	42
Harefield United	38	15	12	11	54	55	42
Kingsbury Town	38	16	10	12	56	40	41
Hoddesdon Town	38	15	10	13	58	54	40
Flackwell Heath	38	11	13	14	45	50	35
Horley Town	38	10	13	15	45	58	33
Edgware	38	12	7	19	48	62	31
Chertsey Town	38	10	10	18	61	88	30
Ruislip Manor	38	12	4	22	55	70	28
Fleet Town	38	8	10	20	38	65	25
Thatcham Town	38	8	6	24	30	85	22
Haringey Borough	38	5	9	24	27	82	19
Camberley Town	38	4	10	24	31	80	16

Kingsbury Town and Fleet Town each had 1 point deducted. Camberley Town had 2 points deducted.
Newbury Town and Grays Athletic both moved to the Isthmian League. Berkhamsted Town and Wolverton Town both joined from the London-Spartan League and Harwich & Parkeston joined from the Isthmian League.

Three points were awarded for a win instead of 2 from the next season.

1983-84

Redhill	40	28	9	3	73	28	93
Chalfont St. Peter	40	27	10	3	88	32	91
Burnham	40	27	7	6	80	29	88
Whyteleafe	40	24	8	8	63	32	80
Flackwell Heath	40	21	7	12	57	37	70
Harefield United	40	20	8	12	62	47	68
Banstead Athletic	40	19	10	11	63	48	67
Marlow	40	17	7	16	65	63	58
Hoddesdon Town	40	15	13	12	53	52	58
Ruislip Manor	40	16	9	15	59	44	57
Kingsbury Town	40	15	12	13	58	52	57
Wolverton Town	40	12	12	16	59	65	48
Edgware	40	13	8	19	47	51	47
Harwich & Parkeston	40	13	9	18	54	66	45
Chertsey Town	40	12	6	22	41	63	42
Berkhamsted Town	40	10	11	19	50	63	41
Thatcham Town	40	8	14	18	65	79	35
Horley Town	40	9	6	25	34	83	33
Haringey Borough	40	8	8	24	44	80	32
Fleet Town	40	6	8	26	31	82	26
Camberley Town	40	4	10	26	35	85	22

Harwich & Parkeston and Thatcham Town each had 3 points deducted.

The Isthmian League expanded its Second Division by forming two regional sections, North and South.

Berkhamsted Town, Chalfont St. Peter, Flackwell Heath, Harefield United, Haringey Borough, Kingsbury Town Marlow and Wolverton Town all joined the North section while Banstead Athletic, Camberley Town, Chertsey Town, Ruislip Manor and Whyteleafe all joined the South Section.

Burnham, Edgware, Redhill and Thatcham Town all joined the London-Spartan League, Fleet Town and Horley Town both joined the Combined Counties League, Harwich & Parkeston joined the Eastern Counties League and Hoddesdon Town joined the South Midlands League.

The Athenian League then closed down.

CORINTHIAN LEAGUE 1945-1963

During the Second World War, a number of clubs in the South-East found themselves playing unfamiliar opponents. Some clubs from such competitions as the London League and Spartan League mixed in with more senior clubs from the Isthmian and Athenian Leagues and this experience meant that when normal football resumed in 1945, they wished to play in a higher standard league than previously. The Isthmian and Athenian Leagues still had their full quota of members and so nine of those ambitious clubs – Epsom Town, Erith & Belvedere, Grays Athletic, London Fire Forces, Maidenhead United, Slough United, Twickenham, Walton & Hersham and Windsor & Eton – formed an entirely new competition, the Corinthian League.

In the last pre-war season: Epsom Town and Grays Athletic had been members of the London League, Maidenhead United and Windsor & Eton had been members of the Spartan League and Erith & Belvedere had played in the Kent League.

Walton & Hersham was a new club formed by the 1945 amalgamation of pre-war clubs Hersham, who lost their ground during the war, and Walton-on-Thames. Both of these two clubs had been members of the London League for the cancelled 1939-40 season.

Slough United had been formed in 1943 by the amalgamation of Slough F.C., who were pre-war members of the Spartan League and Slough Centre who had been pre-war members of the Windsor, Slough & District Junior League.

Twickenham had been formed in 1943 and played in the Middlesex Senior League from 1943-45. The final founder member was London Fire Forces who had no regular ground of their own and played all Corinthian League games away.

1945-46

Grays Athletic	16	14	2	0	59	14	30
Slough United	16	13	1	2	54	24	27
Erith & Belvedere	16	9	2	5	50	28	20
Windsor & Eton	16	8	1	7	56	49	17
Maidenhead United	16	7	0	9	43	44	14
Epsom Town	16	6	1	9	28	37	13
Walton & Hersham	16	5	2	9	31	53	12
Twickenham	16	4	1	11	31	67	9
London Fire Forces	16	1	0	15	16	52	2

Epsom Town left the league after Epsom F.C. (re-formed in 1945), reclaimed their ground which they had leased to Epsom Town while they were inactive. With nowhere to play, Epsom Town disbanded while Epsom F.C. continued to play in the London League.

Twickenham left after their hopes of ground-sharing at Brentford came to nothing and so they dropped back to the Middlesex Senior League.

London Fire Forces were also asked to resign as they had no ground.

Carshalton Athletic, Edgware Town and Uxbridge joined from the London League, Hounslow Town joined from the Spartan League, Bedford Avenue joined from the United Counties League and Hastings & St. Leonard's and Eastbourne both joined from the Southern Amateur League.

1946-47

	P	W	D	L	F	A	Pts
Walton & Hersham	24	19	2	3	88	35	40
Slough United	24	15	4	5	92	49	34
Windsor & Eton	24	14	4	6	83	49	32
Uxbridge	24	13	4	7	92	53	30
Grays Athletic	24	12	5	7	70	59	29
Erith & Belvedere	24	12	2	10	68	51	26
Hounslow Town	24	9	4	11	57	55	22
Maidenhead United	24	8	5	11	50	67	21
Hastings & St. Leonard's	24	6	7	11	42	68	19
Eastbourne	24	8	2	14	57	80	18
Carshalton Athletic	24	6	6	12	59	91	18
Edgware Town	24	6	2	16	40	76	14
Bedford Avenue	24	4	1	19	51	116	9

Slough United demerged, Slough Town continuing to play in Slough United's place in the Corinthian League while Slough Centre joined the Spartan League.
Chesham United joined from the Spartan League.

1947-48

	P	W	D	L	F	A	Pts
Walton & Hersham	26	17	4	5	82	40	38
Hounslow Town	26	16	2	8	68	46	34
Erith & Belvedere	26	15	3	8	67	38	33
Carshalton Athletic	26	15	2	9	70	53	32
Grays Athletic	26	13	5	8	68	56	31
Edgware Town	26	12	5	9	55	46	29
Hastings & St. Leonard's	26	12	3	11	72	57	27
Maidenhead United	26	10	5	11	45	52	25
Eastbourne	26	10	4	12	55	68	24
Uxbridge	26	10	3	13	53	62	23
Chesham United	26	6	9	11	48	60	21
Windsor & Eton	26	9	3	14	42	75	21
Slough Town	26	7	4	15	50	51	18
Bedford Avenue	26	4	0	22	35	106	8

Bedford Avenue moved to the Central Amateur League and Worthing joined from the Sussex County League.

1948-49

	P	W	D	L	F	A	Pts
Walton & Hersham	24	19	1	4	82	32	39
Uxbridge	24	14	5	5	52	36	33
Hounslow Town	24	13	6	5	67	45	32
Erith & Belvedere	24	13	5	6	54	39	31
Grays Athletic	24	12	4	8	73	58	28
Slough Town	24	10	6	8	55	38	26
Worthing	24	7	7	10	49	60	21
Chesham United	24	8	5	11	42	75	21
Maidenhead United	24	8	4	12	34	48	20
Carshalton Athletic	24	7	3	14	48	59	17
Edgware Town	24	4	8	12	35	43	16
Eastbourne	24	6	4	14	49	68	16
Windsor & Eton	24	6	0	18	35	74	12

Hastings & St. Leonard's withdrew after playing one game because of ground difficulties following the formation of the new professional club, Hastings United. Their single game, a 6-0 defeat away to Hounslow Town, was deleted from the table.
Epsom joined from the London League.

1949-50

	P	W	D	L	F	A	Pts
Hounslow Town	26	19	3	4	86	37	41
Walton & Hersham	26	18	4	4	69	31	40
Erith & Belvedere	26	14	6	6	59	30	34
Uxbridge	26	15	3	8	65	47	33
Worthing	26	12	4	10	57	50	28
Grays Athletic	26	10	8	8	63	62	28
Eastbourne	26	10	7	9	52	46	27
Slough Town	26	10	7	9	46	51	27
Edgware Town	26	10	5	11	50	53	25
Maidenhead United	26	7	8	11	43	46	22
Chesham United	26	7	8	11	53	59	22
Carshalton Athletic	26	8	4	14	56	75	20
Epsom	26	2	5	19	38	95	9
Windsor & Eton	26	3	2	21	34	89	8

Walton & Hersham moved to the Athenian League and Windsor & Eton moved to the Metropolitan League. Tilbury joined from the London League and Maidstone United joined from the Kent League.

1950-51

	P	W	D	L	F	A	Pts
Slough Town	26	17	4	5	65	33	38
Hounslow Town	26	17	3	6	80	41	37
Erith & Belvedere	26	13	5	8	59	43	31
Edgware Town	26	14	2	10	65	52	30
Maidenhead United	26	13	3	10	57	49	29
Grays Athletic	26	11	5	10	68	54	27
Chesham United	26	11	4	11	69	61	26
Tilbury	26	11	4	11	42	44	26
Uxbridge	26	10	4	12	64	62	24
Worthing	26	11	2	13	52	75	24
Carshalton Athletic	26	8	4	14	65	75	20
Eastbourne	26	8	3	15	47	65	19
Epsom	26	8	2	16	61	94	18
Maidstone United	26	6	3	17	58	104	15

1951-52

	P	W	D	L	F	A	Pts
Hounslow Town	26	21	1	4	84	28	43
Grays Athletic	26	19	5	2	77	35	43
Slough Town	26	19	3	4	85	37	41
Erith & Belvedere	26	14	1	11	56	50	29
Carshalton Athletic	26	10	7	9	67	59	27
Chesham United	26	12	2	12	64	62	26
Tilbury	26	11	4	11	46	58	26
Eastbourne	26	9	7	10	53	53	25
Epsom	26	9	4	13	45	65	22
Worthing	26	8	6	12	44	68	22
Uxbridge	26	8	5	13	59	58	21
Edgware Town	26	5	5	16	37	60	15
Maidstone United	26	3	7	16	40	80	13
Maidenhead United	26	5	1	20	28	72	11

1952-53

	P	W	D	L	F	A	Pts
Carshalton Athletic	26	19	1	6	70	44	39
Hounslow Town	26	16	4	6	84	46	36
Epsom	26	16	2	8	72	39	34
Maidstone United	26	14	4	8	58	53	32
Uxbridge	26	12	5	9	40	41	29
Grays Athletic	26	11	6	9	58	47	28
Edgware Town	26	11	6	9	65	54	28
Tilbury	26	10	5	11	46	42	25
Maidenhead United	26	9	5	12	44	50	23
Slough Town	26	7	7	12	39	53	21
Eastbourne	26	7	7	12	40	58	21
Erith & Belvedere	26	8	4	14	43	50	20
Chesham United	26	5	4	17	33	64	14
Worthing	26	6	2	18	29	80	14

1953-54

Carshalton Athletic	26	17	5	4	75	41	39
Edgware Town	26	17	4	5	75	41	38
Hounslow Town	26	13	8	5	75	45	34
Maidenhead United	26	13	7	6	60	43	33
Eastbourne	26	11	5	10	47	45	27
Grays Athletic	26	12	2	12	62	50	26
Tilbury	26	10	6	10	60	56	26
Erith & Belvedere	26	10	6	10	45	55	26
Uxbridge	26	11	3	12	45	56	25
Epsom	26	11	1	14	54	64	23
Worthing	26	7	6	13	52	66	20
Maidenhead United	26	7	4	15	46	71	18
Slough Town	26	5	7	14	49	60	17
Chesham United	26	4	4	18	38	90	12

Yiewsley joined from the Delphian League.

1954-55

Hounslow Town	28	22	3	3	80	37	47
Grays Athletic	28	18	3	7	74	41	39
Carshalton Athletic	28	17	4	7	65	38	38
Slough Town	28	12	10	6	58	49	34
Uxbridge	28	11	8	9	62	46	30
Maidenhead United	28	11	6	11	50	63	28
Yiewsley	28	12	3	13	49	46	27
Edgware Town	28	10	7	11	58	60	27
Chesham United	28	12	3	13	56	73	27
Erith & Belvedere	28	10	8	10	57	56	26
Worthing	28	10	4	14	54	62	24
Maidstone United	28	9	5	14	48	50	23
Tilbury	28	9	5	14	47	56	23
Eastbourne	28	3	7	18	24	63	13
Epsom	28	3	6	19	41	83	12

Erith & Belvedere had 2 points deducted.
Hounslow Town moved to the Athenian League.

1955-56

Maidstone United	26	19	3	4	74	37	41
Yiewsley	26	15	5	6	62	31	35
Uxbridge	26	14	5	7	56	34	33
Slough Town	26	14	5	7	59	38	33
Epsom	26	14	3	9	58	42	31
Grays Athletic	26	13	3	10	48	48	29
Maidenhead United	26	12	4	10	56	47	28
Carshalton Athletic	26	12	3	11	50	41	27
Tilbury	26	9	6	11	43	55	24
Edgware Town	26	7	7	12	30	49	21
Worthing	26	7	5	14	57	71	19
Eastbourne	26	6	4	16	29	54	16
Erith & Belvedere	26	6	2	18	32	69	14
Chesham United	26	6	1	19	36	74	13

Carshalton Athletic moved to the Athenian League. Wembley joined from the Delphian League and Dorking joined from the Surrey Senior League.

1956-57

Yiewsley	28	18	6	4	73	35	42
Grays Athletic	28	16	8	4	81	43	40
Maidenhead United	28	17	5	6	88	50	39
Epsom	28	18	2	8	76	37	38
Maidstone United	28	15	6	7	80	40	36
Slough Town	28	12	9	7	63	42	33
Eastbourne	28	12	6	10	67	56	30
Uxbridge	28	12	6	10	54	52	30
Wembley	28	9	8	11	53	55	26
Erith & Belvedere	28	11	3	14	51	66	25
Edgware Town	28	8	5	15	48	72	21
Dorking	28	7	5	16	51	80	19
Tilbury	28	8	3	17	31	78	19
Chesham United	28	4	5	19	38	83	13
Worthing	28	2	5	21	34	99	9

Maidstone United moved to the Athenian League and Tilbury moved to the London League. Dagenham joined from the Delphian League and Horsham joined from the Metropolitan League.

1957-58

Maidenhead United	28	20	3	5	65	39	43
Slough Town	28	18	6	4	72	41	42
Grays Athletic	28	17	6	5	82	28	40
Yiewsley	28	13	8	7	56	36	34
Edgware Town	28	13	5	10	59	54	31
Uxbridge	28	12	7	9	57	53	31
Dagenham	28	11	8	9	38	40	30
Epsom	28	12	5	11	64	60	29
Erith & Belvedere	28	11	2	15	44	57	24
Eastbourne	28	7	9	12	40	50	23
Wembley	28	9	4	15	48	54	22
Chesham United	28	9	4	15	40	50	22
Horsham	28	6	5	17	50	77	17
Dorking	28	4	9	15	37	63	17
Worthing	28	6	3	19	48	98	15

Grays Athletic moved to the Athenian League and Yiewsley moved to the Southern League. Leatherhead joined from the Delphian League.

1958-59

Dagenham	26	19	2	5	70	36	40
Maidenhead United	26	14	7	5	63	38	35
Slough Town	26	14	5	7	75	41	33
Wembley	26	13	4	9	61	44	30
Leatherhead	26	13	4	9	58	54	30
Dorking	26	9	8	9	45	40	26
Uxbridge	26	11	3	12	58	63	25
Edgware Town	26	11	3	12	49	67	25
Horsham	26	9	5	12	66	68	23
Erith & Belvedere	26	8	7	11	43	53	23
Chesham United	26	8	6	12	45	57	22
Epsom	26	8	6	12	44	57	22
Eastbourne	26	5	7	14	28	50	17
Worthing	26	5	3	18	45	82	13

Letchworth Town and Wokingham Town both joined from the Delphian League.

1959-60

Uxbridge	30	20	4	6	72	40	44
Maidenhead United	30	16	6	8	70	40	38
Dorking	30	17	3	10	69	47	37
Epsom	30	17	2	11	70	55	36
Letchworth Town	30	14	6	10	68	62	34
Dagenham	30	13	7	10	50	40	33
Slough Town	30	14	4	12	54	53	32
Horsham	30	13	5	12	68	64	31
Wokingham Town	30	11	7	12	62	51	29
Worthing	30	11	7	12	70	74	29
Erith & Belvedere	30	10	9	11	62	66	29
Leatherhead	30	12	3	15	56	63	27
Chesham United	30	11	4	15	45	60	26
Wembley	30	11	3	16	56	77	25
Eastbourne	30	8	4	18	41	67	20
Edgware Town	30	4	2	24	37	91	10

Epsom merged with Ewell & Stoneleigh F.C. and changed their name to Epsom & Ewell.

1960-61

Maidenhead United	30	19	5	6	65	39	43
Chesham United	30	19	2	9	73	38	40
Edgware Town	30	17	6	7	70	40	40
Dagenham	30	18	3	9	82	55	39
Horsham	30	17	3	10	85	77	37
Uxbridge	30	15	5	10	50	40	35
Worthing	30	14	5	11	85	67	33
Letchworth Town	30	15	3	12	64	66	33
Dorking	30	12	6	12	64	61	30
Erith & Belvedere	30	10	7	13	59	57	27
Eastbourne	30	10	6	14	50	59	26
Epsom & Ewell	30	11	3	16	46	77	25
Leatherhead	30	9	4	17	68	93	22
Wokingham Town	30	8	5	17	44	60	21
Wembley	30	6	6	18	51	80	18
Slough Town	30	4	3	23	48	95	11

1961-62

Maidenhead United	30	23	3	4	77	31	49
Chesham United	30	19	4	7	64	34	42
Horsham	30	18	3	9	88	57	39
Edgware Town	30	15	7	8	47	40	37
Dagenham	30	16	3	11	65	49	35
Uxbridge	30	14	5	11	47	41	33
Erith & Belvedere	30	14	5	11	56	57	33
Slough Town	30	12	5	13	47	49	29
Wokingham Town	30	11	6	13	50	49	28
Leatherhead	30	10	7	13	63	52	27
Letchworth Town	30	8	9	13	55	65	25
Worthing	30	10	5	15	52	67	25
Eastbourne	30	8	6	16	39	57	22
Dorking	30	8	6	16	55	90	22
Epsom & Ewell	30	8	2	20	47	81	18
Wembley	30	7	2	21	40	73	16

1962-63

Leatherhead	30	22	5	3	88	36	49
Erith & Belvedere	30	18	6	6	61	32	42
Wokingham Town	30	18	5	7	53	41	41
Dagenham	30	15	8	7	64	47	38
Uxbridge	30	15	7	8	73	51	37
Letchworth Town	30	16	3	11	75	50	35
Maidenhead United	30	12	9	9	61	46	33
Slough Town	30	12	9	9	62	54	33
Chesham United	30	11	6	13	66	59	28
Worthing	30	12	4	14	63	78	28
Dorking	30	9	6	15	56	70	24
Horsham	30	10	3	17	50	74	23
Edgware Town	30	9	5	16	43	66	23
Eastbourne	30	7	5	18	43	76	19
Epsom & Ewell	30	5	5	20	31	82	15
Wembley	30	4	4	22	46	73	12

The Corinthian League closed as a separate competition in 1963, being absorbed into the Athenian League as its new First Division (second tier). 14 of the Corinthian League's 16 clubs made up the new division, the exceptions being Dagenham and Maidenhead United who moved up to the Athenian League's newly named Premier Division

DELPHIAN LEAGUE 1951-1963

The Delphian League was formed in 1951 on the initiative of Dagenham and of Woodford Town and was aimed at clubs who wanted to play at a higher level than the Spartan League but had been unable to gain entry into the Corinthian League.

The 14 founder members were Aylesbury United, Berkhamsted Town, Bishops Stortford, Brentwood & Warley, Slough Centre, Stevenage Town, Wembley, Willesden and Yiewsley, all of whom joined from the Spartan League; Cheshunt, Rainham Town and Woodford Town, all of whom joined from the London League and Dagenham and Leatherhead, both of whom joined from the Metropolitan League.

1951-52

Brentwood & Warley	26	16	4	6	65	37	36
Dagenham	26	16	3	7	68	35	35
Yiewsley	26	14	5	7	70	48	33
Leatherhead	26	14	4	8	51	43	32
Woodford Town	26	12	7	7	59	44	31
Aylesbury United	26	12	6	8	67	40	30
Rainham Town	26	13	3	10	41	43	29
Slough Centre	26	10	6	10	58	61	26
Willesden	26	10	3	13	48	50	23
Bishops Stortford	26	10	3	13	55	80	23
Berkhamsted Town	26	9	3	14	47	58	21
Stevenage Town	26	6	7	13	50	75	19
Cheshunt	26	5	6	15	46	69	16
Wembley	26	2	6	18	30	72	10

Hemel Hempstead and Upminster both joined from the Spartan League, Upminster changing their name to Hornchurch & Upminster.

1952-53

Dagenham	30	22	3	5	78	34	47
Aylesbury United	30	18	3	9	70	43	39
Yiewsley	30	14	11	5	62	48	39
Slough Centre	30	16	4	10	60	35	36
Stevenage Town	30	17	2	11	63	51	36
Brentwood & Warley	30	15	5	10	60	50	35
Woodford Town	30	14	6	10	66	52	34
Rainham Town	30	14	3	13	47	41	31
Leatherhead	30	12	7	11	53	59	31
Hornchurch & Upminster	30	12	5	13	48	48	29
Berkhamsted Town	30	11	6	13	57	71	28
Wembley	30	8	7	15	52	58	23
Cheshunt	30	9	4	17	48	66	22
Hemel Hempstead	30	7	3	20	46	77	17
Bishops Stortford	30	6	5	19	47	94	17
Willesden	30	4	8	18	29	59	16

Willesden moved to the Parthenon League.

1953-54

Aylesbury United	28	18	5	5	97	45	41
Dagenham	28	18	4	6	64	35	40
Rainham Town	28	17	6	5	64	40	40
Wembley	28	14	4	10	52	49	32
Slough Centre	28	13	5	10	58	52	31
Bishops Stortford	28	12	4	12	64	56	28
Stevenage Town	28	12	4	12	65	61	28
Woodford Town	28	11	5	12	41	59	27
Yiewsley	28	11	4	13	51	45	26
Brentwood & Warley	28	8	9	11	55	62	25
Berkhamsted Town	28	9	7	12	54	61	25
Cheshunt	28	10	5	13	50	59	25
Hemel Hempstead	28	9	5	14	48	66	23
Hornchurch & Upminster	28	6	6	16	46	72	18
Leatherhead	28	4	3	21	45	92	11

Yiewsley moved to the Corinthian League and Tufnell Park Edmonton joined from the Spartan League.

1954-55

Bishops Stortford	28	22	3	3	98	39	47
Dagenham	28	19	3	6	82	29	41
Aylesbury United	28	18	1	9	77	43	37
Rainham Town	28	16	4	8	66	47	36
Slough Centre	28	15	5	8	62	46	35
Hemel Hempstead	28	14	1	13	56	53	29
Woodford Town	28	11	6	11	55	58	28
Wembley	28	11	4	13	48	40	26
Stevenage Town	28	10	6	12	53	72	26
Tufnell Park Edmonton	28	9	6	13	41	61	24
Leatherhead	28	8	5	15	48	65	21
Hornchurch & Upminster	28	9	3	16	49	68	21
Berkhamsted Town	28	9	3	16	42	70	21
Cheshunt	28	6	3	19	37	76	13
Brentwood & Warley	28	4	5	19	36	83	13

Cheshunt had 2 points deducted for fielding an ineligible player.
Hemel Hempstead changed their name to Hemel Hempstead Town.
Cheshunt moved to the London League and Ware joined from the Spartan League.

1955-56

Dagenham	28	20	3	5	83	28	43
Wembley	28	18	6	4	72	32	42
Rainham Town	28	18	3	7	71	45	39
Bishops Stortford	28	16	5	7	84	43	37
Aylesbury United	28	14	4	10	57	63	32
Hornchurch & Upminster	28	13	5	10	60	59	31
Hemel Hempstead Town	28	11	8	9	61	56	30
Leatherhead	28	11	5	12	53	63	27
Tufnell Park Edmonton	28	9	7	12	51	59	25
Ware	28	8	9	11	63	73	25
Berkhamsted Town	28	10	3	15	53	72	23
Woodford Town	28	8	7	13	52	74	23
Slough Centre	28	6	6	16	50	68	18
Brentwood & Warley	28	5	3	20	42	80	13
Stevenage Town	28	2	8	18	35	72	12

Stevenage Town merged with Stevenage Rangers to form Stevenage F.C..
Slough Centre disbanded and Wembley moved to the Corinthian League.
Letchworth Town joined from the Spartan League.

1956-57

Dagenham	26	18	5	3	66	29	41
Rainham Town	26	15	4	7	68	45	34
Brentwood & Warley	26	14	6	6	68	46	34
Aylesbury United	26	11	7	8	55	41	29
Bishops Stortford	26	13	3	10	70	56	29
Ware	26	13	2	11	78	65	28
Letchworth Town	26	12	3	11	57	47	27
Hornchurch & Upminster	26	12	3	11	47	44	27
Leatherhead	26	11	4	11	57	67	26
Hemel Hempstead Town	26	8	6	12	50	56	22
Stevenage	26	6	7	13	39	70	19
Tufnell Park Edmonton	26	5	8	13	40	59	18
Berkhamsted Town	26	6	5	15	35	64	17
Woodford Town	26	5	3	18	43	84	13

Dagenham moved to the Corinthian League. Aveley joined from the London League and Wokingham Town joined from the Metropolitan League.

1957-58

Letchworth Town	28	22	4	2	96	27	48
Aveley	28	18	4	6	77	46	40
Rainham Town	28	17	5	6	67	45	39
Brentwood & Warley	28	15	5	8	78	47	35
Aylesbury United	28	14	6	8	69	49	34
Leatherhead	28	14	4	10	77	56	32
Hornchurch & Upminster	28	13	5	10	50	38	31
Bishops Stortford	28	12	6	10	62	54	30
Tufnell Park Edmonton	28	11	6	11	44	53	28
Woodford Town	28	8	6	14	44	66	22
Ware	28	8	5	15	41	60	21
Wokingham Town	28	8	5	15	44	69	21
Hemel Hempstead Town	28	6	5	17	30	72	17
Stevenage	28	5	3	20	40	79	13
Berkhamsted Town	28	4	1	23	24	82	9

Leatherhead moved to the Corinthian League and Harrow Town joined from the Spartan League.

1958-59

Brentwood & Warley	28	21	1	6	74	39	43
Hornchurch & Upminster	28	19	2	7	73	41	40
Woodford Town	28	15	6	7	60	39	36
Harrow Town	28	14	7	7	70	40	35
Bishops Stortford	28	15	5	8	64	50	35
Rainham Town	28	14	5	9	64	41	33
Aylesbury United	28	16	1	11	57	48	33
Aveley	28	13	5	10	58	52	31
Ware	28	10	7	11	52	49	27
Wokingham Town	28	11	2	15	63	54	24
Tufnell Park Edmonton	28	9	5	14	55	50	23
Letchworth Town	28	7	8	13	52	70	22
Hemel Hempstead Town	28	6	5	17	44	77	17
Stevenage	28	5	4	19	39	94	14
Berkhamsted Town	28	3	1	24	30	111	7

Letchworth Town and Wokingham Town both moved to the Corinthian League and Hornchurch & Upminster moved to the Athenian League. Hertford Town joined from the Spartan League.

1959-60

Brentwood & Warley	24	17	3	4	56	23	37
Hertford Town	24	17	1	6	55	22	35
Harrow Town	24	13	7	4	52	32	33
Bishops Stortford	24	14	3	7	52	35	31
Aylesbury United	24	13	4	7	50	37	30
Woodford Town	24	12	3	9	39	29	27
Rainham Town	24	10	7	7	45	35	27
Aveley	24	8	7	9	41	42	23
Ware	24	8	4	12	38	54	20
Stevenage	24	6	5	13	34	50	17
Tufnell Park Edmonton	24	6	4	14	36	53	16
Hemel Hempstead Town	24	3	3	18	23	63	9
Berkhamsted Town	24	2	3	19	22	68	7

Tufnell Park Edmonton changed their name to Edmonton and Stevenage changed their name to Stevenage Town. Windsor & Eton joined from the Metropolitan League and Histon joined from the Spartan League.

1960-61

Hertford Town	20	20	5	3	65	27	45
Brentwood & Warley	28	21	1	6	86	32	43
Windsor & Eton	28	17	4	7	64	43	38
Hemel Hempstead Town	28	14	5	9	59	44	33
Bishops Stortford	28	14	2	12	67	63	30
Harrow Town	28	12	6	10	65	63	30
Aveley	28	13	3	12	69	55	29
Rainham Town	28	11	4	13	53	46	26
Aylesbury United	28	10	4	14	57	64	24
Histon	28	10	4	14	58	71	24
Ware	28	8	6	14	55	74	22
Edmonton	28	8	5	15	47	64	21
Stevenage Town	28	7	7	14	44	61	21
Woodford Town	28	8	5	15	38	68	21
Berkhamsted Town	28	3	7	18	35	87	13

Woodford Town and Rainham Town both moved to the Metropolitan League.
Harlow Town joined from the London League.

1961-62

Hertford Town	26	18	5	3	84	32	41
Hemel Hempstead Town	26	14	9	3	64	29	37
Bishops Stortford	26	14	6	6	62	36	34
Brentwood & Warley	26	12	8	6	63	55	32
Aylesbury United	26	11	8	7	46	40	30
Windsor & Eton	26	10	7	9	66	53	27
Aveley	26	9	8	9	50	43	26
Edmonton	26	8	9	9	45	43	25
Stevenage Town	26	9	7	10	53	65	25
Berkhamsted Town	26	9	4	13	34	58	22
Ware	26	7	7	12	36	58	21
Harlow Town	26	5	8	13	28	39	18
Harrow Town	26	3	7	16	33	62	13
Histon	26	5	3	18	39	90	13

Tilbury and Wingate both joined from the London League.

1962-63

The table shown is as at 8th March 1963 when the competition was abandoned because the severe winter had caused so many postponements there was no realistic possibility of the league programme being completed.

Hertford Town	17	13	3	1	61	19	29
Bishops Stortford	17	9	5	3	38	29	23
Aveley	17	8	5	4	34	29	21
Stevenage Town	15	7	4	4	21	24	18
Tilbury	16	6	5	5	32	29	17
Windsor & Eton	17	6	5	6	37	35	17
Edmonton	14	7	2	5	40	20	16
Harlow Town	11	7	1	3	25	7	15
Aylesbury United	14	5	5	4	32	29	15
Hemel Hempstead Town	12	5	3	4	31	18	13
Berkhamsted Town	16	6	1	9	27	25	13
Ware	15	5	2	8	28	33	12
Brentwood & Warley	17	5	1	11	27	49	11
Harrow Town	12	3	3	6	23	32	9
Histon	18	4	1	13	21	67	9
Wingate	16	1	4	11	21	53	6

An Emergency Competition was then organised to decide the league title.

Western Section

Edmonton	7	5	1	1	25	6	11
Windsor & Eton	7	4	2	1	14	10	10
Berkhamsted Town	7	3	3	1	16	12	9
Hemel Hempstead Town	7	3	2	2	13	9	8
Harrow Town	7	4	0	3	11	10	8
Aylesbury United	7	2	0	5	12	21	4
Wingate	7	2	0	5	9	17	4
Stevenage Town	7	0	2	5	8	23	2

Eastern Section

Hertford Town	7	5	1	1	15	4	11
Bishops Stortford	7	5	1	1	13	8	11
Harlow Town	7	4	1	2	14	10	9
Aveley	7	4	0	3	11	11	8
Tilbury	7	2	2	3	13	13	6
Ware	7	1	3	3	13	17	5
Histon	7	1	2	4	7	14	4
Brentwood & Warley	7	0	2	5	7	16	2

Championship Play-Off

Hertford Town vs Edmonton	1-1, 1-4 (aet)

Edmonton won 5-2 on aggregate and were declared champions.

The Delphian League closed as a separate competition in 1963, being absorbed into the Athenian League as its new Second Division (third tier).

15 of the Delphian League's 16 clubs made up the new division, the exception being Stevenage Town who turned professional and joined the Southern League.